"Compelling. Insightful. Timely. A landmark book. Writing for theologians, pastors and students, Dr. Litfin harvests the fruit from more than forty years of focused study, showing the difference between the results-oriented persuader and the faithful herald. In a world where the biblical preacher has too often been replaced by the shrewd marketer, the magnetic entertainer and the 'change-the-world campaign strategist,' this book is desperately needed."
Colin Smith, senior pastor, The Orchard EFC, president, Unlocking the Bible

"Paul's disavowal of the use of rhetoric in 1 Corinthians 1:17-21 has perplexed interpreters and spurred considerable debate in recent years. Duane Litfin examines this passage in the context of Greco-Roman rhetorical practice and generates a very convincing thesis. He argues that in his evangelism Paul rejects using rhetorical techniques to persuade his listeners of the truth of the gospel because he does not want their faith to be based on his creative arguments. Rather, he proclaims the gospel, allowing the Holy Spirit to generate faith in the hearts of those who are open to belief. The Holy Spirit, not persuasive arguments, provides a firm ground for faith. Litfin's carefully nuanced study of 1 Corinthians 1–4 in its first-century context provides not only the most plausible interpretation of Paul's disavowal of rhetorical usage to date, but also a model for preaching that is aware of the call and commission of the human herald and the Holy Spirit's role in opening the heart of the hearer to the proclamation of the gospel."
Duane F. Watson, professor of New Testament studies, Malone University, Canton, OH

"Culminating an illustrious career as a pastor, professor and college president, Dr. Duane Litfin delivers his magnum opus in *Paul's Theology of Preaching*. This is ecclesial theology at its finest: scholarly yet not arcane, theological yet not obscure, relevant yet not cookie-cutter. This isn't simply an excellent book on Paul's theology of preaching; it's a prophetic call to a radically God-centered approach to Christian ministry."
Todd Wilson, senior pastor, Calvary Memorial Church, cofounder and chairman, The Center for Pastor Theologians, author of *Real Christian*

"Duane Litfin has identified in Paul and 1 Corinthians 1–4 the kind of rhetoric that I can wholeheartedly endorse. This is not a rhetoric of persuasion that is cozying up to those in Corinth, but Paul is demonstrating a rhetoric of proclamation that relies upon the Holy Spirit for response. This book provides an important introduction to preaching and rhetoric that makes crystal clear that Paul was doing something very different from the rhetoricians around him. Litfin also provides numerous important practical implications and observations. I think that both scholars and pastors will benefit greatly from reading this book."

Stanley E. Porter, president, dean and professor of New Testament, Roy A. Hope Chair in Christian Worldview, McMaster Divinity College, Hamilton, Ontario, Canada

"This book does something too little seen in biblical studies today: it brings together deep learning and contemporary pastoral wisdom. A fresh look at Paul's theology of preaching and what it means for our proclamation of the gospel today."

Timothy George, founding dean of Beeson Divinity School, Samford University, general editor of the Reformation Commentary on Scripture

"In this wise—and provocative—study of Paul, Duane Litfin demonstrates that the apostle's intended meaning has often been seriously obscured by seeing him as engaged in various 'rhetorical ploys.' Making his case with a thorough grasp of ancient rhetoric, as well as with a profound commitment to the church's call to proclaim the gospel with clarity, Litfin exposes the confusion in the kind of preaching that aims at 'results' rather than being founded in an uncompromising desire to be obedient to the biblical text."

Richard J. Mouw, president emeritus and professor of faith and public life, Fuller Theological Seminary

"In *Paul's Theology of Preaching*, Duane Litfin sets forth the Greco-Roman context of ancient Corinth, where the citizens of the city regarded themselves as 'connoisseurs of eloquence.' . . . It was a context where the Apostle Paul's preaching simply did not measure up—and came under withering criticism from some in the Corinthian church. The apostle's resulting defense set it down once and for all that those who preach the gospel are called to proclamation, not rhetorical persuasion. As such, it provides a needed corrective to preachers who uncritically assume that their calling is to persuade their hearers of the gospel. This important, beautifully written book deserves careful reading and wide discussion in the church and the academy."

R. Kent Hughes, senior pastor emeritus of College Church in Wheaton, IL

PAUL'S THEOLOGY *of* PREACHING

The Apostle's Challenge to the Art of Persuasion in Ancient Corinth

DUANE LITFIN

An imprint of InterVarsity Press
Downers Grove, Illinois

InterVarsity Press
P.O. Box 1400, Downers Grove, IL 60515-1426
ivpress.com
email@ivpress.com

Revised and expanded edition © 2015 by Duane Litfin

Original edition © 1994 by Duane Litfin, published by Cambridge University Press under the title St. Paul's Theology of Proclamation: 1 Corinthians 1-4 and Greco-Roman Rhetoric, *Vol. 79 in the Society for New Testament Studies Monograph Series*

All rights reserved. No part of this book may be reproduced in any form without written permission from InterVarsity Press.

InterVarsity Press® is the book-publishing division of InterVarsity Christian Fellowship/USA®, a movement of students and faculty active on campus at hundreds of universities, colleges and schools of nursing in the United States of America, and a member movement of the International Fellowship of Evangelical Students. For information about local and regional activities, visit intervarsity.org.

Scripture quotations, unless otherwise noted, are from The Holy Bible, English Standard Version, copyright © 2001 by Crossway Bibles, a division of Good News Publishers. Used by permission. All rights reserved.

Quotations in the excursus "The Two Dynamics in Galatians" are taken from J. Louis Martyn, Galatians: A New Translation with Introduction and Commentary, The Anchor Yale Bible *(New Haven, CT: Yale University Press, 1997). Used by permission.*

Cover design: David Fassett
Interior design: Beth McGill

Images: column: © Yoeml/iStockphoto
    Greek key mosaic pattern: © RapidEye/iStockphoto
    statue of St. Paul: © Massimo Merlini/iStockphoto
    mosaic: © fmajor /iStockphoto

ISBN 978-0-8308-2471-7 (print)
ISBN 978-0-8308-9855-8 (digital)

 As a member of the Green Press Initiative, InterVarsity Press is committed to protecting the environment and to the responsible use of natural resources. To learn more, visit greenpressinitiative.org.

Library of Congress Cataloging-in-Publication Data

Litfin, A. Duane.
 Paul's theology of preaching : the apostle's challenge to the art of persuasion in ancient Corinth / Duane Litfin.
   pages cm
 Includes bibliographical references and index.
 ISBN 978-0-8308-2471-7 (pbk. : alk. paper)
 1. Bible. Corinthians, 1st, I-IV—Criticism, interpretation, etc. 2. Preaching—Biblical teaching. 3. Rhetoric, Ancient. 4. Rhetoric in the Bible. I. Title.
 BS2675.6.P68L58 2015
 227'.2067—dc23
                                                                                              2015013535

| P | 23 | 22 | 21 | 20 | 19 | 18 | 17 | 16 | 15 | 14 | 13 | 12 | 11 | 10 | 9 | 8 | 7 | 6 | 5 | 4 | 3 | 2 | 1 |
| Y | 34 | 33 | 32 | 31 | 30 | 29 | 28 | 27 | 26 | 25 | 24 | 23 | 22 | 21 | 20 | 19 | 18 | 17 | 16 | 15 | | | | |

In memory of

William R. Haughton,

sine qua non

Contents

List of Excurses — 9

Acknowledgments — 11

Abbreviations — 13

Preface — 15

Introduction — 31

PART ONE: GRECO-ROMAN RHETORIC

  1 The Beginnings — 57

  2 The Goal of Rhetoric — 70

  3 The Power of Rhetoric — 75

  4 The Reach of Rhetoric — 81

  5 The Genius of Rhetoric — 86

  6 The Appraisal of Rhetoric — 95

  7 The Hazards of Rhetoric — 103

  8 The Rewards of Rhetoric — 108

  9 The Grand Equation of Rhetoric — 112

PART TWO: 1 CORINTHIANS 1–4

  10 Paul and Rhetoric in Corinth — 119

  11 The Setting of 1 Corinthians 1–4 — 129

  12 Paul's Argument Introduced: 1 Corinthians 1:1-17 — 161

  13 Paul's Argument Begun: 1 Corinthians 1:17-20 — 182

  14 Paul's Argument Encapsulated: 1 Corinthians 1:21 — 195

  15 Paul's Argument Continued: 1 Corinthians 1:22–2:5 — 214

  16 Paul's Argument Completed: 1 Corinthians 2:6–4:21 — 236

PART THREE: SUMMARY AND ANALYSIS

   17 Paul's Ministry Model   259

   18 Important Questions   285

   19 Appropriate Strategies   307

   20 Conclusion: The Pauline Model   315

Appendix One: Paul, Apollos and Philo   323

Appendix Two: The Book of Acts   327

Appendix Three: Paul's Epistemology   334

Appendix Four: Implications for Preaching   339

Appendix Five: Broader Implications   350

Works Cited   360

Author Index   387

Scripture Index   390

List of Excurses

Avoiding Confusion	39
Augustine's Consistency	51
The Issue of Rhetorical Genre	131
On Letters Versus Speeches	135
Paul and First-Century Literary Culture	145
The Social Stratification of the Corinthian Church	148
Good Rhetoric Versus Bad Rhetoric.1	150
Paul's Eloquence	157
A Common Blind Spot	173
The Two Dynamics in Galatians	179
The Salvific Role of the Herald	186
A Unique Exception	189
The Double Foolishness of the Preaching	191
Chrysostom on the Wise and Foolish	192
Greek Word Formation	199
Paul's Core Concern	203
Roman Heralds	206
Both Ancient and Modern	209
The Demand for Proof	214
The Root Problem	218
Paul's Crucicentric Proclamation	223
Paul's Weakness and Fear	226
Experiential Proof of the Gospel	229
The Apostle as Deceiver	231
An Early Church Echo	235
Good Rhetoric Versus Bad Rhetoric.2	260
The Human Factor in Salvation	267

Paul's Preaching and Paul's Letters	288
Paul's Insincerity	289
Langue and *Parole*	293
Good Rhetoric Versus Bad Rhetoric.3	294
An Ancient Quest	298
Paul's Inconsistency	304

Acknowledgments

There is a kind of book about which you may say, almost without exaggeration, that it is the whole of a man's literary life, the unique child of his thought. Other writings he may have published, on this or that occasion; please God, the work was not scamped, nor was he indifferent to the praise and blame of his critics. But it was all beside the mark. The Book was what mattered—he had lived with it all these years, fondled it in his waking thoughts, used it as an escape from anxiety, a solace in long journeys, in tedious conversations. Did he find himself in a library, he made straight for the shelves which promised light on one cherished subject; did he hit upon a telling quotation, a just metaphor, an adroit phrase, it was treasured up, in miser's fashion, for the Book. The Book haunted his daydreams like a guilty romance. . . .

Strange, that a thing which is so much part of oneself should go out into the world, and lie in shop-windows, and be handled by reviewers! Yet this venture of paternity must be made, in the hope that there is some truth here worth the telling; or, if not that, tinder at least to catch the sparks of another man's fire.

R. A. Knox

Not all writers have in them such a Book. But I understand at least something of what Knox describes (1950, p. v). I will not say that all else has been beside the mark, but, as noted in the following preface, this book has been gestating in me for a long time. Some of its ideas have seen the light in previous, more or less partial (and no longer readily available) versions. Now, finally, their fullest treatment is presented here.

It is less odd for me than Knox would have it, then, to see this Book delivered out into the world. I have known the sensation before; readers are after all the purpose of such writing. Their responses in turn have affirmed that there is indeed some truth here worth the telling. Hence the appearance of this final version. It's the one I envisioned from the outset.

A work so long in the making has inevitably involved numerous contributors, too many to name here. But I must at least acknowledge my gratitude to the staff of Buswell Library at Wheaton College for their unflagging and always congenial support in the completion of this final version. To these and all the other contributors, I am indebted.

Finally, in the passage above Ronald Knox leaves unaddressed one crucial sidelight of having a single project so long percolating in one's mind: the patience and long-suffering of those closest to you who must endure the process secondhand. In my case, my wife, Sherri, has borne the brunt of this decades-long requirement with good cheer. For this, as for so many other things about her, I am deeply grateful.

Abbreviations

AT	Author's translation
SPTOP	Litfin (1994). *St. Paul's Theology of Proclamation*

Augustine

Doctr. chr.	*De doctrina christiana*

Cicero

De fin.	*De finibus*
De inv.	*De inventione rhetorica*
De off.	*De officiis*
De or.	*De oratore*
Opt. gen.	*De optimo genere oratorum*
Or. Brut.	*Orator ad M. Brutum*
Part. or.	*Partitiones oratoriae*

Quintilian

Inst. or.	*Institutio oratoria*

Tacitus

Dial.	*Dialogus de oratoribus*

Preface

I begin this book with a personal account. I offer it not because it's important in its own right but because it will be useful in setting the context for what follows.

THE BEGINNING

I first began thinking on the subject of this book in the early 1970s while pursuing a doctoral program in rhetorical theory at Purdue University. With eight years of biblical and theological studies behind me, and with a special interest in the subject of preaching, I plunged for the first time into the arcane world of Greco-Roman rhetoric. Primed as I was, the intersection of classical rhetoric and Christian preaching—indeed, we may say the clash of these two worlds[1]—at 1 Corinthians 1–4 became immediately apparent.

My first public attempt to explore this clash appeared in a *Christianity Today* article titled (by the editors; it was not a title I would have chosen) "The Perils of Persuasive Preaching."[2] In this article I argued that in 1 Corinthians 1–4 the Apostle Paul was calling into question the use of human persuasive techniques in Christian preaching. The article generated a range of strong responses. Most were positive, but some signaled that if my argument were to stand it would require a good deal more support than such a popular treatment could provide. Thus began an extensive search to find someone, anyone, who had explored the issues in detail. It was a search that would prove futile. No one, it seemed, had produced the study

---

[1]In his book *Classical Rhetoric and Its Christian and Secular Tradition from Ancient to Modern Times*, classicist George Kennedy attempted a survey of the interplay between Christianity and classical rhetoric, in the process of which he quotes 1 Cor 1:17-2:5 almost in full and then declares, "This passage may be said to reject the whole of classical philosophy and rhetoric" (1980, pp. 131-32). Classical scholar E. A. Judge concurred: "It would be hard to find a more momentous or conscious upheaval in all the cultural history of the West" (1960, p. 47; cf. "total confrontation," idem, 1983, p. 11).
[2]Litfin (1977). See appendix four.

I was after.[3] It occurred to me that perhaps I should attempt it.

Looking back it is sometimes difficult to recall that Greco-Roman backgrounds were at that point still out of favor in New Testament studies. Though this ancient cultural milieu had traditionally played a prominent role in the interpretation of the New Testament, and of 1 Corinthians 1–4 in particular, over the previous half century several alternatives had come to the fore. Various theories about Gnosticism or the Philonic Wisdom of the syncretistic Hellenistic synagogue had crowded into the spotlight, particularly among German scholars. As it would happen, a dramatic resurgence of Greco-Roman backgrounds would soon emerge, but as of the 1970s this development was still only a cloud on the horizon. It scarcely seemed a promising time to make the case that Greco-Roman rhetoric might be the appropriate backdrop for Paul's argument in 1 Corinthians 1–4 after all.

Yet, convinced that I was on to something, I decided to give it a try. When the opportunity presented itself in the early eighties, we moved to England to pursue this research at Oxford University.

The Oxford Years

I vividly recall my first meeting with my supervisor, Anthony Harvey. Having by then spent a decade thinking through the relevant issues, both in classical rhetoric and in 1 Corinthians, I had submitted an unusually detailed research proposal. But Canon Harvey—halfway through my program he became a Canon of London's Westminster Abbey, a destination to which I happily commuted for our periodic consultations—was at first skeptical. "I don't know if you have a study here or not," he commented. "What would you like me to do?" To this I remember stammering something like, "Well, you know quality research when you see it. Just look over my shoulder and tell me if I'm doing good work." "I can certainly do that," was his cryptic reply. It was not, it seemed to me at the time, an auspicious beginning.

With a heightened sense of trepidation I nonetheless plunged into my work, and soon in that first Michaelmas term I caught a glimpse of my supervisor's budding interest. I joined a small doctoral seminar with the renowned Pauline scholar G. B. Caird. When I was introduced to Professor Caird he nodded and said, "Ah, you're the fellow Anthony spoke to me about. You must come to my

---

[3]On this point, see "Recovering the Rhetorical View" in the introduction (pp. 35-36). As late as the mid-eighties Betz (1986, p. 16) could still refer to "Paul's rhetoric as he himself practiced it" as "a problem completely unresolved, and even undiscussed, as yet."

rooms and tell me about your work." Flattered, but also wary—*What had Anthony said about me?*—I made an appointment to meet the following week.

On the day of my appointment I knocked on Caird's door in the stately Queens College on Oxford's High Street. Professor Caird greeted me cordially, sat us down and poured tea. Then, filling and lighting his pipe, he leaned back and asked me to describe my project. I recall taking seven or eight minutes to line out my work, during which time Caird said not a word. He just studied me through a wreath of pipe smoke, offering a periodic "Hmmmm." I finished my summary with no idea of what he thought of my proposal.

"So, that's what I'm proposing to do," I said. There followed one of those dramatic moments one never forgets. Professor Caird paused, leaned toward me over the coffee table, tapped out his pipe into the ash tray and said, "No, no, Mr. Litfin, this will never do." It was a withering comment. All of my uncertainties flooded in. *Why did I think I had something to contribute to the important discussion of Paul and his preaching?* I had come halfway around the world to pursue this research, but with Caird's single comment my reason for being at Oxford collapsed like the proverbial house of cards.

It was a deflating moment. But thankfully it didn't last. I had done my homework before venturing into this arena and when Caird began plying me with questions I produced some ready answers. Soon his resistance began to change. An hour later Professor Caird sent me on my way with his encouragement, urging me to keep him apprised of my work. What had momentarily seemed an end became instead a delightful beginning. I left Queens that day reassured that I was on to something worthwhile.

I was only a few months into my work when Anthony, who had quickly moved from skepticism to genuine interest, decided we should bring in a second supervisor. Anthony had read "Greats" (classics) at Oxford but had since focused on the New Testament, and he wanted me to have a professional classicist. Thus he teamed up with Latin scholar Michael Winterbottom to oversee my work. The research and writing went well—with no little credit to my two supervisors—and in the end, when my project was completed, this dual supervision was followed by dual examination in the persons of F. F. Bruce (New Testament) and D. A. Russell (classics).

The dreaded *viva*, the oral examination by a panel of world-class experts on one's topic, is typically a moment of truth for an Oxford doctoral candidate. All hangs in the balance, not only your years of study and writing but also the gaining of the necessary credential for any future in the academy. Everything winnows down to this decisive event. With the stakes so high, the moment can be terrifying.

But this was not my experience. My *viva* proved to be a wonderful occasion. As chair of the proceedings, Professor Bruce began by introducing us to the audience (the examination was conducted in a public setting). Then he turned to me and said, "Professor Russell and I have conferred and we are in agreement that there is no question but that this work is of DPhil quality. So our purposes today are twofold. First, we want to be assured that you are the one who wrote this; and second, we wish to talk to you about your research."

Was I hearing this right? *You pass; now we just want to talk with you about your work?* Thus began a doctoral student's dream *viva*: two hours of conversation with two of the world's leading experts on your subject, both of whom have examined your work in detail, found it convincing and now wish only to explore it with you. I could not have asked for more. I was deeply honored, and their affirming comments on my finished work proved invaluable.

Following the *viva*, as we were preparing to leave I asked Professor Bruce if he thought I should seek to publish my study. He abruptly answered, "Why, of course. I've waited years for someone to write this." He was pleased, he said, to see at least this aspect of Greco-Roman backgrounds emerging from the shadows.[4]

The dissertation's publication may have seemed obvious to F. F. Bruce, but it required his encouragement for it to become obvious to me. Later that year over a pleasant lunch in another part of the world, Bruce graciously volunteered to write a foreword for the work. Regrettably, he died before the other demands on my schedule permitted me to have the manuscript ready for publication.

A Decade Later

It was not until the early nineties that I got around to revising my research for publication. The resulting book was titled *St. Paul's Theology of Proclamation*. By this time, of course, what had been a trickle in the late seventies had grown to a torrent; rhetorical studies of the biblical text were now ubiquitous. During my Oxford years I had discovered considerably more relevant literature than I was aware of when I started—though still no study such as I was attempting—but this was only the beginning. Throughout the 1980s Greco-Roman backgrounds roared back into favor and rhetorical studies began popping up everywhere. So plentiful had the literature become by 1994 that Alan Hauser and Duane Watson

---

[4]See Grass (2012, pp. 190-91) for the context of Bruce's comment.

would compile a comprehensive book-length bibliography titled *Rhetorical Criticism of the Bible*. An impressive proportion of the entries had been published during the previous decade.

What's more, there finally appeared during the early and mid-nineties four book-length studies focused on my passage in particular, 1 Corinthians 1–4. First came Stephen Pogoloff's *Logos and Sophia* (1992); then my own *St. Paul's Theology of Proclamation* (1994; hereinafter *SPTOP*); and then Michael Bullmore's *St. Paul's Theology of Rhetorical Style* (1995). In 1997 Bruce Winter's *Philo and Paul Among the Sophists* joined the group. All four largely independent investigations argued similar theses: namely, that it was not Gnosticism or Philonic Wisdom but Greco-Roman rhetoric that lay at the core of the Corinthian "wisdom of words" (σοφίᾳ λόγου, 1:17) Paul was compelled to address. These were the first book-length studies to make this argument.[5]

The genealogy of these four books is significant. Each was produced in relative isolation from the others. Pogoloff's book showed no awareness of my Oxford research from a decade earlier, and in revising that work for publication I remained unaware of his earlier dissertation. Similarly, Pogoloff's monograph appeared a few months too late to be discovered and used in my revision. Bullmore remained unaware of Pogoloff's work, and my book appeared too late to show up in his bibliography. But Bullmore was aware of my Oxford dissertation and spent several pages summarizing its argument, which he then used as a springboard for his own more specific thesis. Winter's book briefly engaged both my book and Pogoloff's but not Bullmore's.

It is significant, then, that these four books, while reflecting important differences, nevertheless held in common the conviction that Greco-Roman rhetoric played a crucial role in the problems Paul faced in Corinth, especially as those

---

[5]Much later another book would be added to the list: Corin Mihaila's *The Paul-Apollos Relationship and Paul's Stance Toward Greco-Roman Rhetoric* (2009). Earlier, the only book-length treatments to focus on the early chapters of 1 Corinthians were Ulrich Wilckens's *Weisheit und Torheit* (1959), Rolf Baumann's *Mitte und Norm des Christlichen* (1968) and James A. Davis's *Wisdom and Spirit* (1984). Wilckens argued against rhetorical backgrounds in favor of a gnostic interpretation, as he did again later in his influential *TDNT* article on σοφία. Baumann insisted that the problem in Corinth was "enthusiasts" who overvalued spiritual gifts and the personalities connected with their manifestation. Davis argued for a Jewish "Torah-centric" background to the Corinthian wisdom. More recently five other treatments, while in some ways supportive of our own thesis, all focus on other dimensions of the passage: Jeffery Lamp's *First Corinthians 1–4 in Light of Jewish Wisdom Tradition* (2000); Hans-Christian Kammler's *Kreuz und Weisheit* (2003); L. L. Welborn's *Paul, the Fool of Christ* (2005); H. H. Drake Williams's *The Wisdom of the Wise* (2010); and Harm-Jan Inkelaar's *Conflict over Wisdom* (2011).

problems are reflected in the early chapters of 1 Corinthians. That four largely unrelated studies should emerge during such a short period is testimony to the power of this historic understanding of 1 Corinthians 1–4. Once the freeze on Greco-Roman backgrounds began to thaw, it was only a matter of time before studies such as these would appear. Today the rhetorical dimension of what Paul experienced in Corinth is almost universally granted, due at least in part to the influence of one or more of these four books.

It would be a mistake, however, to conclude that these four studies merely duplicate one another. They are in large agreement that Greco-Roman rhetoric formed an important backdrop to 1 Corinthians 1–4, but what they do with that assumption leads them in different directions. These differences will emerge as we proceed, but for the moment let us focus on the unique nature of this present work.

The Present Book

This book constitutes an exploration of the origins of a crucial Pauline insight for ministry. This ancient insight is sounded throughout the apostle's writings, and if we are alert enough to catch them, we can hear its echoes down through church history to the present day. But this insight receives its fullest biblical exploration in 1 Corinthians 1–4. What is this insight? Why is it important? What are its implications? These are the issues that will occupy us in this book.

An exploration of Paul's important insight constituted the core of my original research and the book that grew out of it. In both instances this key Pauline insight was gleaned from a study of 1 Corinthians 1–4 (buttressed by a range of other passages) as seen against the backdrop of Greco-Roman rhetoric. Absent this backdrop, Paul's central insight is easily missed by modern readers. The lack of the appropriate contrast, not to mention the insight's deeply counterintuitive nature, renders it difficult for us to discern. But lay out the appropriate background and the image changes. The Apostle's ministry-shaping argument emerges with clarity and power.

For his original readers, of course, the effort to recover this ancient backdrop was scarcely necessary. The relevant cultural background was *their* background; it was an inescapable dimension of their everyday life, part and parcel of their own thinking. But not so for us. In our case it is something we must work to reconstruct. If we are unwilling to put forth this reconstruction effort, the history of the interpretation of 1 Corinthians 1–4 suggests that we will likely fail to appreciate this important dimension of the Apostle's thought. This book is designed to recover that background, display the Apostle's argument against it, and then provide some analysis for the church's contemporary thought and practice.

It is, as we shall see, essentially this threefold treatment that is unique to this present book. Why had no such treatment appeared previously? First, focused studies such as this one (called monographs) are a fairly recent development in biblical scholarship. They were largely unknown in earlier generations when the rhetorical issues at stake in 1 Corinthians 1–4 were widely appreciated by scholars educated in the classics. But then just as these sorts of monographs were coming onto the scene, Greco-Roman backgrounds fell out of favor in biblical studies. Thus the early- to mid-twentieth-century reluctance to give attention to Greco-Roman backgrounds became the new culprit. This was the primary reason for the blind spot I originally stumbled across and set out to address in my Oxford research, not to mention the chilly reception my research proposal initially received.

Even after Greco-Roman rhetorical backgrounds swerved back into favor during the twentieth century's second half, however, two other factors continued to obscure Paul's point. For starters, current fashions in contemporary biblical criticism tend to divert scholars from engaging the relevant dimensions of Paul's thought.

CRITICAL THEORIES

In the waning years of the nineteenth century, the focus of biblical scholarship had shifted. From studying the letters of the New Testament primarily for their historical and theological contributions, following the lead of scholars such as Adolf Deissmann the writings themselves and their authors increasingly became the focus of study.[6] This led to the rise of a variety of technical approaches to the text such as structural analysis, form criticism and rhetorical criticism. As the twentieth century unfolded, this shift of focus conspired with developing theories of language, epistemology and hermeneutics[7] to discourage biblical scholars from focusing on the dimensions of Paul's thought we are after.

---

[6]As scholars grew increasingly skeptical about the ability of texts to convey information about their ostensible referents—the objects, ideas or events to which their language appears to refer—they turned their attention to what is directly accessible: the "verbal reality" of the text that lay before them (Kennedy, 1984, p. 119). Gitay (1991, p. 13) characterizes this shift as a move from classical biblical scholarship's focus on the "content" or "first meaning" of a text to what he aptly calls "the art of the final product," a study of the phenomena of the text itself. But see Witherington (2009b, pp. 2-3, 12-13) for a contemporary apologetic for a more classical approach.

[7]For documentation and a succinct summary of these complex trends, see Lampe (2010, pp. 4-7).

For many critics today, readers are viewed as having little access to an author's meaning in a text, first because it is naive to credit an author with actually meaning *simpliciter* what he says, and second because the author's meaning—to the extent we may even speak of such a thing—is in any event unavailable to us.[8] Among other things, texts are exercises in *portrayal*, and especially *self-portrayal*. Thus the only author a reader encounters in a text is not the real author but the implied author; that is, the author as displayed in the text, who may be very different from the real author. Moreover, because every use of language is essentially an exercise in influence or power, the one wielding language is always in one form or another seeking to shape the recipient to the author's will.[9] The critic's challenge is thus to bring this rhetorical intent to the surface. In this way the focus shifts from what an author is *saying* in a text to what an author is *doing* there; that is, how he or she is using language functionally to accomplish his or her rhetorical purposes. For such a task rhetorical criticism is the ideal tool. The ascendance of these critical theories is one of the key reasons for the massive resurgence of interest in ancient and modern rhetoric that has characterized the last half century of biblical studies.

Ever since the work of J. L. Austin and John Searle, of course, modern readers have been reminded of the performative function of language. One need only think of the title of Austin's posthumous book, *How to Do Things with Words*. It is often useful indeed to inquire about what an author intends his or her words to *accomplish*, a point students of ancient and modern rhetoric have long appreciated.[10] The problem, therefore, is not the insightful claim that humans use language not simply to "mean" things but also to "do" things. The problem arises when the latter winds up eclipsing the former; that is, when we take refuge in the performative functions of language because contemporary hermeneutical theories have trapped us in a "methodological impasse" when it comes to discerning an author's meaning. Says Raymond Pickett,

> One conceivable way through this methodological impasse would be to suppress the urge to discern which meanings are preeminent, and to focus in-

---

[8]For a detailed analysis of the relevant issues, see Vanhoozer (1998).

[9]For example: "The study of the pragmatics of texts has shown that in persuasive texts the real (empirical) author sets out to manipulate his real readers towards a specific objective by means of encoding himself and his readers in such a way and applying such textual strategies as will expedite the desired effect." Thus for the reader there is "the danger of uncritically identifying the encoded author and readers with their empirical counterparts. The encoded interlocutors are constructs of the writer; there does not exist a one-to-one relationship between them and their referents in the real world" (Du Toit, 1989, pp. 192, 196).

[10]For a helpful summary on this topic, see Briggs (2001).

stead on how each meaning contributes to a particular rhetorical strategy. Instead of asking what a specific theme or symbol meant for Paul, the focus would be on the function of its various expressions within the discourse [of] a given letter(s). The objective of such an approach would be to ascertain how Paul's statements relate to what he is trying to *accomplish* through his written correspondence, which is different from attempts to delineate what his statements disclose about his theology. The method being proposed here . . . is more concerned with the performance of his utterances than with what they reveal about his thought.[11]

For a classic instance of this approach, consider 2 Corinthians 11:6. When we hear Paul acknowledge there that he is ἰδιώτης τῷ λόγῳ—that is, he is "unskilled" or amateurishly unimpressive when it comes to public speaking—we are regularly warned against taking this acknowledgment at face value. Instead of what it appears to be—a humble admission that by the exalted standards of Greco-Roman eloquence his critics were, at least on this point, essentially right (2 Cor 10:10)—this statement is commonly treated as a well-known rhetorical ploy,[12] akin to a sly and crafty attorney seeking to disarm the jury by passing himself off as "just an ol' country lawyer." On this view, Paul's statement is not to be interpreted as providing reliable information about its ostensible subject, the Apostle's speaking abilities. In fact, it assumes the opposite: that Paul understood his humble acknowledgment to be false, just as the canny lawyer knows his humble self-deprecation to be false. As a rhetorical ploy Paul's statement shows the curtain of *appearance* he was seeking to erect, but it cannot for that very reason be examined for much behind that curtain. The identification of Paul's self-description as rhetorical artifice undermines the attempt to credit any face value to the statement itself.

What is peremptorily ruled out of bounds in this line of thinking, of course, is the possibility that, in the what-you-see-is-what-you-get spirit of the exhortation to "let your 'yes' be yes and your 'no' be no,"[13] when Paul claimed to be unskilled in speech he meant pretty much what he said. This was no mere ploy

---

[11]Pickett (1997, pp. 25-26). From an either-or, "language is performative, not descriptive" stance, some scholars go so far as to reject even the more fundamental idea that Paul possessed a stable and coherent underlying theology of which his arguments were an expression. By this reading Paul made up his theology on the fly so as to accomplish his rhetorical purposes. See Vos (2010) for a survey of this scholarship.

[12]E.g., see Quintilian, *Inst. or.* 4.1.8-9; Dio Chrysostom, *Discourses* 12.9, 16; 19.4; 35.1; 42.1-3; 47.1, 8. On this tactic, see Dover (1974, pp. 25-26); North (1979, p. 163); Ober (1989, pp. 174-77).

[13]Jas 5:12; Mt 5:37; cf. the use of δόλος ("cunning contrivance for misdirection, guile") in Jn 1:47.

designed to misdirect his readers. Paul's use of this language, like all language, was agenda driven; but his was not a *hidden* agenda. His statement was a sincere expression of the truth—a truth cited indeed with a goal of disarming his readers, but in this instance not by rhetorical artifice but by the statement's earnest candor and authenticity.[14] Paul's unflinching acknowledgment—in a letter designed to be read publicly—of his critics' scathing assessment of the centerpiece of his apostolic calling, his preaching (2 Cor 10:10), suggests a high level of transparency and candor; so why must we credit him with anything less just a few verses later? Paul understood all too well that by the exacting standards of Greco-Roman eloquence he was indeed "unskilled when it comes to speech."[15] As such he was no match for the polished orators so popular in Corinth. But then, he did not aspire to match them. Paul was determined to operate according to a different standard. "Our conscience testifies," he wrote to the Corinthians, "that we have conducted ourselves in the world, and especially in our relations with you, with integrity and godly sincerity [εἰλικρινείᾳ]. We have done so, relying not on worldly wisdom but on God's grace" (2 Cor 1:12 NIV; cf. 2:17).

Of course, one can always argue that this last self-portrayal is but another example of Paul's rhetorical guile and is no more to be credited than the others, and so on. But this level of skepticism[16] renders the biblical text impenetrable.

---

[14]See, e.g., Olbricht (2005, p. 158) on the role of "frankness" in Paul's "ideal person." Cf. Collins's (2009) treatment of Paul's other self-references in the Corinthian epistles.

[15]R. Dean Anderson (1998, p. 278): In this instance Paul's statement "should be taken seriously and not as rhetorical understatement"; cf. also Henderson (2011, p. 30). As we have noted, however, many contemporary critics are disinclined for theoretical reasons to allow this possibility. As Beardslee (1994, p. 367) says, "The older literary criticism assumed that writing was 'about' something." That is, it was "referential" in the sense that it referred to some thing or state of affairs external to itself. Increasingly skeptical of such views, contemporary treatments often turn their attention to the structural or rhetorical forms of the text itself, or what Beardslee calls "the pragmatics of the text, that is, the study of its intended effect on the audience" (p. 370). Hence the inclination to view Paul's reference as a rhetorical ploy rather than descriptive of an actual state of affairs.

[16]This fashionable stance, which forces a shift of focus away from *what* an author is saying to *why* he or she is saying it, is reminiscent of the shift from substance to function that C. S. Lewis addressed in his essay "Bulverism" (1970, p. 273): "You must show *that* a man is wrong before you start explaining *why* he is wrong. The modern method is to assume without discussion *that* he is wrong and then distract his attention from this (the only real issue) by busily explaining how he became so silly. In the course of the last fifteen years I have found this vice so common that I have had to invent a name for it. I call it 'Bulverism.' Someday I am going to write the biography of its imaginary inventor, Ezekiel Bulver, whose destiny was determined at the age of five when he heard his mother say to his father—who had been maintaining that two sides of a triangle were together greater than a third—'Oh you say that *because you are a man*.' 'At that moment,' E. Bulver assures us, 'there flashed across my opening mind the great truth that refu-

What's more, in the case of the Apostle Paul it seems an unnecessarily cynical reading of a man who claimed to have renounced hidden strategies (τὰ κρυπτὰ τῆς αἰσχύνης) in favor of a much more straightforward approach. His determination, he said, was to commend himself not by artifice (πανουργίᾳ) but "by the open statement of the truth [φανερώσει τῆς ἀληθείας] ... to everyone's conscience in the sight of God" (2 Cor 4:2).[17] Only a determined hermeneutic of dour suspicion would require us to treat such claims as contrived rhetorical strategies rather than honest expressions of the Apostle's heart.[18]

One thing is certain: delimiting our focus to the rhetorical *function* of Paul's language in 1 Corinthians 1–4 is a surefire way to forfeit the core insight for ministry the Apostle explores there. But there is also a second reason this insight is sometimes overlooked. Different readings of the rhetorical background itself have conspired to obscure the Apostle's point. We will explore this problem in the process of our examination of 1 Corinthians 1–4, but for now it is enough to note that, while (as stated above) there are other works that have focused on the rhetorical background to 1 Corinthians 1–4, our threefold treatment of these chapters remains unique to this work. This is emphatically *not* to claim that the core insight that animates Paul's argument through this passage is itself unique to this book; were that the case it would render this work highly suspect. The truth is the opposite: this insight is a historic one, surfacing repeatedly throughout church history from Paul to the present. This present book is unique only in its treatment of that insight—that is, in the extent to which it documents Paul's insight and then turns to its analysis and application.

Broken Linkages

I am aware, of course, that not all will find such a turn congenial. Both my original research and *SPTOP* hinted (but only hinted) at my interest in the contemporary implications of 1 Corinthians 1–4, "not merely for the Corin-

---

tation is no necessary part of argument. Assume that your opponent is wrong, and explain his error, and the world will be at your feet. Attempt to prove that he is wrong or (worse still) try to find out whether he is wrong or right, and the national dynamism of our age will thrust you to the wall.' That is how Bulver became one of the makers of the Twentieth Century."

[17]Cf. Jn 7:18: "The one who speaks on his own authority seeks his own glory; but the one who seeks the glory of him who sent him is true, and in him there is no falsehood." Note the background for this comment in Jn 5:41-44.

[18]An interpreter's philosophical precommitments (including, we should note, our own) inevitably shape his or her reading of Paul. My own commitments promt me toward something closer to the "hermeneutics of affirmation" discussed by Patrick and Scult (1999, pp. 76-83).

thians but for ourselves."[19] This present book presses the discussion further. It not only updates and reworks those previous efforts, but also gives much more attention (see part three) to analyzing the ideas that render Paul's argument so relevant today. Yet this very notion of contemporary relevance is off-putting to some who have drunk deeply at the philosophical fountains of modern and postmodern criticism. The move from Paul to contemporary implications requires a set of linkages which for these critics do not exist. To which I say, fair enough. But these linkages do exist for many others.

Readers who are not able to keep abreast of contemporary trends in New Testament criticism may be startled to see what happens when such linkages are severed. In the interpretation of 1 Corinthians, for example, the result is what one might conclude are three *different* Pauls.

Paul the First (*Paul.1*) is the iconic apostle of church history, Paul with the linkages intact. The goal of studying a letter such as 1 Corinthians is first and foremost to engage his ideas. The structure of the letter, problems in the Corinthian church and the broader cultural influences that may have informed and fed into them are important primarily insofar as understanding them deepens our ability to appreciate Paul's response. The working assumption behind this version of Paul is that due to his apostolic calling he had a unique access to religious truth. Thus his ideas bear a divinely ordained authority. This is why, as the hand-picked representative of the risen Christ, *Paul.1* stands at the privileged center of the interpretational enterprise.

But what happens when this working assumption is jettisoned or rendered irrelevant by modern theories of language and hermeneutics? The result is a deprivileged *Paul.2*. This nonapostolic Paul is just an ordinary man now, and one, moreover, who has taken a step back into the shadows. The Paul of 1 Corinthians can no longer be identified as the real Paul. The Paul we encounter there is essentially a persona created by the real Paul to accomplish his rhetorical purposes. But this also means that the real Paul has retreated from us. He has become a grayed-out figure, only dimly discerned. In any case, since he lacks any special divine authority and is as vulnerable to his own failings as any of the rest of us, this Paul no longer merits a privileged place in our interpretation anyway. The

---

[19]*SPTOP*, p. 18. In a curious contemporary burst of Bulverism, Eriksson (1998, p. 36) found even this mild sentiment discrediting. Said he of my argument in *SPTOP*, "Litfin himself has been persuaded by Paul's statements in 1 Cor 2:1-5.... This is possibly because of his desire to develop a contemporary theology of preaching."

idea of trying to wrestle with his ideas, were they even available, is of less interest to us.[20] Other objects compete for our attention. For example, now that the Corinthian community need no longer take a back seat to an authoritative Paul, that community itself can become our object of attention, not as a step toward understanding Paul but as fully deserving of its own turn in the spotlight. Even those who opposed Paul in Corinth must be granted their due, for they too have a right to be understood on their own terms, not just Paul's. In this way the dim figure of *Paul.2* becomes increasingly irrelevant to the interpretation of his own letter. We study 1 Corinthians not to learn from him but to learn about others.

And then there is *Paul.3*. This is the Paul of those who resent the canonical status the Apostle has enjoyed for all these centuries. Their *Paul.3* is not only the deprivileged Paul; he is the villain of the drama in Corinth. This Paul may have been an ordinary man, but he was a genius when it came to leveraging his outsized apostolic claims into social power, power he often wielded to silence other legitimate voices. The goal of the interpreter therefore is to rediscover those whom Paul has silenced, side with them against Paul and then hand them the microphone so their disenfranchised voices can finally be heard. Ironically, the proponents of *Paul.3* are also interested in the contemporary implications of 1 Corinthians. In this case, however, what they have in mind are the social and political implications stemming from their *repudiation* of Paul.[21]

It is important to keep in mind, of course, that these second and third versions of Paul owe their existence precisely to the towering figure of Paul the First. This is the apostolic Paul of the early church. He is the iconic Paul of the Roman Catholic, Orthodox and Reformation communions alike. This Paul is the one who has inspired Christianity's greatest teachers, theologians, musicians and artists, and it is his ongoing significance that energizes not only our finest biblical commentaries but also vigorous theological debates such as that surrounding the so-called New Perspective. This Paul is the once-embittered Jew who was driven

---

[20]E.g., see Amador (1999).
[21]Still further down this path is a fourth, and apparently ultimate, shift of focus wherein the work of the critic him- or herself becomes the prime interest. This "emancipatory paradigm shift" frees us from outmoded notions about obligations to the text and author so that we can focus on what are perceived as more relevant issues such as "the theoretical contributions of the margins, such as feminism, postcolonialism, and critical race and ethnic-cultural studies" (Fiorenza, 2005, p. 10; cf. 2007). Pippin (1997, p. 273): "When New Testament scholars read the Bible, they invent ideologies. Liberatory readings are creations of new (utopian) narratives. Does the reader submit to or revolt against the ideologies of a text? Ideological and liberatory criticisms allow the readers choices and the chance to break out of any hegemonic interpretative discourse."

to the ground on that Damascus road, transformed into the indefatigable servant of the One he was persecuting and then sent out to change the world by preaching the good news of Jesus Christ. This is the Paul of this book.

If the embrace of this canonical Paul reflects the interpreter's willingness to acknowledge Paul's apostolic authority (which it does[22]), in the same way the shift to *Paul.2* or *Paul.3* reflects the interpreter's willingness to wear the bridle of contemporary critical theories. This is a bridle, however, that comes with built-in blinders. Such blinders can serve a useful temporary function, but if worn permanently they become a form of blindness. It's important to see that the so-called hermeneutic of suspicion, so characteristic of so much modern criticism, is not a necessary entailment of a historical understanding of the rhetorical character of human discourse. It is, rather, a byproduct of a particular set of epistemological and hermeneutical commitments, none of which, despite their current prevalence in the academy, is indubitable or beyond criticism.[23] Thus we are under no obligation to don these blinders as a permanent fixture.

From my own background in rhetorical theory I find the pronounced skepticism toward Paul of many rhetorical critics overdone and underwarranted. In my estimation, the so-called face value of Paul's statements deserves more credit than it sometimes receives.[24] I do not argue for naiveté in our reading of Paul—language, including Paul's, is after all astonishingly complex and often used to mean things it does not on the surface seem to mean—but I do think a bit more empathy[25] is often in order, not to mention a damping down of the arrogance,

---

[22]As Mitchell (2002, p. 409) observes, exegesis "is inherently interwoven with portraiture." This is an important point. Every treatment of Paul is working from, and contributing to, some particular portrait of this historical figure, and ours is no exception. For the necessary context, however, see Mitchell's brief but useful survey (pp. 407-39) of how exegetes have portrayed Paul over the centuries, from late antiquity (Chrysostom and Augustine) to the discordant world of twentieth-century scholarship. Troy Martin (2010) offers a still more bewildering summary of the confusion in current biblical studies. Perhaps with time these debates will winnow out into some semblance of consensus, but at present the cacophony should make us wary of the overly dogmatic conclusions of some of the participants. By contrast, see Young (1997) for the earliest foundations of the age-old "reading community" of those who continue to look to the Scriptures as their "rule of faith and practice."

[23]These commitments are both ancient and newly (post)modern; cf. p. 295 below.

[24]*Face value* is not to be equated, of course, with literal. Nor is it to deny rhetorical intent (see pp. 291-306). But as Caird (1980, p. 39) says, "To understand why a speaker says what he does is not the same thing as understanding what he is saying." My goal will be to guard against allowing the former—a version of the old "intentional fallacy" that is all too common in contemporary Pauline studies—to cut us off from the latter.

[25]For example, see Young (1985, pp. 351-52) on John Chrysostom's empathetic approach to Paul: If Chrysostom overly "idealises" Paul, Young says, "yet his mode of empathy has, I think, enormous potential for discerning the fundamental thrust of what Paul was getting at. Chrysostom

Preface

superiority and condescension critics sometimes exude. We should not withhold from Paul the same courtesy we wish others to grant to us: the right to mean what we say. In this book my goal is to listen to the Apostle in 1 Corinthians 1–4, try to understand what he has to say there and then offer some contemporary analysis.

Issues of Method

These several purposes, however, present a practical difficulty. They require that this book bridge some of the demands of both academics and practitioners. The celebrated New Testament scholar C. K. Barrett addressed this problem in the preface to his work *The Signs of an Apostle*. That book was the printed version of his academic Cato Lecture for the 1969 Brisbane Conference in Australia, and the preparation of the book, he said, "has caused me great perplexity."

> One thing is clear to me. I cannot put out of my mind the vast crowd that thronged the church, and overflowed it, that warm May evening. I did my best to speak to them, and I wish to write for them now. At the same time I cannot forget my obligation to the professional theologians of Australia, the ministers and the students of theology. It is not easy to combine two purposes in one book; not easy, but I hope not impossible, if my readers will be tolerant of one another, as well as of me.[26]

This book will also require tolerant readers. I wish to address some of the implications of the Apostle's argument in 1 Corinthians 1–4 that are of genuine importance for practitioners. But to do so will require some effort in reconstructing the proper background to Paul's argument. What's more, we cannot in the process bypass a series of scholarly debates that, depending on how they are decided, determine the nature of that argument. The relevance of Paul's point for practitioners can only be developed by *engaging* those debates, not avoiding them. Hence the dual focus of this book.

To make things easier for these two audiences I have adapted an approach

---

was asking the right questions. He was not much interested in piecing together historical jig-saw puzzles of the kind that preoccupy modern critics, but rather in discerning what Paul was saying and why.... Chrysostom approaches Paul expectantly, and listens to the text in order to learn. For that very reason, he often discerns Paul's meaning the more clearly. Lack of expectancy, indeed deliberate distancing of oneself from the text in the interests of historical objectivity, accompanied by concentrating on obscure or incompatible statements in the interests of finding clues as to the genesis of the material, has been regarded as essential in modern research: but could it not be an important factor in distorting our reading of the material? Involved listening to what the text has to say may be the only way to hear and understand."

[26]Barrett (1970, pp. 5-6).

other writers facing a similar dilemma have found useful. For example, in his attempt to address both specialists and a broader audience in his *Where the Conflict Really Lies: Science, Religion, and Naturalism*, philosopher Alvin Plantinga employs "two sizes of print: the main argument goes on in the large print, with more specialized points and other additions in the small."[27] In his book *The Global Carbon Cycle*, author David Archer opts for a different approach. Though he wished to keep his book as accessible to the average reader as possible, he could not adequately address his complex subject without plunging at times into technical matters. Thus throughout the book he encapsulates the more specialized material in text boxes. Closer to our own study, Jacob Milgrom and Daniel Block also employ text boxes to set apart various scholarly digressions ("excursuses") in their commentary on the biblical text of Ezekiel. In this present book I will follow adapted versions of these approaches to bridge the interests of both kinds of readers. Those who are interested primarily in the overall argument of the book can follow the larger font, skipping over the more technical material. Readers who wish to engage the contested issues can dip as desired into the excurses, footnotes and appendices.

Finally, because this volume stands on the shoulders of my previous book, *St. Paul's Theology of Proclamation*, I will avoid duplicating that work's copious documentation except where necessary. As a part of the well-known Society for New Testament Studies Monograph Series (SNTS, #79), *SPTOP* is widely available in libraries, and specialist readers who require its fuller documentation can quite easily find it. The documentation in this book will focus mainly on works actually cited or materials published since the 1994 appearance of *SPTOP*.

---

[27]Plantinga (2011, p. xv). The widely used *Theological Dictionary of the New Testament* (*TDNT*) (like the *Theologisches Wörterbuch zum Neuen Testament* before it) employs a similar approach, apparently for space-saving reasons.

Introduction

No theory of discourse stands alone; each is rooted in the soil of its author's presuppositions.

This may seem at first blush an abstract point, of peculiar interest to theorists perhaps, but of little relevance to the rest of us. Yet like so many other first impressions, this one would be mistaken. This observation embodies an important truth, one we must be willing to engage if we are to grasp the Apostle Paul's theology of preaching.

Put simply, when it comes to human communication, presuppositions and practice tend to be organically related—the practice developing naturally from the presuppositions that generate and support it. This is especially the case when the subject is *moral* or *religious* discourse. For instance, listen to the conclusion of Raymond Anderson on the subject of Søren Kierkegaard's theory of "edifying discourse." According to Anderson, Kierkegaard's ideas clearly demonstrate "the intimate relation which exists between a theory of discourse and the philosophic outlook which underlies and nourishes it. . . . One can point to any aspect of Kierkegaard's theory of communication and rather easily relate it to the basic categories and presuppositions of his philosophy."[1]

To understand Kierkegaard's approach to communication, says Anderson, we must understand the presuppositions that shaped that approach. Why? Because in the realm of human discourse, and in religious or moral discourse in particular, presuppositions and practice tend to reflect one another rather closely. To understand the practice we must understand the presuppositions. Only then can we fully appreciate the communicator's chosen mode of discourse.

The Apostle Paul's approach to preaching is a particularly clear expression of this relationship. If we are to make sense of the Apostle's practice as a preacher,

---

[1]Anderson (1963, pp. 12-13); cf. Mason (1989); Duhamel (1965, pp. 91-92).

we must grasp the theological presuppositions that, in Paul's mind, gave rise to that practice. In other words, we must answer these two questions: How did Paul conceive of his preaching, and in what ways was this conception shaped by the basic presuppositions of his thought? It is in the answers to these two questions that we find embedded Paul's theology of preaching.

The Central Passage

To answer these questions we are obviously driven to the Apostle's writings. But when we arrive there we discover an interesting point. Only one passage in Paul's extant epistles was written specifically to answer these questions; that is, despite the fact that preaching was one of Paul's regular topics, there remains only one section in Paul's letters in which we discover anything like a *reasoned exploration* of how the Apostle operated as a preacher and why. This section is 1 Corinthians 1–4, and the subsection 1:17–2:5 in particular. In this sense, 1 Corinthians 1–4 stands unique in Paul's writings. Hence it is to these verses we must turn if we are to appreciate Paul's understanding of his own *modus operandi* as a preacher.

It is perhaps due to this uniqueness that immediately upon turning to 1 Corinthians 1–4 we discover a thicket of interpretational questions. Chief among them is the meaning of the important word σοφία ("wisdom") as introduced in 1 Corinthians 1:17. This term was so widely used in Paul's day and in such a variety of contexts, most of them interwoven with one another in the fabric of Greco-Roman society, that the interpretational possibilities are exceptionally rich. Indeed, this richness appears to have engendered much of what N. A. Dahl called the "chaos"[2] that attends the modern exegesis of 1 Corinthians 1–4. Yet we cannot hope to come to grips with how Paul understood his own behavior as a preacher without sorting the matter out.

The most important step in sifting through the questions is the realization that we must distinguish between σοφία in the mouth of the Corinthians and σοφία in the mouth of Paul. Both Paul and the Corinthians were impressed by and committed to σοφία, and both could use the term with ease. Yet the two sides seemed diametrically opposed in their meanings. Hence the semantic confusion and the difficulty in interpreting σοφία in 1 Corinthians 1–4.

I do not mean to suggest, however, that the difficulty lies in deciphering when Paul uses σοφία in the Corinthian sense and when he uses it in his own. For the most part commentators have had little trouble distinguishing the two. Nor,

---

[2]Dahl (1967, p. 317).

perhaps surprisingly, does the difficulty lie in discovering the background of Paul's own use of σοφία.³ This is an important investigation for other purposes—for instance, inquiry into the origins of Paul's Christology⁴—but the term σοφία does not play a large role in the Apostle's description of his own missionary methods. The main difficulty in sorting through Paul's argument in 1 Corinthians 1–4 lies in determining what was behind the Corinthian use of σοφία, and hence what it was to which Paul was responding. And to this question modern scholarship has offered multiple answers.

Prior to the twentieth century exegetes typically interpreted the crucial phrase σοφία λόγου ("wisdom of words," 1 Cor 1:17) with primary reference to Greco-Roman rhetoric and philosophy.⁵ According to this view, Paul was criticized by some in Corinth because his preaching did not measure up to the standards of a culture profoundly influenced by an unparalleled rhetorical heritage. In 1 Corinthians 1:17–2:5 Paul defends himself against this charge, a charge that he took seriously because of the centrality of preaching to his apostolic calling. Hence, according to this view, the Corinthian σοφία must be understood against the backdrop of the Greco-Roman rhetorical/philosophical tradition.

During the first half of the twentieth century, however, this traditional view was eclipsed by newer approaches to σοφία in Corinth. For example, some interpreted wisdom mainly in the light of gnostic mythological themes. The gnostic interpretation is rooted in the History of Religions School and can be traced back to late nineteenth- and early twentieth-century scholarship. According to this view, Paul's references to wisdom and knowledge in the Corinthian correspondence belong in the context of early Hellenistic Gnosticism. Opposing Paul in

---

³On this important subject, see Lamp (2000, pp. 117-88). Lamp embraces a rhetorical understanding of the Corinthian use of σοφία, and then focuses his own study on the Apostle's use of the term. In doing so, his findings somewhat parallel our own.

⁴On which, see Fee (2007, appendix A).

⁵One late but important exception was Baur's influential work (1863) in delineating competing strains of Petrine and Pauline Christianity in the early church. In working out his thesis, Baur reduced the "parties" in Corinth to these two camps, which in turn required him to interpret the Corinthian σοφία Paul was challenging (including the σοφία λόγου of 1:17) in Jewish terms (cf. Baur, 2003, vol. 1, pp. 268-320). This interpretation proved untenable, and Baur's views eventually fell out of favor. But see Goulder's attempts (1991, 2001) to revive them. Says Goulder (2001, p. 65), "The 'words of wisdom' that Paul forswore in 1.17; 2.1, 13 were the words that poured forth from the rabbis."..."Wisdom was the whole culture of Judaism.... The authorities to whom the Petrines appealed were the sages and scribes and debaters ... in Jerusalem." Goulder's renewed argument is no more persuasive than its predecessors, however, and has not gained many followers. It cannot compete with the Greco-Roman backgrounds, which lie so ready to hand and are so much more clarifying.

Corinth were gnostic "pneumatics" who voided the significance of the cross. Paul was writing to refute and counteract their pernicious influence.[6]

Another approach held that the Corinthian σοφία must be understood against the backdrop of the later Hellenistic-Jewish tradition represented by Philo and the *Wisdom of Solomon*. On this view the Corinthians had embraced, perhaps under the influence of Apollos, a Philonic type of heavenly Wisdom as the means of attaining the highest spiritual status or even salvation itself. These Wisdom enthusiasts considered Paul simply another Wisdom teacher and evaluated him accordingly, finding his wisdom deficient. In this light, 1 Corinthians 1:17–2:5 is construed as Paul's defense against these Corinthian criticisms and a rebuke of the low estimate of the cross of Christ in their Wisdom theology.

These two perspectives, including various admixtures of the two, held sway over a large proportion of Pauline studies for much of the middle of the twentieth century, particularly in Germany.[7] Both Gnosticism and Wisdom theology were

---

[6] In recent years this view has fallen out of favor. In fact, M. A. Williams (1996) has called into question the entire conception of Gnosticism on which these earlier studies were erected.

[7] For full documentation on these and other competing background options, see Kwon (2010). Not discussed by Kwon, however, is the Stoic option.

Brookins's treatment (2011; cf. Brookins 2010) is the latest in a series of efforts to argue for a Stoic philosophical background to the Corinthian wisdom; see Paige (1992); on Paul and Stoicism more generally, see Engberg-Pedersen (2000). But like his predecessors, Brookins's case, at least insofar as 1 Cor 1–4 is concerned, is weak. Brookins's working assumption (i.e., that "the best answer as to the nature of the Corinthians' divisive 'wisdom' is that which provides a unifying explanation for the whole of the letter") leads him to reject "the rhetorical thesis" because it "fails to demonstrate what close relation the presumably rhetorical wisdom which takes front and centre over the first four chapters of the letter has to do with the remaining twelve chapters" (p. 76). But what grounds do we have for demanding any such "unifying explanation"? See, e.g., Stirewalt's discussion (2003, pp. 64-77) of ancient "seriatim" letters; and Stamps (2002, p. 449): "I see 1 Corinthians as a 'pastoral' letter which addresses a primary issue and a number of subsidiary issues, some of which are directly related to the primary issue and some are not." It is widely observed that 1 Cor 1–4 is an unusually discrete literary unit within 1 Corinthians as a whole; indeed, see De Boer's argument (1994, p. 231) that chapters 1–4 and 5–16 are so distinct that they may best be viewed as "a composite of two letters, a composite of Paul's own making" as he responds first to the information received from Chloe's people (1 Cor 1:11) and then later to the information (and letter, 1 Cor 7:1) he received at the subsequent arrival of Stephanas, Fortunatus and Achaicus (1 Cor 16:17). Thus it is entirely possible that the "rhetorical wisdom" issue that dominates chapters 1–4 is left behind as the Apostle shifts to the topics that will control the remainder of the epistle, with rhetorical concerns appearing again only as echoes in 2 Corinthians (and perhaps in 1 Clement). In any case, Brookins's attempt to develop a Stoic explanation for the rhetorical concerns that he acknowledges stand "front and centre" in chapters 1–4 is strained and unpersuasive. On the approach to rhetoric generated by Stoic philosophy, see pp. 277-78 below.

Sounding a different note, Tomlin (1967) argues for an Epicurean background to the conflicts in Corinth. While his case may have something to say to the larger situation in Corinth, it bears little relevance to the issues Paul is dealing with in chapters 1–4. Thus it need not occupy us here.

undoubtedly in the process of shaping, and being shaped by, first-century thought, and a clearer understanding of both has added to our insight into the Pauline letters and the milieu in which they were written. Yet today both have fallen out of favor with most New Testament scholars. As the twentieth century waned and now well into the twenty-first century, the older rhetorical view has recovered new life.

Recovering the Rhetorical View

How could these other options have eclipsed the earlier rhetorical interpretation and dominated the field for so long during the twentieth century? For years there seemed to be little inclination to give the rhetorical option its due.[8] To be sure, some of the older commentators provided still-useful contributions,[9] and a number of twentieth-century commentators at least left room for or actually gave some weight to rhetorical concerns. But in no instance did these earlier writers bring out the full force of the traditional rhetorical view. Prior to 1980 the literature remained devoid of concentrated attempts to investigate the full implications of Greco-Roman rhetoric for understanding Paul's argument in 1 Corinthians 1–4.[10]

The absence of such investigations inevitably contributed to the confusion that marked the mid-twentieth-century interpretation of 1 Corinthians 1–4. Consider, for example, the extraordinary range of scholarly responses the rhetorical interpretation received during this period. This range was nicely summarized by Ulrich Wilckens in his influential article on σοφία in *TDNT*.[11] On the one hand, Wilckens referred to the rhetorical alternative as the "customary interpretation" of "most exegetes," thus acknowledging that over the centuries this view had enjoyed wide (though we might add, in the light of the lack of thorough scholarly attention it received, not particularly deep) support. At the other end of the spectrum, Wilckens spoke for a host of contemporary New Testament scholars in rejecting the rhetorical interpretation outright. All the more surprising, then, was the absence prior to the 1980s of any thorough attempt to focus on this subject and resolve the issues, particularly in light of the importance of the early chapters of 1 Corinthians for understanding Paul's thought in general and his view of preaching in particular.

---

[8]See Peterson (1998, pp. 8-15) for a helpful survey of the nineteenth- and twentieth-century treatments of rhetoric in biblical studies that lay behind this problem; cf. also Witherington (2009a, pp. 214-15); Betz (1986, p. 20).
[9]See Betz (1986, pp. 16-20) for a survey of this older literature.
[10]On this point, see the documentation in *SPTOP*, pp. 4-8.
[11]Wilckens (1965, vol. 7, p. 522).

Since 1980, of course, the picture has changed dramatically. Rhetorical analysis of the biblical text has become widely popular. The intervening years have witnessed a veritable explosion of such studies. So profuse has been this outpouring that we will not again see a book-length bibliography on the subject such as that of Hauser and Watson (1994). Not only have such bibliographical works become superfluous in the digital age, where search engines can deliver targeted information much more quickly; such a book could no longer do justice to the volume of relevant studies.

Yet it is crucial for our purposes to recognize that for the most part these studies have consisted of *rhetorical criticism*; that is, they attempt to identify recognizable rhetorical patterns[12] in the text and then use those insights to shed light on the writer's strategies, style, intent or, to a lesser extent, his ideas. What has been consistently overlooked by New Testament scholars, however, is that there are other types of rhetorical investigations that may also prove useful in biblical studies, particularly when the subject is preaching. To understand the distinction I have in mind, we must begin with our terminology.

Clarifying Our Terms

The terms *rhetoric* or *rhetorical* occur everywhere in biblical studies these days. Yet it is not always clear in what sense they are being used. In fact, it is frequently unclear that the users themselves understand in what sense they are employing the terms.[13] The result is widespread semantic confusion, particularly around questions such as whether Paul himself employed "rhetoric." This question is much discussed in the literature, often with little awareness that, given the ambiguity inherent in the term, the participants are talking past one another. They are using similar language to refer to distinguishably different things, or at least distinguishably different dimensions of the same thing.

This sort of semantic disarray poses a special challenge for those who are new to the subject of rhetoric. It's a challenge with which I can sympathize. I was months into a university doctoral program in rhetorical theory before I finally

---

[12]Especially those of the ancient Greco-Roman culture; see on this approach Porter's helpful summary (2013, pp. 320-24).

[13]Stamps (1999, p. 257) correctly observes, "Rhetorical criticism may be in a bit of a muddle because it is not always clear what it means by rhetoric." Yet on another issue, Stamps creates something of a muddle of his own when in his attempt to identify a distinctively "Christian rhetoric" he fails to observe the crucial distinction—well explicated by Porter (1999) in the essay immediately preceding Stamps's own—between Paul's letters and his missionary preaching (on which issue, see below, pp. 39-40, 135-37, 304-6).

began to find my way through the linguistic fog that surrounds this ancient term. What follows is a quick primer designed to help the reader clear away some of that fog. A bit of effort here will pay dividends in clarifying the relevant issues that will occupy us later on.

What is rhetoric? A typical academic definition sounds like this: *Rhetoric is a particular type of response to particular kinds of situations; namely, it is a persuasive response to situations that are susceptible to influence.* Hence the confusion. With such a broad and abstract definition of such a complex and multidimensional subject, the term *rhetoric* inevitably falls victim to a perplexing array of nuances.[14]

To help sort through this array, philosopher Maurice Natanson categorized the "the different aspects of rhetoric" as follows, ranging from the narrowest to the broadest: (1) rhetorical intention in speech, (2) the technique of persuasion, (3) the general theoretical rationale of persuasion and (4) the philosophy of rhetoric. Says Natanson,

> Rhetoric in the narrower aspect involves rhetorical intention [1] in the sense that a speaker or writer may devote his effort to persuade for some cause or object. Since much of what is commonly called "bad" rhetoric frequently is found in such efforts, the field of rhetoric understood as the technique of persuasion [2] is systematically studied and taught. Here the teacher of rhetoric investigates the devices and modes of argument, the outline for which is to be found in Aristotle's *Rhetoric* or other classical rhetorics. Reflection of a critical order on the significance and nature of the technique of persuasion brings us to rhetoric understood as the general rationale of persuasion [3]. This is what might be termed the "theory" of rhetoric in so far as the central principles of rhetoric are examined and ordered. The emphasis is on the general principles of rhetoric as rhetoric is intimately related to functional, pragmatically directed contexts. Finally, we come to the critique of the rationale of rhetoric which inquires into the underlying assumptions, the philosophical grounds of all the elements of rhetoric. It is here that a philosophy of rhetoric [4] finds its placement.[15]

---

[14]In addition to the following clarifications, see below, pp. 292-306. Confusion among these nuances is one of the persistent flaws of Resner's treatment (1999), which in his case is compounded by a similar equivocation in his use of the term *preaching*. Contemporary usage employs this common English word to refer to both Paul's missionary activity and the modern pastor's sermon to a Sunday morning congregation. But careful thinking about the issues surrounding Paul's κήρυγμα requires recognizing the crucial differences between these two settings; see Hunter (1943, pp. 24-26), and cf. below, pp. 304-6, 339-40.

[15]Natanson (1965, p. 65).

Here Natanson provides us with a helpful taxonomy of concepts. (I have added the bracketed numbers to help distinguish his four aspects of rhetoric.) Rhetorical situations, defined by their persuasive possibilities, give rise to rhetorical intentions in a communicator (aspect 1). To help communicators follow through on these intentions, thinkers over the centuries have wrestled with rhetoric at the level of behavior (rhetorical "technique," aspect 2); or more abstractly at the level of theory ("rationale," aspect 3); or more abstractly still, at the level of relating such behavior and theory to underlying philosophical assumptions (aspect 4). This last aspect Natanson calls "the philosophy of rhetoric."

> The philosophy of rhetoric . . . has as its subject matter the application of the critique of presuppositions to those presuppositions which characterize the fundamental scope of rhetoric: Presuppositions in the relationship of speaker and listener, the persuader and the one persuaded, judger and the thing being judged. The specific object of inquiry here is not the technique of speaking or persuading or judging, but the very meaning of these activities.[16]

The Distinctive Focus of This Study

What distinguishes this present book is that it is, to use Natanson's terms, a study in the Apostle Paul's *philosophy of rhetoric*, or better for our purposes, his *theology of preaching*. This means that, while we will trace in some detail Paul's core argument through 1 Corinthians 1–4, this book is not to be confused with a general commentary on 1 Corinthians, nor even a general commentary on these four chapters. Even more important, neither is this book an exercise in *rhetorical criticism*. Rhetorical critics tend to focus on Natanson's first two categories: the writer's rhetorical intentions (aspect 1) and the rhetorical techniques ("devices and modes of argument," aspect 2) employed to implement those intentions. Such criticism is often useful as far as it can reach. But it is important to see that when it comes to the study of 1 Corinthians 1–4 this limited focus does not reach far enough. Natanson's first two categories do not exhaust the relevance of rhetoric to these important chapters. The uniqueness of 1 Corinthians 1–4 is due precisely to the degree to which its argument plunges us deeper into the subject of rhetoric; that is, into an encounter with Natanson's third and fourth aspects of rhetoric as well.[17]

---

[16]Ibid.
[17]This is the essential point missed by Frestadius (2011, p. 56) when he says, "Thus, it does not make a significant difference whether one assumes the Corinthian wisdom to be related to

AVOIDING CONFUSION

One of the challenges in any discussion of Paul and rhetoric is to keep the specific object of our focus clear. Failing to do so is a prescription for confusion, a problem that arises when commentators slide unwittingly, not only from one to another of Natanson's four aspects of rhetoric, but also from one to another of at least *six interrelated but distinguishable topics*.

The three primary topics in this discussion are (a) Paul's practice as a preacher, (b) the form of Paul's letters and (c) Paul's argument in 1 Corinthians 1–4. Several potential relationships among these three then lead to a further set of topics: (d) Paul's rhetorical practice in his preaching compared to that in his letters, (e) Paul's argument in 1 Corinthians 1–4 compared to his actual practice as a preacher and (f) Paul's argument in 1 Corinthians 1–4 compared to his use of rhetoric in his letters.

Each of the first three topics can be legitimately investigated in its own right. This is an important observation for our present study. In the above paragraphs I have stated that this present book is not a work of rhetorical criticism. The focus of rhetorical criticism is typically topics (a) and (b), while our focus is topic (c). Our goal is to engage Paul's *theology of preaching* (or, if one prefers, his *philosophy of rhetoric*) as expressed in this seminal passage on the subject, 1 Corinthians 1–4. What's more, just as resolving topic (c) is not inherently necessary to the examination of topics (a) and (b), so also resolving the issues of topics (a) and (b) is not inherently necessary for addressing topic (c). Thus, until our summary and analysis section, the first two general topics will not occupy much of our attention.

Yet these three primary topics are intimately related, and work on any one of them obviously raises questions about the others. Thus it is that topics (d), (e) and (f) enter the picture. But note that each of these secondary topics requires assumptions about the first three, and this is where the discussion often becomes convoluted and confusing. Tenuous arguments based on other tenuous arguments make for still more tenuous and fragile conclusions.

For example, consider the issue of Paul's missionary preaching in comparison to his letters (d). Some commentators seek to minimize or eliminate this distinction based on arguments about the oral and aural quality of first-century Greco-Roman culture. The claim is that Paul's letters were meant to be read aloud and thus are essentially comparable to his oral discourse.

But against this argument see Porter (1999), and pp. 135-37 below. For a variety of reasons the distinction between Paul's λόγοι and his ἐπιστολαί cannot be so easily dismissed. Not least among these reasons is the fact that Paul's evangelistic λόγοι

---

proto-Gnosticism, Jewish-Hellenistic Wisdom, Sophistry, Cynicism, or social class, because the lowest common denominator of these philosophies is their elevation of the εγώ."

were delivered to distinguishably different audiences than were his ἐπιστολαί (see the documentation in Olbricht, 2005; cf. also p. 304-6 below). Both Paul and his critics observed a strong contrast between these two forms of communication (2 Cor 10:10) and apparently measured them by different yardsticks. Commentators who brush this explicit assessment aside typically do so because it does not comport with their larger reading of Paul. In our case, however, Paul's observation in 2 Corinthians 10:10 supports entirely our larger reading of the situation in Corinth, including the picture of Paul's missionary preaching in Acts (see appendix two).

Yet if Paul's λόγοι and his ἐπιστολαί are not to be collapsed into one, as if in studying the latter we are *ipso facto* hearing the former, this also means that while we have extended examples of Paul's ἐπιστολαί, we lack any comparable record of his missionary λόγοι. We have what Paul and others said *about* his preaching, and we have the abridged examples of his preaching in Acts (on which, see Porter, 2013, pp. 344-47), plus whatever patches in the Epistles may plausibly reflect that preaching. But we do not have any extended examples of Paul's actual λόγοι. Thus our conclusions about Paul's missionary preaching must be based on something other than direct evidence.

Then there is topic (e), the issue of Paul's purported repudiation of rhetoric in 1 Corinthians 1–4 versus his use of rhetoric in his missionary preaching. Because we lack full examples of Paul's actual missionary preaching, much less multiple examples, the claim that Paul's practice as a preacher contradicted his own analysis in 1 Corinthians 1–4 cannot bear much weight. We can understand clearly enough Paul's concerns in 1 Corinthians 1–4, but erecting the other side of this proposed contrast requires so much extrapolation and supposition as to render the exercise dubious. Dogmatic claims about contradictions between Paul's argument in 1 Corinthians 1–4 and his practice as a preacher must be viewed with skepticism.

Finally, there is topic (f), the much-discussed issue of Paul's repudiation of rhetoric in 1 Corinthians 1–4 versus his use of rhetoric in his letters. Given that we have in hand both 1 Corinthians 1–4 and multiple examples of Paul's letters, this discussion would seem to stand on much firmer grounds. Even so, the questions abound. What is Paul affirming about his preaching in 1 Corinthians 1–4? What is Paul challenging in 1 Corinthians 1–4? Is it "rhetoric," or something more specific, or something else altogether? And what about Paul's letters? Does Paul actually use rhetoric there? If so, what do we mean by "rhetoric"—that is, in what sense are Paul's letters "rhetorical"? Of what kind is Paul's rhetoric? How do we account for what we find Paul challenging in 1 Corinthians 1–4 and what we see in his letters?

On these and other related questions the commentators are conflicted, as the documentation in this book will amply testify. But this much is certain: equivocation in our use of the terms *rhetoric* or *rhetorical*, or unwittingly conflating the above six issues, can only muddy the water. If we can keep our focus and terminology clear, we can at least minimize the potential for confusion.

We began this introduction by observing that every theory of discourse is anchored in the soil of its author's presuppositions, whether philosophical or theological, and that the Apostle Paul's approach to preaching is a particularly clear expression of this relationship. With Natanson's categories in hand we are in a position to see the relevance of these observations for our study of 1 Corinthians 1–4. Nowhere else in Paul's writings do we find more thoroughly explored the relationship between the Apostle's theological premises and his understanding of his preaching practice. In these unparalleled chapters Paul is at pains to defend his approach to discourse (that is, his own preaching) against an alternative preferred by some of the Corinthians. To do so he contrasts his communication approach with their alternative and takes recourse to his theological presuppositions to explain and defend why he must practice the one and not the other. This argument is what renders 1 Corinthians 1–4 unique in Paul's writings.[18]

What we have in 1 Corinthians 1–4, then, if we have the eyes to see it, is nothing less than a study in Natanson's fourth aspect of rhetoric, the *philosophy of rhetoric*. In Paul's case, the corresponding term is the Apostle's *theology of preaching*. Does not 1 Corinthians 1–4 constitute a critique of the presuppositions of those who were criticizing Paul's preaching, and an exposition of Paul's own? Is not Paul grappling here with, among other things, "the relationship of speaker and listener, the persuader and the one persuaded, judger and the thing being judged" (aspect 4) in Christian preaching? And in basing his approach to these things on God's own *modus operandi* in the world, does Paul not strike to "the very meaning of these activities"? In each case the answer is yes.[19] Paul's argument through this first major unit of the epistle constitutes a unique record of his critical reflections on "the general rationale of persuasion" (aspect 3). As such, it provides a Pauline "critique of the rationale of rhetoric which inquires into the underlying assumptions" of the art (aspect 4). Whatever else 1 Corinthians 1–4 may be, these pivotal chapters constitute a unique study in the Apostle Paul's own philosophy/theology of rhetoric/preaching.

---

[18]In his treatment of the closely related issue of Paul's epistemology (see appendix three), Scott (2006, p. 15) cites 1 Cor 1:17–2:16 as one of only two "explicit statements about human reasoning" in the Pauline corpus. The other is Rom 1:18-32, the argument of which, unlike 1 Cor 1–4, was not generated by criticisms of Paul's preaching. Thus, while its epistemological stance mirrors that of 1 Cor 1–4, Rom 1 lacks any comparable discussion of Paul's missionary preaching.

[19]First Cor 1–4 offers us Paul's insight into how he wants his readers to view his *preaching*; see also Mitchell (2003) on Paul's insight into how to view his *letters*.

Plan of the Book

Part one: Greco-Roman rhetoric. My goal in this book is to provide readers the full resources required for an in-depth engagement with this aspect of Paul's argument in 1 Corinthians 1–4. This will require us to come to grips with the rhetorical challenge Paul faced in Corinth. Unfortunately, from our distant vantage point in history we will not fully appreciate that challenge unless we are willing to develop a fairly sophisticated understanding of what ancient rhetoric was about and what made it such a powerful cultural force. In other words, we must understand classical rhetoric as it was taught, practiced and experienced in the Greco-Roman culture Paul and the Corinthians inhabited. Only then can we appreciate the Apostle's forceful response in 1 Corinthians 1–4. This crucial material will constitute part one of our study. There is much one does not need to understand about ancient rhetoric in order to appreciate Paul's concerns; the following chapters are focused on what one *does* need to understand.

Avoiding rhetorical stereotypes. In this discussion we will attempt to shake ourselves free from some common stereotypes of classical rhetoric. In today's popular usage *rhetoric* is often a negative term, as in "mere rhetoric" or "empty rhetoric." But in the Apostle Paul's world and that of the Corinthians, rhetoric was often considered a noble thing. It is in fact this more positive understanding of rhetoric that we must rehabilitate if we are to do justice to Paul's argument in 1 Corinthians 1–4. Thus our study will attempt to avoid four common pitfalls in the study of ancient rhetoric.

1. *Wearisome minutia.* First, we will avoid being caught up in, indeed, overwhelmed by, the interminable and often tedious minutia of classical rhetoric. Spending a casual half-hour with resources such as Dean Anderson's *Glossary of Greek Rhetorical Terms*, or Stanley Porter's *Handbook of Classical Rhetoric in the Hellenistic Period*, or Heinrich Lausberg's *Handbook of Literary Rhetoric*, or Richard Lanham's *A Handlist of Rhetorical Terms*, not to mention E. W. Bullinger's classic *Figures of Speech Used in the Bible*, can leave one's eyes glazed over. We will spend little time with the seemingly endless classifications of the ancient rhetorical handbooks. What we are after is the far more important and fascinating *essence* of the rhetorical art.

By way of analogy, consider our English words *weather* and *climate*. *Weather* reports tend to describe immediate details and change dramatically from day to day, whereas descriptions of a region's *climate*, distilled from many weather reports over extended periods, address prevailing conditions or tendencies. In the

Introduction 43

same way, our goal will be to examine a wide range of rhetorical sources, drawn from before, during and after the first century, to demonstrate the prevailing rhetorical *climate* within which Paul conducted his ministry in Corinth. It is in the essential features of this rhetorical climate that we will find the key to understanding Paul's concerns in 1 Corinthians 1–4.

2. *Rhetoric as manipulation.* We will also try to avoid reducing classical rhetoric to not much more than techniques for manipulation.[20] For example, one writer expressed the views of many when he wrote,

> Rhetoric, as antiquity understood it, has little to do with the "truth," but it is the exercise of those skills which make people believe something to be true. For this reason, rhetoric is pre-occupied with demonstrations, persuasive strategy, and psychological exploration of the audience, but it is not interested in establishing the truth itself. Consequently, people who are interested in the truth itself must be distrustful of the "art of persuasion," because they know of its capacity for intellectual manipulation, dishonesty and cynicism. The effectiveness of rhetoric depends primarily upon the naiveté of the hearer, rather than upon the soundness of the case. Rhetoric works only as long as one does not know how it works.[21]

As we shall see, this description, common though it may be, represents a skewed caricature of classical rhetoric. It is rhetoric viewed, so to speak, through the jaundiced eye of Plato.[22] It does not do justice to the central and more noble dimensions of the rhetorical tradition. Quintilian, a late contemporary of the Apostle Paul who was the leading teacher of rhetoric in first-century Rome and as honorable a pagan as one was likely to find in the empire, would have been scandalized by such a sour and tendentious definition of the art he taught. He would have rejected it out of hand as a serious distortion of what rhetoric was about.[23] There were certainly those who conceived of and practiced rhetoric in

---

[20]Attempts to reduce Paul's rhetorical challenge in Corinth to the influence of first-century "sophists" tend to fall into this trap. On this mistake see below, pp. 150-53, 260-61, 294-97.
[21]Betz (1975, p. 378).
[22]See Jasper (1990, p. 134). It is important to remember that Plato's critique of rhetoric grew out of, and was fully valid only within the framework of, his epistemological stance. This point is too often ignored by those who relish the former but would never embrace the latter.
[23]E.g., consider this passage from Quintilian (*Inst. or.* 11.1.8-11): "Too much insistence cannot be laid upon the point that no one can be said to speak appropriately who has not considered not merely what it is expedient, but also what it is becoming to say. I am well aware that these two considerations generally go hand in hand. For whatever is becoming is, as a rule, useful. . . . Sometimes, however, the two are at variance. Now, whenever this occurs, expediency must yield to the demands of what

this cynical one-sided manner—too many, in fact—but it will hardly do to paint the ancient rhetorical tradition per se in such negative terms. Walter Ong was closer to the truth when he spoke of the classical tradition of rhetoric as

> one of the most consequential and serious of all academic subjects and of all human activities. As the art of persuasion, the art of producing genuine conviction in an audience, rhetoric affected the entire range of human action as nothing else in theory or in practice quite did. The study and use of rhetoric enabled one to move others, to get things done. . . . The study of rhetoric required engagement in the totality of human affairs, in politics and other decision making fields, in real life. . . . Rhetoric conferred power, and admirably humane power, for its power depended on producing conviction in others, on giving others grounds to act on out of free human decision resulting from deliberation. Such power befitted human beings. It was radically different from the brute power exerted by war and other uses of physical force.[24]

3. Rhetoric as mere ornamentation. Equally common is the tendency to treat classical rhetoric as if it were nothing more than a body of literary devices for stylistic embellishment. This too represents a misunderstanding of what rhetoric was about. For the ancients classical rhetoric involved issues far more substantial than how to generate purple prose. As classicist D. A. Russell points out,

> Rhetoric was always a rigorous discipline. It had arisen in a period of unparalleled inquisitiveness and doubt. It encouraged hard thinking, verbal and logical ingenuity, and shrewd psychological observation. In its long centuries of arid scholasticism, it never quite lost its edge. It is therefore something of a misunderstanding when writers on ancient literature treat the influence of

---

is becoming. Who is there who does not realize that nothing would have contributed more to secure the acquittal of Socrates than if he had employed the ordinary forensic methods of defence and had conciliated the minds of his judges by adopting a submissive tone and had devoted his attention to refuting the actual charge against him? But such a course would have been unworthy of his character, and, therefore, he pleaded as one who would account the penalty to which he might be sentenced as the highest of honours. The wisest of men preferred to sacrifice the remnant of his days rather than to cancel all his past life. And since he was but ill understood by the men of his own day, he reserved his case for the approval of posterity and at the cost of a few last declining years achieved through all the ages life everlasting. . . . This instance alone shows that the end which the orator must keep in view is not persuasion, but speaking well, since there are occasions when to persuade would be a blot upon his honour. The line adopted by Socrates was useless to secure his acquittal, but was a real service to him as a man; and that is by far the greatest consideration."

[24]Ong (1983, p. 1). See Booth (1963) for a brief, winsome and readable version of the nobler rhetorical tradition; for a much longer and more thorough discussion, see Perelman and Olbrechts-Tyteca (1969).

the rhetorical schools as entirely negative and destructive. The mistake, now less common than it was, comes partly from taking Plato's polemic as a decisive condemnation, partly from regarding rhetoric as basically an art of verbal embellishment, not of reasoning.[25]

A failure to appreciate Russell's point has left many with not much more than a caricature of classical rhetoric, a caricature, moreover, which on occasion in New Testament studies has served as a straw man, easily bowled over and dismissed. The truth is that the genius of classical rhetoric encompassed matters considerably more weighty than such caricatures allow. Our goal will be to focus on both the nobler and baser elements of Greco-Roman rhetoric as the mainstream of the ancient world understood it.

4. Underestimating ancient rhetoric. This too is a common tendency, one that is particularly costly in the interpretation of 1 Corinthians 1–4. It will be crucial when we arrive at the Corinth of Paul's day to have seen the sheer, overwhelming power of the rhetorical tradition in Greece. The practice of eloquence was not something that merely existed during Paul's day; it was pervasive in Greece and had been for centuries. It was a prime ingredient in the cultural heritage that defined Hellenism and gave the Greek mind its shape. There can be no question of anachronism or establishing channels of influence. The reach of rhetoric was all but inescapable during the life of Paul, from city to town to village. The Greco-Roman people thrived on eloquence and lionized its practitioners as moderns do their movie stars. For the average first-century citizens of the Greco-Roman world, this popular rhetorical tradition represented the most common context in which they conceived of or used the crucial term σοφία. To understand the role rhetoric played in Corinth, we must attempt to empathize with the passion for oratory that characterized this period.[26] Only then can we begin to grasp its importance to the first-century Corinthians. And more importantly, only then will we fully appreciate the Apostle's argument in 1 Corinthians 1–4.

For all of these reasons, the first section of this book will focus on the essential core of classical rhetoric, the alternative approach to discourse Paul was forced to disavow. In this section we will lean heavily on the primary sources.

---

[25]Russell (1981, p. 119).
[26]This is not easy for some to do. As Fantham (1997, p. 111) observed, "Both the vast scale of modern political societies and the overwhelming increase in communication by images or through the intimacy of electronic media explain why the concept of oratory has become alien and archaic, needing a social commentary to explain it to the modern reader."

Our goal will be to provide the reader with a firsthand encounter with the essential features of the ancient rhetoric tradition.

Part two: 1 Corinthians 1–4. The second section of the book will focus on the situation Paul encountered in Corinth and the apostolic response that situation elicited. Our goal will be to show the extent to which Greco-Roman rhetoric prompted the problems Paul faced in Corinth, and in what ways understanding this background sheds light on the full significance of the Apostle's argument. In this section our aim will be to clarify Paul's understanding of his own *modus operandi* as a preacher as expressed especially in 1 Corinthians 1:17–2:5. We will also, however, treat 1 Corinthians 1–4 in its entirety so as to give due weight to the full literary unit that forms the context of this central passage.

It may be tempting for readers interested primarily in Paul and his preaching to bypass the early chapters on rhetoric (part one) and move directly to this second section. But there will be a price paid in doing so. I have wrestled with the issues raised in this study for years, and it is my experience that Paul's argument in this crucial passage is so inimical to our contemporary Western ways of thinking that we are unprepared to appreciate what he is saying unless we are forced, so to speak, by the data to do so. We must be willing to prepare ourselves with a relatively sophisticated understanding of the genius of classical rhetoric if we intend to do justice to Paul's argument and its implications.

In part one we will focus on the rhetorical heritage that shaped the challenge Paul faced in Corinth. We will examine the pervasive cultural role of eloquence and observe its constant associations with status, power and influence in Greco-Roman society. In part two we will focus on Paul's engagement with that rhetorical tradition in Corinth. In doing so we will observe the close interaction of the rhetorical terms that play such a crucial part in 1 Corinthians 1:17–2:5: σοφία, λόγος, δύναμις, πίστις and ἀπόδειξις. In the process it will become clear that the background of 1 Corinthians 1–4 can scarcely be other than this rhetorical tradition. Without this background—a background, we should remind ourselves, that we must take pains to reconstruct but that was second nature to the Corinthians—significant dimensions of the Apostle Paul's argument in 1 Corinthians 1–4 remain inconspicuous. But against this background these dimensions rise to the surface and Paul's argument becomes vividly apparent.

Part three: Summary and analysis. In the final section of this book we summarize the issues and provide some analysis designed to help us make sense of them. Here we will finally be in a position to appreciate more fully some of the challenges of Paul's ministry model. For it is not until we discover the essence of classical rhetoric and the human psychological dynamic on which it is based—and we begin to see that this fundamental human dynamic has not changed but rather is something we all value and depend on in much of modern life, and then we observe that it is precisely this dynamic that in 1 Corinthians 1–4 the Apostle is calling into question for the purposes of ministry—that our thinking is challenged rather than reinforced. It is at this point that the first two parts of this study become so valuable. They will not permit us to sidestep the Apostle's concern. We must confront it and weigh it, not merely for the Corinthians but for ourselves.

The Natural Paradigm

In parts one and two we will focus primarily on Paul's preaching, for criticism of that preaching was the presenting problem that prompted Paul's response in 1 Corinthians 1–4. But as we do so it will also become clear that the Apostle was working with presuppositional issues that are much wider in their implications. In these important chapters Paul is operating from premises that comprise a Pauline paradigm or model for ministry in general. He applies this pattern to his preaching, but as we will see it is a pattern that applies equally to all Christian ministry. It is this paradigm that Paul sets over against its alternative.

A paradigm is a general way of thinking about something that provides a pattern or model for decision making. The paradigm Paul wished to call into question—let us call it the *natural paradigm*, named after the "natural person" (ψυχικὸς ἄνθρωπος) of 1 Corinthians 2:14—is one that is familiar to us all. The natural paradigm works in concert with our native inclinations, and countless individuals, including those in ministry, function unreflectively within its framework every day. This widespread use in turn reinforces this paradigm's dominant status.

According to the *natural paradigm*, we begin by determining what we wish to accomplish. What results are we after? Then we strategize so as to accomplish these results. We ask ourselves, what means should we employ to achieve these goals? Manipulative, unethical or dishonest means are obviously out of bounds, but within appropriate ethical boundaries, what must we do if we expect to achieve our aims? This is the question that guides our ministry planning. We build our strategies so as to achieve the goals we've set.

The utility of this approach is easily apparent. We decide what we're after and then orient our plans accordingly. What could be more obvious? The advantages of this pattern are so evident that it's difficult even to conceive an alternative—

which is why we operate within its framework every day. Every businessman decides what he wants to accomplish and then builds his business plan to achieve it. Every lawyer determines what decision she wants from the jury and then organizes her case accordingly. Every advertiser decides what he wants the customer to do and then shapes his message so as to achieve that aim. Every politician judges how she wants the voters to think and vote and then designs her communication strategy appropriately. In the same way those in ministry may strategize so as to accomplish their preset goals. The wisdom of this approach is self-evident. It is universally employed, patently effective, glaringly obvious. What could be more natural?

Yet therein lies the proverbial rub. What if the very *naturalness* of this paradigm, from a Pauline point of view, is the problem?

Challenging the Natural Paradigm

Suppose that we wished to call this natural paradigm into question precisely on these grounds; that is, however useful and legitimate it may be elsewhere, its very *naturalness* renders it fundamentally flawed as an approach to Christian ministry. Our complaint against the natural paradigm would not be that it is immoral or dishonest—at least not inherently. The complaint would focus on a more penetrating, but also more subtle, concern about this paradigm's sheer humanness. The problem with the natural paradigm, we would argue, is not that it is unethical but precisely that it is so quintessentially... *natural*. It's worth asking, were we to voice this sort of appeal, what welcome might our complaint receive? Our hearers would likely be those who have long found the natural paradigm useful. It may never have occurred to them that such an approach to ministry might be problematic. They would have no grounds on which to call it into question, or any alternative to consider in its place. So what would be their response to our complaint?

The answer is, our complaint would likely fall on stony ground. In fact it might well be met with considerable resistance. If the natural paradigm is not unethical and it is capable of achieving results, we might hear in response, what's the problem? On what grounds must we shy away from something so valuable? Having never grappled with the deeper issues at stake—or perhaps even realized that there *are* any deeper issues at stake—many would likely resist relinquishing something so obviously useful.

We should not underestimate the strength of such resistance. This issue was, after all, a key aspect of Paul's argument with the Corinthian church, and his mixed success in that endeavor suggests how entrenched the natural paradigm can be. What's more, the natural paradigm's alternative—let us call it the *Pauline paradigm*—is one that cuts painfully cross-grain to our typical ways of thinking and doing. It is deeply counterintuitive, not to mention countercultural. Like so many other topsy-turvy aspects of the gospel, where the way up is down and we find ourselves precisely by losing ourselves, this very contrariness constitutes the Pauline paradigm's greatest strength. Yet Paul's experience in Corinth, not to mention the regular recurrence of these issues throughout church history, suggests that this advantage is not everywhere appreciated. The natural paradigm is a difficult thing to relinquish. A willingness to call it into question and a readiness to embrace a radically different, Spirit-dependent alternative, one that is foreign to most of our natural inclinations, requires considerable discernment. The Apostle's success, or lack thereof, in making the case against the natural paradigm with his ancient Corinthian readers should give us pause.

Yet the ministry stakes are high enough that the responsibility to explore these issues anew is always with us, in our generation no less than any other. This debate has bubbled to the surface many times and in countless places throughout church history, and it remains pertinent for twenty-first-century Christians as well. It may in fact be especially pertinent for contemporary Christians, particularly in our Western, Americanized culture where pragmatism is so prized and the natural paradigm is so taken for granted. In such settings Christians may be uniquely susceptible to being captivated by this pragmatic approach to ministry, wooed by its promise and oblivious to its pitfalls.

Clashing Paradigms

Paul's extended argument in 1 Corinthians 1–4 constitutes the New Testament's *locus classicus* on the clash of these two paradigms. The roots of his argument reach deep into the Old Testament prophetic calling and the ministry of Jesus as portrayed in the Gospels, and its branches stretch into the remainder of the New Testament and early church literature. But 1 Corinthians 1–4 remains the seminal text on the subject. Not until the early fifth-century Book IV of St. Augustine's *De Doctrina Christiana*, "the first manual of Christian rhetoric,"[27] do we find a treatment that devotes more concentrated attention to the relevant

---

[27]Sullivan (1930, p. iii). Unless otherwise indicated, as here, patristic quotations are taken from the appropriate volumes of the Eerdmans (and later, Hendrickson Publishers) reprints of *The Ante-Nicene Fathers* and *The Nicene and Post-Nicene Fathers*.

issues. Augustine's treatment, in fact, offers another cautionary insight into just how stubborn our attachment to the natural paradigm can be.

A millennium before Augustine, Callicles sought to convince Socrates of the indispensability of rhetoric in defending the truth (*Gorgias* 486). Plato's Socrates remained stubbornly unconvinced. But one cannot say the same for Plato's erstwhile pupil, Aristotle. In his famous treatise *Rhetoric*, Aristotle argued that it would be "absurd" to resist the use of rhetoric in defense of the truth if others use it in service of error.[28] A thousand years later, St. Augustine, himself a former teacher of rhetoric[29] and now a Christian, found himself following Aristotle rather than Socrates:

> Since rhetoric is used to give conviction to both truth and falsehood, who could dare to maintain that truth, which depends on us for its defence, should stand unarmed in the fight against falsehood? ... Who could be so senseless as to find this sensible? No, oratorical ability, so effective a resource to commend either right or wrong, is available to both sides; why then is it not acquired by good and zealous Christians to fight for the truth, if the wicked employ it in the service of iniquity and error, to achieve their perverse and futile purposes?[30]

According to Sr. Thérèse Sullivan, Book IV of *De Doctrina Christiana*, which she calls "a handbook of Christian rhetoric,"[31] was designed as "a word aiming to fit the Christian orator for his important duty of inculcating the truths of religion."[32] How odd, then, that despite their obvious relevance to his topic, the reservations Paul expressed in 1 Corinthians 1–4 play no part in Augustine's discussion. He cites Scripture profusely throughout *De Doctrina*'s four books, but he essentially ignores the early chapters of 1 Corinthians. Augustine apparently found irresistible the natural paradigm's perfectly logical argument that if

---

[28]*Rhetoric* 1.1.12. This was the gist of the famous line attributed to Aristotle, "It would be shameful for me to be silent and suffer [the sophist] Isocrates to speak" (cited by Quintilian, *Inst. or.* 3.1; cf. Diogenes Laertius, *Lives* 5.3).

[29]In his *Confessions*, Augustine (Outler, 1955) refers to his former profession as that of a "word-merchant" (9.5.13): "During those years I taught the art of rhetoric. Conquered by the desire for gain, I offered for sale speaking skills with which to conquer others" (4.2.2). But after his conversion Augustine made the decision, "not to snatch my tongue's service abruptly out of the speech market, but to withdraw quietly, so that the young men who were not concerned about thy law or thy peace, but with mendacious follies and forensic strifes, might no longer purchase from my mouth weapons for their frenzy" (9.2.2).

[30]IV.2.3 (Green, 1997). J. J. Murphy (2008, pp. 205-18) demonstrates that Augustine was out of step on this point with many of his most illustrious Christian predecessors and contemporaries, men such as Lactantius, Cyprian, Titian, Justin Martyr, Clement of Alexandria, Tertullian, Synesius of Cyrene, Ambrose, Jerome and Basil.

[31]Sullivan (1930, p. 5).

[32]Ibid., p. 4.

Introduction

the enemies of the truth use the techniques of human persuasion to promote their error, Christians must use those same techniques in setting forth the truth.

AUGUSTINE'S CONSISTENCY

Significantly, this pattern follows throughout Augustine's larger corpus. His extant writings demonstrate a prodigious knowledge of both the Old and New Testaments and include innumerable biblical references—especially to the Apostle Paul, on which, see Thomas Martin (2000). Yet unlike most of his patristic contemporaries (e.g., St. John Chrysostom, who engages Paul's concerns at length), Augustine nowhere demonstrates, so far as I can discover, any interest in Paul's worries about the potential pitfalls of "persuasive words of wisdom" (1 Cor 2:4 AT). Even other relevant Pauline references—such as the critics' assessment of Paul's speech as contemptible (2 Cor 10:10) or Paul's assessment of himself as an unaccomplished speaker (2 Cor 11:6)—are essentially ignored. One looks in vain for a discussion of the relevant issues by the prolific former teacher of rhetoric, St. Augustine of Hippo.

Augustine's determined avoidance of these issues is striking. As noted above, even in the one place it would seem he would be required to interact with the argument of 1 Corinthians 1–4—Book IV of *De Doctrina Christiana*, a veritable "exposition of Christian rhetoric" (Sullivan, p. 5)—Augustine leaves the Apostle's concerns unaddressed. He makes only one passing reference (28.61) to the σοφίᾳ λόγου Paul rejects in 1 Corinthians 1:17, but this he minimizes by associating it with the instruction to Timothy to teach his flock to avoid "quarrelling about words" (μὴ λογομαχεῖν, 2 Tim 2:14). Even then, Augustine is quick to clarify that this warning "is not said to the end that we should say nothing in defense of truth whenever opponents attack it" (Sullivan, 1930, p. 185). The problem Paul is warning against, he says, is not the defense of the truth; it's a self-centered concern about "how your style may be preferred to another's" (ibid., p. 187). In any case, this much remains clear to Augustine: "Whether he expresses himself in the subdued, or in the moderate, or in the grand style, [the preacher] has this aim in speaking, that truth be made clear, that truth be made pleasing, that truth be made convincing" (ibid.). Hence, in his single reference (7.15) to Paul's assertion that he was deficient in public speaking (2 Cor 11:6), Augustine brushes the notion aside as a temporary concession to his Corinthian detractors.

Unlike so many of the church fathers who were trained in the art of persuasion but who followed the Apostle Paul in calling it into question for the purposes of preaching, Augustine seemed oblivious to the potential pitfalls in his position. Says Kolbert (2006, p. 150), "Although Augustine abandoned his secular career as an orator and came to look upon his former self as a mere 'seller of words' that was paid 'in the markets of rhetoric' to tell lies and teach others to lie persuasively, he kept and refined the very skills that brought him from provincial North Africa to the proximate edges of imperial power in Milan. In this way, he benefited from centuries of reflection by Hellenistic philosophers on the capacity of speech to influence human souls." Whether Augustine's failure to appreciate Paul's concerns about this human capacity was the reason for, or the result of, his avoidance of 1 Corinthians 1–4, we cannot know.

Instead of embracing the Apostle's critique, Augustine preferred an adapted version of the Ciceronian model[33] of the "*officia*" of the orator (12.27), emphasizing the preacher's threefold obligation to instruct (*docere*), to please or charm (*delectare*) and to persuade (*flectere*; often elsewhere, *movere*).

> It is necessary ... that the sacred orator, when urging that something be done, should not only teach in order to instruct, and please in order to hold, but also move in order to win. For indeed, it is only by the heights of eloquence that that man is to be moved to agreement who has not been brought to it by truth.[34]

To his credit, Augustine believed strongly in the necessity of prayer. In fact the preacher's effectiveness would come, he said, "more through the piety of his prayers than through his orator's skill, so that by praying for himself and for those whom he is going to address, he is a petitioner before a speaker" (15.32). This was because Augustine understood that even with the best of human efforts, only God can give the increase (1 Cor 3:7). "No one learns aright the things which pertain to life with God, if he becomes not through God, docile to God." Yet for Augustine, this did not eliminate the need for human persuasion in preaching. Just as medicine, "administered to men by men, is of no avail except to those to whom God restores health"—God can cure even without it and without him the medicine cannot cure—we do nonetheless administer the medicine. In the same way, human persuasive efforts, when contributed "by men, are of help to the soul when God makes them of help, who could have given his Gospel to man even without man's agency or help" (16.33).

This is an eminently plausible line of argument. Its only weakness is its failure to appreciate how radically and completely the Pauline ministry paradigm calls it into question. Paul certainly did not deny the human element in ministry. It is Paul whom Augustine cites to the effect that God's plan included the Apostle's

---

[33] 13.29; here and following, Sullivan (1930). On Augustine's adaptation of Ciceronian doctrines, see Fortin (2008); Thomas Martin (2000, p. 248).
[34] See Thomas Martin (2000, pp. 244–48) on Augustine's commitment to persuasion.

"planting" and Apollos's "watering," without which there would be no crop to increase. What Augustine missed were Paul's much more searching concerns about the circumscribed role humans are to play *within* God's plan, and the potential hazards of overstepping the boundaries of that role. Having failed to engage Paul's argument in 1 Corinthians 1–4, Augustine, like the Corinthians before him and countless others after him, seemed scarcely aware that there were any boundaries to overstep.

Augustine is one of my heroes of the faith, and I hold him in the highest regard. All the more sobering, then, to see how difficult it was for him to relinquish the natural paradigm. To be willing to abandon something so intuitively useful we must open ourselves to being instructed by the Apostle Paul. We must grasp the deeper issues at stake and embrace the Apostle's radical assessment of those issues. We must be willing to enter into the Apostle's critique of the natural paradigm so as to appreciate that critique's depth and passion. And then we must willingly rise to the Pauline alternative. Nothing short of a thorough engagement with that apostolic critique and its implications for Christian practice will suffice. Anything less is too easily and conveniently sidestepped. Either we will be willing to hear Paul's assessment of the natural paradigm in this central passage and be ready to embrace the alternative he puts on offer, or the issues will likely be lost on us.

Conclusion

In the concluding section of this book we will examine some of the implications of the Pauline ministry paradigm entailed in the theology of preaching we discover in 1 Corinthians 1–4. But we cannot begin there. Our beginning must be with the historical circumstances that prompted the Apostle to write. Then we will turn to Paul's argument itself. To understand that argument aright we must be willing to see it for what it is. In 1 Corinthians 1–4 we find Paul describing both the shape of his own preaching and his theological rationale for why it must take that shape. It will be in understanding these two things—Paul's own *modus operandi* as a preacher and his theological rationale for why this approach was the only one available to him—that we will discover the relevance for the church's ministry today. To facilitate that discovery we must begin by exploring the alternate approach Paul was at pains to disavow, for only against that backdrop will it become clear what the Apostle was driven to put in its place.

Part One

Greco-Roman Rhetoric

1

The Beginnings

In the introduction to his work on early Greek politicians, W. R. Connor says of the term *demagogy*, "The word can deceive us. It need not inevitably refer to specious or corrupt ways of appealing to the masses; indeed the early uses of the word are far more neutral and much less emotional. Today, however, the word has become unavoidably pejorative."[1] Connor thus chooses to shun the term altogether.

Unfortunately, we cannot follow suit. Though we face a similar dilemma with the word *rhetoric*, the term is too central to our discussion to be replaced. Despite the fact that moderns tend to associate rhetoric with purple prose at best or shameful manipulation at worst, we shall have to begin at the beginning and see if we can recover some of this ancient word's lost value.

What do we mean, then, by the term *classical rhetoric*? Answering this question will require some effort, but it is effort well spent. It will be crucial when we arrive at the Corinth of Paul's day to have explored the sheer, overwhelming influence of this rhetorical tradition in Greece. Rhetoric was not something that merely existed during Paul's day; it was pervasive in his Hellenized world and had been for centuries. In fact, the first-century poet Juvenal could use its presence as proof positive of civilization's reach: "Today the whole world has its Greek and its Roman Athens," he said. "Eloquent Gaul has trained the pleaders of Britain, and distant Thule talks of hiring a rhetorician."[2] Where Greeks and Romans were, says Juvenal, there was rhetoric.

This pervasive rhetorical tradition was a prime ingredient in the cultural heritage that defined the Greco-Roman world and gave the ancient mind its shape. The people thrived on eloquence and treated its practitioners as celeb-

---

[1]Connor (1971, p. 3).
[2]Juvenal, *Satires* 15.110-12. Except where otherwise indicated, citations from classical sources are taken from the appropriate volume of the Loeb Classical Library.

rities. To grasp the role rhetoric played in ancient Corinth, we must attempt to understand and empathize with this passion for the spoken word. This need not mean, thankfully, that we must attempt a full-scale history of ancient rhetoric. Splendid examples of such histories are widely available elsewhere,[3] and this goal would in any case take us too far afield. But to understand classical rhetoric as the ancients did, it will be important to examine at least its beginnings and some of its most relevant features. For those who wish to engage Paul's argument in 1 Corinthians 1–4, this material is important reading.

What follows, then, constitutes a short course in classical rhetoric. It represents a distillation of the key insights we must understand if we wish to grasp the preaching challenges Paul faced in Corinth. I have attempted wherever possible to allow the ancient voices to speak for themselves. Listening to these voices is the best way to prepare our modern ears to hear and appreciate the concerns of the Apostle Paul. So let us begin at the beginning.

ATHENS, THE BIRTHPLACE OF ELOQUENCE

It is to Cicero that we owe the citation from Aristotle to the effect that the first stirrings in the study of rhetoric began in ancient Syracuse.[4] Aristotle was no doubt correct, and his view was widely held throughout antiquity. Yet for our purposes the point is little more than a historical technicality. It is to Greece we must turn, and to Athens in particular, if we are to understand what became of rhetoric. Why? Because, as Cicero himself put it, it was in fifth-century B.C. Athens, "that city where eloquence was born and grew up to maturity,"[5] that rhetoric first genuinely thrived.

In the midst of one of the most extraordinary centuries any nation has known, the kindling of an interest in rhetoric appears to have been a complex instance of spontaneous combustion. The place was right, the people ready, the time prepared. With conditions so ripe, it seems in retrospect scarcely avoidable that what has come to be known as classical rhetoric should first have flourished in ancient Athens.

There was already in Greece by the fifth century, of course, a considerable tradition of delight in the spoken word. To be a man of action and eloquence had long been the ideal of the Greeks. Physical prowess counted for a great deal

---

[3]E.g., see Habinek (2005).
[4]Cicero, *Brutus* 46.
[5]Ibid., 39; cf. 27, 49-50, 255; *De or.* 1:13.

in Greece, but scarcely more than verbal prowess. By tradition the Greeks always reserved a portion of their highest respect for the one who, like the venerable lord Echeneus in Homer's *Odyssey*, was "well skilled in speech."[6]

By the fifth century, however, this deeply ingrained cultural appreciation of eloquence reached a new stage of crystallization. The Greeks had become connoisseurs of their own language, possessed of a taste and appetite for its rich expressiveness that only the eloquence of poets or orators could satisfy. Moreover, the potential of this extant market was vastly expanded by the political and social developments of the fifth century.

In the political realm the trends toward democracy that had begun with Hesiod and Solon were coming to full flower. Such factors as the increase in the number of elected positions, limitations on the length of terms, and the extension of both the right to vote and eligibility for office to lower classes combined to give oratory an ever-increasing role in public life. Sovereignty had come to rest in the Assembly, which decided issues by majority vote after prolonged deliberations. It was an unprecedented forum for public address in which every citizen was expected to participate either directly or indirectly.

For not a few ambitious young men, and especially those who lacked the credentials of nobility, these political developments opened up avenues to power, position and wealth that had heretofore been closed to all but the few. Social and political mobility became a genuine possibility. What these young hopefuls lacked, however, were the skills required to take advantage of their opportunities, skills that centered and depended on the ability to speak persuasively before a crowd.

Athens had also developed a complex legal system in which large (averaging perhaps four to five hundred), randomly selected juries were addressed in extended speeches, not by trained lawyers, which as a profession did not yet exist in Athens, but by the plaintiffs and defendants themselves. These public trials became one of the leading entertainments in Athenian life, effectively parodied by Aristophanes in *The Wasps*. Crowds would daily gather to hear the impassioned pleas for and against conviction, and their reactions would in turn sway the decisions of the jury. Powerful speakers gained repute, while weak speakers suffered not only defeat but ridicule. In a litigious society such as Athens the capacity to move an audience came to be valued at a premium, for therein lay the pathway to success and honor, or, as the case might be, to survival.

---

[6]Homer, *Odyssey* 7.158; cf. Cicero, *Brutus* 40.

Conspiring with these social and political developments were the philosophical trends of the day. The fifth century witnessed a major sea change in Greek thought. Prior to the time of Socrates, Greek philosophy had been dominated by the physical philosophers who were struggling to understand the nature of the material universe. But during Socrates's generation a significant shift took place. The spotlight of philosophy edged away from abstract analyses of the physical world toward seemingly more pertinent considerations of humans themselves and human affairs in general.

The apparent overload of the physicists' speculations, as brilliant as some of them seem in retrospect, thus combined with the developing political opportunities of the day to whet the appetite of the ordinary citizen for an understanding of the principles governing the human arena, and of the arts that promised successful participation therein. Inevitably this provided a strong impetus to the development of the formal study of rhetoric, that most utilitarian of social skills. In the debates over matter versus form, being versus becoming, unity versus diversity, rhetoric could play little role. But in the decisions of city life, in matters of public justice or policy or honor, rhetoric found a cultural medium in which it could flourish. As these questions of human conduct came increasingly to the attention of the Athenian people, so did the already attractive subject of eloquence, and the τέχνη ("art" or "craft") of rhetoric by which it was produced, grow in importance.

We have said that eloquence had long been prized by the Greeks. Yet the τέχνη by which it could be consciously produced was not born until sometime early in the fifth century. This distinction is an important one. The Greek word τέχνη does not translate easily into English since there exists no simple equivalent that bears just the right connotations. The core meaning of the word has to do with the notion of skillfulness according to design, in contrast to randomness or chance. The one who possesses a systematic understanding of a subject that leads to skill in its application possesses the τέχνη of the subject. A mere knack or aptitude that is neither derived from nor governed by such understanding, but stems instead from a natural flair or handiness, does not constitute a τέχνη. A τέχνη involves something studied, grasped and under conscious control. It consists of a system of rules or a method of making or doing that can be discovered, mastered and taught. Thus the English terms "art," "craft" or "skill" come closest to the ancient meaning of τέχνη.

Though persuasion had always been honored among the Greeks—the divine Πειθώ ("Persuasion") was one of the Greek goddesses—until the fifth century no one had yet articulated or taught a τέχνη of eloquence. Greek speakers had long produced powerful speeches, but never according to a systematic knowledge of what makes eloquence effective. This was what began to change during the fifth century. Because of the confluence of factors mentioned above, there emerged during this period an intense interest in the τέχνη of rhetoric, that art by which skill in this most crucial of activities, public speaking, could be propagated.

Though on the surface this was seemingly a small step, in reality it was a revolutionary social development. That *sine qua non* of effective leadership in Greece, the ability to speak persuasively before an audience, was brought within range of the ordinary man. Always before, this ability had seemed beyond the grasp of most since the gods, or more likely, social position, appeared to bestow it on so few. But the discovery of a τέχνη of rhetoric raised irreversibly in the minds of many less privileged men a new question: Was it indeed possible that these crucial skills could actually be *taught*, and in turn *learned* by anyone? This was an iconoclastic idea in more ways than one, not least because of its social implications. It jolted Socrates, Plato and the elite of Athens to respond and motivated generations of ambitious young men to begin looking for an education in rhetoric.

This desire for formal training in rhetoric was supplied in two important ways, and at two distinguishable levels: the written and the oral. At the written level there began to appear early in the fifth century rhetorical handbooks, known as τέχναι, which were designed to teach simple, practical techniques for persuasive argumentation primarily for use in the law courts. At the oral level there developed the important educational movement known as the *sophists*.

THE RHETORICAL HANDBOOKS

The first rhetorical handbooks were specialized and utilitarian documents. As a result they were highly prescriptive and often trivial. They were not, and did not deserve to be, preserved as quality literature. We know that most of the older handbooks were still available to Cicero (106–43 B.C.), for in writing *De Inventione* he states, "I was able to set out before me the store of wisdom of all who had written from the very beginning of instruction in rhetoric down to the present time."[7] But subsequently almost all of these handbooks perished. Yet they were the progenitors of a body of literature on the subject of persuasion that was to grow over the centuries to enormous proportions. Evolving not

---
[7]Cicero, *De inv.* 2.5. This is something of an overstatement on Cicero's part, however. By his own testimony not all sources were available to him; e.g., see *De inv.* 2.7. On Cicero's method of research, see *De inv.* 2.4-5.

uniformly but in fits and starts, this literature has not yet ceased to expand and ripen. The early handbooks were merely the first seedlings in this vast and in some ways wearisome forest of books.

Much has changed in the field of rhetoric over the centuries since these first textbooks were published, but perhaps more importantly much has remained the same. This is due to the deeper truth that while people change with time, in another weightier sense they also remain the same. If it were possible to compare an audience of ancient Greece with an audience drawn from contemporary Western society, one would obviously discover profound differences. Yet we would also discover, at the core of things, certain crucial similarities rooted in fundamental characteristics of human psychology, characteristics that will not change without transforming human beings into something other than what they have always been. Since the essence of the art of rhetoric is itself tied to these very characteristics of human psychology, it too remains at the core unchanged. The external garb of rhetoric has modulated radically with the times; in fact, a nimble adaptation to the ever-changing kaleidoscope of situational demands may be said to be the genius of the art. But at its core the essence of rhetoric, like the elementary human nature to which it conforms, does not much change. The ancient handbooks and the most modern textbooks on public speaking tread common ground.

The Sophists

If the handbooks promulgated rhetoric at the written level, the sophists taught it at the oral level. Exactly what the sophists were is difficult to describe. For our purposes it will suffice to use W. K. C. Guthrie's definition of the sophists as a loosely defined and largely self-appointed group of "professional educators who gave instruction to young men, and public displays [ἐπίδειξις] of eloquence, for fees."[8] Such a class of educators could scarcely have existed in Greece one hundred years earlier, but with the developments of the fifth century there emerged a market for their services, which they confidently—indeed, often shamelessly—thrust themselves forward to supply.

The skills the sophists claimed to teach they called ἀρετή, which is often rendered "virtue." But this translation is particularly deficient due to the limited connotations of this English word. For the Greeks ἀρετή meant excellence of any sort and was closely related to notions of skill or proficiency. Thus the word enjoyed a bewildering array of uses. Every activity, it seems, from shoemaking

---

[8]Guthrie (1971, p. 35).

to waging war to living life, had its own ἀρετή. By itself the word was therefore incomplete. It always required, at least implicitly, a genitival limitation; it always referred to the ἀρετή *of* something. Possessing ἀρετή simply meant that one was good at something, manifesting some form of excellence.

When the sophists claimed to teach ἀρετή, the excellence they had in mind was that of public life, and especially that of the politician and public speaker. Their ἀρετή was career oriented, says G. B. Kerferd, comprising "all those qualities in a man which made for success in Greek society and which could confidently be expected to secure the admiration of a man's fellow-citizens, followed in many cases by substantial material rewards."[9] Rhetoric, therefore, lay at the heart of the sophists' formula for success. Whatever differences they displayed among themselves, the key thing they had in common was their emphasis on the art of persuasion. In fact, at least one of the sophists, Gorgias, insisted that effective speaking was all he taught.[10] The reason for the sophists' unanimity at this point reaches back to the crucial role played by oratory in the public life of Athens. As classicist Werner Jaeger put it, to be successful in that arena "the prime necessity was to master the art of public speaking."[11] This was the key to both social advancement and political power.

Yet for many of the sophists the matter reached deeper than the issue of political power. For them rhetoric harnessed for political and social ends a more elemental power: the δύναμις λόγου, the power of persuasive discourse. This was a force that for many was the closest their skepticism ever came to things divine. The sophists were not alone even in their own day, of course, in their awareness of the power of the spoken word, and others would follow in their wake. As Xenophon put it, "Many supporters are necessary to him who ventures to use force; but he who can persuade needs no confederates, having confidence in his own unaided power of persuasion."[12]

The emergence of a group who could channel such a powerful force unavoidably aroused opposition in Athens. The most famous attacks on the sophists came from those who, along with Socrates and Plato, viewed their moral and philosophical influence as pernicious. In *The Clouds* Aristophanes wickedly portrays the decadent sophists as both a symptom and a cause of the

---

[9]Kerferd (1981, p. 131).
[10]Plato, *Philebus* 58a; *Meno* 95c; *Gorgias* 495C.
[11]Jaeger (1945, vol. 1, p. 290).
[12]Xenophon, *Memorabilia* 1.2.11.

Athenian decline. But perhaps more importantly, and certainly more dangerously, the sophists were perceived by the elite of Athens as social threats. They were promoting a social mobility that was undermining established social patterns. This was not to be tolerated; hence the series of trials during the second half of the fifth century on trumped up charges of ἀσέβεια, or impiety.

It is a testimony to the power and usefulness of what the sophists taught that they thrived despite their opposition. If they were not the best friends rhetoric has ever had, they nevertheless did a great deal, for better or worse, to popularize it and give it substance.

Plato

Plato was born at Athens in 427 B.C. His parents, evidently people of means, were able to provide him with the best available education. It was during the period of Plato's upbringing that the sophists flourished in Athens, and he no doubt heard them all. Yet their teachings fell on stony ground in the mind of the sensitive young scholar, and there is nothing to suggest that sophistic doctrines ever held any appeal for him. Instead Plato was drawn to the more eccentric teachings of Socrates. After the death of Socrates in 399, Plato's ideas continued to ferment. Further study and teaching eventually led to the founding of his Academy (387 B.C.) and to the writing of some of the most widely read literature ever composed.

Plato was alarmed by the teaching of the sophists and rose to resist it. As Kerferd says, "Virtually every point in Plato's thought has its starting point in his reflection upon problems raised by the sophists, virtually every dialogue in one way or another has one or more sophists either visibly present at or covertly influencing its discussions."[13] Yet Plato's real concern was not the persuasive techniques the sophists taught; it was their epistemology, their views of truth and knowledge. Plato was not inherently opposed to rhetoric, but neither was he interested in moving an audience as an end in itself. Working to persuade an audience was valid, he believed, only if one moved them toward where they ought to go, that is, toward the truth. But how could one move toward the truth if one did not know what it was?

Isocrates

Yet Plato's lifelong struggle with the sophists was one he was destined to lose. It was not his educational ideals that would come to dominate Greco-Roman education but those of his rival, the sophist Isocrates.

---
[13]Kerferd (1981, p. 173).

Isocrates was born in 436, a full generation before the death of Socrates. He first studied under the sophist Gorgias and later competed against his younger rival, Plato, in the education of young men in Athens. Yet Isocrates outlived Plato by almost a decade; indeed, he came within sixteen years of outliving Aristotle, who was also something of an opponent. He died in 338, having fallen short by only two years of a full century of life, spanning a period of wildly fluctuating Athenian fortunes. By his death Isocrates had seen or heard the best the ancient world had to offer, and the worst.

Isocrates was one of the professional teachers of Athens; that is to say, he was a sophist. As such he offered a popular alternative to Plato's Academy. At first his students were largely Athenians, but as his fame spread pupils began coming to him from across the Mediterranean world. Even more than the other sophists, Isocrates's instruction covered a broad spectrum of practical matters designed to produce what might be called the cultured sophisticate. But like the rest, at the core of it all was training in eloquence.

As it would happen, it was Isocrates's sort of education, not Plato's, that would come to dominate the educational systems of the Greco-Roman world. This trend began with Isocrates and increased during the Hellenistic period. Then under the influence of the Romans it became virtually universal. By the first century B.C. rhetoric had come to be considered the crown of a liberal education and rhetorical proficiency the telltale mark of a formally educated man.[14] Thus it was Isocrates, not the more famous Plato, who would become the educator of the Greco-Roman world.

This comes as a surprise to many who have never heard of Isocrates. Isocrates's massive contribution to our Western educational tradition deserves more attention than it has received. According to the renowned French historian of education H. I. Marrou,

> When Plato and Isocrates are studied consecutively Isocrates necessarily gets left in the shade and is more or less sacrificed to his brilliant rival. . . . [Yet there] is no doubt that Isocrates has one claim to fame at least, and that is as the supreme master of oratorical culture, the literary kind of education that was to become the dominant feature of the classical tradition. . . . On the whole it was Isocrates, not Plato, who educated fourth-century Greece and subsequently the Hellenistic and Roman worlds; it was from Isocrates that,

---

[14]See Morgan (1998, pp. 190-97).

"as from a Trojan horse," there emerged all those teachers and men of culture, noble idealists, simple moralists, lovers of fine phrases, all those fluent, voluble speakers, to whom classical antiquity owed both the qualities and the defects of its main cultural tradition.[15]

This point is important for our study. The struggle between Plato and Isocrates bore implications for first-century Corinth. If we are to understand the rhetorical background to the problems Paul faced there, we must come to grips with the Isocratean tradition cited by Marrou.

> The thing that really showed whether a man was cultivated or not was not whether he had studied science or medicine—things that only interested a narrow range of specialists—but whether he had received either of the two rival and allied forms of advanced education which were still the most widespread and characteristic—the two forms of culture typified by Plato and Isocrates: the philosophical and the rhetorical.[16]

Of these two forms of culture, Marrou says,

> the dominant member was unquestionably the second, which left a profound impression on all manifestations of the Hellenistic spirit. For the very great majority of students, higher education meant taking lessons from the rhetor, learning the art of eloquence from him. This fact must be emphasized from the start. On the level of history Plato had been defeated: posterity had not accepted his educational ideals. The victor, generally speaking, was Isocrates, and Isocrates became the educator first of Greece and then of the whole ancient world. His success had already been evident when the two were alive, and it became more and more marked as the generations wore on. Rhetoric is the specific object of Greek education and the highest Greek culture.[17]

THE RHETORICAL TRADITION

Thus began what we have come to call *classical rhetoric*. In the centuries to follow, towering figures would emerge in this classical tradition, Aristotle, Cicero and Quintilian preeminent among them. These and countless lesser figures would

---

[15]Marrou (1956, p. 79). Marrou's reference to the Trojan horse is from Cicero, *De or.* 2.94: "Then behold! There arose Isocrates, the Master of all rhetoricians, from whose school, as from the Horse of Troy, none but leaders emerged."
[16]Marrou, p. 194.
[17]Ibid.

extend the range of rhetoric to the entire Western world, and we will examine their work in what is to come. Yet it must also be said that little of significance emerged within the Greco-Roman rhetorical tradition during these later centuries that cannot in some way be traced back to fourth-century Greece and to Isocrates in particular. By the close of the fourth century B.C. the central core of rhetoric had been articulated. While later writers could and did subtract from it, settling for something less, none was able to add to it or modify it in any lasting or substantial way. For the most part, later rhetoricians only elaborated, refined or further systemized what they had received.

Five Historical Developments

Our goal in the following chapters is to highlight some of the most relevant features of this central rhetorical tradition as a way of setting the stage for our study of 1 Corinthians 1–4. But before doing so, let us briefly observe five historical developments in particular that will be relevant to our study of Paul in Corinth.

First, Cicero (106–43 B.C.) eventually codified the orator's training into what came to be called the five "canons" of rhetoric (see *De inv.* 1.7). These canons, developed at length by Quintilian (A.D. 35–100) in his *Institutes of Oratory*, were designed to instruct orators in the skills and choices required to achieve their goals with an audience. The canons were as follows: (1) *invention* (*inventio*) covered the discovery and development of persuasive arguments to be used in the substance of the speech; (2) *arrangement* (*dispositio*) treated the organization of the speech's substance so as to achieve its desired effect; (3) *style* (*elocutio*) focused on the effective wording of the speech; (4) *memory* (*memoria*) emphasized stocking the mind with memorable ideas and language and taught mnemonic devices for remembering the speech; and (5) *delivery* (*pronuntiato* or *actio*) covered the orator's use of voice and gestures to communicate the speech to an audience. These five headings were still used in the teaching of public speaking well into modern times.

Second, from the time of Aristotle public speeches in the Greco-Roman world were divided into three types. According to Aristotle, these three types corresponded to three kinds of hearers who faced three kinds of decisions: "A member of the general assembly is a judge of things to come; the dicast ["juror"], of things past; the mere spectator, of the ability of the speaker. Therefore there are necessarily three kinds of rhetorical speeches, deliberative, forensic, and epideictic."[18]

---

[18]Aristotle, *Rhetoric* 1.3.1-3.

In the centuries to follow teachers and practitioners tended to embrace Aristotle's threefold division. They viewed *deliberative* oratory as that which took place in the public realm. It was focused on the future as orators sought to persuade or dissuade assemblies regarding better or worse courses of action. *Forensic* rhetoric was the oratory of the courts. It was focused on what had or had not taken place in the past. It was about issues of justice or injustice and involved accusing defendants or defending the accused. *Epideictic* (from ἐπίδειξις, "exhibition, display, demonstration") was the oratory of ceremonial occasions such as festivals or funerals. It was focused on the present, offering praise or blame of individuals or assessments of virtue or vice. During the first century, Rome's greatest teacher of rhetoric, Quintilian, was skeptical of this threefold analysis because he rightly viewed it as oversimplified.[19] Yet in the end even Quintilian capitulated to the weight of tradition, concluding that on this issue "the safest and most rational course seems to be to follow the authority of the majority."[20]

Third, from the earlier demonstration speeches of the older sophists there emerged during the Hellenistic period (that century-and-a-half transition from the death of Alexander to the final conquest by Rome) and proliferated during the Roman centuries the widespread use of practice exercises, for both the inculcation and maintenance of rhetorical skills. The Greek term for this practice speech was μελέτη, the Latin, *declamatio*.[21] With time these declamations, which originally served a largely pedagogical role,[22] became something more: popular public exhibitions designed for show. They tended to emphasize form over content and as such became virtual caricatures of what many moderns associate with the term *rhetoric*.

Fourth, there arose during the Hellenistic period and persisted well into the Christian era what came to be called the Asianist-Atticist controversy. It was essentially a debate over rhetorical style. Asianism, an artificial, flamboyant and undisciplined style fed by "foreign" elements from the East, emphasized the new, the startling, the bold. Atticism, by contrast, represented an attempt to recover the classical simplicity of the ancient Athenian style of speaking. It was restrained, spare and in its own way equally artificial as speakers attempted to affect a stilted dialect that belonged to the past.

---

[19]Quintilian, *Inst. or.* 3.4.
[20]Ibid., 3.4.12.
[21]See Russell (1983).
[22]They were designed, as Bloomer (2011, p. 179) says, to prepare students for "ascending the pinnacle of Roman society, becoming a master of persuasive speech, another Cato or Cicero."

The Beginnings 69

Finally, there arose a movement that came to be called, following Philostratus, the New or Second Sophistic.[23] This movement represented a reflowering of the ancient Greek interest in the sophists. Once again the land witnessed an upsurge of famous orators who went about teaching rhetoric to others, giving demonstration lectures and declaiming on various public occasions—all for a fee. Some of these orators undertook ambassadorial tasks for their native cities. In their immense popularity and great wealth, many of these latter-day sophists rivaled their famous counterparts of ancient Athens. Largely a second- to fourth-century A.D. Greek phenomenon,[24] the Second Sophistic nevertheless began developing momentum during the latter half of the first century, as seen in figures such as Nicetes (ca. A.D. 50–100) and Dio of Prusa (ca. A.D. 40–115).

---

[23] Philostratus, *Lives* 481.
[24] On the difficulty of defining the boundaries of the Second Sophistic, see Whitmarsh (2005, pp. 4-22). On Winter's attempt to locate the movement back into first-century Corinth, and its implications for our own study, see "Good Rhetoric Versus Bad Rhetoric.1" in chapter eleven.

2

The Goal of Rhetoric

Aelius Aristides (A.D. 117–181), a popular Greek orator during the so-called Second Sophistic, claimed that oratory was "of all human things . . . [the] greatest, first, and most perfect, and if it is possible to say so, the greatest thing to be prayed for."[1] Why such reverence for oratory? Because oratory is

> the bond of maintaining life for mankind, so that matters should not be decided for anyone by force, weapons, anticipation, numbers, size, or any other inequality; but that reason should calmly determine justice. This is the beginning and nature of oratory, the desire to save all men and to repel force through persuasion.[2]

Aristides had it right. From the beginning persuasion was viewed as the alternative to coercion. Hence the importance of the art of rhetoric, which claimed to harness and teach the skills of persuasion. There did eventually emerge, of course, a tamed, caged rhetoric, rhetoric that had been domesticated for mere exhibition, what George Kennedy calls "secondary rhetoric."[3] But this type of rhetoric was always a derived and diminished thing, like a powerful lion expending its enormous strength padding impotently behind bars. At its core the underlying art was always about what Kennedy calls "primary rhetoric"; that is, the art of moving your listeners where you want them to go. Given this audience, given the possibilities inherent in this subject matter, given this occasion, how can I achieve my predetermined purposes? This was the essential question classical rhetoric was designed to answer.

The concern for marshaling rhetorical possibilities to achieve some predetermined effect may be viewed as the defining feature of rhetoric. Persuasion,

---

[1] Aristides, *To Plato in Defense of Oratory* 204.
[2] Ibid.
[3] Kennedy (1980, p. 4).

victory, success in winning a particular result lay at its center. Rhetoric is, said Plato, the art (τέχνη) that "leads the soul [ψυχαγωγία] by means of words."[4] The goal of all the speaker's efforts, he said, is "to produce conviction [πειθώ ... ποιεῖν] in the soul."[5] Plato believed that "oratory is the maker of persuasion," said Aristides; that is, it "aims at things and guides its words, according to its aim."[6] This was an assumption with which Aristides was not only prepared to agree but on which he insisted: "Taking aim is an attribute of oratory."[7]

As we have noted, Plato was skeptical of rhetoric on epistemological grounds. Yet in his assessment of the essence of rhetoric he stood in agreement with the larger rhetorical tradition: primary rhetoric was about the deliberate inducing of beliefs, decisions and actions within audiences. "No one can be called an orator," says Messalla in Tacitus's *Dialogus De Oratoribus*, who cannot speak "in a manner fitted to win conviction [*ad persuadendum*]."[8] Quintilian could thus speak of "the purpose for which oratory was above all designed," that is, to "speak with profit and with power to effect [the orator's] aim."[9]

The great Roman orator Cicero agreed. At the outset of his life's work he says in *De Inventione*, "The function of eloquence seems to be to speak in a manner suited to persuade an audience, the end is to persuade by speech."[10] This perspective never changes in Cicero's writings.[11] Persuasion is portrayed as the essential art taught in the rhetorical schools. In *Partitiones Oratoriae*, which is little more than a rhetorical catechism, to the question, What is the aim of the speaker? comes the answer, "To discover how to convince the persons whom he wishes to persuade."[12] The business of oratory, says Cicero in *Brutus*, is persuasion;[13] the speaker's aim is "to win the assent of the throng."[14] How does one win this assent? Through the three functions of oratory: "The supreme orator ... is the one whose speech instructs [*docere*], delights [*delectare*] and

---

[4]Plato, *Phaedrus* 261A. ψυχαγωγία (metaph., "winning of men's souls, persuasion").
[5]Ibid., 271A, cf. 271C; *Gorgias* 452D-453A.
[6]Aristides, *To Plato in Defence of Oratory* 138.
[7]Ibid., 140.
[8]Tacitus, *Dial.* 30.5.
[9]Quintilian, *Inst. or.* 12.10.72. Quintilian preferred to view "speaking well" as the true goal of rhetoric (see 2.15.38; 2.17.23-25), but it was an idiosyncratic view he could not maintain. He regularly defaulted to the standard view, as above. See *SPTOP* (pp. 100-105) for a discussion of why Quintilian lapsed into this inconsistency.
[10]Cicero, *De inv.* 1.6.
[11]See Quintilian, *Inst. or.* 2.15.5.
[12]Cicero, *Part. or.* 1.6.
[13]Cicero, *Brutus* 59.
[14]Ibid., 191.

moves [*movere*] the minds of his audience. The orator is duty bound to instruct; giving pleasure is a free gift to the audience, to move them is indispensable."[15] As Brutus puts it, a speaker who lacks the "ability to influence the minds of his hearers and to turn them in whatever direction the case demands" thereby "lacks the one thing most essential."[16]

The most well-known ancient source on how this process actually works is Aristotle's *Rhetoric*. Rhetoric, Aristotle says, may be defined as "the faculty of discovering the possible means of persuasion in reference to any subject whatever."[17] For Aristotle the art of rhetoric centers on the ability to discover, in any given situation, the potential instruments of persuasion. Persuasion is the goal, and rhetoric is designed to "to promote this end as far as possible."[18]

Aristotle viewed rhetoric as the counterpart of dialectic, or "a sort of division or likeness of Dialectic, since neither of them is a science that deals with the nature of any definite subject, but they are merely faculties [δύναμις] of furnishing arguments [λόγοι]."[19] (Note these rhetorical terms: we will hear them and those that follow echoed in 1 Cor 1–4.) These arguments take the form of proofs (πίστεις). What constitutes a proof, or, in so many words, how are people persuaded? Aristotle states his basic assumption this way: "Proof [πίστις] is a sort of demonstration [ἀπόδειξις], since we are most strongly convinced when we suppose anything to have been demonstrated [ἀποδεδεῖχθαι]."[20] In other words, we believe what we see, or think we see. Persuasion always rests on some form of demonstration; conversely, that which demonstrates is most persuasive. The task of the speaker is to discover these means of demonstration and make use of them to effect belief within the audience. To instruct in how to do so is the purpose of Aristotle's *Rhetoric*.

Like Plato, Aristotle held that it is the task of speakers to produce (ποιέω, "to

---

[15] Cicero, *Opt. gen.* 4.
[16] Cicero, *Brutus* 279.
[17] Aristotle, *Rhetoric* 1.1.1.
[18] Ibid., 1.1.14. But for a critique of this view of rhetoric, see Quintilian, *Inst. or.* 2.15.13.
[19] Aristotle, *Rhetoric* 1.2.7. Cf. 1.1.1, 14.
[20] Ibid., 1.1.11. The term πίστις is part of the family of words related to the verb πιστεύειν, which means to trust, put faith in, to believe that or believe in. The semantic shadings of πίστις are therefore subtle. For our purposes the relevant meanings of πίστις are "faith," "belief" or "conviction." The word refers to the state of trusting someone or something, or having been persuaded of something. In some settings, πίστις shifts to that which *generates* faith, belief or conviction; that is, that which creates a basis for trust. Hence: "a pledge" or "guarantee"; or in a rhetorical context, a "means of persuasion" or a "proof." But see also in the *Rhetoric* πίστις as "conviction," 1.2.8; 2.1.3, 5. Quintilian (*Inst. or.* 5.10.8) understands πίστις as the equivalent of the Latin *fides* (faith, or credibility). In this way "faith" and the "basis for faith" shade into one another in the term πίστις.

create, bring into existence") belief.[21] Hence in his discussion of the parts of a speech he concludes that there are really only two: the statement of the speaker's subject and the proof (πίστις) through demonstration (ἀπόδειξις). These are the only necessary parts of every persuasive speech.[22] There is perhaps no single sentence in the *Rhetoric* that encapsulates this dynamic better than this one: "Persuasion is produced by the speech itself, when we establish the true or the apparently true from the means of persuasion applicable to each individual subject."[23] Here, explicitly stated, is the dynamic on which the persuader depends. The audience believes when the speaker establishes or appears to establish the truth by means of the persuasive resources available to him. The heart of it is this: they believe when we demonstrate.

To create or produce belief in their listeners, orators must possess a grasp of fundamental human motives. As a keen observer of human psychology Aristotle devoted an extended section of the *Rhetoric* to the essentials of what moves people to behave as they do. These underlying motives then became the sources of rhetorical argument. If an orator can show his listeners that his proposals will enhance their ability to achieve the good things they desire, his arguments are more likely to persuade. Aristotle was here simply carrying out Plato's observation in the *Phaedrus* that any serious teacher of rhetoric must describe the soul, "say what its action is and toward what it is directed, or how it is acted upon and by what."[24]

Will the speaker always be able to produce belief? Not necessarily, says Aristotle. Usually he can only be expected to come as close to success as the circumstances will allow. Nevertheless, when he is handling the truth the speaker does bear responsibility for failure. Says Aristotle, "Rhetoric is useful, because the true and the just are naturally superior to their opposites, so that, if decisions are improperly made, they must owe their defeat to their own advocates; which is reprehensible."[25]

It is important, then, to see the closed psychological system within which ancient rhetoric operated. There is nothing magical about the transaction. Aristotle uses the term δύναμις constantly with regard to rhetoric, but unlike earlier thinkers such as Gorgias, who portrayed the power of persuasion in explicitly mystical terms, it now refers to the ability or power of the orator to utilize the fundamental psychological dynamic of rhetoric to produce belief.

---

[21] Aristotle, *Rhetoric* 1.2.8; cf. 2.1.1-7.
[22] Ibid., 3.13.1, 4.
[23] Ibid., 1.2.3-6.
[24] Plato, *Phaedrus* 271A; cf. Aristotle, *Rhetoric* 1.2.7; 2.12.1.
[25] Aristotle, *Rhetoric* 1.1.12.

The speaker's task is to marshal the logical, emotional and ethical means of persuasion so effectively that he produces conviction within the audience, or that he come as close as humanly possible.

The demands of oratory were therefore heavy and complex because the rhetorical possibilities the orator must be prepared to discern and manipulate toward success are potentially infinite in variety. This is why eloquence requires the most stringent and exhaustive training, not least the close study of great orators from the past. Quintilian, for example, constantly urged his students to analyze and imitate the persuasive strategies of their predecessors:

> Imitation (for I must repeat this point again and again) should not be confined merely to words. We must consider the appropriateness with which those orators handle the circumstances and persons involved in the various cases in which they were engaged, and observe the judgment and powers of arrangement which they reveal, and the manner in which everything they say, not excepting those portions of their speeches which seem designed merely to delight their audience, is concentrated on securing the victory over their opponents.[26]

It was just this sort of training that the ancient teachers of rhetoric put on offer. All of classical rhetoric rested like an inverted pyramid on this point: to teach speakers how to discover and then use with persuasive success the rhetorical possibilities within any situation, within any audience, within any subject. Whether their goal was to move nations or merely to entertain, whether the orator's fate hung in the balance or merely his ego, the purpose of the rhetorician's art was to enable speakers to have their way with their audiences. In one form or another, however momentous or trivial, persuasion remained the persistent object of ancient rhetoric.

---

[26]Quintilian, *Inst. or.* 10.2.27.

3

The Power of Rhetoric

Oratory carried a strong dramatic appeal to the ancient Greeks. For a people who had been nursed on heroic figures singlehandedly facing fearsome challenges, the drama of oratory was immensely attractive. The earlier Greeks would have had little stomach for the gore of the later Roman gladiators, but they would surely have understood their dramatic appeal.

For the Greeks this appeal was embodied in oratory: the challenge laid down and not to be escaped, the lone figure rises to the occasion, a hush falls over the audience. The suspense, the anticipation, the delight of watching the speaker succeed through the astonishing brilliance of his words and ideas—it was a drama more or less reenacted on each new occasion. Moreover, it was not a drama of long ago and far away in which the audience participated vicariously; it was here and now, and they were directly playing their crucial part. It was only to be expected that they thrived on eloquence and submitted themselves willingly to the sway of orators.

It was this power to sway, granted by audiences and brandished by orators, that the early rhetoricians claimed to be harnessing. For them, as for most Greeks, persuasion was at least in one sense a magical thing. It was not, to be sure, the magic of incantation, the shamanistic use of words in ritual or chant to conjure up external forces. But in a different sense this power of eloquently expressed ideas to move the human mind may also be considered a form of magic, at least metaphorically, and there is strong evidence to suggest that the early Greeks conceived of rhetoric just so. Jacqueline de Romilly has traced the association of rhetoric and magic from its beginnings and shows that the relationship was not broken until Aristotle.[1]

For the early Greeks the power of persuasion was an awesome, relentless thing, often positive but sometimes evil or demonic. Hence the adjective δεινός was

---

[1] Romilly (1975, pp. 69-88).

regularly used of persuasive speakers. Originally derived from a word meaning "fear," δεινός carried with it a suggestion of the strange, the awesome, the uncanny; it was applied to that which was powerful but not fully understood and therefore to be feared. The word usually meant "clever" when applied to persuaders, but not merely so. An aura of the uncanny seemed to persist around the power of λόγοι.

This conviction of the power of persuasion came to its most forceful expression in Gorgias's *Encomium to Helen*. But it was also evident from the beginning in even the most prosaic of the early handbooks. Plato, for example, cites Tisias, along with Gorgias, in a discussion of the amazing—and, to Plato, largely reprehensible—things that can be accomplished "through the force of words" (διὰ ῥώμην λόγου).[2] Later the term most often used was not ῥώμην but δύναμις, a word that must often be translated "faculty," "capacity" or "function," but which never quite loses its core meaning of "power." According to Quintilian it was roughly the equivalent of the Latin *vis*.[3] Whether in Greek or Latin, however, the conviction was the same: the spoken word could be an awesomely potent force. Thus for Socrates, the contrast to being skilled in speech (ῥητορικός) was to be ἀδύνατος (without power).[4] Eloquence was, as Philostratus later put it, a "power in word and thought alike, a power of persuasion that is . . . truly formidable, which you call rhetoric, a power that holds sway both in the forum and on the rostrum."[5]

So central was the notion of power to the exercise of rhetoric that Quintilian could build it into the very definition of the art. Says he, the most common (*frequentissimus*) definition of rhetoric was *vis persuadendi*, "the power to persuade."[6] To ensure that no one misreads his terminology, Quintilian immediately clarifies his thought: "What I call a power (*vis*), many call a capacity (*potestas*), and some a faculty (*facultas*). In order therefore that there may be no misunderstanding I will say that by power (*vis*) I mean δύναμις."[7] Thus did Quintilian set out for us a taxonomy of rhetoric and power.

Whatever one called it, the power of rhetoric was anchored in the orator's ability to adapt to his audience for the sake of persuasion. This is Aristides's point when he says that the capacity to choose from among the many options "all that

---

[2]Plato, *Phaedrus* 267B.
[3]Quintilian, *Inst. or.* 2.15.3-4.
[4]Plato, *Phaedrus* 239A.
[5]Philostratus, *Discourses* 33.1.
[6]Quintilian, *Inst. or.* 2.15.3.
[7]Ibid.

is better to be said" is the key to the power of persuasion.⁸ This power of persuasion was not to be taken lightly, for as Dio observed, it is by the δύναμις of this persuasion, a most δρῖμύς ("piercing") and δεινός ("fearful") power called rhetoric, that men prevail "in the forum [ἀγορά] and on the rostrum [βῆμα]."⁹ By his sheer power, says Dio in another place, the orator may overwhelm his listeners.¹⁰ With the δύναμις of his eloquence he can turn even the law to his own use.¹¹

The Force of Eloquence

According to Cicero, this ability to sway the audience constitutes "the orator's chief source of power (*vis*)."¹² Indeed it was the grand style of speaking, as against the less demonstrative styles, that produced *vis maxima*:

> I mean the kind of eloquence which rushes along with the roar of a mighty stream, which all look up to and admire, and which they despair of attaining. This eloquence has power to sway men's minds and move them in every possible way. Now it storms the feelings, now it creeps in; it implants new ideas and uproots the old.¹³

In a similar vein Quintilian speaks of that orator "whose eloquence is like to some great torrent that rolls down rocks and 'disdains a bridge' and carves out its own banks for itself."¹⁴ This is the speaker, he says, who,

> will sweep the judge from his feet, struggle as he may, and force him to go whither he bears him. This is the orator that will call the dead to life.... This is he that will inspire anger or pity, and while he speaks the judge will call upon the gods and weep, following him wherever he sweeps him from one emotion to another, and no longer asking merely for instruction.¹⁵

This sort of rhetorical power was considered the mark of great oratory. Thus "Longinus" compared Cicero with Demosthenes:

> Demosthenes' strength is usually in rugged sublimity, Cicero's in diffusion. Our countryman [Demosthenes] with his violence, yes, and his speed, his

---

⁸Aristides, *To Plato* 185; cf. 382.
⁹Dio Chrysostom, *Discourses* 33.1; cf. "Longinus," *On the Sublime* 1.4, 12.4, 34.4.
¹⁰Dio Chrysostom, *Discourses* 33.5.
¹¹Ibid., 76.4; cf. 18.5.
¹²Cicero, *Brutus* 276; cf. 89.
¹³Cicero, *Or. Brut.* 97.
¹⁴Quintilian, *Inst. or.* 12.10.61.
¹⁵Ibid., 12.10.61-63.

force, his terrific power of rhetoric, burns, as it were, and scatters everything before him, and may therefore be compared to a flash of lightning or a thunder-bolt. Cicero seems to me like a wide-spread conflagration, rolling along and devouring all around it: his is a strong and steady fire, its flames duly distributed, now here, now there, and fed by relays of fuel.[16]

For his part, Quintilian made a similar argument, but in his case championing especially his hero Cicero:

> Cicero, having devoted himself entirely to the imitation of the Greeks, succeeded in reproducing the forcefulness of Demosthenes, the abundance of Plato, and the elegance of Isocrates. But he did more than reproduce by study the excellences of each: most, or rather all, of his virtues are the self-generated product of the happy richness of his immortal genius. He does not, as Pindar says, "collect the rainwater," but wells forth with a living flood; for he was born, by the favour of Providence, to be the man in whom eloquence could try out all her powers. Who can give information more precisely, or stir feelings more deeply? Who had ever such a gift of charm? You believe him to be winning by consent what he is really extorting by force; and when he sweeps the judge along with his violence, the judge feels not that he is being hijacked, but he is going along of his own accord. Indeed such is the authority in everything Cicero says that one is ashamed to disagree.[17]

This ability to move the minds and hearts of one's listeners was what Quintilian considered "the splendour of eloquence" (*claritas orationis*).[18]

> Few indeed are those orators who can sweep the judge with them, lead him to adopt that attitude of mind which they desire, and compel him to weep with them or share their anger. And yet it is this emotional power that dominates the court, it is this form of eloquence that is the queen of all. . . . The peculiar task of the orator arises when the minds of the judges require force to move them. . . . The verdict of the court shows how much weight has been carried by the arguments and the evidence; but when the judge has been really moved by the orator he reveals his feelings while he is still sitting and listening to the case. When those tears, which are the aim of most perorations, well forth from his eyes, is he not giving his verdict for all to see? It is to this, therefore, that

---

[16]"Longinus," *On the Sublime* 12.4.
[17]Quintilian, *Inst. or.* 10.1.109-11.
[18]Ibid., 2.16.10.

the orator must devote all his powers, "There lie the task and toil!" Without this all else is bare and meager, weak and devoid of charm. For it is in its power over the emotions that the life and soul of oratory is to be found.[19]

A Different Kind of Power

Finally, we should observe one further connection between rhetoric and power. The δύναμις to persuade provided the foundation for a still broader kind of political and social power. As Dio says, an ambitious man may aspire "to be admired for his eloquence and by this means to have greater power than his fellows."[20] In his *Olympic Discourse* Dio notes that the students of the sophists, "having been properly educated and having grown wise, may thenceforth be renowned among all Greeks and Barbarians, being pre-eminent in virtue and reputation and wealth and in almost every kind of power [δύναμις]."[21] Dio offers this observation somewhat sarcastically, but he nonetheless admired those who reached for and gained this sort of influence. Hence his affirmation, as evidence of his "devotion to wisdom," of one man's desire to gain "training in eloquent speaking" so as to enhance his social influence:

> And you, as it seems to me, are altogether wise in believing that a statesman needs experience and training in public speaking and in eloquence. For it is true that this will prove of very great help toward making him beloved and influential and esteemed instead of being looked down upon. For when men are afraid, what does more to inspire them than the spoken word? And when they wax insolent and uplifted in spirit, what more effectively brings them down and chastens them? What has greater influence in keeping them from indulging their desires? Whose admonitions do they endure more meekly than the man's whose speech delights them? Time and again, at any rate, there may be seen in our cities one group of men spending, handing out largess, adorning their city with dedications, but the orators who support these measures getting the applause, as though they and not the others had brought these things about. For this same reason the poets of the earliest times, who received their gift of poetry from the gods, never spoke of either the strong or the beautiful as being "looked upon as gods," but reserved this praise for the orators. So it is because you not only have observed all this, but are also endeavouring to put it into practice that I commend and admire you.[22]

---

[19]Ibid., 6.2.3-4, 5, 7.
[20]Dio Chrysostom, *Discourses* 68.4.
[21]Ibid., 12.11.
[22]Ibid., 18.2-3.

How was it that the art of persuasion could bestow such societal affirmation and influence? In the *Dialogus* Messalla gives the historic answer. There he describes the pathway by which eloquence was translated into political power:

> In times past, a speaker's political wisdom was measured by his power of carrying conviction [*persuadere poterat*] to the unstable populace.... All this ... provided a sphere for the oratory of those days and heaped on it what one saw were vast rewards. The more influence a man could wield by his powers of speech, the more readily did he attain to high office, the further did he, when in office, outstrip his colleagues in the race for precedence, the more did he gain favour with the great, authority with the senate, and name and fame with the common people.... With [such influential figures], moreover, it was a conviction that without eloquence it was impossible for anyone either to attain to a position of distinction and prominence in the community, or to maintain it.... So it was that eloquence not only led to great rewards, but was also a sheer necessity; and just as it was considered great and glorious to have the reputation of being a good speaker, so on the other hand, it was accounted discreditable to be inarticulate and incapable of utterance.[23]

---

[23]Tacitus, *Dial.* 36.3-8.

4

The Reach of Rhetoric

One scarcely needs to read between the lines to conclude that the people of the Greco-Roman world luxuriated in public speaking. Fame, power, wealth, position—all were available to the orator. And it was the appetite of the people for eloquence that made it possible. They loved the eloquent man and were willing to shower upon him all that society could grant. Most of all, they were willing to give him their applause and praise, which to many orators became addictive. On the other hand, the crowd was equally quick to punish rhetorical weakness. As Socrates put it, in a rueful comment on his society, "The disgrace, I fancy, consists in speaking or writing not well, but disgracefully or badly."[1]

A generation before Socrates, Thucydides's Cleon, an Athenian statesman and military general, complained during the famous Mytilenian Debate of what he considered the fickleness of the Athenian people, due to their susceptibility to powerful speakers. "It is your wont," he said, "to be spectators of words and hearers of deeds, forming your judgment of future enterprises according as able speakers represent them to be feasible." The Athenians were more easily swayed by eloquence, he lamented, than they were by what they had seen with their own eyes. "You are adepts not only at being deceived by novel proposals but also at refusing to follow approved advice, slaves as you are of each new paradox and scorners of what is familiar."

> Each of you wishes above all to be an orator himself, or, failing that, to vie with those dealers in paradox by seeming not to lag behind them in wit but to applaud a smart saying before it is out of the speaker's mouth; you are as quick to forestall what is said as you are slow to foresee what will come of it. You seek, one might say, a world quite unlike that in which we live, but give too little heed to that which is at hand. In a word, you are in thrall to the

---

[1] Plato, *Phaedrus* 258D.

pleasures of the ear and are more like men who sit as spectators at exhibitions of sophists than men who take counsel for the welfare of the state.²

Cleon was no philosopher, but his complaint was a forerunner to that of Plato a century later. Thucydides presents Cleon, who wound up losing the debate, in an unfavorable light, and but for Thucydides Cleon's criticism would have been long forgotten. But Plato is a different matter. His concerns, much more thoroughly argued, have proven to have staying power. One can hear their echoes to this day in contemporary debates about rhetoric.

Plato mistrusted the crowd because he believed only the few were capable of true philosophy. The corrupt majority he compared to a partially blind and deaf shipmaster who has no idea where he is going and who is constantly surrounded by a group of sailors wrangling among themselves for control of the helm. These sailors represented the various public speakers appealing to the democratic majority.³ Yet the crowd was not for Plato some powerful but innocent tool merely manipulated by the orators. He saw the great ignoble mass as the ultimate corrupter of the good. How could society's hope for the future, the budding young philosopher, resist being dragged down, he asks,

> when . . . the multitude are seated together in assemblies or in court-rooms or theatres or camps or any other public gathering of a crowd, and with loud uproar censure some of the things that are said and done and approve others, both in excess, with full-throated clamour and clapping of hands, and thereto the rocks and the region round about re-echoing redouble the din of the censure and the praise. In such a case how do you think the young man's heart, as the saying is, is moved within him? What private teaching do you think will hold out and not rather be swept away by the torrent of censure and applause, and borne off on its current, so that he will affirm the same things that they do, and be even such as they?⁴

If the orator played the audience, it was the audience who called the tune, and it was this overwhelming power of the crowd that Plato feared most. He believed such power could and inevitably would be directed against the truth by "the man who thinks that it is wisdom to have learned to know the moods and the

---

²Thucydides, *History of the Peloponnesian War* III.33.4, 6-7. Cf. Acts 17:21 on the Athenians five centuries later: "Now all the Athenians and the foreigners who lived there would spend their time in nothing except telling or hearing something new."
³Plato, *Republic* 488B-C.
⁴Ibid., 492D.

The Reach of Rhetoric 83

pleasures of the motley multitude in their assembly."[5] Says he,

> It is as if a man were acquiring the knowledge of the humours and desires of a great strong beast which he had in his keeping, how it is to be approached and touched, and when and by what things it is made most savage or gentle, yes, and the several sounds it is wont to utter on the occasion of each, and again what sounds uttered by another make it tame or fierce, and after mastering this knowledge by living with the creature and by lapse of time should call it wisdom [σοφία], and should construct thereof a system and art and turn to the teaching of it.[6]

The picture that emerges from Plato is thus a disapproving one. The motley multitude is a blind and deaf shipmaster who must look to others for direction; a great strong beast who delights in being roused or charmed. For the orator its wrath was immediate and painful, but its blessing was the key to success, power and prestige.

This delight in being roused or charmed continued into the Roman centuries unabated. Despite a widely noted decline in eloquence during the first century A.D.,[7] public speaking remained highly popular. For their part, audiences continued to lionize the orators. As Tacitus put it, the decline in eloquence was not for lack of votaries.[8] The Greek orators in particular were extremely popular, students as well as audiences flocking about their every appearance. The walls of Ephesus and Mytilene shook with rounds of applause for them, says Messalla.[9]

Moreover, the popularity of oratory was extremely broad based. It permeated the entire Greco-Roman world, from the emperors to the man in the street. For example, Philostratus says that the interest in the sophist Favorinus at Rome was universal, and that all of Greece acclaimed the eloquence of Polemo.[10] People appeared to possess a passion for rhetoric, as Tacitus in fact says of himself.[11] Hence Dio was putting into words the feelings of the multitude as much as his

---

[5]Ibid., 493D.
[6]Ibid., 493A-B.
[7]This decline, however, is often overstated (see Dominik, 1997; Kennedy, 1972, chaps. 6–7), a mistake that might have surprised Quintilian, the first century's greatest Roman teacher of rhetoric. He expected otherwise: "Subsequent writers on the history of oratory will find abundant material for praise among the orators who flourish today: for the law courts can boast a glorious wealth of talent. Indeed, the consummate advocates of the present day are serious rivals of the ancients, while enthusiastic effort and lofty ideals lead many a young student to tread in their footsteps and imitate their excellence" (*Inst. or.* 10.1.122).
[8]Tacitus, *Dial.* 28.2; cf. Seneca, *Epist. Mor.* 114.12ff.
[9]Tacitus, *Dial.* 15.3.
[10]Philostratus, *Lives* 539; cf. 562 on Herodes; or 567 on Aristocles.
[11]Tacitus, *Dial.* 2.1.

own when he spoke of "the uncontrolled craving which possesses me for the spoken word."[12] "Like the fawns and calves listening to Orpheus, . . . this is the way I have nearly always been affected when listening to sophists and orators."[13]

As a result of its popularity, oratory was ubiquitous in the Greco-Roman world of the first century. Though the opportunities tended to ebb and flow with the changes of emperor, all sorts of rhetoric could still be found to flourish. And despite Tacitus's gloomy assessment of the state of forensic rhetoric—"the speaker has only two or three for an audience, and the hearing goes forward in what is a scene of desolation"[14]—Pliny could write to a friend,

> Rejoice, I tell you, on my account and your own, and no less for our country; for oratory is still held in honour. When I was on my way the other day to plead before the Centumviral Court, there was no room left for me to reach my place except by way of the magistrates' bench, through their assembled ranks, as the rest of the floor was crowded. And then a young patrician who had had his clothing torn, as often happens in a crowd, stayed on clad in nothing but his toga to listen for seven hours—which was the length of the speech I made.[15]

Pliny describes another such occasion as follows:

> One hundred and eighty judges were sitting, the total for the four panels acting together; both parties were fully represented and had a large number of seats filled with their supporters, and a close-packed ring of onlookers, several rows deep, lined the walls of the courtroom. The bench was also crowded, and even the galleries were full of men and women leaning over in their eagerness to see and also to hear, though hearing was rather more difficult. Fathers, daughters and stepmothers all anxiously awaited the verdict.[16]

The aura of excitement and suspense in such situations was palpable. Pliny captured something of this dynamic tension when he spoke of the "warmth and spirit" of the speeches being

> fed from the atmosphere of court: the bench of magistrates and throng of advocates, the suspense of the awaited verdict, [the] reputation of the different speakers, and the divided enthusiasm of the public; and they gain too from

---

[12]Dio Chrysostom, *Discourses* 19.4.
[13]Ibid.
[14]Tacitus, *Dial.* 39.3.
[15]Pliny, *Letters* 4.16.1-2.
[16]Ibid., 6.33.3-4.

the gestures of the speaker as he strides to and fro, the movements of his body corresponding to his changing passions.[17]

It should not be surprising that audiences and orators alike found such scenes exhilarating. Said the enthusiastic Aper,

> What a supreme delight it is to gather yourself to your feet, and to take your stand before a hushed audience, that has eyes only for you! Think of the growing crowd streaming round about the speaker, and taking on any mood in which he may care to wrap himself, as with a cloak. It is the notorious delights of speech-making that I am enumerating—those that are full in view even of the uninitiated.[18]

---

[17]Ibid., 2.19.2; cf. 2.10.6.ff.
[18]Tacitus, *Dial.* 6.4.

5

The Genius of Rhetoric

The ability to adapt nimbly to the rhetorical demands of the situation was from the beginning the mark of the effective orator. It could hardly be otherwise. All speakers, to be effective, must shape themselves to their listeners. The question is, to what end? Merely to please, or to persuade?

That flatterers accommodated themselves to their audience had been taken for granted since Plato. The essence of flattery was to discover what the crowd wanted and then give it to them. It was just this of which the sophists and rhetoricians were constantly accused by their critics. Says Dio, "The sophists . . . can't help adopting the thought of their listeners, saying and thinking such things as fit the nature of those listeners, whatever it happens to be."[1] Seneca's Votienus Montanus was describing just such self-serving accommodation when he said, "If you prepare a declamation beforehand, you write not to win but to please. You [search] out all possible allurements; you throw arguments overboard, because they are bothersome and much too sober; you rest content with epigrams and developments. Your aim is to win approval for yourself rather than for the case."[2]

In a similar vein Agamemnon, the rhetorician-teacher in Petronius's *Satyricon*, criticized other teachers of rhetoric for using this approach with their students:

> No wonder the teachers are to blame for these exhibitions. They are in a madhouse, and they must gibber. Unless they speak to the taste of their young masters they will be left alone in the colleges, as Cicero says. Like mock toadies (of Comedy) cadging after the rich man's dinners, they think first about what is calculated to please their audience.[3]

But is Agamemnon's suggested alternative an improvement? He continues, "They

---

[1]Dio Chrysostom, *Discourses* 35.8; cf. 4.124-27.
[2]Seneca the Elder, *Controversiae* 9.Pr.1.
[3]Petronius, *Satyricon* 3.

will never gain their object unless they lay traps for the ear. A master of oratory is like a fisherman; he must put the particular bait on his hook which he knows the little fish will make for, or he may sit waiting on his rock with no hope of a catch."[4]

In each of these instances the speaker adjusts to his audience merely to gain their approval by giving them what they already want. But is this the sort of adaptation recommended by Isocrates, Aristotle, Cicero or Quintilian? Clearly some distinctions are in order.

Aristides provides these distinctions. In the most complete discussion of the subject to be found in ancient literature, Aristides rejects Plato's accusation that rhetoric is mere flattery. Crucial to his refutation is Plato's admission that the goal of rhetoric is persuasion. Aristides's argument hinges on the fact that an orator cannot persuade an audience while being at the same time under their sway. He may lead them, or they may lead him, but both cannot be the case simultaneously. In what sense, then, do those who genuinely persuade adapt to their audience? The people understand this intuitively, says Aristides:

> They go to [the orators'] doors, beseech them, grovel, believing that oratory is a curative for everything, death, exile, their terrors, the wrath of the jurors, the contentiousness of the people, everything. Why? Because they know that orators do not practise to say what their seated audience approves ... but ... practise to speak as the situation demands, conjecturing its nature, not that of the audience, and if that of the audience too, not so as to serve their desires, nor to say all that they wish to hear, but by saying all that is better to be said, so as to have the power of persuasion; just as we see doctors conjecturing the nature of the body, not indeed so as simply to gratify the desires, but so as not at random to apply the best treatment, but in what way the patient would be most receptive. . . . If this, Plato, is to conjecture men's natures and to address them after observing them, then we have not escaped the charge, all orators will say. But if you say that they yield to the multitudes and do what they are commanded, but do not command, you have taken the servant-girl for the mistress, and in blaming the public slaves, you think you blame the orators. The public slaves are not proud because they serve the will of the city, while it is a source of pride for orators that they do not say what the people approve, but what they think is the best.[5]

Aristides articulates here the classical concept of rhetorical adaptation. Knowing what he wants to achieve, the persuader analyzes the complex of possibilities

---

[4]Ibid., 3-4.
[5]Aristides, *To Plato* 184-88; cf. Plutarch, *Lives*, Pericles 15.

inherent in the subject matter, the occasion and the audience, weighing which strategy and tactics are most likely to be effective. The orator cannot bring these possibilities to the rhetorical situation; he must discover them within the situation and then be prepared to use whatever he finds with maximum effectiveness. This had always been the essence of the rhetorical art, and Aristides was correct in insisting that it not be glibly brushed aside as flattery.

It was, in fact, precisely this feature that prompted so many medical analogies throughout the ancient literature. For example, in Plato's *Phaedrus* Socrates himself argues that true rhetoric, when rightly understood, will be seen to involve, like medicine, at least three steps. First, says Socrates:

> In both cases you must analyse a nature, in one that of the body and in the other that of the soul, if you are to proceed in a scientific manner, not merely by practice and routine, to impart health and strength to the body by prescribing medicine and diet, or by proper discourses and training to give the soul the desired belief and virtue.... So it is clear that Thrasymachus, or anyone else who seriously teaches the art of rhetoric, will first describe the soul with perfect accuracy and make us see whether it is one and all alike, or, like the body, of multiform aspect; for this is what we call explaining its nature.
>
> *Phaedrus*: Certainly.
>
> *Socrates*: And secondly, will say what its action is and toward what it is directed, or how it is acted upon and by what.
>
> *Phaedrus*: To be sure.
>
> *Socrates*: Thirdly, he will classify the speeches and the souls and will adapt each to the other showing the causes of the effects produced and why one kind of soul is necessarily persuaded by certain classes of speeches, and another is not.[6]

ADAPTATION FOR PERSUASION

Classical rhetoric, then, was designed to teach a speaker to apply Socrates's medical analogy. It focused on how to adjust to the exigencies of the rhetorical situation so as to achieve a predetermined result. The key to this process was effective audience adaptation. Says Cicero's Crassus, "The eloquence of orators

---

[6]Plato, *Phaedrus* 270B-271B.

has always been controlled by the good sense of the audience, since all who desire to win approval have regard to the goodwill of their auditors, and shape and adapt themselves completely according to this and to their opinion and approval."[7] Since no single kind of speech suits every occasion, the speaker must be prepared both to analyze what is required and then to carry it out. The prudent and cautious speaker is controlled by the reception of the audience, always ready to modify his tactics. Like Socrates, in *De Oratore* Antonius says that the speaker must often be "like a careful physician, who before he attempts to administer a remedy to his patient, must investigate not only the malady of the man he wishes to cure, but also his habits when in health, and his physical constitution." This is why, says Antonius, shifting to a different analogy,

> when setting about a hazardous and important case, in order to explore the feelings of the tribunal, I engage wholeheartedly in a consideration so careful, that I scent out with all possible keenness their thoughts, judgements, anticipations and wishes, and the direction in which they seem likely to be led away most easily by eloquence. If they surrender to me, and . . . of their own accord lean towards and are prone to take the course in which I am urging them on, I accept their bounty and set sail for that quarter which promises something of a breeze. If however an arbitrator is neutral and free from pre-disposition, my task is harder, since everything has to be called forth by my speech, with no help from the listener's character. But so potent is that Eloquence, rightly styled, by an excellent poet, "soulbending sovereign of all things," that she can not only support the sinking and bend the upstanding, but, like a good and brave commander, can even make prisoner a resisting antagonist.[8]

"The universal rule, in oratory as in life," said Cicero, "is to consider propriety."[9] All aspects of the speech—content, style, delivery—must be adapted to the subject and to the character of both the speaker and the audience. This is the secret of effective speech:

> Since I am not seeking a pupil to teach, but an orator to approve, I shall begin by approving of one who can observe what is fitting. This, indeed, is the form of wisdom that the orator must especially employ—to adapt himself to occasions and persons. In my opinion one must not speak in the same style at all

---

[7]Cicero, *Or. Brut.* 24.
[8]Cicero, *De or.* 3.186-87.
[9]Cicero, *Or. Brut.* 71.

times, nor before all people, nor against all opponents, nor in defence of all clients, nor in partnership with all advocates. He, therefore, will be eloquent who can adapt his speech to fit all conceivable circumstances.[10]

Because adaptation with a view to achieving a specified result lay at the heart of rhetoric, Quintilian held that the "all-important gift for an orator is a wise adaptability."[11] This enabled the speaker to be prepared for any contingency, ready to make the appropriate rhetorical choice. For example, Titus Livius was praised for the fact that "his speeches are eloquent beyond description; so admirably adapted is all that is said both to the circumstances and the speaker."[12] In the end, no set of rules can capture this rhetorical sensitivity, particularly in regard to word choice; we must follow, says Quintilian, "the dictates of our own judgement, which will tell us what it is sufficient to say and how much the ears of our audience will tolerate."[13] Similarly, delivery must be appropriate to the situation: "Such appropriateness obviously lies in the adaptation of the delivery to the subjects on which we are speaking."[14] Even the content is shaped to the listener: "It is most important that we should know how the judge is disposed to listen, and his face will often (as Cicero reminds us) serve as a guide to the speaker. Consequently we must press the points that we see commend themselves to him, and draw back from those which are ill-received."[15] Should the orator use the grand, mediate or plain style of speaking? Says Quintilian,

> Eloquence has . . . a quantity of different aspects, but it is sheer folly to inquire which of these the orator should take as his model, since every species that is in itself correct has its use and what is commonly called style of speaking does not depend upon the orator. For he will use all styles, as circumstances may demand, and the choice will be determined not only by the case as a whole but by the demands of the different portions of the case.[16]

IMPRESSIVE SKILLS

This ability to adapt to the demands of the rhetorical situation, whatever they might be, was a valuable and indeed a genuinely impressive skill. It required

---

[10]Ibid., 122-25.
[11]Quintilian, *Inst. or.* 2.13.2; cf. 11.1.46-56.
[12]Ibid., 10.1.101.
[13]Ibid., 11.1.91.
[14]Ibid., 11.3.61; cf. 10.1.17.
[15]Ibid., 12.10.56.
[16]Ibid., 12.10.69.

knowledge, training and gift, as Messalla points out in the *Dialogus*.

> It is only from a wealth of learning, and a multitude of accomplishments, and a knowledge that is universal, that his marvelous eloquence wells forth like a mighty stream. The orator's function and activity is not, as is the case with other pursuits, hemmed in all round within narrow boundaries. He only deserves the name who has the ability to speak on any and every topic with grace and distinction of style, in a manner fitted to win conviction, appropriately to the dignity of his subject-matter, suitably to the case in hand, and with resulting gratification to his audience.[17]

How does one become such an orator? We must follow the path of the ancients, says Messalla.

> For them the one thing needful was to stock the mind with those accomplishments which deal with good and evil, virtue and vice, justice and injustice. It is this that forms the subject-matter of oratory. Speaking broadly, in judicial oratory our argument turns upon fair dealing, in the oratory of debate upon advantage, in eulogies upon moral character, though these topics quite frequently overlap. Now it is impossible for any speaker to treat them with fullness, and variety, and elegance, unless he has made a study of human nature, of the meaning of goodness and the wickedness of vice. This is the source from which other qualifications also are derived. The man who knows what anger is will be better able either to work on or to mollify the resentment of a judge, just as he who understands compassion, and the emotions by which it is aroused, will find it easier to move him to pity. If your orator has made himself familiar with these branches by study and practice, whether he has to address himself to a hostile or a prejudiced or a grudging audience, whether his hearers are ill-humoured or apprehensive, he will feel their pulse, and will handle them in every case as their character requires, and will give the right tone to what he has to say, keeping the various implements of his craft lying ready to hand for any and every purpose. There are some with whom a concise, succinct style carries most conviction, one that makes the several lines of proof yield a rapid conclusion: with such it will be an advantage to have paid attention to dialectic. Others are more taken with a smooth and steady flow of speech, drawn from the fountain-head of universal experience: in order to make an impression upon these we shall borrow from the Peripatetics their stock arguments, suited and ready in advance for either side

---

[17]Tacitus, *Dial.* 30.5.

of any discussion. Combativeness will be the contribution of the Academics, sublimity that of Plato, and charm that of Xenophon; nay, there will be nothing amiss in a speaker taking over even some of the excellent aphorisms of Epicurus and Metrodorus, and applying them as the case may demand.[18]

What is noteworthy in this extended passage is its persistent emphasis on the orator's resources to adapt to whatever he meets in order to achieve persuasion. Tacitus, too, understood the genius of rhetoric.

Messalla's tendency was to look to the past to find genuine oratory. Yet it seems that even the most elaborate oratory, for all its bombast and display, could retain a core of primary rhetoric. It was possible, of course, to relinquish persuasion altogether and sink into pure entertainment, flattery or self-interest, and Dio's criticisms of the sophists seem to suggest that they sometimes did precisely this. But not even all of the sophists pandered to their audiences. As Dio says on one occasion after castigating the group as a whole, "My remarks are not leveled at all sophists, for there are some who follow that calling honourably and for the good of others, men to whom we should pour libation and offer incense."[19] Tacitus's spokesman on behalf of first-century oratory, Aper, actually argues that the newer and more expansive styles of oratory, so disdained by the purists as decadent, were due precisely to a kind of audience adaptation designed in the end to persuade. Hence in defense of Cassius Severus he says,

> Now as to Cassius, who is the object of their attack, and who according to them was the first to turn away from the straight old path of eloquence, my argument is that it was not from defective ability or want of literary culture that he went in for that style of rhetoric, but as the result of sound judgement and clear discrimination. He saw that with altered conditions and a variation in the popular taste, . . . the form and appearance of oratory had also to undergo a change.[20]

Back in the olden days audiences were unsophisticated and had nothing better to do than listen to boring speeches, says Aper. But contemporary, highly informed audiences would never tolerate such things.

> Nowadays your judge travels faster than counsel, and if he cannot find something to engage his interest and prejudice him in your favour in a good going proof, or in piquant utterances, or in brilliant and highly wrought pen-

---

[18]Ibid., 31.1-7; cf. 34.4.
[19]Dio Chrysostom, *Discourses* 35.10.
[20]Tacitus, *Dial.* 19.1-2.

pictures, he is against you. The general audience, too, and the casual listeners who flock in and out, have come now to insist on a flowery and ornamental style of speaking; they will no more put up with sober, unadorned old-fashionedness in a court of law than if you were to try to reproduce on the stage the gestures of Roscius or Ambivius Turpio. . . . The adornment of the poet is demanded nowadays also in the orator, an adornment not disfigured by the mouldiness of Accius or Pacuvius, but fresh from the sacred shrine of a Horace, a Virgil, a Lucan. It is by accommodating itself to the taste and judgement of hearers such as these that the orators of the present day have gained in grace and attractiveness. And the fact that they please the ear does not make our speeches any the less telling in a court of law. Why, one might as well believe that temples are not so strongly built today because they are not put together out of coarse uncut stone and ugly-looking bricks, but glitter in marble and are all agleam with gold.[21]

The last argument in this passage is significant. Aper has not given up persuasion; he is arguing that stylistic standards must change with the times so as to win a hearing. Later, somewhat adjusting his analogy, he says again,

My own view is that the orator, like a prosperous and well-found householder, ought to live in a house that is not only wind and weather proof, but pleasing also to the eye; he should not only have such furnishings as shall suffice for his essential needs, but also number among his belongings both gold and precious stones, so as to make people want to take him up again and again, and gaze with admiration.[22]

The utilitarian aspects of Aper's house refer to the persuasive dimensions of the speech and seem to be taken for granted. His point is that persuasive goals are not incompatible with oratorical forms the audience finds pleasing and to which they will be receptive. *Delectare* ("to please") was, after all, considered one of the three *officia oratoris*, which taken together were designed to persuade. Aper's emphasis on form and on gaining the admiration of the audience—the seemingly unnecessary intrusions designed to reveal rather than conceal the presence of an author—may well raise suspicions of an underlying rot. But to give Aper his due we must not conclude that he had relinquished primary rhetoric or embraced a purely pandering form of adaptation. The problem of the orator's

---
[21] Ibid., 20.2-7.
[22] Ibid., 22.4.

winning a hearing fits comfortably within the legitimate concerns of the mainstream of classical rhetoric. To the extent that this was Aper's motive for embracing the more contemporary style, his argument to these classicists was not without merit. Such adaptation lies at the heart of genuine rhetoric.

6

The Appraisal of Rhetoric

When the ancient orator stood to his feet to address an audience, he was thereby making an open bid for evaluation. The speaker willed to risk the audience's disapproval for the potential of winning their approbation. The orator could not know for sure what their response would be; he could only trust his rhetorical skills and then invite them to render their judgment. And this the ancient audiences did with enthusiasm and relish.

Greek and Roman audiences from the beginning had grasped and reveled in their role as judges. Indeed, this can only be what we mean when we say that oratory flourished in antiquity. It was the audience's function as the final arbiters of oratory that rendered the exercise such a delight. Their attitude seemed to be that when an orator took to his feet he was fair game for whatever he received, whether applause or derision. If he was unwilling to endure such judgment, he ought not enter the lists.

THE AUDIENCE AS JUDGE

The goal of persuasion inherently involved an invitation on the part of the orator for evaluation by the listeners. As Aristotle had put it, "He who has to be persuaded is a judge."[1] Cicero later stated the inevitable converse: "Judgement is

---

[1] Aristotle, *Rhetoric* 2.1.2; cf. also 1.3.1ff. What is sometimes overlooked in this generalization is that Aristotle intended it to apply to all types of rhetoric, whether deliberative, forensic or epideictic. Hence Freese's summary (1925, p. xxxvii) of Aristotle's treatment of these three types of speeches: "There are three kinds of rhetoric, corresponding to the three kinds of hearers; for the hearer must be either (1) a judge of the future; or (2) a judge of the past; or (3) a mere 'spectator' (critic) of the orator's skill. Hence the three kinds of rhetoric are: (1) deliberative; (2) forensic; (3) epideictic." Even in the most self-centered epideictic the orator is intent upon a verdict, and Aristotle provides extended counsel on strategies designed to achieve it (1.9.1-41). Effective epideictic requires shrewd audience adaptation every bit as much as deliberative or forensic oratory, for, as Aristotle says, if we expect our encomiums to be successful we had better "consider in whose presence we praise" (1.9.30).

passing upon us as often as we speak."[2] The awareness of this judgment was always before the effective speaker. Insensitive speakers might be oblivious to it—and often failed as a result—but the better speakers were minutely sensitive to their audience, playing them like a grand instrument. Cicero's Vopiscus gives expression to this hypersensitivity:

> As the orator's chief stage seems to be the platform at a public meeting, it naturally results that we are stimulated to employ the more ornate kind of oratory; for the effect produced by numbers is of such a kind that a speaker can no more be eloquent without a large audience than a flute-player can perform without a flute. And as there are a number of different ways of falling foul of the public, one must be careful not to arouse the disapproving outcries of the people, who are aroused either by some error in the speech, if a remark is thought to be harsh or arrogant or base or mean or to show some fault of character, or by personal annoyance or dislike that is either deserved or arises from slander and rumour, or if the subject is unpopular, or, if the public is in a state of excitement arising out of some desire or alarm that it feels.[3]

According to Cicero, not the verdict of the critics but the audience's response was the final arbiter:

> This discussion about the reasons for esteeming an orator good or bad I much prefer should win the approval of you and of Brutus, but as for my oratory I should wish it rather to win the approval of the public. The truth is that the orator who is approved by the multitude must inevitably be approved by the expert. What is right or wrong in a man's speaking I shall be able to judge, provided I have the ability and knowledge to judge; but what sort of an orator a man is can only be recognized from what his oratory effects. Now there are three things in my opinion which the orator should effect: instruct his listener, give him pleasure, stir his emotions. By what virtue in the orator each one of these is effected, or from what faults the orator fails to attain the desired effect, or in trying even slips and falls, a master of the art will be able to judge. But whether or not the orator succeeds in conveying to his listeners the emotions which he wishes to convey, can only be judged by the assent of the multitude and the approbation of the people. For that reason, as to the question whether an orator is good or bad, there has never been disagreement between experts

---

[2]Cicero, *De or.* 1.125.
[3]Ibid., 2.338-39.

and the common people.... For this is the very mark of supreme oratory, that the supreme orator is recognized by the people. Thus, while Antigenidas the flutist may very well have said to a pupil, whom the public had listened to coldly, "play for me and for the Muses"; I would say rather to our Brutus here, addressing as he does commonly a great audience, "play for me and for the people, my dear Brutus." They will recognize the effect, I shall understand the reason for it. When one hears a real orator he believes what is said, thinks it true, assents and approves; the orator's words win conviction. You, sir, critic and expert, what more do you ask? The listening throng is delighted, is carried along by his words, is in a sense bathed deep in delight. What have you here to cavil with? They feel now joy now sorrow, are moved now to laughter now to tears; they show approbation detestation, scorn aversion; they are drawn to pity to shame to regret; are stirred to anger wonder, hope fear; and all these come to pass just as the hearers' minds are played upon by word and thought and action. Again, what need to wait for the verdict of some critic? It is plain that what the multitude approves must win the approval of experts.[4]

The ancient audiences were highly responsive to the orators. They delighted in even the finer points of oratory and let the speakers know it. "I have often seen the whole assembly," said Cicero, "burst into a cheer, in response to a happy cadence."[5] In another place Crassus comments,

Although we hope to win a "Bravo, capital!" as often as possible, I don't want too much of "Very pretty, charming!"—albeit the actual ejaculation "Couldn't be better!" is one I should like to hear frequently; but all the same, this applause in the middle of a speech and this unlimited praise had better have some shadow and background to make the spot of high light appear to stand out more prominently.[6]

Perhaps most interesting of all is this scene painted by Cicero:

This is what I wish for my orator: when it is reported that he is going to speak let every place on the benches be taken, the judges' tribunal full, the clerks busy and obliging in assigning or giving up places, a listening crowd thronging about, the presiding judge erect and attentive; when the speaker rises the whole throng will give a sign for silence, then expressions of assent, frequent

---
[4]Cicero, *Brutus* 184-88.
[5]Cicero, *Or. Brut.* 168.
[6]Cicero, *De or.* 3.101.

applause; laughter when he wills it, or if he wills, tears; so that a mere passer-by observing from a distance, though quite ignorant of the case in question, will recognize that he is succeeding and that a Roscius is on the stage.[7]

This was the type of setting in which public speakers exercised their talents. Audiences were knowledgeable and eager to evaluate, to show their approval or disapproval. Their standards were high, and speakers were expected to meet them. For their part the speakers gave their best efforts to moving such audiences. The key to the orator's success lay in his ability to manage the rhetorical possibilities in such a way as to fit the exigencies of the situation and win the result he was after. His efforts constituted the variable by which the rhetorical equation either worked or failed.

INFORMED LISTENERS

The problem the speakers of the first century faced, however, was that their listeners had become increasingly experienced, and therefore increasingly astute, judges of oratory. By its nature the artfulness of rhetoric usually remains hidden. Like great athletes who fool the spectator's eye by making their sport look easy, the best orators also concealed their craft. Their hard-won eloquence often appeared effortless and natural. In the orator's case, however, the artfulness was kept out of sight for a second reason: the craft of rhetoric was most effective when it accomplished its purposes without drawing attention to itself.[8]

This is not unique to oratory, of course; it's the same for any art form. In the process of entertaining us, for instance, the well-honed craft of an accomplished comedian does not draw attention to itself. We experience the effects of his or her artfulness and respond in laughter, but the art itself remains covert, not so much concealed as *transparent*. The same can be said of the artistry of poets or novelists; it best achieves its effects when it does not draw attention to itself. So also, the art of the orator depended on his ability to win the result he was after without drawing the audience's attention to how he was doing it.

Yet as the ancient audiences grew in their understanding of the orator's art, this became ever more difficult to accomplish. As Aper observed, "Now . . . everything has become common property," and "there is hardly any casual auditor in the well of the court who, if he has not had a systematic training in the

---

[7]Cicero, *Brutus* 290. Roscius was a famous Roman actor.
[8]Classen (1992, p. 343): "The best orator disguises his knowledge of the theory." Similarly (idem, 2002, p. 44): "The first rule of rhetoric any speaker observes is to conceal the art."

rudiments of the art, cannot show at least a tincture of it."[9] Such astuteness was not new, of course. According to Messalla, orators had long functioned under conditions "in which any stupid or ill-advised statement brings prompt retribution in the shape of the judge's disapproval, taunting criticism from your opponent—yes, and from your own supporters expressions of dissatisfaction."[10] Later Messalla speaks in a similar vein of past audiences, "always numerous and always different, composed of friendly and unfriendly critics, who would not let any points escape them, whether good or bad."[11] Yet with the passage of time the sophistication of the audiences only deepened, making the task of the orator ever more challenging. Messalla himself insisted at one point that the Roman audiences of his own day were highly perceptive,[12] and Pliny specifically praised one such audience for its critical abilities.[13] To the east the sophist Polemo reminded the Athenians of the fact that, as everybody knew, they were σοφοί judges of oratory,[14] and still further east Dio could say to an obscure audience in Phrygia, "You are devoted to oratory to a degree that is remarkable, I may even say excessive, and you tolerate as speakers only those who are very clever."[15] In short, the typical Greco-Roman audiences of the day consisted of people who had been fed a rich diet of oratory from birth. The result was that even if they could not themselves produce powerful speeches, they certainly expected them from the public speakers.

In the end, as Aristotle had said, the listeners were the orator's judge; they held his fate in their hands. Cicero's experienced and respected orator Crassus discusses this point at length in *De Oratore*. Says he,

> Great indeed are the burden and the task that he undertakes, who puts himself forward, when all are silent, as the one man to be heard concerning the weightiest matters, before a vast assembly of his fellows. For there is hardly a soul present but will turn a keener and more penetrating eye upon defects in the speaker than upon his good points. Thus any blunder that may be committed eclipses even those other things that are praiseworthy.[16]

---

[9]Tacitus, *Dial.* 19.5.
[10]Ibid., 34.3.
[11]Ibid., 34.5.
[12]Ibid., 32.2.
[13]Pliny, *Letters* 3.18.8.
[14]Philostratus, *Lives* 535.
[15]Dio Chrysostom, *Discourses* 35.1.
[16]Cicero, *De or.* 1.116.

How is it that ordinary audiences with little or no formal training could be so astute in judging orators? Cicero believed that the ability to discriminate effective speech from ineffective was virtually innate. Thus Cicero's spokesman Crassus says,

> But do not let anybody wonder how these things can possibly make any impression on the unlearned crowd when it forms the audience, because in this particular department as in every other nature has a vast and indeed incredible power. For everybody is able to discriminate between what is right and what wrong in matters of art and proportion by a sort of subconscious instinct, without having any theory of art or proportion of their own; and while they can do this in the case of pictures and statues and other works to understand which nature has given them less equipment, at the same time they display this much more in judging the rhythms and pronunciations of words, because these are rooted deep in the general sensibility, and nature has decreed that nobody shall be entirely devoid of these faculties. And consequently everybody is influenced not only by skillful arrangement of words but also by rhythms and pronunciations. For what proportion of people understands the science of rhythm and metre? Yet all the same if only a slight slip is made in these, making the line too short by a contraction or too long by dwelling on a vowel, the audience protests to a man. Well, does not the same thing take place in the case of pronunciation, so that if there are not only discrepancies between the members of a troupe or chorus but even inconsistency in the pronunciation of individual actors, the ordinary public drives them off the stage? It is remarkable how little difference there is between the expert and the plain man as critics, though there is a great gap between them as performers.[17]

The audiences of the Greco-Roman world were thus very knowledgeable. The orator must be meticulous because they miss very little. "Just as the public sees a mistake in versification, so it notices a slip in our oratory."[18] They may allow the orator to get away with it, but not because they missed it; someone will have caught the mistake. Cicero acknowledges a certain limited role for professional criticism of oratory, but in the end, he says, the only criticism that matters is that of the audience. This is due again to the explicitly utilitarian nature of rhetoric. A speech is not intended to be fine art and cannot be judged as such. It is designed to move listeners and must be judged by this standard.

---

[17]Ibid., 3.195-97.
[18]Ibid., 3.198.

This is not to suggest, of course, that the rhetorical judgment of common man was in any final sense "correct." Most listeners lacked the sophisticated criteria of the professional judges or literary critics and so could still be taken in by the more superficial aspects of oratory. This was Pliny's complaint when he said, "There are certainly very few members of an audience sufficiently trained to prefer a stiff, close-knit argument to fine-sounding words. Such a disparity shocks, but it exists; for in general a bench of magistrates and an audience have very different demands."[19] Yet in the end the Greco-Roman audiences rendered their verdicts anyway, whether sound or not. As listeners they were sometimes swayed by aspects of speeches that should not have carried weight, and they no doubt missed other aspects that ought to have influenced them deeply. But they gave their decisions nonetheless.

Ancient orators and oratory existed to be evaluated, and relentlessly evaluated they were, not merely on the occasion of the speech but seemingly ever afterward by those who heard of or read the oration later. Comparing and contrasting orators was a favorite pastime, with some preferring one orator and others preferring another. Whole volumes of literature—from Cicero's *Brutus* and Dionysius's *Critical Essays* to the Elder Seneca's *Controversiae* and *Suasoriae*, the pseudo-Plutarchian *Lives of the Ten Orators*, "Longinus's" *On the Sublime* and Philostratus's *Lives of the Sophists*—were given over to the weighing of rhetorical strengths and weaknesses. Countless smaller sections in writers such as Quintilian, Tacitus, Pliny, Plutarch, Dio Chrysostom and Suetonius lapse into a similar exercise.

Interestingly, Pliny repeatedly submitted his own oratory to criticism by friends in hopes of ironing out wrinkles that would certainly be criticized by the public.[20] But it probably did not work. Even such an accomplished orator as Herodes recognized the impossibility of satisfying his judges. Said he, in reply to being lauded for his life's words and works, "All this that you speak of must decay and yield to the hand of time, and others will plunder my speeches and criticize now this, now that."[21] Herodes understood that it was in the nature of things that speaker and speeches alike would be judged by their audiences.

In the end, the orator needed his listeners and could not function without them. Brutus confesses as much when he says, "If I am abandoned by the circle

---

[19] Pliny, *Letters* 2.19.6; cf. Cicero, *Brutus* 184ff.
[20] E.g., see *Letters* 7.17.
[21] Philostratus, *Lives* 552; cf. the treatment afforded Scopelian, 515.

of listeners, I am quite unable to speak."²² To which Cicero replies,

> Yes, . . . this is inevitably the case. Thus, for example, if the wind instrument, when blown upon does not respond with sound, the musician knows that the instrument must be discarded, and so in like manner the popular ear is for the orator a kind of instrument; if it refuses to accept the breath blown into it, or if, as a horse to the rein, the listener does not respond, there is no use of urging him.²³

It was "the multitude and the forum" for whom eloquence existed, not the literary critic.²⁴ Without a cooperative audience the orator could accomplish nothing. They were the ones the orator must satisfy. On the other hand, there may come a point in the speech when the listeners set aside their role as judge and simply give themselves to the speaker. This is the point where the audience has been won by the speaker: "They no longer are intent on watching or catching him, but are now on his side, and wish him success; overcome with admiration for the vigour of his oratory, they do not seek points to criticize."²⁵ This is the point at which the orator knows that victory is his. The audience is no longer his judge, precisely because they have already given him their verdict.

---

²²Cicero, *Brutus* 184-88.
²³Ibid., 192.
²⁴Ibid., 283.
²⁵Cicero, *Or. Brut.* 210.

7

The Hazards of Rhetoric

The early twentieth-century orator and editor Glenn Frank once memorably described the audience's relationship to the speaker. "His audience is to him," said Frank, "what the tiger is to its trainer; he must become either the master or the victim of its moods."[1] It is a sentiment every first-century Greco-Roman orator would have endorsed.

The rhetorical astuteness of first-century audiences meant that they were anything but compliant, malleable entities shaped at will by the orator. Though the crowd delighted in rhetoric, they were also suspicious of it. As Philostratus says, "Even while they praise [rhetoric] they suspect it of being rascally and mercenary and constituted in despite of justice."[2] This ambivalence, a curious amalgam of approval and skepticism, seemed to manifest itself in an astonishingly wide range of responses to the orators: the audience might cheer and applaud with enthusiasm,[3] or raise an uproar, shouting the speaker down;[4] they might sit, silent and indulgent,[5] or pelt the speaker with stones out of rage;[6] they might listen raptly in awe,[7] or respond with jeering, hissing, derisive laughter or crude jokes.[8] In short, the audience had it in its power to terrify and dominate the speaker if it cared to, a fact that was not lost on speakers.

Orators knew on the one hand that they needed the crowd, but they also genuinely feared the crowd and what it could do. Dio used the image of the

---

[1] Frank (1919, p. 414).
[2] Philostratus, *Lives* 499. This has always been the case. Says Ober (1989, p. 169) of ancient Athens, "There can be little doubt that, although the Athenians delighted in rhetorical displays, they remained suspicious of the expert orators and their verbal skills"; cf. idem, pp. 187-91.
[3] Tacitus, *Dial.* 32.2; 15.3; Dio Chrysostom, *Discourses* 40.6.
[4] Dio Chrysostom, *Discourses* 7.25, 39; 38.6-7; 32.11; 48.3; 32.22.
[5] Ibid., 34.6; 7.25.
[6] Ibid., 34.6; cf. 32.26.
[7] Ibid., 33.5.
[8] Ibid., 43.3; 32.11, 22.

rulers to explain this phenomenon to the Alexandrians. Some rulers, he said, are like kindly kings, honored for "the general safety of their realm, real guardians and good and righteous leaders of the people, gladly dispensing the benefits." These dish out hardships "among their subjects rarely and only as necessity demands, rejoicing when their cities observe order and decorum." But other rulers "are harsh and savage tyrants, unpleasant to listen to and unpleasant to meet; their rage is prompt to rise at anything, like the rage of savage beasts, and their ears are stopped, affording no entrance to words of fairness, but with them flattery and deception prevail."

> In like manner democracy is of two kinds: the one is reasonable and gentle and truly mild, disposed to accept frankness of speech and not to care to be pampered in everything, fair, magnanimous, showing respect for good men and good advice, grateful to those who admonish and instruct; this is the democracy which I regard as partaking of the divine and royal nature, and I deem it fitting that one should approach and address it, just as one directs with gentleness a noble steed by means of simple reins, since it does not need the curb. But the more prevalent kind of democracy is both bold and arrogant, difficult to please in anything, fastidious, resembling tyrants or much worse than they, seeing that its vice is not that of one individual or of one kind but a jumble of the vices of thousands; and so it is a multifarious and dreadful beast, like those which poets and artists invent, Centaurs and Sphinxes and Chimaeras, combining in a single shape of unreal existence attributes borrowed from manifold natures. And to engage at close quarters with that sort of monster is the act of a man who is truly mad or else exceedingly brave and equipped with wings, a Perseus or a Bellerophon.[9]

Dio's portrait of the vagaries of the audience was not exaggerated. He knew from firsthand experience what it was to face a hostile crowd. The account he adduces in his Euboean Discourse of one actual audience suggests that the above description was not far fetched:

> Now at first the crowd deliberated on other matters for a considerable while, and they kept up a shouting, at one time in gentle fashion and all of them in cheerful mood, as they applauded certain speakers, but at other times with vehemence and in wrath. This wrath of theirs was something terrible, and they at once frightened the men against whom they raised their voices, so that

---

[9]Ibid., 32.25-28; cf. 4.122.

> some of them ran about begging for mercy, while others threw off their cloaks through fear. I too myself was once almost knocked over by the shouting, as though a tidal wave or thunder-storm had suddenly broken over me. And other men would come forward, or stand up where they were, and address the multitude, sometimes using a few words, at other times making long speeches. To some of these they would listen for quite a long time, but at others they were angry as soon as they opened their mouths, and they would not let them so much as cheep.[10]

This graphic description of an apparently typical day of oratory "practically in the center of Greece"[11] gives some idea of what orators might be called on to face. It explains Galaxidorus's sympathy for the public speakers of the day, men who, as he put it, were "compelled to live at the caprice of a self-willed and licentious mob."[12] It also supplies a bit more weight to the witticism of Polemo recorded by Philostratus: "On seeing a gladiator dripping with sweat out of sheer terror of the life-and-death struggle before him, Polemo remarked: 'You are in as great an agony as though you were going to declaim.'"[13]

The ancient orator perceived himself as vulnerable to the whims of the audience. The stakes were high: he could be plunged to the depths of ridicule or lifted to the heights of praise, and the distance between the two was sometimes deceptively brief. Hence the two extremes often came together in discussions of rhetoric, expressed almost in the same breath:

> Nobody ever admired an orator for correct grammar, they only laugh at him if his grammar is bad, and not only think him no orator but not even a human being; no one ever sang the praises of a speaker whose style succeeded in making his meaning intelligible to his audience, but only despised one deficient in capacity to do so. Who then is the man who gives people a thrill? whom do they stare at in amazement when he speaks? who is interrupted by applause? who is thought to be so to say a god among men? It is those whose speeches are clear, explicit and full, perspicuous in matter and in language, and who in the actual delivery achieve a sort of rhythm and cadence—that is, those whose style is what I call artistic.[14]

---

[10]Ibid., 7.24-26.
[11]Ibid., 7.1.
[12]Plutarch, *Moralia* 580A.
[13]Philostratus, *Lives* 541.
[14]Cicero, *De or.* 3.52-53.

The potential displeasure of the audience placed a heavy weight on the sensitive speaker, and "the better the orator, the more profoundly is he frightened of the difficulty of speaking, and of the doubtful fate of a speech, and of the anticipations of the audience."[15] Crassus admits that even as an experienced orator, "I very often prove it in my own experience, that I turn pale at the outset of a speech, and quake in every limb and in all my soul."[16] At this point Antonius chimes in with an explanation of this phenomenon; that is, why it is that the greater the orator's ability, the more profoundly nervous he is:

> I discovered this twofold explanation: first, that those who had learned from experience and knowledge of human nature understood that, even with the most eminent orators, the fate of a speech was sometimes not sufficiently in accordance with their wish; wherefore, as often as they spoke, they were justifiably fearful, lest what could possibly happen sometime should actually happen then. Secondly there is something of which I often have to complain, that, whenever tried and approved exponents of the other arts have done some work with less than their wonted success, their inability to perform what they knew how to perform is explained by their being out of the humour or hindered by indisposition (people say, "Roscius was not in the mood for acting to-day," or "He was a little out of sorts"); whereas, if it is an orator's shortcoming that is being criticized the same is thought due to stupidity. But stupidity finds no apology, since no man's stupidity is set down to his having been "out of sorts" or "that way inclined." And so in oratory we confront a sterner judgement. For judgement is passing upon us as often as we speak; moreover one mistake in acting does not instantly convict a player of ignorance of acting, but an orator, censured on some point of speaking, is under an established suspicion of dullness once for all, or at any rate for many a day.[17]

Audiences were sometimes cruel to speakers who failed to measure up, even formerly great ones. Quintilian considered Domitius Afer to be "by far the greatest of all the orators whom it has been my good fortune to know." Yet, says Quintilian,

> I saw him, when far advanced in years, daily losing something of that authority which his merits had won for him; he whose supremacy in the courts had once been universally acknowledged, now pleaded amid the unworthy

---

[15]Ibid., 1.120.
[16]Ibid., 1.121.
[17]Ibid., 1.123-25.

laughter of some, and the silent blushes of others, giving occasion to the malicious saying that he had rather "faint than finish."[18]

Under such conditions it is not surprising that fear of the audience became a common peril to the orator. Yet, said Quintilian, the true orator must rise above such fear to "that loftiness of soul which fear cannot dismay nor uproar terrify nor the authority of the audience fetter further than the respect which is their due."[19]

For although the vices which are its opposites, such as arrogance, temerity, impudence and presumption, are all positively obnoxious, still without constancy, confidence and courage, art, study and proficiency will be of no avail. You might as well put weapons into the hands of the unwarlike and the coward. ... I am not unwilling that the man who has got to make a speech should show signs of nervousness when he rises to his feet, should change colour and make it clear that he feels the risks of his position: indeed, if these symptoms do not occur naturally, it will be necessary to simulate them. But the feeling that stirs us should be due to the realisation of the magnitude of our task and not to fear: we should be moved, but not to the extent of collapsing.[20]

---

[18]Quintilian, *Inst. or.* 12.11.3.
[19]Ibid., 12.5.1.
[20]Ibid., 12.5.2, 4.

8

The Rewards of Rhetoric

Just as in ancient Greece, Roman society held out its highest rewards to the eloquent. Said Cicero, "From eloquence those who have acquired it obtain glory and honour and high esteem,"[1] not to mention reputation and applause.[2] "Will anyone ever doubt, that in peaceful civil life eloquence has always held the chief place in our state, and jurisprudence has been of secondary importance? The reason is that the former brings with it a large measure of popularity, glory and power."[3] In a section in the *De Officiis* on how to win a good name, Cicero similarly says, "The eloquent and judicious speaker is received with high admiration, and his hearers think him understanding and wise beyond all others."[4]

Though the finest of Greece always represented the standard, Cicero believed that at its best Rome could match Greece orator for orator. To demonstrate this seems to have been one of the prime purposes of the *Brutus*. In *De Oratore* Cicero says that as in Greece, so in Rome, "Assuredly no studies have ever had a more vigorous life than those having to do with the art of speaking."[5]

> For as soon as our world-empire had been established, and an enduring peace had assured us leisure, there was hardly a youth, athirst for fame, who did not deem it his duty to strive with might and main after eloquence. At first indeed, in their complete ignorance of method, since they thought there was no definite course of training or any rules of art, they used to attain what skill they could by means of their natural ability and of reflection. But later, having heard the Greek orators, gained acquaintance with their literature

---
[1] Cicero, *De inv.* 1.5.
[2] Cf. Cicero, *Brutus* 159.
[3] Cicero, *Or. Brut.* 141.
[4] Cicero, *De off.* 2.48.
[5] Cicero, *De or.* 1.13.

and called in Greek teachers, our people were fired with a really incredible enthusiasm for eloquence.[6]

Eloquence prospered as a result: "The number of students is very great, the supply of masters of the very best, the quality of natural ability outstanding, the variety of issues unlimited, the prizes open to eloquence exceedingly splendid."[7] The Roman people stood in close agreement with Crassus:

> There is to my mind no more excellent thing than the power, by means of oratory, to get a hold on assemblies of men, win their good will, direct their inclinations wherever the speaker wishes, or divert them from whatever he wishes. In every free nation, and most of all in communities which have attained the enjoyment of peace and tranquility, this one art has always flourished above the rest and ever reigned supreme. For what is so marvelous as that, out of the innumerable company of mankind, a single being should arise, who either alone or with a few others can make effective a faculty bestowed by nature upon every man? Or what so pleasing to the understanding and the ear as a speech adorned and polished with wise reflections and dignified language? Or what achievement so mighty and glorious as that the impulses of the crowd, the consciences of the judges, the austerity of the Senate, should suffer transformation through the eloquence of one man? What function again is so kingly, so worthy of the free, so generous, as to bring help to the suppliant, to raise up those that are cast down, to bestow security, to set free from peril, to maintain men in their civil rights?[8]

The potential rewards for eloquence were unrivaled. Audiences could raise an orator to the heights and bestow on him every benefit of society. Fame, admiration, honor, glory, wealth, privilege, power, advancement—such were the proffered rewards of oratory, a point never driven home more forcefully than by Tacitus's Aper. Oratory, he says, is

> a profession than which you cannot imagine any in the whole country more productive of practical benefits, or that carried with it a sweeter sense of satisfaction, or that does more to enhance a man's personal standing, or that brings more honour and renown here in Rome, or that secures a more brilliant reputation throughout the Empire and in the world at large.[9]

---
[6]Ibid., 1.14.
[7]Ibid., 1.16.
[8]Ibid., 1.30-32.
[9]Tacitus, *Dial.* 5.4.

Later Aper makes his point with a series of rhetorical questions:

> Where is there a profession whose name and fame are to be compared with renown in oratory? What class of men enjoys greater prestige here in Rome than our public speakers, in the eyes not only of busy men, engrossed in affairs, but also of younger persons and those who have not yet come to a man's estate—provided always that they are of good natural disposition and have some outlook? Are there any whose names are dinned at an earlier age by parents into their children's ears? Are there any to whom the plain man in the street, our citizens in their working-clothes, more frequently point as they pass by, saying, "There goes So-and-so"? Visitors also and nonresidents, as soon as they set foot in the capital, ask for the men of whom in their country towns and colonies they have already heard so much, and are all agog to make them out.[10]

These and many other benefits besides, concludes Aper, "are the honours and distinctions and resources which we find to repletion in the houses of those who from youth up have dedicated themselves to the practice of law and the profession of oratory."[11] This explains why Lucian could portray "Lady Rhetoric" as

> sitting upon a high place, very fair of face and form, holding in her right hand the Horn of Plenty, which runs over with all manner of fruits. Beside her imagine, pray, that you see Wealth standing, all golden and lovely. Let Fame, too, and Power stand by; and let Compliments, resembling tiny Cupids, swarm all about her on the wing in great numbers from every side.[12]

With such an array of rewards at stake it is not surprising that speakers would aspire to eloquence. Rhetoric was perceived as an avenue to success, and many were determined to make the best of it. This was Dio's point when he commented on the various motives for pursuing oratory:

> There are many well-born men and, in public estimation, ambitious, who are whole-heartedly interested in it, some that they may plead in courts of law or address the people in the assembly in order to have greater influence than their rivals and have things their own way in politics, while the aim of others is the glory to be won thereby, that they may enjoy the reputation of eloquence.[13]

For not a few such men eloquence became the ruling passion of their lives. Phi-

---
[10]Ibid., 7.2-4.
[11]Ibid., 8.4; cf. also 38.4-6.
[12]Lucian, *A Professor of Public Speaking* 6.
[13]Dio Chrysostom, *Discourses* 24.3; cf. also 6.21, 66.12, 69.3.

lostratus reports with some wonderment, for example, that Herodes coveted the ability to speak extemporaneously even more than the rank of consular.[14]

Inevitably such driving ambition led to jealousies and rivalry among the orators. The competition for the favor and esteem of the people was often fierce, as can be seen from Philostratus's description of the quarrel between Polemo and Favorinus. It began, he says,

> in Ionia, where the Ephesians favored Favorinus, while Smyrna admired Polemo; and it became more bitter in Rome; for there consulars and sons of consulars by applauding either one or the other started between them a rivalry such as kindles the keenest envy and malice even in the hearts of wise men.[15]

According to Quintilian, the Roman people of the first century, like their predecessors, held the orators in highest honor (*summa dignitas*).[16] They showered on them every reward. When orators give a speech that "awakens the clamorous applause of the audience," he says, "they are escorted home through the forum, perspiring at every pore and attended by flocks of enthusiastic friends."[17] It would not "be difficult to produce either ancient or recent examples to show that there is no other source from which men have reaped such a harvest of wealth, honour, friendship and glory, both present and to come."[18] The crowd was by no means an infallible measure of excellence in oratory, Quintilian insists, but they knew what they liked, and giving them what they liked was in a sense what motivated the orator:

> The desire to win approbation kindles and fosters our efforts. So true it is that there is nothing which does not look for some reward, that eloquence, despite the fact that its activity is in itself productive of a strong feeling of pleasure, is influenced by nothing so much as the immediate acquisition of praise and renown.[19]

To be sure, Quintilian makes it clear that the orator must be careful not to let this desire for applause interfere with winning the day. Rather, he should be assured instead that in winning the day will come the only genuine tribute to oratory: "the praise accorded when the task is done."[20]

---

[14]Philostratus, *Lives* 536; cf. 565.
[15]Ibid., 490; cf. Pliny, *Letters* 6.33.1.
[16]Quintilian, *Inst. or.* 2.16.8.
[17]Ibid., 12.8.3.
[18]Ibid., 12.11.29.
[19]Ibid., 10.7.17.
[20]Ibid., 12.9.4.

9

The Grand Equation of Rhetoric

Rhetoric, then, played both a powerful and pervasive role in first-century Greco-Roman society. It was a commodity of which the vast majority of the population were either producers or, much more likely, consumers, and not seldom avid consumers. Though the self-centered potential of fine-sounding words came to be encouraged to an unhealthy degree during this period, leading to a partial decay of genuine eloquence, by no means did this involve a waning in the popularity of oratory. If anything the reverse was true: oratory became more prevalent than ever.[1] In both the Roman and Greek settings, the frequency with which speakers rose to address audiences seemed to be on the rise during the first century. The quality of oratory may have declined but the quantity had not.

As had always been the case, speakers went about their business so as to have their way with their audiences. They approached the speaking situation with predetermined goals and adapted themselves accordingly. That the goals of many first-century orators were sometimes petty, narcissistic and in the end unworthy of their art must not be allowed to obscure the fact that functional rhetoric was still to be found in the public gatherings of the Roman Empire. Primary rhetoric had not died.

Yet in the final analysis it must be said that to the average listener the distinction between functional and decorative (that is, *primary* and *secondary*) rhetoric probably would not have meant much. He thrived on oratory, but there is no evidence that he was much given to analyzing why. On the whole, first-century audiences were highly knowledgeable listeners in the sense of having seen—and seen through—most of the rhetorical tricks. But theirs was nevertheless the taste of the common man, not the purist. They enjoyed the merely

---

[1] As Kennedy (1972, p. 428) says, "Any fair estimate would judge the early Roman empire as one of the most eloquent periods in human history." See ibid., chaps. 6–7, for full documentation.

decorative as well as the genuinely persuasive and probably did not distinguish overmuch between the two. Both were considered powerful.

There was, so to speak, a transaction that took place between speaker and audience, an unspoken agreement wherein orators offered themselves and their efforts for the listeners' evaluation. The issues at stake might be important, as in a court case, or they might be trivial, involving nothing more than a judgment about the speaker's facility with words. But for his part the orator hoped to win the day for his cause, even if that cause was only himself. The potential rewards were such that he was willing to risk failure for the possibility of success.

It was a gamble, with the odds depending very much on the orator's rhetorical abilities. For their part the audience was granted each time the heady power of judgment, the opportunity to decide not only the issues at stake but also, in a certain sense, the fate of the orator. Every indication suggests that, like the crowds in the Coliseum giving thumbs up or down to the gladiators, the audience relished their role as judge. It was a transaction on which both sides seemed to thrive.

As to the dynamic of rhetoric itself, it was as if the orator worked with a Grand Equation in which everything was fixed except his own contribution. The audience and the subject matter were what they were; he could not change them. And even the goal of the speech was something independent, something external to himself. It was fixed by him, but also in a sense for him. Only the orator's own efforts were completely under his control. Leaning solely on his own brilliance, he had to become the supple variable by which the equation was made to work. His task was so to discover and manipulate the mix of rhetorical possibilities inherent in the audience, subject and occasion that his purpose would be accomplished—or, to cite Aristotle's important qualification, that he come as close to success as circumstances would allow. Indeed, teaching the orator how to find and use these possibilities was what classical rhetoric was about.

A THREE-PART EQUATION

The persuader was thus always working within the boundaries of this Grand Equation. It typically encompassed three primary parts: the audience, the desired results and the speaker's efforts. The audience for the persuader was a *Given*. He could not change them; the point was to adapt to what he found there in order to achieve his goals. This sends us to the opposite end of the equation: the results. These constituted the *Independent Variable*; that is, the results are independent in the sense that, once set, they determine the remainder of the equation. What was it the persuader wished to accomplish with his audience? It was the answer to this question that determined the *Dependent Variable*, the speaker's efforts. The persuader must adapt his efforts in whatever way necessary to achieve *this* result with *this* audience, and all of his rhetorical education was designed to train him in how to do so. It was his skill in successfully adapting himself and his efforts to the needs of the moment that made the rhetorical equation work.

Notice that the persuader's efforts were inherently results driven. Once set, the desired result governed the equation.[2] That is why so much attention was paid in ancient rhetorical literature to the mindset of the audience, to their belief systems, to their likes and dislikes, and to what will most likely win particular responses from them. To be successful in achieving his desired result the persuader was required to adapt himself to his audience; in fact, the ability to do so constituted the genius of classical rhetoric. Without this ability there was little hope of achieving the desired goal. But with it, the rhetor could strategize effectively to achieve his desired effect. Since he was methodologically uncommitted, the persuader was free—within the bounds of honesty, generally—to choose from his full repertoire of methods whatever would most likely achieve his purposes. This capacity to mold one's efforts to the demands of the given situation so as to achieve a particular result was what ancient rhetorical theory and training was designed to teach.

The Demands of Rhetoric

So then, what was required to produce an orator who could fulfill these high demands? Quintilian provides the best answers. Born in Spain around A.D. 35, this late contemporary of the Apostle Paul was educated in Rome, where he eventually returned to become the city's leading pedagogue. He was the first to hold an official chair of rhetoric that included a stipend from the State. Though he sometimes practiced forensic oratory in the courts, Quintilian's life's work consisted mainly of training others for public speaking. How seriously he took this task may be gauged from an examination of his *Institutes of Oratory*. Its twelve books, detailing the training of the first-century orator virtually from birth, constitute the largest treatise on rhetoric to have survived from antiquity. George Kennedy acclaimed it as simply "the finest statement of ancient rhetorical theory" available to us.[3]

---

[2]Ong (1983, p. 2): "Rhetoric starts with the conclusion, the position it wants to convince others to take, for which it must find supporting reasons.... Rhetoric knows its conclusions in advance, and clings to them."

[3]Kennedy (1972, p. 496).

Quintilian's approach to rhetoric may be fairly summed up as Ciceronian. Though he was not afraid to differ with Cicero, Quintilian believed that "for posterity the name of Cicero has come to be regarded not as the name of a man, but as the name of eloquence itself." Therefore, says Quintilian, "let us ... fix our eyes on him, take him as our pattern."[4] Quintilian followed his own advice and cites Cicero over and over again. In almost every important way Quintilian's rhetorical theory is a faithful reflection of the great Ciceronian ideal, an ideal that dominated first-century rhetoric.

What was that ideal? The true orator must possess an encyclopedic knowledge of a wide variety of subjects, a profound understanding of his listeners and an ability to express himself masterfully in language. And he must be able so to marshal each of these on any given occasion as to achieve victory.

> The man of eloquence whom we seek ... will be one who is able to speak in court or in deliberative bodies so as to prove, to please and to sway or persuade. To prove is the first necessity, to please is charm, to sway is victory; for it is the one thing of all that avails most in winning verdicts. For these three functions of the orator there are three styles, the plain style for proof, the middle style for pleasure, the vigorous style for persuasion; and in this last is summed up the entire virtue of the orator. Now the man who controls and combines these three varied styles needs rare judgement and great endowment; for he will decide what is needed at any point, and will be able to speak in any way which the case requires. For after all the foundation of eloquence, as of everything else, is wisdom.[5]

Who could master such a task? Cicero is unapologetic about his standards and is fully aware that those who fulfill them are, to say the least, rare: "In an orator we must demand the subtlety of the logician, the thoughts of the philosopher, a diction almost poetic, a lawyer's memory, a tragedian's voice, and the bearing almost of the consummate actor. Accordingly no rarer thing than a finished orator can be discovered among the sons of men."[6]

First-century orators were required to be craftsmen of ideas and language. Purity of diction was crucial.[7] "No word will fall from the orator's lips that is not well chosen or impressive."[8] In fact, the whole effort should be so finely and ar-

---

[4]Quintilian, *Inst. or.* 10.1.112; cf. 12.Intro.4; 12.1.19, 20; 3.1.20.
[5]Cicero, *Or. Brut.* 69-70.
[6]Cicero, *De or.* 1.128.
[7]Cf. Cicero, *Brutus* 258-59.
[8]Cicero, *Or. Brut.* 134.

tistically constructed that "if you break up the well-ordered structure of a careful orator by changing the order of the words: the whole thing would be ruined."[9] This is the sort of verbal artistry that was required of first-century orators.

These are high demands indeed. They are in fact demands the itinerant Jewish Apostle could not meet. Nor did he aspire to. As we shall see, Paul's goals as a missionary preacher were not those of the Greco-Roman persuader. They were the goals of a simple herald, goals that were dramatically different from those of the polished orators so popular in the Greco-Roman world of the first century.

---

[9] Ibid., 232; cf. Dionysius of Halicarnassus, *De compositione verborum* 4.

Part Two
---

1 Corinthians 1-4

10

Paul and Rhetoric in Corinth

With this summary of Greco-Roman rhetoric in hand, we may now turn our attention to the New Testament. Before doing so, however, we must briefly address two important questions: (1) What did the Apostle Paul, a Hellenistic Jew trained as a rabbi in Jerusalem, know of this rhetorical culture? (2) What role did the Greek rhetorical tradition play in the city of Corinth?

What Did the Apostle Paul Know of Greco-Roman Rhetoric?

The question of whether Paul was educated first in Tarsus and then in Jerusalem, or whether he moved to Jerusalem at an age that was early enough to render unimportant anything he might have received in Tarsus, has engendered much debate over the years. The first option would presumably have afforded the young Saul an opportunity to become conversant early on with Hellenistic ideas and authors, while the second would have given his education a more decidedly Jewish slant.[1]

The arguments for and against these options have been well explored by others and need not be rehearsed here. Fortunately we need not decide between them,[2]

---

[1] Given the Hellenizing influences at work in first-century Judaism, Judge (1983, p. 9) observes, "Paul would have had the opportunity of a Greek education even in Gamaliel's school in Jerusalem"; see the documentation in Litfin (1994, pp. 137-39).

[2] Either option will suit our purposes, but my own sympathies lie with Tarsus. The German classicist Eduard Norden (1909, p. 495) was famously critical of conclusions based on the Apostle's youthful experience at Tarsus. Yet there are good reasons why Tarsus has continued to play a role in the discussion. Tarsus was no mere backwater; it was the "metropolis" (μητρόπολις) of the Anatolian Peninsula (see Kaster, 1988, pp. 3-4). Rhetorical education was particularly strong there. Strabo, writing around the time of Paul's birth, emphasizes the rhetorical elements within the Tarsian culture: "The people at Tarsus have devoted themselves so eagerly not only to philosophy, but also to the whole round of education in general, that they have surpassed Athens, Alexandria, or any other place that can be named where there have been schools and lectures of philosophers" (*Geography* 14.5.13). When it is remembered that rhetoric was the crown of "the whole round of education" during this period, Strabo's comment becomes significant. In fact, Strabo does not leave his meaning ambiguous. He states that "the city of Tarsus has all kinds of schools of rhetoric." Later Strabo describes how the Tarsian Boethus had endeared himself to

not to mention the vexed questions of Paul's social class[3] or the quality of his literary style.[4] Our treatment of 1 Corinthians 1–4 requires us to assume on the part of the Apostle a certain limited understanding of the broad stance of Greco-Roman rhetoric, but only this and no more. In contrast to many who take up the subject of Paul and rhetoric, we will not argue that Paul intentionally used Greco-Roman persuasive strategies in his epistles or discourses. Those who so argue must assume a much more specific knowledge of rhetoric on the part of the Apostle[5]

Caesar "by the facility prevalent among the Tarsians whereby he could instantly speak offhand and unceasingly on any given subject" (14.5.14). Little wonder that Apollonius went to Tarsus to study rhetoric (Philostratus, *Life of Apollonius* 1.7; 6.34). Smith (1974, p. 9) ranks Tarsus over Alexandria and alongside Rome and Athens for the prevalence of its "many rhetorical schools." With their passion for education, their many schools for rhetoric and the general prevalence of eloquence among the Tarsians, Paul would not need to have spent long years of formal training there to have learned something about Greco-Roman rhetoric. Unless it can be demonstrated that Paul left Tarsus for Jerusalem at a very tender age indeed, he probably had his first taste of Greek eloquence here. For a detailed summary of the Tarsian argument, see Porter (2013, pp. 330-37). See also Du Toit (2000); Hengel (1989); Pitts (2008).

[3]See Gerd Theissen's minimalist conclusions that as a tentmaker Paul belonged to a "circle of privileged craftsmen"; that the possession of both Tarsian and Roman citizenship meant that Paul had a privileged legal status; that this also meant that Paul was probably "moderately prosperous"; and that Paul must have had an education that was "beyond the elementary school level and at least comparable to that of the grammar school," though this last would have been gained most likely in a Jewish synagogue school rather than "a pagan grammar school" (2003, pp. 372-74). Meggitt (1998, pp. 75-97) argues that even this assessment of Paul's social and economic standing exaggerates the facts. For the ongoing discussion of Paul's tentmaking as evidence of his social class, see Hock (2008).

[4]On which, see pp. 141-47 below.

[5]Ben Witherington is probably the leading proponent of the idea that Paul was a master rhetorician. Says he, "Sometimes it is urged that Paul's rhetoric is somewhat rudimentary. This sort of critique is usually leveled by those who think that one can only find in Paul's letters micro-rhetoric, the use of simple rhetorical devices like rhetorical questions, and the like. Nothing could be further from the truth. In fact, Paul's letters reflect the use of some of the most sophisticated and complex rhetorical moves imaginable" (2009a, p. 131; cf. idem, 2009b, pp. 7-17). This claim obviously requires Witherington to argue that Paul had a thorough education in Greco-Roman rhetoric (2009a, pp. 99-104, 120-21); cf. Hock (2003); Neyrey (2003).

But against Witherington's arguments, see Porter and Dyer (2012). Porter and Dyer reverse Witherington's argument by claiming that "no clear case can be made for Paul's formal knowledge of rhetoric—and thus also its formal use in the composition of his letters. At best, one might say that Paul acquired the type of rhetorical knowledge that any intelligent and widely travelled citizen of the Hellenistic world may have had." This suggests to Porter and Dyer that we should be skeptical about the notion that Paul's letters are masterpieces of Greco-Roman rhetoric. "Without the assurance of Paul's formal rhetorical training—a study that required years of work and included much theorizing (as reflected in the handbooks) and practice (as found in various rhetorical exercises)—one cannot make the claim . . . that Paul was not only well-versed in ancient rhetoric but was a master rhetorician. Even if rhetoric was 'in the air' (so to speak) in the NT era, this cannot account for the level of knowledge and application suggested for Paul by Witherington and others" (pp. 334-35). Porter and Dyer are surely right on this point. As Marrou (1981, p. 197) says, "The acquisition and mastery of so complex and elaborate a technique [as the art of Greco-Roman rhetoric] called for prolonged effort. Isocrates was already insisting

than is required here. They may or may not be correct, but for our purposes a more modest assumption will do.

Aper, Tacitus's first-century spokesman, claimed that the practice of oratory was so pervasive in his day that one could scarcely find even among "casual listeners" anyone who, "if he has not had a systematic training in the rudiments of the art [of rhetoric], cannot show at least a tincture of it."[6] So also with the Apostle Paul. We will assume of Paul nothing more than one would expect of an intelligent and literate man who was born a Roman citizen in Tarsus, was trained in an increasingly Hellenized Jerusalem, spoke fluent Greek, and lived and moved perceptively in the Hellenistic world of the first century, a world in which rhetoric and oratory were common features of daily life.

The modesty of this assumption means that either of the above theories about Paul's education will suffice. If Paul was first educated in the Hellenistic educational setting of Tarsus, then this alone would be more than enough to account for the level of understanding we see in Paul. But our assumption by no means requires a Tarsian education. For example, there is ample evidence to suggest that by the time of Paul, Greek culture—and Greek rhetoric in particular—had been assimilated by the Jews and was in discreet use among the Pharisees in Jerusalem.[7] Thus Paul may have learned something of Greco-Roman rhetoric from this source. Such a supposition is speculative but reasonable.

What is not speculative, however, is the fact that by the time he wrote the Corinthian epistles Paul had spent years moving widely in the Hellenistic world. However long he may have remained in Tarsus, Paul later lived not sporadically but for extended periods of time among the people who made up the Greco-Roman culture. The language, practices and thinking of the Hellenistic world were forced on him, and he could not have avoided them had he tried. If nothing

---

on three or four years of study, and in the Hellenistic and Roman periods the time was extended up to eight years." The notion that Paul possessed such an education stretches credulity.

In his essay "Paul and the Terminology of Ancient Greek Rhetoric" (2002, pp. 29-44), classicist C. J. Classen winds up closer to Porter and Dyer than to Witherington: "Paul was familiar with a number of technical terms of Greek rhetoric. Where he knew them from I do not venture to decide; their use, however, together with that of technical terms of philosophy signify a standard of education which warrants the assumption that Paul was familiar through theory (handbooks) or practice (actual application) with the rules and precepts of ancient rhetoric" (p. 44). In another place Classen (1992, p. 323) says: "Anyone who could write Greek as effectively as Saint Paul did must have read a good deal of works written in Greek, thus imbibing applied rhetoric from others, even if he never heard of any rules of rhetorical theory; so even if one could prove that Saint Paul was not familiar with the rhetorical theory of the Greeks, it can hardly be denied that he knew it in its applied form."

[6]Tacitus, *Dial.* 19.5.
[7]See Kinneavy (1987, pp. 56-100).

else, this exposure alone easily accounts for the general understanding of Greco-Roman rhetoric we observe in Paul's argument throughout 1 Corinthians 1–4. As Eduard Norden put it, it is virtually "self-evident" (*selbstverstandlich*) that Paul's mission in the Hellenistic world alone was enough to provide him an understanding of the how these things worked.[8]

In the final analysis, then, speculations about where Paul was educated need not occupy us. Beyond the above minimalist assumptions, we will avoid speculating about where Paul may have gained his insights. Our goal is to explore the Apostle's argument without recourse to complex hypotheses regarding the sources that may or may not have shaped his thoughts. The precariousness and inconclusiveness of many of these reconstructions are well-known. For our purposes we can pass by such speculations, substituting for them instead a simple and unremarkable conclusion about the Corinthians.

What Role Did the Greek Rhetorical Tradition Play in the City of Corinth?

The history of the city of Corinth is too familiar to require more than the briefest summary, especially since excess historical detail adds little to our present discussion. It will be enough to note the broad outlines of the city's heritage.[9]

Located on an isthmus at a juncture of north-south traffic between central Greece and the Peloponnesus on the one hand, and east-west traffic between the seas on the other—"at the cross-roads of Greece," as Dio Chrysostom put it[10]—ancient Corinth became a thriving center of commerce, industry and wealth. In the kaleidoscope of Greek politics throughout the classical and Hellenistic periods, the city played an important role, but never more tragically than when it became the chief city of the Achaean League during the second century B.C. Once Rome set out to crush the League, Corinth was the last bastion to fall, and its demise was virtually total. Under the consul Mummius the Romans utterly destroyed Corinth in 146 B.C., razing the city quite literally to the ground and sending its people into slavery.[11] Old Corinth was dead. Its ruins were to lay undisturbed for over a century.

---

[8]Norden (1909, vol. 2, p. 493; cf. p. 507). See also Dibelius (1953, pp. 30-31).
[9]For a more detailed yet concise and accurate summary of what we know of first-century Corinth, see Adams and Horrell (2004), pp. 2-8.
[10]Dio Chrysostom, *Discourses* 8.5.
[11]See Dio Cassius, *Roman History* 21 (Zonaras 9.31); Strabo, *Geography* 8.6.23; Pausanias, *Descriptions of Greece* 2.1-5; 7.16.7ff.

In 44 B.C., however, Corinth was resurrected as a Roman colony by Julius Caesar. Because of its strategic location, New Corinth quickly began to thrive and Augustus eventually (ca. 27 B.C.) made it the capital of the province of Achaia. By the middle of the first century A.D. Corinth had once again become a prosperous[12] and cosmopolitan seaport.

Because the city was situated crucially in the center of Greece and continued to uphold many long-established Greek traditions—for example, the Isthmian Games and various other festivals were held here[13]—Corinth quickly reclaimed much of its Greek identity, becoming once more, as Favorinus put it, "thoroughly Hellenized."[14] With its deeply rooted Greek heritage, its close proximity to other distinctively Greek cities such as Athens, and its unavoidable location for north-south travel in Greece, it is hardly surprising that Hellenism firmly reasserted itself, once again making Corinth the very "promenade of Hellas."[15]

Yet the Roman influence in Corinth also remained important, shaping everything from the layout of the new city to its civil and legal systems. Rome was simply too much a part of New Corinth to be shaken off. Dio Chrysostom criticized the Corinthians, for example, for their love of the Roman gladiatorial displays.[16] Imperial visits were not uncommon, and Nero's interest in an isthmian canal in particular dictated a strong Roman influence in mid-first-century Corinth.[17] Moreover, because Corinth was an important stop for sea travelers, various other groups from around the empire were also drawn here

---

[12]Strabo notes that Old Corinth was famous for its wealth (*Geography* 8.6.19-20, 23); the recovered wealth of the rebuilt Corinth is emphasized by Dio Chrysostom, *Discourses* 37.36.
[13]Cf. Strabo, *Geography* 8.6.20; Pausanias, *Description of Greece* 2.1.7; 2.2.2.
[14]See Dio Chrysostom, *Discourses* 37.26; on the Favorinian authorship of this discourse, see below.
[15]Dio Chrysostom, *Discourses* 37.7. The strong Greek identity of Corinth is reinforced by the description of Corinth by Pausanias (*Description of Greece* 2.1-5). Moreover, Dio Cassius seems to indicate that this was Caesar's intention from the beginning. Apparently Caesar not only founded Corinth as a Roman colony but restored it specifically in memory of its brilliant Greek heritage, leaving its name intact as a tribute to its past (*Roman History* 43.50.3-5). Not surprisingly, then, the Greek aspects of New Corinth were strongly emphasized by Roman historian A. H. M. Jones (1940, pp. 60-63): "The emperors made no attempt to romanize the Greek-speaking provinces." Why then the colonies? "These settlements were clearly too few and far between seriously to modify the predominantly Greek culture of the regions in which they were planted, and in point of fact they for the most part gradually took the tone of their surroundings; Greek supplanted Latin on their inscriptions and even on their coins the Latin legends, engraved by Greek artists, became progressively more illiterate and ultimately in some cases became Greek." Speaking specifically of Corinth, Jones notes the "rapidity with which the majority of the colonies were hellenized" and says that even at the beginning, "Caesar's colonists at Corinth were for the most part freedmen, and to the majority of them Greek was probably more familiar than Latin."
[16]Dio Chrysostom, *Discourses* 31.121.
[17]Cf. Dio Cassius, *Roman History* 42.16.1-2; 42.14.2-4; Philostratus, *Life of Apollonius* 4.24.

and many of them stayed on. Most notably for our purposes, there was a community of Jews in Corinth, a fact noted in Acts 18:4 and substantiated by a partial inscription indicating that Corinth had its own synagogue.[18]

In short, the populace of Corinth was made up of an alloy of peoples drawn from across the Mediterranean. Though no doubt dominated by Greeks and Romans, with its various travelers and minority residents Corinth represented as much of a cross section of the empire as one was likely to find. More Greek than Rome, more Roman than Athens, if any city of the first century deserved the hyphenated designation Greco-Roman, it was Corinth.

This simple and widely acknowledged conclusion about first-century Corinth is important for our discussion because it discourages us from constructing an interpretation of the Corinthian epistles on any fanciful distinctives of the city. For example, even the much emphasized immorality of the city may have been overdone by commentators. Old Corinth was infamous for its licentiousness, but can the same be said of New Corinth? Despite the presence of the cult of Aphrodite, C. K. Barrett wisely concludes that the Corinth of St. Paul's day "was probably little better and little worse than any other great sea port and commercial center of the age."[19] This is a sound conclusion unless we have clear first-century evidence to the contrary. Thus we will assume nothing more about Corinth than the obvious: it was a Greco-Roman city that partook in an ordinary way of the features of Greco-Roman culture.

In the light of this assumption, our treatment of 1 Corinthians 1–4 will draw on what we have learned about the role of rhetoric and eloquence in the Greco-Roman world as a whole. We will assume that, as was the case in the surrounding culture, eloquence was prevalent in mid-first-century Corinth. Like their neighbors, the people of Corinth thrived on it and participated enthusiastically in their role as auditors. We may assume that the orators who addressed Corinthian audiences were in no way unique but were essentially similar to—in fact, often identical with—the speakers who addressed crowds from Rome to Asia. The delight in eloquence that characterized the rest of the Greco-Roman world characterized Corinth as well, and the association of eloquence with fame,

---

[18]This widely cited inscription, however, is dated "considerably later than the time of St. Paul" (Merritt, 1931, p. 79). Still, none question that an earlier synagogue existed, and the reference in Acts is corroborated by Philo, *Embassy to Gaius* 281-82.

[19]Barrett (1968, p. 3). Conzelmann (1975, p. 12) discounts as mere fable the "often-peddled statement that Corinth was a seat of sacred prostitution," and disputes the notion that "behind the Aphrodite of Corinth lurks the Phoenician Astarte."

power, status and wealth was as obvious and deep-seated here as anywhere.[20]

None of these assumptions about the rhetorical climate in Corinth requires specific corroboration. They stand on the reasonable claim that, unless we have grounds to believe otherwise, we should suppose that Corinth generally mirrored the broad values of the Greco-Roman culture of which it was a part. The burden of proof would lie with anyone who wished to argue differently. Nevertheless, external corroboration of the Corinthian attitude toward eloquence does in fact exist.

Quite beyond the most obvious sorts of evidence—such as the existence of the platform-like βῆμα in the center of the South Stoa of Corinth, a structure that was consciously modeled after the *Rostra* at Rome[21] and that served as a podium from which speakers could address audiences gathered in the ἀγορά ("place of assembly, marketplace")—quite beyond such general indicators as this of the centrality of public speaking to the life of Corinth, we have much more specific evidence in the form of a discourse addressed to the Corinthians by the sophist Favorinus (ca. A.D. 80–150).[22] This discourse merits close attention.

FAVORINUS AND THE CORINTHIANS

Favorinus had apparently visited Corinth twice before. On his first occasion, nearly ten years previous to the present discourse, he had given the crowd a sample of his eloquence (λόγος) and had been well received. On the second visit some years later the response of the Corinthian people was stronger still. Favorinus refers to the "enthusiasm of the populace" with which his λόγος was embraced and says that because of it the people considered him "the noblest among

---

[20]See the excellent discussion of this point by Clarke (2006, pp. 23–39).

[21]Scranton (1951, p. 91). The identification of the Corinthian βῆμα and the Roman *Rostra* is made explicit in a second-century inscription; see Broneer (1939, p. 185), who calls the βῆμα at Corinth the "speaker's platform" and says, "We know that this building . . . was used by the Governor of Achaia for the transaction of public affairs and for the delivery of speeches addressed to the people of the city"; see also Broneer (1937, pp. 125ff); cf. Herod's use of a βῆμα for oratorical purposes in Acts 12:21. Elsewhere Broneer (1951, p. 91), who supervised most of its excavation, calls this Corinthian structure "an outdoor speakers' stand." Interestingly, the proconsul Gallio of Acts 18:12-16 had himself "been adopted by his father's friend, Junius Gallio, the great rhetorician, and taken on his name" (Meinardus, 1973, p. 65) and was thus well named to make use of this platform.

[22]This speech has come down to us as part of Dio Chrysostom's *Discourses*. However, the bulk of scholarly opinion has long attributed it to the sophist Favorinus. In passing we should also note, however, that Favorinus was not the only sophist interested in Corinth. The wealthy Athenian sophist Herodes built the theater at Corinth; see Graindor (1930, pp. 202-9). According to Graindor, after Athens, Corinth was the city Herodes loved best (p. 209). Philostratus claimed that Herodes and Favorinus were intimate acquaintances (*Lives* 490). We may also note that Herodes had as one of his more advanced pupils one Sceptus of Corinth (Philostratus, *Lives* 573).

the Greeks" (ὡς ἄριστος Ἑλλήνων) and importuned him to stay in Corinth.[23] So impressed were the Corinthians with Favorinus's eloquence that they caused a bronze statue to be cast in his likeness and then placed it in the most prestigious position in the city's library, a location where, as Favorinus put it, the Corinthians felt "it would most effectively stimulate the youth to persevere in the same pursuits as myself."[24] Unfortunately for Favorinus, however, on his third visit to Corinth he made a painful discovery. Due to unspecified charges of immorality his statue had been removed from its place of honor and destroyed. To the egotistical sophist this was the unkindest cut of all. Deeply crushed, he responded with the rhetorical defense that has come down to us.

The fate of Favorinus need not detain us. Philostratus portrays him as a profligate and says that the Athenians also rid themselves of his statue.[25] Of greater interest are the Corinthians themselves. The picture of the people of Corinth that emerges from this discourse is one of deep enthusiasm for oratory. They loved eloquence, lionized its practitioners and were concerned that their own youth excel in it. Moreover, this attitude was broadly based among the Corinthian populace. It was "the city" (ἡ πόλις) that dedicated the statue to Favorinus—not just the "Council" but the citizenry as well.[26] Favorinus seems to go out of his way to make this point when he says of the unfounded slander against him that it was rooted in jealousy, a resentment of "the charm of [my] eloquence (λόγος), or whatever one should call that gift to which you yourself, along with women and children, give approval."[27] Like their counterparts throughout the Greco-Roman world, the Corinthian population reveled in the spoken word and granted to its proponents their highest accolades, in this case a bronze statue set in the place of honor, a statue that the chastened Favorinus forlornly recalled as "a mute semblance of my eloquence."[28]

There is one passage in this discourse that deserves to be quoted in full because of the insight it offers into the makeup and thinking of the Corinthian populace. Commenting on the relation of the Romans to the Greeks, the Roman poet Horace (65–27 B.C.) had observed that "Greece, the captive, made her savage victor captive,

---

[23]Philostratus, *Lives* 37.8, 22.
[24]Ibid., 37.8. As Winter (2003, p. 293) observes, Corinthian bronzes "were highly prized in the ancient world so that a statue, not in stone but in bronze, was the greatest honor that could be given."
[25]Philostratus, *Lives* 489-90.
[26]Ibid., 37.20; cf. 37.9.
[27]Ibid., 37.33.
[28]Ibid., 37.46.

and brought the arts into rustic Latinum" (*Epistles* 2.1.156). Favorinus represented the epitome of this cultural captivity. Born in Rome, Favorinus had come to embrace all things Greek. Significantly, he felt that this should stand him in good stead in Corinth especially. Said he, referring to himself in the third person,

> Well, if some one who is not a Lucanian but a Roman, not one of the masses but of the equestrian order, one who has affected, not merely the language, but also the thought and manners and dress of the Greeks, and that too with such mastery and manifest success as no one among either the Romans of earlier days nor the Greeks of his own time, I must say, has achieved—for while the best of the Greeks over there may be seen inclining toward Roman ways, he inclines toward the Greek and to that end is sacrificing both his property and his political standing and absolutely everything, aiming to achieve one thing at the cost of all else, namely, not only to seem Greek but to be Greek too—taking all this into consideration, ought he not to have a bronze statue here in Corinth? Yes, and in every city—in yours because, though Roman, he has become thoroughly hellenized, even as your own city has; in Athens because he is Athenian in his speech; in Sparta because he is devoted to athletics; in all cities everywhere because he pursues the study of wisdom and already has not only roused many of the Greeks to follow that pursuit with him but also attracted even many of the barbarians. Indeed it seems that he has been equipped by the gods for this express purpose—for the Greeks, so that the natives of that land may have an example before them to show that culture is no whit inferior to birth with respect to renown; for Romans, so that not even those who are wrapped up in their own self-esteem may disregard culture with respect to real esteem; for Celts, so that no one even of the barbarians may despair of attaining the culture of Greece when he looks upon this man. Well then, it is for some such reasons as these that I have been erected—not to expose myself to opprobrium by naming more.[29]

In this passage Favorinus strongly emphasizes the Greek tendencies of the Corinthians. Though like Favorinus himself New Corinth had been born Roman, it, like him, had by now become thoroughly Hellenized. Favorinus focuses on this Greek identity of the Corinthian populace—he addresses them as a whole, with no indication that he is singling out some subgroup—sets it off against Romanism and then uses it in his own defense. He considered himself an exponent *par excel-*

---

[29]Ibid., 37.25-27.

lence of Greek culture, a culture that had at its heart the pursuit of λόγος and σοφία. In fact he claims that it was specifically because of his excellence in these two virtues, as perceived by the Corinthians, that his statue had been erected at Corinth in the first place.[30] In other words, these were the things he emphasized in his attempt to become thoroughly Greek, and they were the very things that endeared him to the Corinthians in their own love of things Greek. Hence his dismay at how quickly and dramatically the situation had been reversed.

Favorinus's portrait of the Corinthians should not be used to argue that Latin influence had been eclipsed in Corinth during the time of Paul. To be sure, in his book on Tacitus the Roman historian Ronald Syme portrays the latter half of the first century and the early part of the second as a general time of turning by Romans to things Greek: "If Latin letters declined, Greek civilization now rose again and flourished exuberantly."[31] In fact, when Syme writes of a man having an "addiction to all things Greek" it is not of Favorinus he speaks but Nero![32] Yet Favorinus's account does foster for us a familiar and entirely predictable picture. As one of the leading cities of Greece, and such a cosmopolitan one at that, it would have been remarkable were Corinth anything other than representative of contemporary Greco-Roman culture.

The Corinthians of the early Christian era, like their contemporaries across the Roman Empire, loved and rewarded λόγος and σοφία. On the other hand, they had not the slightest compunction about standing in judgment over the speakers who came before them. They thrived on eloquence and encouraged it among their youth. The love of λόγος and σοφία came easily to them as part of an inherited culture, a παιδεία as old as Isocrates. It was a culture the Romans in many ways borrowed and adapted, but it remained rooted in the soil of Greece. To discover anything different in first-century Corinth would be surprising indeed.

---

[30]Cf. ibid., 37.1, 8, 26-27, 33, 46.
[31]Syme (1958, vol. 2, p. 505).
[32]Ibid., p. 515. Habinek (2005, pp. 35-36): "It is interesting to note that the ancient biographies of emperors still make much of their successes or failures as public speakers. Indeed, mastery of oratory, associated as it was with deliberation, analysis, respect for the audience, and acknowledgement of the history and procedures of the state, serves as a mark of a 'good' emperor in the eyes of the Roman elite; disdain for eloquence, on the other hand, signals unreliability and worse."

The Setting of 1 Corinthians 1–4

Every treatment of the Corinthian epistles begins with assumptions about Paul and the epistles themselves, and ours is no exception. It will be useful to make these assumptions explicit at the outset. The following suppositions are simple and straightforward, and they conveniently allow us to skirt several scholarly debates that may be crucial for other purposes but are at most tangential to our own.

Our treatment of 1 Corinthians 1–4 assumes that Paul wrote 1 and 2 Corinthians, and that 1 Corinthians 1–4 stands as a distinguishable literary unit. The first assumption requires little comment since the genuineness of the Corinthian epistles is undisputed. We will turn to the second in a moment. But first we should note something of the debate we are skirting.

THE STRUCTURE OF THE LETTERS

Scholars have expended prodigious efforts in modern times wrestling with the literary structure of the Corinthian epistles. The questions basically are, should the two epistles that have come down to us be considered distinct and essentially unified letters, written on two separate occasions, or must the structure of our two epistles be viewed as the work of some later editor(s) who combined fragments of more than two epistles to form the letters as we know them? By far the greater structural challenges are to be found in 2 Corinthians, and scholars have propounded a variety of more or less complicated partition theories to account for them. Inevitably these theories, whether of unity or partition, are tied up with complex suppositions regarding the history of Paul's dealings with the Corinthian church.

We are again in the fortunate position of not having to decide this issue in order to proceed. This is due to the singular focus of our discussion. We are not attempting a full-scale commentary on the Corinthian epistles; we are pursuing only one important aspect of the Apostle's thought, a limitation that affords us the luxury of leaving some of these issues unresolved. As we shall see, our reading of 1 Corinthians 1–4 does not depend on any particular structural theory or any one reconstruction of Paul's contacts with the Corinthians. In the final analysis any of them will do.

Here then is the essentially undisputed scenario that produced 1 Corinthians 1–4. Based on the reference to Gallio in Acts 18:12-17, it seems clear that Paul initially visited Corinth sometime around the mid–first century, and that he remained there for an extended period of ministry (Acts 18:11, 18). Then sometime after leaving Achaia, Paul wrote the Christians in Corinth the "previous letter" of 1 Corinthians 5:9. Subsequently Paul was visited, apparently unofficially, by members of the church of Corinth (the household of Chloe, 1 Cor 1:11) who brought him news of the situation there. He also received what appears to have been an official delegation from the church itself (1 Cor 16:17). These messengers may have brought with them a written communication from the church, or it may have come to Paul via some other channel about which we have no information. In either case Paul received a written communication, which seems to have consisted of questions for clarification, particularly about matters of Christian conduct (1 Cor 7:1). In response to both the informal report and the formal questions from the Corinthians, Paul wrote the epistle we know as 1 Corinthians.

The Nature of Chapters 1–4

As for our second assumption, in an article on the literary integrity of 1 Corinthians 1–4, N. A. Dahl famously summed up scholarly opinion regarding this section of Paul's writings.[1] His summary has not been improved upon since it was written a half century ago. We need perhaps do no more than cite Dahl's general observations. It seems clear (1) that in 1 Corinthians 1–4 Paul is addressing the Corinthian church as a whole; (2) that this section was prompted primarily by the informal report of Chloe's people (though it need not because of this be unrelated to the church's more formal questions); and (3) that the passage stands relatively unified and distinct in its subject matter within the letter as a whole. Each of these assumptions is easily demonstrated and therefore generally agreed on by scholars.

On the other hand, one matter that has found little agreement is the relationship of chapters 1–4 to the remainder of the epistle.[2] Yet this too is a debate

---

[1] Dahl (1967, pp. 313-35).
[2] E.g., at one end of the spectrum Kümmel (1965, p. 199) argues that 1 Cor "clearly has no connected train of thought, and there are no connecting links between the separate sections"; cf. De Boer (1994), who argues that chapters 1–4 and 5–16 are so distinct that they should be thought

we need not engage. Few question the integrity of 1 Corinthians 1-4, and the relationship of this section to the rest of the epistle can for our purposes remain an open question. The aspect of Paul's thought we are after is so thoroughly concentrated within the literary unit of chapters 1-4 that the bulk of our attention will be focused there. Echoes of the ideas found in 1-4 are certainly heard elsewhere in the Corinthian correspondence (especially 2 Cor) and we will not ignore these echoes in our own study. Our point is that any one of the viable theories of the relationship of 1-4 to the rest of the Corinthian correspondence will suffice to account for such reverberations. For our purposes we need no more than Dahl's two relatively obvious observations: (1) that we should "understand 1 Corinthians 1:10-4:21 as an introductory section with a definite purpose within the letter as a whole"; and (2) that "the section 1 Corinthians 1:10-4:21 is correctly, even if not exhaustively, to be characterized as an apology for Paul's apostolic ministry."[3]

THE ISSUE OF RHETORICAL GENRE

These minimalist assumptions allow us to bypass another issue that has prompted much critical attention in recent years. It relates to the "rhetorical genre" of 1 Corinthians, or what Witherington calls the letter's *macro-rhetoric*: "the use of rhetorical categories and divisions used in ancient speeches" to shape "the overall structure of some NT documents" (Witherington, 2009b, p. 13; cf. idem, 2009a, pp. 7-8). The question is, should 1 Corinthians be considered *epideictic* ("praise or blame"), *forensic* ("accusatory or defensive") or *deliberative* ("hortatory or dissuasive") rhetoric? Scholars do not seem to be able to agree. For example, contrast the conclusions of Wuellner (1979) and Mitchell (1991). The lack of consensus on this point (see Watson, 2010b; Porter, 2013, pp. 337-44) is perhaps due to the fact that 1 Corinthians does not fit neatly into any of these oversimplified (cf. Quintilian, *Inst. or.* 3.4.1-16) categories. As Bird (2008, p. 379) says, "A conscious or unconscious amalgam and adaptation of epistolary structures, Jewish exegetical techniques, traditional Christian material, biographical self-references, Greco-Roman rhetorical forms, sermonic exhortations,

---

of as two different letters conjoined before dispatch by Paul himself. At the other end of the spectrum, Witherington (1995, p. 74) views 1 Cor as a deliberative discourse with a unified argument; cf. Hall (2003, pp. 29-50) on "The Unity of 1 Corinthians." Stirewalt (2003, p. 75) comes closer to Kümmel than Witherington in concluding that 1 Cor is a "seriatim" letter ("a letter made up of a series of responses to problems and questions"), a point he demonstrates by analyzing 1 Cor alongside a secular example written by Emperor Claudius to the people of Alexandria. My own view is somewhat equidistant between the two poles. But as noted above, for our present purposes almost any point on this spectrum will suffice.
[3]Dahl (1977, pp. 44, 55; but see n. 50). Cf. also Chance (1982) on this point.

apocalyptic and wisdom motifs, evangelistic zeal and pastoral concern make Paul's letters what they are." Hence Watson's conclusion (2010b, p. 44): "The rhetorical species of Paul's epistles conform to epistolary and rhetorical conventions only when they meet his rhetorical purposes. Otherwise he is creating something new." This uniqueness is part of the reason many scholars have resisted the underlying premise that Paul's epistles should be treated as essentially oral discourses (speeches) disguised as letters. For detailed discussions of the issues, see Porter and Dyer (2012); Weima (1997; 2000, pp. 123-31); Kern (1998); Reed (1993).

Our study does not require us to decide these issues, but I tend to identify with J. Louis Martyn's comment (1997, pp. 20-21) on the overabundance of ingenious but also contradictory and inconclusive analyses of Paul's epistles. Speaking of Galatians, Martyn says, "We may doubt that Paul would have fully recognized as his own any of the modern structural analyses of Galatians. . . . The document is a letter from beginning to end, not merely a speech enclosed between epistolary prescript and subscript." Martyn then adds a wry footnote in which he observes of one such analysis that it "is so fanciful as to have the effect of suggesting a moratorium of some length in this branch of research."

THE CENTRALITY OF PAUL'S PREACHING

Paul's relationship with the Corinthians was often a stormy one. The problems were many and Paul's attempts to address them complex. Preliminary to all of these problems, however, was the difficulty addressed in 1 Corinthians 1-4—namely, criticisms on the part of some of the Corinthians of Paul's preaching. This difficulty plagued the Apostle's relationship with the Corinthians almost from the outset, and there is evidence to suggest that it was never fully resolved.

While, as we shall see, the issue of Paul's preaching animates and unifies 1 Corinthians 1-4, it is important to remember that references to this problem are by no means isolated to 1 Corinthians 1-4. The conflict over the Apostle's preaching surfaces repeatedly throughout the Corinthian correspondence. As a prelude to our discussion of 1 Corinthians 1-4, therefore, it will be useful to survey what the Corinthian epistles show us of the problem. This will enable us to gain a better grasp of the true nature of the conflict. It will also guard us against special pleading as we explore 1 Corinthians 1-4.

An examination of the relevant passages leads to several successive observations regarding Paul's preaching and its reception in Corinth.[4] Foremost among

---

[4]The following reflects the interplay between the "rhetorical situation" and "historical situation" of 1 Cor 1-4. On this type of interplay in interpretation, see Watson (1999).

these observations is the simple yet crucial assertion that public speaking lay at the core of Paul's ministry.⁵ According to his own testimony he engaged in other forms of ministry—baptism, intercessory prayer, collecting aid for the impoverished saints in Jerusalem—but there is nothing to suggest that he considered such activities a part of his essential apostolic mandate. On the contrary, Paul flatly states that the task assigned to him was nothing other than a ministry of public speaking: Christ did not send me to baptize, he says, but "to preach the gospel" (εὐαγγελίζεσθαι), that is, to promulgate a message via the spoken word (1 Cor 1:17). Whatever else might be said about Paul's ministry, at the behavioral level public speaking is what he actually did. Whether his audiences were formal or informal, large or small, indoors or out of doors, the use of speech to communicate a verbal message to listeners dominated his activities.

This activity was not unique to Paul, of course; others proclaimed the message as well.⁶ But it is important to see that Paul's ministry was singularly focused on his role as a public speaker. The verbs εὐαγγελίζω, κηρύσσω, καταγγέλλω, λαλέω, παρακαλῶ and μαρτυρέω monopolize Paul's references to his ministry, virtually to the exclusion of anything else.⁷ Paul held that he had been entrusted with a precious treasure, a message of good news from God (2 Cor 4:4, 7). His task as the steward of this treasure was not to hoard it but to disseminate it as widely as possible via the spoken word. According to 1 Corinthians 9:16-18, the public communication of this message obsessed and compelled Paul. In his view he existed to function as a public speaker, a proclaimer of a message to all who would listen. Everything else must be adjusted to this role, including his own personal desires. He claimed to do all things "for the sake of the gospel" (διὰ τὸ εὐαγγέλιον, 1 Cor 9:23), lest having preached (κηρύσσω) to others he himself might wind up "disqualified" (ἀδόκιμος, 1 Cor 9:27) before God. In short, Paul viewed himself, and wanted others to view him, as nothing other than a servant of Christ who had been entrusted with the stewardship of a message. Of such ones, he says, it is required only that they be found faithful in carrying out their stewardship; that is, they must disseminate this message to others (1 Cor 4:1-2; cf. 9:17). To the Apostle this simple picture was enough to capture the essential core of his ministry.

---

⁵Dickson (2003, p. 86): "One activity emerges from the Pauline epistles as the central, and all-consuming, mission duty for Paul, that of 'preaching the gospel.' . . . For Paul, this is the 'default' missionary idea."
⁶Cf. 1 Cor 9:14; 15:11; 2 Cor 1:19; cf. παραδίδωμι in 1 Cor 15:3.
⁷See in the Corinthian correspondence alone: 1 Cor 1:23; 2:1, 4, 6, 7, 13; 3:1; 9:16, 18, 27; 15:1, 2, 11, 14, 15; 2 Cor 1:19; 2:17; 4:5, 13; 5:18-20; 7:14; 10:16; 11:4, 7.

We must not belabor this point, because it is all but universally granted. But we emphasize it here because the centrality of public speaking to the ministry of Paul looms so large when we come to Corinth. It is crucial to realize that the resistance to Paul reflected in 1 Corinthians 1–4 was primarily triggered by, and centered on, negative responses to his public speaking. We can see the cogency of this point by highlighting three further observations.

(1) It is clear that the Corinthians subjected Paul and his ministry to stringent evaluation, or judgment, and that for significant segments of the church the verdict was at least in part a negative one. This negative verdict grew out of a comparison of Paul with one or more other leaders whom some of the Corinthians found more to their liking, prompting them to divide up "in favor of one against another" (ὑπὲρ τοῦ ἑνὸς . . . κατὰ τοῦ ἑτέρου, 1 Cor 4:6).

The Apostle's response to this situation is threefold: (a) While professing to be little troubled personally by the fact that the Corinthians were evaluating him (1 Cor 4:3), Paul nevertheless instructs them to cease doing so (1 Cor 4:5), asserting that God will make the appropriate judgment at the appropriate time. (b) Paul also sporadically attempts to defend himself outright against their critical judgments (1 Cor 9:3 NIV, "my defense to those who sit in judgment on me"; cf. also 2 Cor 12:19), albeit with some reluctance. The Apostle seemed uncomfortable in defending himself to the Corinthians, evidently because such justifications appeared self-serving. His real purpose in defending himself, he says, is to give the Corinthians the opportunity to be proud instead of ashamed of him (2 Cor 1:14; 5:12). In the end his argument is not a defense to them at all, he claims, but a defense before God, laid out to them for their edification (2 Cor 12:19).

But the fundamental problem that runs right through the Corinthian epistles was that the Corinthians viewed Paul from the wrong perspective. The standards against which they measured him were altogether the wrong standards, leading to criticism rather than commendation (cf. 2 Cor 12:11). We will examine this problem in detail later, but for now we need only note that (c) Paul's predominant response to the Corinthians' negative evaluations was to criticize their worldly standards of judgment, recommending instead a set of values that he believed were more firmly rooted in Christ. These different standards would lead inevitably to a reappraisal of himself and his ministry. Paul was genuinely concerned about how he was viewed by the Corinthians, and for mixed reasons. He wished to be approved by them (cf. 2 Cor 1:13-14; 12:20; 13:6), but more importantly he wanted them to understand and practice the truth even if it meant that they would disapprove of him (2 Cor 13:7). In the final analysis, however, Paul was confident that if he could shake the Corinthians free of their worldly standards and ground them firmly in genuinely Christlike values, his ministry would, ipso facto, be vindicated against their judgments.

(2) If it is clear that the Corinthians subjected Paul's ministry to judgment, it is equally clear that this judgment focused in large measure on the Apostle's public speaking. The extent to which this was the case can only be gauged by a careful examination of the text, but for the present we need simply acknowledge the fact of it. Paul's critics in Corinth judged his public speaking to be deficient and explicitly criticized him for it. In the one passage in the Corinthian epistles where Paul most directly cites their assessment (2 Cor 10:10), the appraisal focuses sharply on his speech: Paul's written efforts (ἐπιστολαί) are effective enough, the critics grant, but his physical presence is weak and his speech (λόγοι) is contemptible. Paul's shortcoming according to the Corinthian critics, even as late as 2 Corinthians 10–13, is that he was "unskilled in speaking" (ἰδιώτης τῷ λόγῳ, 11:6). This complaint lay at the core of the Corinthian resistance from early on, and it explains to a large extent Paul's recurrent references to his public speaking throughout both of the Corinthian epistles.

Paul viewed his speaking activities as the keystone of his ministry. To be found wanting here was to be touched on his most sensitive nerve. Hence the Apostle was eager to vindicate his approach to public speaking against the complaints of his critics. This vindication runs like a thread throughout the Corinthian correspondence but finds its fullest statement in 1 Corinthians 1–4.

ON LETTERS VERSUS SPEECHES

Greco-Roman standards of evaluation for speeches (λόγοι) and epistles (ἐπιστολαί) were different. The great Roman orator Cicero set the contrast in a letter to his friend Papirius Paetus: "But tell me now, how do you find me as a letter writer? Don't I deal with you in colloquial style? The fact is that one's style has to vary. A letter is one thing, a court of law or a public meeting quite another. Even for the courts we don't have just one style. In pleading civil cases, unimportant ones, we put on no frills, whereas cases involving status or reputation naturally get something more elaborate. As for letters, we weave them out of the language of everyday" (*Letters to Friends* 188.1).

This contrast was why ancient writers often distinguished between how letters and speeches were to be judged. See, for example, Aristotle, *Rhetoric* 3.12.1; Pliny, *Letters*

5.8; compare also the explicit section on the appropriate characteristics of a personal letter over against a formal treatise or oration in Demetrius, *On Style* 223-35. Nor are Quintilian's words, "Well, you ask, is an orator then always to speak as he writes? If possible, always" (*Inst. or.* 12.10.55), to be weighed against Demetrius. The "writing" Quintilian refers to is the manuscript or the published version of the speech and has nothing to do with the epistolary genre; cf. 53-54. Indeed, a comparison of these two passages (Quintilian and Demetrius) serves to emphasize the differences between what was expected of a public speech and of a genuine epistle. As Demetrius points out, one can head a formal treatise "My dear so and so," as did Plato and Thucydides, but this does not transform it into an epistle (228). People were conscious of the differences and did not appreciate the one masquerading as the other.

The fact is, Paul's letters were directed to very different audiences (see Olbricht, 2005, pp. 138-47) than his evangelistic λόγοι. If they were considered weighty and strong to the Corinthians, they were considered weighty and strong as ἐπιστολαί, not as λόγοι; see Porter (1999). Forbes (2010) rightly stresses the unique hybrid quality of Paul's epistles due to the fact that they were typically "congregational letters" designed to be read (Forbes's "performed" is unduly dramatic) aloud to the gathered Christians (p. 159). But this point is often overplayed. For a succinct summary of the issues, and contra Witherington in particular, see Porter (2013, pp. 327-28); see also Stirewalt (2003, p. 120); idem (1969, pp. 193-94); Porter (1999, pp. 101-8); Porter and Dyer (pp. 323-24); Marshall (1987, pp. 390-93); Reed (1993, pp. 322-23). See also Watson (2010b, pp. 41-42), and classicist C. J. Classen's repeated warnings about conflating ancient letters and speeches (1992, pp. 319-44). For an attempt to bridge the divide between epistolographical and rhetorical camps, see Lampe (2010, pp. 12-17).

In the end, however, it must be acknowledged by all that first-century written materials—whether written versions of speeches (such as Pliny's), letters or even "congregational letters"—all shared this in common: they were not oratory, and were not judged as such by audiences. Socrates had viewed writings as inferior to the liveliness of oral discourse: "If you question them, wishing to know about their sayings, they always say only one and the same thing" (*Phaedrus* 275D). Orators, by contrast, could animate their audiences, "playing on them like the strings of a lyre" (Cicero, *Brutus* 200). Oral and written materials were thus weighed differently. Texts served their purposes, but oral discourse had to be *delivered*, which added all of the nonverbal dimensions of human communication. This is why, as Hudson (1965, p. 23) says, "in ancient times persuasion was carried on almost entirely by the spoken word." Fantham (1997, pp. 124-25) makes the point well: "Cicero echoes Demosthenes: performance was the first, second, and third most important factor of any speech (*De Or.* 3.213; *Orat.* 56). The good orator needed powerful lungs to make himself heard in the open, a commanding presence and eloquent gestures to convey his meaning to those at a distance, and a sense of theatre." He may have prepared at least parts of his speech in writing, but he would know how to deliver it "as if it were spontaneous. . . . Once in front of an audience he would play on [the audience] like an instrument, sensing its mood, entertaining it with humour or placating it with sympathy if the jury were weary from the ranting of the prosecution; he would conciliate it at the beginning, seize its attention by a clear and lively narrative of the facts, and wait until it was under his control before pulling out the stops of indignation or compassion."

The Corinthians were used to this sort of oratory in the speakers who paraded before them. It was part of what some of the Corinthians apparently wanted from Paul. Hence their disappointment and criticism. By the yardstick by which they measured letters, Paul's ἐπιστολαί appeared "weighty and strong." But by the critics' standards for oral discourse, his appearance was judged unimpressive and his performance embarrassing (2 Cor 10:10).

---

(3) If it can be said that the Corinthians were critical of Paul's public speaking, it must also be stressed that these criticisms were directed in large measure against the *form* or *manner* of that speaking. Hence in the apologetic sections of the Corinthian epistles we observe the Apostle repeatedly defending or explaining issues of *form* or *manner*.

This important observation is underappreciated by many commentators and even controversial with others. But it is *crucial* for our own study. Hence we must take a moment to substantiate it. The point is fairly easily demonstrated by a schematic comparison of the ten statements in the Corinthian letters where Paul directly or indirectly refers to his *modus operandi* as a preacher. The following statements are laid out in such a way as to emphasize and coordinate constructions that express the form, appearance or manner of Paul's behavior (AT throughout):

1. 1 Corinthians 1:17
[Christ sent me] . . . to preach the gospel
    οὐκ | ἐν σοφίᾳ λόγου
        in order that (ἵνα μὴ) the cross of Christ not be voided

2. 1 Corinthians 2:1
When I came to you, I came . . . announcing to you the testimony of God
    οὐ | καθ' ὑπεροχὴν λόγου ἢ σοφίας

3. 1 Corinthians 2:3
and I . . . was with you
    | ἐν ἀσθενείᾳ
        and
    | ἐν φόβῳ
        and
    | ἐν τρόμῳ πολλῷ

4. 1 Corinthians 2:4-5
my speech and my preaching [were]
    οὐκ | ἐν πειθοῖς σοφίας λόγοις [or πειθοῖ σοφίας]
        but
    | ἐν ἀποδείξει πνεύματος καὶ δυνάμεως
        in order that (ἵνα) your faith . . . might be
    μὴ . . . ἐν σοφίᾳ ἀνθρώπων
        but
    ἐν δυνάμει θεοῦ

5. 1 Corinthians 2:13
which things . . . we speak
    οὐκ | ἐν διδακτοῖς ἀνθρωπίνης σοφίας λόγοις
        but
    | ἐν διδακτοῖς πνεύματος [λόγοις]

6. 2 Corinthians 1:12
    | ἐν ἁπλότητι [or ἁγιότητι] καὶ εἰλικρινείᾳ
    οὐκ | ἐν σοφίᾳ σαρκικῇ
we have conducted ourselves in the world
    and especially toward you

7. 2 Corinthians 2:17
we are
    οὐ | ὡς οἱ πολλοὶ
        hawking the word of God
        but
    | ὡς ἐξ εἰλικρινείας

>   but
> | ὡς ἐκ θεοῦ
>   in the sight of God in Christ
> we speak

8. 2 Corinthians 4:2

> not walking
> | ἐν πανουργίᾳ
> nor adulterating the word of God
>   but
> commending ourselves
> | τῇ φανερώσει τῆς ἀληθείας
>   to every man's conscience in the sight of God

9. 2 Corinthians 4:7

> we have this treasure
> | ἐν ὀστρακίνοις σκεύεσιν
>   in order that (ἵνα) the excellence of the δυνάμεως
>   might be of God and not from ourselves

10. 2 Corinthians 10:3-4

> though walking
> | ἐν σαρκὶ
> we wage war
> οὐ | κατὰ σάρκα
>   for
> the weapons of our warfare [are]
> οὐ | σαρκικὰ
>   but
> | δυνατὰ τῷ θεῷ

We will examine these statements more closely later, but for now we should observe the following points. First, we note again that each of these statements is to be found in an apologetic section where Paul's ministry is under question and he is on the defensive. No similar or parallel statements are to be found, for example, in 1 Corinthians 5–16, where the subject matter is something other than Paul's ministry.[8]

Second, no fewer than five of these ten statements refer explicitly to Paul's speech (1, 2, 4, 5, 7). A sixth, statement 3, is so closely wedded to its context (statements 2 and 4) that it unquestionably also is related to Paul's speech. Two more statements (6 and 8) indirectly refer to or include Paul's speech. This may be seen by a comparison of these two statements with the above five explicit references to Paul's preaching. For example, the phrase οὐκ ἐν σοφίᾳ σαρκικῇ in statement 6 can only be fully understood in the light of the similar phrases in statements 1–2 and 4–5; and the phrases in statement 8, "adulterating the word of God ... in the sight of God," clearly parallel the phrases "hawking the word of God ... in the sight of God" in statement 7. Thus the close affinities of statements 6 and 8 with the other statements referring directly to Paul's speech suggest that these two statements are expressing similar thoughts. Finally, the metaphors of statements 9 and 10 also include or touch on Paul's speech. In both cases the matter of the Apostle's preaching is part of the immediate context, and in both cases the thoughts expressed appear to be metaphorical echoes of the theme of 1 Corinthians 2:1-5.[9]

Third, we may note that the five most explicit statements (1–5) regarding Paul's speech, fully half of the total, are to be found in the section 1 Corinthians 1–4. In 2 Corinthians the statements (with the exception of statement 7, which is expressly about Paul's speaking) broaden out slightly, indicating that Paul is addressing here the same principle as in 1 Corinthians 1–4 but on a somewhat wider front. Even though Paul's speech is never far from sight, we see in 2 Corinthians the use of more general verbs such as ἀνεστράφημεν (6) and περιπατοῦντες (8, 10), along with the inherently ambiguous metaphors of treasure in earthen containers (9) and weapons of warfare (10). In 1 Corinthians 1–4, on the other hand, the focus remains tightly and explicitly on the matter of Paul's preaching (εὐαγγελίζω, καταγγέλλω, λαλέω), that is, on his λόγος and κήρυγμα.

Fourth, Paul's stress on form, appearance or manner in these ten statements is highlighted by the repeated constructions utilizing ἐν with the dative (1, 3–6,

---

[8]Though 1 Cor 9 is also apologetic in nature, the subject there is not Paul's preaching but his right to receive financial support as a servant of Christ. The statements of accommodation and the repeated ἵνα clauses of 9:19-23 are therefore not unrelated to our discussion but are of a different order than the examples we are examining here.

[9]Compare, for example, the ἵνα clauses in statements 9 and 4; the references to δύναμις and δυνατά in 4, 9 and 10; and the οὐ κατὰ phrases of 2 and 10, or the οὐ ... ἀλλὰ constructions of 4 and 10.

8; cf. 1 Corinthians 4:21), κατά with the accusative (2, 10), and the comparative adverb ὡς (7).[10] Paul was evidently in the position of having constantly to explain or defend the manner or form of his ministry to the Corinthians. He states repeatedly what that form was and what it was not. This is especially evident in 1 Corinthians 1–4. Hence no interpretation that neglects this aspect of the Corinthian problem can succeed in doing justice to 1 Corinthians 1–4.[11]

Paul's Central Challenge

Paul was forced by the situation in Corinth to explain and defend his *modus operandi* as a preacher. Why was this? What were the criticisms in Corinth that prompted such defensive responses from the Apostle? As we have said from the beginning, we do not propose to draw a comprehensive picture of the Corinthian situation. Such a task is beyond the scope of this study. The following discussion is designed to highlight those aspects of the Corinthian situation that called forth the Apostle's core argument throughout 1 Corinthians 1–4. As George Kennedy says, "In many rhetorical situations the speaker will be found to face one overriding *rhetorical problem*."[12] The present chapter is designed to pinpoint the particular overriding problem reflected in 1 Corinthians 1–4.

When Paul originally preached the gospel in the city of Corinth, a sizeable group of Corinthians responded in faith. To be sure, their response was not because they found Paul to be such an eloquent preacher—at least, not by the standards of eloquence they were used to—but because they recognized through the inner confirmation of the Spirit that the gospel Paul preached was true (1 Cor 1:6; 15:1-11; cf. 1 Thess 1:5; 2:13). Hence they embraced this gospel, became followers of Jesus Christ (1 Cor 1:30) and eventually, under the tutelage of Paul, formed a church.

With the subsequent departure of the Apostle and the advent of Apollos, however, the attitude toward Paul of some within the congregation began not

---

[10]Cf. also the use of the dative without ἐν in statement 8 (τῇ φανερώσει); and the contrast between the adjectives σαρκικά and δυνατά in statement 10.

[11]According to Kennedy (1980, pp. 131-32), the argument of 1 Cor 1–2 was designed to challenge "the whole of classical philosophy and rhetoric." R. Dean Anderson (1998, p. 276) disagrees: "Paul's characterisation of his own preaching in [1 Cor 1–4] should not be interpreted against the specific background of Graeco-Roman rhetorical theory." Anderson's treatment, however, is flawed by idiosyncrasy, overconfidence (how many modern commentators will claim to know Cicero better than Quintilian did?) and special pleading. Thus few New Testament scholars have followed his lead.

[12]Kennedy (1984, p. 36). Cf. Bitzer (1974) on the topic of the "rhetorical situation."

so much to change as to solidify. The reservations they had harbored about Paul perhaps from the beginning—reservations about him *personally*, despite the fact that they found the gospel he preached worthy of acceptance—became in Paul's absence more pronounced. What had been before merely nagging embarrassments, perhaps kept to oneself, now crept to the surface and became the object of more or less open discussion.

These embarrassments centered on Paul's public speaking. The Apostle had sustained a relatively visible profile during his stay in Corinth. But in some ways it was scarcely an impressive profile. Both his physical appearance and his speaking itself were plainly deficient, even contemptible, by the sophisticated standards of Greek rhetoric. Paul was simply out of his league. These people were accustomed to the eloquence (εὐγλωττία) of orators of the caliber of Favorinus, that paragon of Greek culture whose eloquence was both σοφός and πότιμος ("sweet, pleasant, fresh").[13] According to Philostratus, "even those in [Favorinus's] audience who did not understand the Greek language shared in the pleasure that he gave; for he fascinated even them by the tones of his voice, by his expressive glance and the rhythm of his speech."[14] Such a one as this could impress the Corinthians. But by this standard the Apostle was an embarrassing figure. Whatever else one could say for him, he fell woefully short by the stringent criteria of genuine Greek eloquence.

Paul was simply ἰδιώτης ("unskilled") as a public speaker (2 Cor 11:6). There is no indication here, as some have claimed, that Paul intended this reference as irony. According to T. R. Glover, when Paul said,

> he was "rude (*idiotes*) in speech" (2 Cor. xi.6), his meaning is quite plain. Elsewhere he speaks of the *idiotes* (1 Cor. xiv.16, 23, 24) in exactly the sense which Greeks gave to the word—the "unlearned," the "layman," the "outsider," the "ordinary person." It is, above all, the man who has not had the education, which was summed up in the name Rhetoric, but which included literature—a scheme of culture which was first thought out and practiced by Isocrates at Athens.[15]

---

[13]Philostratus, *Lives* 489, 491; cf. Rom 16:18. Hence Judge's reference (1968, p. 48) to Paul's "rhetorically fastidious converts" in Corinth.

[14]Philostratus, *Lives* 491.

[15]Glover, (1925, p. 19); cf. Acts 4:13. This understanding of Paul's self-portrayal in 11:6 was typically shared by the church fathers; e.g., on 2 Cor 11:6 see the former teacher of rhetoric John Chrysostom (2 *Corinthians* 23.3). Of Paul's expressions of weakness in 1 Cor 2:3, Chrysostom says it's little wonder Paul was fearful: "Not only are the believers unlearned (ἰδιῶται) persons; not only is he that speaketh unlearned (ἰδιώτης); not only is the manner of the teaching of an unlearned (ἰδιωτείας) cast throughout; not only was the thing preached of itself enough to stagger people; . . . but together with these there were also other hindrances, the dangers, and the

This need not imply, of course, that Paul did not use relatively good Hellenistic Greek. As W. H. Simcox says,

> It is [the] lack of art, rather than any ignorance or positive awkwardness, that made him seem to Hellenic critics ἰδιώτης τῷ λόγῳ (2 Cor xi.6), and made him rather glory in than repudiate the criticism. . . . If St. Paul intentionally avoided the artifices of rhetoric, he did not, like the seer of the Apocalypse, intentionally strain the rules of grammar. But it is probable that he knew as little of the formal rules in grammar as rhetoric; that his general correctness is a matter of instinct rather than of care.[16]

Blass and Debrunner put the balance this way in their discussion of rhetorical "periods":

> The period, i.e., the organization of a considerable number of clauses or phrases into a well-rounded unity, is rare in the N.T. Since the period belongs to the more elegant style, it is most frequently met in Hebrews, which certainly is to be regarded as artistic prose by reason of the composition of its words and sentences. Paul, the ἰδιώτης τῷ λογῳ (2 Cor 11:6), does not generally make the effort required by so careful a style; artistic periods, therefore, in spite of all his eloquence, are not to be found in his writings, while harsh parentheses and anacolutha abound.[17]

To the Corinthians, Paul lacked the high-powered ability of the orators to sculpt ideas at will into irresistible phrases. He came far short of the polish and sophistication in word choice, diction, voice, physical charm and self-possession that was indispensable to impress and move a Greco-Roman crowd. By contrast, Apollos proved to be an "eloquent man" (ἀνὴρ λόγιος) and through this something of a champion in Corinth (Acts 18:24-28); he was no embarrassment. But Paul was a different story.[18]

---

plots, and the daily fear, and the being hunted about" (1 *Corinthians* 6.2; 6.1); and so throughout Chrysostom, 1 *Corinthians* 4-7; *On the Priesthood* iv.5-7. But see also Mitchell (2002, pp. 241-45, 278-91) on Chrysostom's inconsistencies between this claim and his treatment of Paul's practice. In any case, Chrysostom's reading of ἰδιώτης is to be preferred over Winter's unconvincing argument (1997, pp. 213-18) that in portraying himself as ἰδιώτης τῷ λόγῳ Paul is saying he was fully trained in rhetoric, just not an orator by profession.

[16]Simcox (1890, p. 31).

[17]Blass and Debrunner (1961, p. 242). On Paul's style in general see Watson (2010a).

[18]Pogoloff's notion (1992, pp. 188-89) that because Apollos was from Alexandria he must have practiced a florid, boisterous, more rough-hewn Asianist style of rhetoric that appealed to the tastes of the masses but offended the more cultured members of the Corinthian church, while Paul, being better educated in rhetoric, practiced a more refined style of eloquence that appealed to more sophis-

Without attempting to describe Paul's physical stature or appearance,[19] it is nonetheless instructive to contrast the description of Paul in 2 Corinthians 10:10 with Philostratus's picture of the sophist Alexander: "Alexander had a godlike appearance, and was conspicuous for his beauty and charm. For his beard was curly and of modest length, his eyes large and melting, his nose well-shaped, his teeth very white, his fingers long and slender, and well fitted to hold the reins of eloquence."[20] This was the sort of appearance the Greco-Roman audiences approved, as Philostratus observes when describing a speech Alexander gave in Athens: "The Athenians thought his appearance and costume so exquisite that before he spoke a word, a low buzz of approval went round as a tribute to his perfect elegance."[21] But by such standards the traveling Jewish rabbi came across to the rhetorically attuned Corinthians rather differently. His critics found Paul's physical appearance ἀσθενής ("weak, feeble") and his speech ἐξουθενημένος ("paltry, contemptible").[22]

What was it about Paul's speech they found inadequate? Among other things, it was his use of the Greek language. Far from the exquisite word choice of the orators, Paul's Greek was typically that of the common man. While fluent, it was nonetheless the ordinary language of the marketplace, not the glorious rhythms of the rostrum.[23] This is what prompted Nigel Turner to observe in his volume on Greek style that "it is unlikely that [Paul] attended a Hellenistic teacher of rhetoric, for his anacolutha and solecisms are too numerous."[24] This sort of

---

ticated tastes, must be treated with a high degree of skepticism on both counts. Regarding Apollos, Pogoloff's portrayal is based on a multistoried argument that requires reading so much between the lines that the case scarcely bears its own weight; regarding Paul it flies in the face of both the Apostle's and some of his opponents' explicit statements to the contrary (1 Cor 1:17-2:5; 2 Cor 10:10; 11:6). Based on little more than the presence of some standard linguistic conventions in Paul's epistles, Pogoloff concludes far too much about the Apostle's missionary proclamation in Corinth; see "Two Important Implications," chapter 16 below. For less speculative assessments of Paul's relationship to Apollos, see Ker (2000); Mihaila (2009).

[19]The late second-century apocryphal work *The Acts of Paul and Thecla* may (or may not) reflect an older oral tradition in its description of the Apostle as short, bald, hollow eyed, with a long misshapen nose and crooked legs (1.7). The evidence, in any case, is unreliable.

[20]Philostratus, *Lives* 570. On the physical appearance and dress expected of the orators, see Whitmarsh (2005, pp. 23-32). At the end of his own treatment of this subject, Winter (2002, p. 222) says, "The judgement of Paul's opponents that 'his bodily presence was weak' was rendered according to the canons of rhetoric. It meant that his presence constituted such a liability as to all but guarantee his failure as an effective public orator."

[21]Philostratus, *Lives* 571.

[22]For a discussion of Paul's tentmaking and its implications here, see Hock (1980).

[23]On this point, see R. Dean Anderson (1998, pp. 280-82).

[24]Turner (1976, p. 86). Solecisms (σολοικισμός) were usually defined as linguistic mistakes involving more than one word, that is, syntactical errors. Anacolutha, a type of solecism, are grammatical

verbal awkwardness would not have been lost on rhetorically astute audiences. Cicero's Crassus put it this way:

> Everyone, not just the rhetorically trained, is influenced not only by skillful arrangement of words but also by rhythms and pronunciations. For what proportion of people understands the science of rhythm and metre? Yet all the same if only a slight slip is made in these, making the line too short by a contraction or too long by dwelling on a vowel, the audience protests to a man.[25]

By such exacting standards it should not surprise us that Paul, the former Saul of Tarsus, did not measure up. One is reminded of similar complaints against the rhetorically challenged Epictetus: "Then you leave," he protested to his listeners after one of his discourses, "with the remark: 'Epictetus was nothing at all, his language was full of solecisms and barbarisms!'"[26]

PAUL AND FIRST-CENTURY LITERARY CULTURE

It is important to view this unfavorable assessment of Paul's literary qualities against the backdrop of the similar reception the biblical writings in general received during Christianity's earliest centuries. Says Graves (2010, p. 161), "The Christian church came into being and developed within a cultural context that cared deeply about the stylistic qualities of language. When confronted with the claims of the Gospel, educated Romans wanted to know how the sacred writings upon which the Gospel was based compared to the great literary works that set the standard for Graeco-Roman high culture." Not surprisingly, for many of the cultured elites the Bible failed the test. The early critics of Christianity were scathing in their assessment of its literary faults. "The charge that the Christian writings, notably the Bible versions, reeked with barbarisms of language and style were [sic] common" (McCracken, 1949, p. 295).

The Old Testament, which most knew only in Greek or Latin translation, came in

---

inconsistencies brought about by abrupt shifts from one construction to another within a single sentence. As T. R. Glover (1945, p. 190) interestingly observed, "Solecism is still in our vocabulary, a word coined by the satirical to describe the speech of the people of Soloi, a Cilician town not far from Tarsus"; cf. Diomedes (Keil, 1857, vol. 1, p. 453). Aelius Donatus, by contrast, claimed *solecism* was derived from the name of the ancient Greek lawgiver Solon, whose pure Greek was corrupted by foreign travel (Keil, 1857, vol. 5, p. 327). Polybius believed σολοικισμός was formed by conflating several Greek words referring to the injury or mutilation of pure speech (Nauck, 1867, p. 285).
[25]Cicero, *De or.* 3.195-97.
[26]Epictetus, *Discourses* 3.9.14. Solecisms and barbarisms commonly traveled together. If solecisms represented awkwardness in syntax, barbarisms (βαρβαρισμός) were mistakes in spelling or pronouncing single words. Both faults were considered by ancient rhetoricians to be linguistic corruptions associated with ignorance or "foreign" elements.

for particularly rough treatment. The Hebrew language from which it was translated was considered coarse and unsophisticated, features the early translations scarcely improved upon. And the New Testament fared little better. Critics such as the second-century philosopher Celsus repeatedly (e.g., see Origen's *Contra Celsum*) railed against the lowly cultural status of its authors, its vast literary shortcomings and the sorry segments of the population who were drawn to it. The late third- and early fourth-century Arnobius, a former teacher of rhetoric who became a Christian apologist, cited the critics as follows: Your Scriptures, they say, "were written by uneducated and ordinary men and therefore they should not be believed without question as soon as heard. . . . Your narratives . . . are overrun with barbarisms and solecisms and vitiated by ugly faults" (*The Case Against the Pagans* 1:58-59; McCracken, 1949, p. 1043). Lactantius (ca. 240–320), a student of Arnobius who followed in his teacher's footsteps by also becoming a professor of rhetoric cum Christian apologist, explained the reason for the critics' disdain: "An oration running along with smoothness, seizes the minds and impels them where it will." Thus educated listeners, "accustomed to sweet and polished speeches . . . , spurn the simple and direct speech of the divine writings as mean. They seek that which may please the sense of hearing, for whatever is sweet persuades, and settles deep within the mind while it delights" (*The Divine Institutes* 6.21; M. F. McDonald, 1964, p. 455).

In the earliest centuries, during which Christians remained cultural outsiders, Christian apologists readily conceded the Bible's lack of artistic quality and then offered various justifications for why this should be so. Significantly, within these explanations the Pauline argument of 1 Corinthians 1–4 played a prominent role. God's preference for using means the world considered low status so as to confound the worldly wise, an emphasis on the humble message of the gospel rather than rhetorical eloquence, a desire to depend on the power of God rather than human persuasion so as to avoid false results, the importance of having a message that could transcend the sociocultural segments of society—these arguments were widely deployed in defending the Bible against its critics. In this way the inelegant qualities of Scripture were portrayed as an asset rather than a liability.

Beginning in the late third century, however, this Christian apologetic began to change. With the Christianization of the Empire, Christians were moving toward the center of power. Freed from their defensive position, the apologists began to challenge the literary standards by which the Scriptures were judged inadequate and to insist that the Bible deserved to be evaluated on its own terms. The early church historian Eusebius (ca. A.D. 265–340), for example, rose in defense of the literary quality of the Old Testament (*Preparation for the Gospel* 11.5). St. Jerome (347–420) was originally put off by the Bible's lack of sophistication, but once he learned Hebrew his assessment began to change; his much-improved Latin translation of the Old Testament revealed the Hebrew language's hidden beauty. Similarly, Augustine (354–430) was also initially offended by the Bible's lack of literary quality, but by the time he wrote Book IV of his *On Christian Doctrine* he was convinced that the Scriptures demonstrated a splendid beauty of their own (cf. Ambrose, *Letters to Bishops* 21). "Instead of accepting that pagan literature was of a higher literary quality than the Bible, Augustine argued that Scripture was equal in eloquence to secular literature, but also different and unique" (Graves, 2010, p. 177). Augustine's analysis deeply influenced the centuries to follow and is echoed today by those who insist that the Apostle Paul was an eloquent communicator in his own right.

This revised approach to assessing Paul has much to be said for it; see Roukema (2013, p. 67). But we must not allow it to obscure the fact that this was not how the Apostle was originally measured by the Corinthians, who, as it turned out, were the precursors of the early church's later critics. To them Paul's preaching appeared to lack the polish and sophistication of their day's elitist culture. By such standards Paul was recognized, not only by the Corinthians but also by his strongest early church apologists, to be "unskilled in speaking" (2 Cor 11:6). The difference between their respective treatments of Paul—the former critical, the latter supportive—may have been that unlike Paul's earlier Corinthian critics, the later apologists were the beneficiaries of the rationale Paul had spelled out in 1 Corinthians 1–4.

Yet the difficulty was that these Corinthian Christians were inevitably associated with Paul—stuck with him, so to speak. In fact, he was in a sense perceived as their leader, their teacher. Hence their embarrassment. Like so many of their Greco-Roman neighbors, connoisseurs of eloquence and wisdom and acutely conscious of the related matters of status and esteem, some of the Corinthians found Paul's all-too-public deficiencies a painful liability. After all, they supposed, and with justification, it was difficult enough to attain a reputation as a cultured person in Corinth without being associated with someone at once so visible and so culturally lacking as Paul.

These status-conscious Corinthians apparently harbored few reservations about rendering a negative judgment of Paul's abilities as a speaker. They perceived the wandering Jewish rabbi in this respect in much the same light as they perceived other itinerant speakers: as fair game for their evaluations.[27] How could they embrace the gospel Paul preached while yet remaining critical of Paul's rhetorical deficiencies? The inconsistency seems in retrospect odd, and so it was. In fact it is precisely this inconsistency and the misplaced values that allowed it to exist that Paul addresses in 1 Corinthians 1–4.

---

[27]On this point, see Forbes (2003); Winter (2001, pp. 31-43).

THE SOCIAL STRATIFICATION OF
THE CORINTHIAN CHURCH

The subject of the social makeup of the Corinthian congregation has engendered a great deal of debate in recent years. Initiating what has come to be called a "new consensus" on the subject, Theissen (1974; see especially pp. 232, 264, 268) argued that the issue of social status played a prime role in the Corinthian church. With a meticulous examination of the available data Theissen showed that the Corinthian congregation was characterized by a pronounced social stratification. According to Theissen, the educated upper-class minority tended to dominate the lower-class majority; for their part the lower-class elements looked to the higher-status minority to set the standards. Hence Theissen speaks of the strongly developed status consciousness ("*allzu stark entwickeltem Status-bewusstsein*," p. 235) that existed in Corinth and explores at length the social implications of Paul's terminology regarding the wise, powerful and wellborn. In short, the picture that emerges from Theissen's analysis can be summarized as follows: a few trendsetting community members from the upper class standing over against a large number of Christians from the lower classes (p. 232). See also Wuellner (1973); Meeks (1982; 1983; 2009). Adding their own contributions to this picture, Welborn (1987; 1997, pp. 1-42) stresses the political dimensions of the social discord in Corinth, while Dutch (2005) argues for the role of the ancient gymnasium as a source of an educated elite in the Corinthian congregation. Clarke (2006) makes a case for assuming that at least some from the Corinthian social elites were numbered among the church's leadership.

But see also Meggitt's dissent (1998) from this "new consensus." Meggitt argues that the Corinthian congregation may not have been as stratified as some have concluded; see also Dale Martin's (2001, pp. 51-64) and Theissen's (2001, pp. 65-84) responses to Meggitt, along with Meggitt's response to their critique (2001, pp. 85-94). Meggitt concludes: "I am still not convinced that we can determine with any precision the nature of social diversity within the Pauline communities and what part it can legitimately be said to play in their conflicts" (2001, p. 94). Finally, we may note Theissen's somewhat moderated criticism (2003) of Meggitt two years later; see also C. K. Robertson (2001) for a different form of dissent from the "consensus."

For our purposes, thankfully, it can be said that our analysis is not dependent on any particular resolution of this debate. The overall result of these and other studies gives a picture of the Corinthian society, and even the Corinthian church, as to one degree or another socially stratified, divided along the very cultural fault lines we have described in our own much more focused study of the role of rhetoric in the Greco-Roman world. What is important for our purposes is the recognition that a passion for eloquence transcended these social divisions. This passion, shared by high and low alike, was what generated the criticisms of Paul's preaching in Corinth, however the stratification question is resolved.

How Churches Were Viewed

We can fully grasp the thinking of these Corinthians only through an examination of Paul's response to it, but for now it may help to be reminded of how Paul and his churches must have appeared in their first-century context. In a famous two-part article titled "The Early Christians as a Scholastic Community," E. A. Judge concluded that the early churches must have been viewed as "a school of disciples under the instruction of a rabbi, or a devout sect committed to the study and preservation of the law, or finally . . . a society formed to attend upon the teachings of a travelling preacher."[28] It is this last category that interests us. Judge argues that "the churches we know of from the New Testament were founded and to some extent carried on under the auspices of visiting professional preachers, which makes them parallel in some respects to the philosophical movements of the day."[29] This brings Judge to the observation that Paul must have been viewed as a "sophist."

> The hey-day of sophistry was undoubtedly the second century A.D. when opulence and an insatiable passion for words maintained a constant stream of touring lecturers around the Greek world. The sophists found a ready entree into private salons, and were engaged publicly by the Greek states from time to time to address their assemblies or to lecture in the gymnasium. The Roman Caesars were notable patrons of the art. Since versatility was a prime test of rhetorical skill, the sophists needed to be much more learned than their critics have credited them with being. At their worst they were undoubtedly tedious and pedestrian, as the extant works of Maximus of Tyre show, but at their best, as in the case of Herodes Atticus, they were intellectual leaders of great eminence, not only in preserving the classical heritage but in guiding public policy and private morality in their own day.[30]

The term *sophist* was thus fairly elastic, so much so that Lucian, a second-century rhetorician, could even refer to Jesus as "that crucified sophist."[31] Judge

---

[28]Judge (1960–1961, p. 136).
[29]Ibid., p. 125.
[30]Ibid.
[31]Lucian, *The Passing of Peregrinus* 13.

lumps into the category of sophist such diverse figures as Aelius Aristides, Dio Chrysostom, Epictetus, Apollonius of Tyana and the charlatan Peregrinus, and then argues that "this is the class to which St. Paul belonged."

> This is not to say that [Paul] modelled himself on any of them, nor that he would have approved of this categorization. Indeed none of them would; the various schools and traditions insisted upon rigid distinctions among themselves. Nevertheless they belong together by force of circumstance; they were all travellers, relying upon the hospitality of their admirers, all expert talkers and persuaders, all dedicated to their mission and intolerant of criticism. Just as Jesus by general consent acquired the status of a rabbi, and the disciples at Jerusalem seem to have settled down to sect life of a routine kind, so it may be argued that St. Paul provided himself with a secure social position, consciously or unconsciously, by adopting the conventions of the sophistic profession.[32]

Judge follows this section with a detailed examination of Paul's ministry, demonstrating that the Apostle was in superficial ways similar to other traveling speakers. The Corinthians were used to a more or less steady stream of such speakers and typically registered in some way their own judgments about these speakers' eloquence or lack of it. As "Longinus" put it, such judgment was "the last fruit of ripe experience."[33] In this light it should not be surprising to discover a willingness, if not an inclination, among some of the Corinthian believers—and particularly among those who were most impressed with professional rhetorical standards—to subject Paul's speech to judgment. They were merely doing, so to speak, what came naturally. Their judgments need not have been overly harsh; we have called them merely embarrassments. Paul simply did not measure up to their standards, and they became unreserved in saying so.

GOOD RHETORIC VERSUS BAD RHETORIC.1

In the section quoted above, Judge locates "the hey-day of sophistry" in the second century A.D. The hey-day Judge was referring to is what came to be known, following Philostratus (*Lives of the Sophists* 481), as the "Second Sophistic." Winter (2002) argues that this traditional dating is mistaken. The early stirrings of this sophistic movement were already what lay behind the challenges to Paul's preaching in mid-first-century Corinth.

---

[32] Judge (1960–1961, p. 126).
[33] "Longinus," *On the Sublime* 6.

Winter's study powerfully reinforces our own thesis that the values and practices of Greco-Roman rhetoric were what prompted some of the Corinthians to criticize Paul's preaching, and that 1 Corinthians 1–4 is Paul's primary response to this criticism. But Winter's use of the term *sophistic* raises the question of definition. What is it that renders something "sophistic" as against merely "rhetorical"?

Winter's brief discussion of the sophists of old, along with their practice and training (pp. 3-5), is generic enough to describe the rhetorical tradition itself, from Isocrates to Quintilian. Regardless of when the so-called Second Sophistic may have come into bud, the general rhetorical features (and criticisms) Winter uses to demonstrate its presence during the first century long predated the first century. In fact, they were perennial in the rhetorical tradition. So what is gained by labeling the problems in Corinth specifically "sophistic"?

There may be a workable answer to this question, but if so it will not be a short or simple one. The evidence is too elusive. The ancient term *sophist* was notoriously difficult to pin down; see Bowersock (1969, pp. 10-15) or Stanton (1973, pp. 350-58) on the elasticity of its usage. Similarly, the boundaries of the Second Sophistic itself are amorphous and equally difficult to define both chronologically and culturally; see Graham Anderson's helpful explanation of why this is the case (1993, pp. 1-12). So what does it mean, and how valid can it be, to identify the rhetorical problem in Corinth as specifically "sophistic"?

How we answer these questions would be merely a matter of labeling and of little consequence for our own study were it not for what often occurs when Paul's rhetorical opponents in Corinth are labeled *sophistic*. The sophists, old and new, always had their detractors, particularly among philosophers such as Plato and Aristotle. Labeling the problem in Corinth *sophistic* thus introduces this negative spin. We too easily wind up with "good" rhetoric, so to speak, and "bad" (sophistic) rhetoric, with the problem in Corinth being the latter (see further on this problem, pp. 260-61, 294-97 below). According to Winter, the sophistic tradition Paul encountered in Corinth was marked by its egotistical boasting and its use of ornamental rhetoric—contra Kennedy's claim (1972, p. 553) that "sophists were generally Atticists in style and spread Atticist standards"—for the purposes of personal gain and deception. Paul's criticism therefore was not of rhetoric itself but of the *misuse* of rhetoric by the "sophists."

At times Winter appears to appreciate a deeper apostolic critique of persuasion itself, as when he says, "Paul refused to anchor the confidence of the Corinthian converts in the persuasiveness of rhetorical argumentation" (p. 164). But in other places Paul's concerns are reduced to deceptiveness: "It . . . appears that . . . Paul may not have felt compelled to renounce rhetoric per se but the 'deceit' . . . which all too often accompanied its spoken manifestation, especially of the sophists" (p. 227). Elsewhere Paul's concern is reduced further to a repudiation of the "grand style" of speaking in favor of the "plain style" (e.g., p. 164). Yet in the end these come together in Winter's conclusion that it was only that persuasion brought about by deceit and ornamentation, what he calls "the sophistic means of persuasion," that Paul found "unsuitable for securing belief in the gospel" (p. 164).

This way of identifying the rhetorical problem Paul faced in Corinth has become popular. It appears to offer a handy solution to the question of how to reconcile Paul's critique of rhetoric with his own use of rhetoric. But this facile solution suffers from several debilitating weaknesses. First, it sets up "sophistic" rhetoric as something of an apostolic straw man, easily bowled over and dispatched. Asserting that Paul was against deceit and self-aggrandizement amounts to little more than keen insight into the obvious; of course he was. Reducing Paul's penetrating argument in 1 Corinthians 1–4 to such a simplistic knock-down conclusion borders on the banal.

Second, this approach leads to a strange conclusion. What does this definition of the Corinthian problem say about all those persuasive strategies advocated by the practitioners of "good" rhetoric? Throughout this book it has been the persuasive strategies of this nobler, nonsophistic rhetorical tradition—what Winter calls "rhetoric per se"—that we have traced from their beginnings. Are we to conclude that Paul found these human strategies entirely "suitable" for securing belief in the gospel? According to the "good" versus "bad" rhetoric approach, the πίστις engendered by these human psychological techniques was unproblematic for the Apostle. It was only the "sophistically" induced πίστις that troubled him.

Third, this is an odd conclusion precisely because it does such a disservice to the evidence of 1 Corinthians 1–4. It completely misstates the emphasis of Paul's critique. While the Apostle certainly did eschew deception and self-aggrandizement (e.g., see 2 Cor 4:2), this is not his focus in 1 Corinthians 1–4. The Apostle's critique in this crucial passage cuts much deeper. Paul says not a word about deceitfulness or ego-centric verbal pyrotechnics in 1 Corinthians 1–4; his concern there is the potential for engendering false results (false πίστις) by employing human persuasive techniques in the preaching of the gospel (1 Cor 2:5). Far from valorizing good rhetoric over bad, Paul was concerned *most* with precisely those effective but also purely human powers to generate πίστις that could be found even, perhaps we should say *especially*, in the best rhetoric of the first century.

The narrowing of Paul's concern to "bad" rhetoric severely underestimates the Apostle's concerns. Winter's book makes a strong contribution to our understanding of the rhetorical background to 1 Corinthians 1–4 (not to mention its other strengths), but its failure to justify and maintain a workable definition of *sophistic*, in contrast to the merely *rhetorical*, is a serious weakness. This weakness in turn renders tenuous the book's secondary conclusions about what it was that troubled the Apostle. For a very different approach to resolving the question of Paul's purported use of rhetoric, see part three of of our study below.

Finally, we must comment on what's missing in Winter's book. For all its worthwhile contributions, it inexplicably ignores, as do many other works, a rich vein of insight into the Apostle's essential concerns: his proposed *alternative* to the art of persuasion. Winter's detailed attention to the language of the rhetorical/sophistic tradition leaves no available stone unturned, perhaps to a fault. But the deep significance of the non-rhetorical terms Paul consistently chooses to describe his own preaching—the language not of the persuader but of the proclaimer, annunciator or testifier—is left puzzlingly untouched. This language, which we will explore later, is a flashing arrow pointing to the essential issue Paul wants his readers to grasp. When we follow its direction we discover the essence of not only what the Apostle was determined to avoid, but more importantly of what he was intent on affirming. This language is a clear indicator that what Paul was rejecting was not merely the deceitful and self-aggrandizing aspects of the rhetoric of his day. It was no less than that, but, with equal certainty, it was also more. As we shall see, what Paul rejected was the results-driven dynamic of Greco-Roman persuasion itself; that is, the use of human psychological techniques, sophistic or otherwise, to generate πίστις in his listeners.

It is important to note that we need not conclude that there were many in the Corinthian congregation who were themselves finished orators. Perhaps some were; perhaps not. But for our purposes it scarcely matters. Our description is addressed more to the values of the Corinthian Christians than to their accomplishments. Some might have been capable or even eloquent speakers, but more likely the average member of the congregation merely wanted to be one. He was, like so many of his fellow citizens, an aficionado of eloquence rather than a practitioner, a reverer of the cultured and influential set rather than a member of it. The Corinthians were for the most part little people with mere pretensions of culture and status.

In his book *Greek Popular Morality in the Time of Plato and Aristotle*, K. J. Dover exposed the roots of this tendency in Greek society.[34] For example, he concludes his discussion with a list of what every "poor Athenian" wanted to possess ("wealth, a great name, distinguished ancestors") and to be ("educated, cultured, well-dressed and well-groomed, with the physique and poise of a man trained in fighting, wrestling and dancing"). Though they were themselves on the outside—or perhaps even in a few cases, still more tantalizingly, on the fringe—of the circles of status, influence and sophistication in Corinth, they exalted those on the inside and themselves put on the airs of aristocracy, affecting the stance of sophisticated critics as best they could.

---

[34]Dover (1974, pp. 34-45).

Dover's picture is by no means far-fetched. We know in fact that these sorts of pretensions were not uncommon. As A. D. Nock pointed out, "The small man in antiquity suffered from a marked feeling of inferiority and from a pathetic desire for self-assertion, of which the epitaphs supply abundant illustrations."[35] In his *Themes in Greek and Latin Epitaphs*, Richmond Lattimore quotes this very sentence from Nock to explain his own point that the epitaphs often represent "boasts," especially in the "numerous cases where the dead man himself declares, or is made to declare, his excellencies."[36] We may cite a pair of these Greek epitaphs as examples:

> Titus Phaneus Modestus, a rhetorician (σοφιστὴς),
> one to be ranked with the seven sages.[37]

> I, a small tomb, conceal no small man,
> Because he was an orator (ῥήτωρ) as regards speaking,
> a philosopher (φιλόσοφος) as to what ought to be thought.[38]

Pathetic indeed is the picture of a man who must apologize for the meager size of his tomb by boasting of his eloquence and wisdom. Lattimore's point is that had he genuinely possessed such qualities during his lifetime they would not have had to be trumpeted so loudly from his gravestone.

What is significant here is the image of the little man with pretensions or affectations of being associated with the great, the eloquent, the wise of society, those who in the Greco-Roman world garnered the respect of all. Recall that because of his λόγος and σοφία Favorinus was considered by the Corinthians "as the noblest among the Greeks." Such an image suggests that in a city like Corinth much of the population looked on with a mixture of awe and envy as the inner ring of those who actually possessed such nobility—the wise and powerful, the wellborn and the cultured, the aristocrats of society known among other things for their eloquence and wisdom[39]—paraded before them, and that not a few of this majority would

---

[35]Nock (1933, p. 212).
[36]Lattimore (1942, p. 285).
[37]Ibid.
[38]Ibid., pp. 285-86. Cf. the man's additional claims to wisdom in the fuller citation in Kaibel (1878, p. 36).
[39]Peter Brown (1992, pp. 41-42) on the social reality that persisted from ancient Greece to the late Roman Empire: "Those who passed through the school of a rhetor were considered to have developed a more lively intelligence, a more refined speech, and a more harmonious and impres-

very much like to have been ranked among the elite.

It was from just such a majority that the Corinthian church was drawn—some of them, no doubt, to use Nock's words, small men suffering from feelings of inferiority and a pathetic desire for self-assertion. Akin to the lowly sports fan who could never personally compete but finds significance by lionizing and identifying with those who do, they were susceptible to inflated but false pride. Despite their smallness—or perhaps the reverse, because of it—they envisioned themselves, in an exercise of reflected glory, "wise by the standards of this age" (σοφὸς . . . ἐν τῷ αἰῶνι τούτῳ, 1 Cor 3:18), somehow distinguished (1 Cor 4:7), possessing wisdom and power and therefore honor among their fellow Corinthians (1 Cor 4:10). But this was for most of them self-deception. Some few of the Corinthians may have possessed these qualities to a degree, but as for the rest, Paul unequivocally states that "not many" of the Corinthians could claim such grounds for pride. They were not viewed as wise, powerful or wellborn (σοφοί, δυνατοί, εὐγενεῖς), whatever their pretensions. They did not belong to the high-status influential class of society, and everyone knew it. Hence their self-deceived boasting was especially vain and empty, something Paul repeatedly emphasizes by referring to them as "puffed up" (1 Cor 4:6, 18, 19; 5:2). They were, to use a related English colloquialism, "full of hot air."

It was because of these false pretensions among some of the Corinthians that the reactions against Paul, and in favor of others, arose. An examination of the three references in chapters 1–4 to the Corinthians being "puffed up" makes this clear and gives some indication of what prompted these reactions.[40] In 1 Corinthians 4:6 Paul speaks of the Corinthians being puffed up "in favor of one against another." Thus the contentions were two-sided. Pro: They were boasting in their chosen personality (1 Cor 3:21). Con: They were examining and reaching a critical verdict against the others, especially Paul (1 Cor 4:3-5). In 4:18 Paul relates their being puffed up to his own absence. It was when Paul did not come to them that "some" were puffed up. And finally, in 4:19 their being puffed up is associated with their speech, or perhaps better, their elo-

---

sive bearing than anyone else. This would mark them out for the rest of their lives. In the later empire a rhetorical training that had flourished in the Greek world since the fourth century B.C. retained unabated importance."

[40]The remaining three uses of φυσιόω in 1 Cor (5:2; 8:1; 13:4) remain consistent. The Corinthians were prone to self-inflated pride, a tendency that manifested itself not only in the problems discussed in chapters 1–4 but in other areas as well (cf. 1 Cor 8:1-3).

quence.⁴¹ When he arrives in person, Paul says, he will discover not the λόγος of the ones who are puffed up but their true δύναμις, for the kingdom of God is not ἐν λόγῳ but ἐν δυνάμει. An emphasis on λόγος was apparently one of the defining characteristics of this group.⁴²

The picture that emerges here is a coherent one. Some of the Corinthians were avid devotees of eloquence and wisdom.⁴³ When Paul brought them the gospel they had genuinely embraced the crucified Christ and become Christians, despite the rhetorical deficiencies of Paul's preaching. Yet like countless Christians after them, they failed to see the full implications of their conversion, and their old value system remained basically intact. While Paul was present the force of his leadership kept the problem from erupting, but upon his departure—and perhaps exacerbated by the arrival of the eloquent Apollos (Acts 18:24)⁴⁴—the age-old cultural appeal of παιδεία, of eloquence and

---

⁴¹Barrett (1968, p. 118).

⁴²The Corinthian fascination with λόγος apparently outlasted the Apostle Paul. *1 Clement*, written by the church in Rome to the church in Corinth years later, during the last two decades of the first century, warns against the danger of trying to impress foolish men who "boast in the pride of their λόγος rather than in God" (1 Clem 21:5). "Does he that is a good speaker (εὔλαλος) think that he is righteous?" asks the writer (30:4) in a loose quotation of Job 11:2-3. Later he exhorts the Corinthians: "Let the wise (ὁ σοφός) manifest his σοφία not in λόγοι but in good deeds" (38:2). And still later: "Learn to be submissive, putting aside the boastful and the haughty self-confidence of your tongue, for it is better for you to be found small but honorable in the flock of Christ, than to be pre-eminent in repute but to be cast out from his hope" (57:2; cf. also the contrast with God's σοφία and λόγοι in 57:3ff.). On the relation of *1 Clement* and the rhetorical tradition, see Van Unnik (1971, pp. 39-40).

⁴³Similar, e.g., to the ancient Athenians: "Each of you wishes above all to be an orator himself, or, failing that, to vie with those dealers in paradox by seeming not to lag behind them in wit but to applaud a smart saying before it is out of the speaker's mouth" (Thucydides, *History of the Peloponnesian War* III.33.4, 6-7).

⁴⁴In his review of *SPTOP*, James Dunn (1996, p. 117), despite supporting my central argument, found "least convincing" my suggestion that it may have been "an unwitting contrast between the eloquence of Apollos and Paul" that "triggered the sort of divisions we discover in rhetorically attuned Corinth." Though this point was explored merely as a possibility and played, then and now, no necessary role in my argument, it is worth noting that with the renewed appreciation for the rhetorical background of the issues of 1 Cor 1-4, this very traditional idea has found strong support. E.g., see Mihaila's summary (2009, pp. 186-89); cf. also Pogoloff (1992, pp. 180-96); Ker (2000); Hays (1997, p. 22). Says Witherington (1995, p. 130), after Paul left Corinth "Apollos came and 'watered' Paul's mission field. Unfortunately, the method of watering he used amounted to pouring fuel on an already existing fire." Strangely, even Dunn's own words from the previous year (1995, p. 30) might be cited in favor of this view: "The attractiveness of this... hypothesis [that 1 Cor 1-4 'as a whole is directed primarily against an Apollos faction'] is enhanced when we recall that, according to Acts 18.24 and 28, Apollos was from Alexandria and was an eloquent and powerful expositor of the Scriptures. For the Jewish community in Alexandria was famed for its wisdom literature and Paul's elder contemporary, Philo of Alexandria, for his allegorical expositions of the Scriptures. It is an easy step of the historical imagination, therefore, to identify those rebuked consistently throughout 1.17-3.23 for their false evalu-

wisdom, began to reassert itself. In the insecurity of their empty quest for social approval Paul came to be viewed as an embarrassment among them, a social liability.⁴⁵

Not everyone in the Corinthian congregation felt this way about Paul, of course, but some did. These were the ones who were most puffed up with the twin Greek virtues of λόγος and σοφία and with the status these conferred on their possessors. Others, to whom Paul's unpretentious and straightforward approach may have carried more appeal, attempted a defense of the Apostle. We do not know much about this group beyond their partisanship for Paul, but perhaps they pointed out that in his own way the Apostle could be very impressive indeed. In any case, the result was that because of his shortcomings as a speaker when measured against the lofty standards of Greek eloquence, Paul found himself and his ministry the objects of much discussion in the Corinthian church. This was, at least in part, the distressing picture Paul gained from the report of the household of Chloe.

PAUL'S ELOQUENCE

The above scenario is in many ways corroborated by Stephen Pogoloff's dissertation become monograph, *Logos and Sophia: The Rhetorical Situation of 1 Corinthians* (1992). Yet a closer look shows some important differences between Pogoloff's treatment and our own.

First, Pogoloff's work is primarily focused on the role rhetoric played in the status-oriented factions reported in 1 Corinthians 1–4, while our interest is Paul's theology of preaching. This contrast makes for two quite different, though overlapping, projects. Pogoloff's book is essentially a work of rhetorical criticism, while ours is a study in the philosophy of rhetoric.

---

ation of wisdom and clever speech with Apollos or with an Apollos faction. These would be the Apollos party, including some of Paul's own converts won over by Apollos' impressive rhetoric (cf. 3.6-8), as well, presumably, as others converted by Apollos himself (cf. 1.13-15)."

⁴⁵Given this lack of regard by some of the Christians, not to mention the rough treatment Paul received at the hands of the synagogue Jews and the Roman authorities in Corinth (Acts 18:1-17), we should not pass by the delicious irony of the following modern development. In 2007 the city of Corinth convened an international conference on the subject of "Saint Paul and Corinth." Two years later the city published the conference's papers, in the prologue of which publication we read this: "The time came, finally, for Corinth to fulfill its great debt. A spiritual debt to Paul, the Apostle to All Nations; the Apostle that opened up the horizon of the Divine Revelation for the city and also endowed the city with so much prestige with his presence that Corinth today is known everywhere in the world mainly through Paul's work and his extremely significant epistles to the Corinthians" (Papadopolos, 2009).

Second, while Pogoloff focuses extensively, and for the most part helpfully, on the rhetorical terms that feature so prominently in the Apostle's response to his Corinthian critics, like so many other commentators he ignores the non-rhetorical language Paul uses to describe his own discourse. Yet this language—that of the proclaimer, testifier or annunciator—is replete with significance for Paul's argument. We are unlikely to do justice to the contrast Paul is after by ignoring one whole side of it.

Third, neglecting this line of investigation represents a serious blind spot in Pogoloff's otherwise insightful treatment. It is, in fact, a blind spot that leads to at least one important area of misinterpretation. Pogoloff rightly emphasizes that the Corinthians' deepest problem was their misplaced values, and that this problem in turn displayed itself publicly in their personality-centered quarrels. Where Pogoloff departs from the picture we have painted is in his supposition that the "I am of Paul" group championed the Apostle precisely *because* of his eloquence, not his lack of it.

Pogoloff is drawn to this reading by what has become a common assumption. Though he acknowledges that interpreters have traditionally "concluded that [Paul] rejected rhetorical devices of all kinds," Pogoloff argues that "today we must take account of the relative sophistication of Paul's rhetoric" (p. 120). Thus Pogoloff attempts to replace the "traditional" view—that Paul rejected rhetoric for the purposes of his preaching, which resulted in a message that by first-century standards was rhetorically unimpressive, which in turn prompted some of the rhetorically attuned but worldly Corinthians to call the Apostle and his ministry into question—with an alternate reading. According to Pogoloff, some of the Corinthians were drawn to Paul and championed him just *because* they "perceived him as possessing the status indicator of eloquence" (p. 119).

This argument, however, represents a significant misreading of the situation in Corinth, one that both suffers from and reveals a number of shortcomings: (1) It fails to credit Paul's own assessments of his preaching as rhetorically deficient (1 Cor 2:1-4; 2 Cor 11:6). (2) It dodges Paul's opponents' equally negative assessment of Paul's preaching (2 Cor 10:10), an assessment that Paul never attempts to challenge. (3) It ignores the witness of the first three centuries of Paul's early church defenders that by the rhetorical standards of the day he was indeed deficient; see Graves (2010). (4) It overinterprets the significance of Paul's purported use of "rhetoric." To leap from the presence of common linguistic conventions in Paul's letters to the claim that his missionary preaching met the cultural standards for "eloquence" is a non sequitur on stilts. The evidences for and the significance of Hellenistic communicative conventions in Paul's letters must be handled with much more care and nuance; see our discussion of this problem below, pp. 292-306. (5) Pogoloff's reading seriously underestimates the Greco-Roman world's stringent rhetorical criteria for what could be considered eloquent (see chap. 6 above). There is little in Paul's letters to justify the notion that the Corinthian aficionados of oratory would have viewed Paul's preaching as meeting these criteria—and much to suggest the opposite. Indeed, part of the Apostle's argument in support of his nonrhetorical approach was precisely the fact that God prompted the Corinthians to respond to his message *despite* its lack of eloquence (1 Cor 2:1-4). (6) Pogoloff's reading forces him into the awkward claim that "Paul rejects not rhetoric, but the cultural values wedded to it" (p. 121), as if such a wedding could be annulled. Paul knew better: Greco-Roman eloquence was one of the prime expressions of those cultural values. The idea that Paul could use "rhetoric" to preach a message that called into question the cultural values on which that "rhetoric" was based requires an untenable division between rhetoric's form and its content. The two cannot be disentangled; each is implicated in the other. Paul argues that he could not pour the gospel into the mold of Greco-Roman eloquence without thereby emptying the cross of its power (1 Cor 1:17). (7) Having to argue the case that the "I am of Paul" faction championed Paul because he was so eloquent leads Pogoloff into a quagmire. On the one hand he says, "Paul persuaded the Corinthians to receive his gospel." On the other, Paul "insists . . . that this persuasion was not due to his personal eloquence" (p. 136). Yet on the third hand, Paul's persuasive skills were required after all: "To persuade his audience of the truth of the gospel, [Paul] had to speak in a way persuasive to those whose ears and values were Hellenistic and therefore rhetorical" (p. 190). This is confusing; but more importantly, in portraying the Apostle as a sophisticated persuader Pogoloff seems oblivious to Paul's central conviction about his preaching: his determination to depend for its results on the δυνάμει θεοῦ (1 Cor 2:5) rather than on the psychological dynamic of the art of persuasion. On the question of Paul persuading his audience, see below, pp. 292-306.

Upon receiving this unofficial report, combined in some way with an official written request for clarification of some of his previous teaching, Paul determined to write the Corinthian church another letter, the epistle we know as 1 Corinthians. Paul had given much thought to the manner of his preaching because of the centrality of public speaking to his apostolic commission. What the Corinthians did not understand was that Paul had consciously and intentionally embraced his form of preaching—in contrast to the persuaders of his day—for theological reasons. As C. K. Barrett argues, Paul had made this decision before ever arriving in Corinth.[46] Somehow the Corinthian critics must be made to see this point and to understand that dividing among themselves over such an issue was entirely inappropriate. Hence the first part of Paul's letter (1 Cor 1-4) was designed to address their criticism of his ministry and is therefore apologetic in nature. Its goal was to defuse the Corinthian divisiveness by eliminating Paul's preaching as an occasion for contentions.

---

[46]Barrett (1982, p. 24). Whether this should be related to Acts 17 and Paul's experience in Athens is a matter of speculation. It's a question we will not try to resolve.

The above scenario[47] suggests that the defense of matters of form—that is, the form of Paul's preaching—was uppermost in the mind of the Apostle in 1 Corinthians 1–4, and that he raises matters of theological content precisely to explain and justify this form. In other words, rather than seeking to correct theological errors among the Corinthians, Paul actually assumes a basic agreement with the Corinthians on theological matters and uses this agreement to explain and defend his *modus operandi* as a preacher. Some modern interpreters continue to postulate a variety of more or less serious theological differences between Paul and the Corinthians that Paul is attempting to correct. Matters relating to Paul's *modus operandi* are either slighted, ignored or dismissed as irrelevant. Which of these interpretations represents the best reading of 1 Corinthians 1–4 can only be resolved by turning to the text itself.

---

[47]In framing this picture we have intentionally avoided drawing on 2 Cor 13:3, where Paul warns that when he arrives for the third time in Corinth he will spare no one, "since you seek proof that Christ is speaking in me. He is not weak in dealing with you, but is powerful among you." Wherever one places 2 Cor 10–13 in the sequence of Paul's interactions with the Corinthians, it comes well after, and potentially rather long after, 1 Cor 1–4. Much has occurred in the interim to muddy the water. Hence it is doubtful that we should attribute such sentiments to the Corinthians as early as the writing of 1 Cor 1–4. The problem of Paul's speech is still present in 2 Cor 13:3, but this particular criticism is something new, something beyond the earlier problem. In fact, 2 Cor 13:3 may best be understood as a reflection of the Corinthians' response to Paul's argument in 1 Cor 1–4 and therefore at least one full interchange beyond it. In other words, the sentiments expressed in 2 Cor 13:3 are a result of 1 Cor 1–4, not a contributor to it. As Witherington (1995, p. 74) says, "It is a mistake to read all of the situation of 2 Corinthians back into 1 Corinthians. In particular, it is unlikely that a group of anti-Pauline agitators are already causing problems for the Corinthian *ekklēsia* at the time of 1 Corinthians."

12

Paul's Argument Introduced

1 Corinthians 1:1-17

We turn now to examine the details of 1 Corinthians 1–4. Our goal will be to trace the argument of this literary unit, giving closest attention to the section that most explicitly spells out the Apostle's theology of preaching, chapters 1–2. To begin our discussion, however, let us highlight a crucial feature of the Apostle's thought.

A FUNDAMENTAL CONTRAST

To understand Paul's argument in 1 Corinthians 1–4 it is important to grasp a fundamental contrast or antithesis that undergirds much of the Apostle's thinking. This contrast provides the conceptual framework for his appeals throughout this section. It is a contrast Paul emphasizes repeatedly in the Corinthian correspondence, which indicates that understanding it may have been as difficult for the Corinthians as it was important for Paul. The Apostle captures this contrast with a variety of language so that choosing a particular set of terms to describe it runs the risk of oversimplification. For our needs it will be enough to cite Paul's own language, allowing his terminology to speak for itself. Below is a selected list of some of his most explicit references to this contrast in the Corinthian epistles. In some instances the opposite member of the antithesis is left implicit.

The antithesis highlighted in these references is one of realm (cosmos-heaven), of time (this age–the age to come), but most of all of person (man-God). Paul portrays here a basic two-sidedness of things, a fundamental dualism, not of ontology but of viewpoint. There is God's perspective,[1] and over against this there is another perspective comprising all the rest, the perspective "of the world" (τοῦ

---

[1] Hays (1997, p. 28) refers to this as the "apocalyptic perspective," hearkening back to his description of the gospel as "an announcement about God's apocalyptic intervention in the world, for the sake of the world."

κόσμου). The nature of the constructions in both columns varies, yet each holds in common—in fact, each depends upon—the same general presupposition: the existence of a dichotomy of viewpoint, a "this side" over against "that side" type of antithesis.

Table 12.1

1 Corinthians		
1:20	…	… of this age
1:20	God	… of the world
1:21	… of God	… the world
1:26	…	… by human standards
1:27-28	God	… of the world
2:5	… God	… human
2:6-8	… God	… the rulers of this age
2:12	… from God	… of the world
3:18	…	… of this age
3:19	…	… of this world
7:31	…	… of this world
7:33-34	… of the Lord	… of the world
9:8	…	… according to human judgment
13:12	then	now
15:19	…	… in this life only
15:32	…	… from human motives
15:40-49	heavenly, imperishable	earthly, perishable
2 Corinthians		
4:7	… from God	… from us
4:17	eternal …	momentary …
4:18	… the things not seen	… the things seen
4:18	eternal …	temporary …
5:1	from God … in the heavens	earthly
5:16	…	… according to the flesh
10:2-3	…	… according to the flesh
11:18	…	… according to the flesh

Furthermore, despite the obvious diversity within the τοῦ κόσμου side of the contrast, Paul seems to treat it monolithically, as if any diversity here is ultimately less important than its basic coherence. As Conzelmann says, "The cosmos appears as a collective subject, the bearer of 'its' wisdom."[2] The complexity inherent in such descriptions as "τοῦ κόσμου" or "κατὰ ἄνθρωπον" does not seem to trouble Paul. He is apparently dealing with his subject at a level of theological abstraction that transcends such diversity.

Regarding Paul's treatment of these twin perspectives we must underscore several initial observations.

(1) The Apostle's constant repetition of the antithesis suggests a fundamental opposition of the two perspectives. God's perspective is that of deity, of heaven, of eternity, while from this side the perspective is that of mortal flesh, the world, this age. The two represent divergent ways of perceiving reality, and according to Paul they often clash. From out of the restricted viewpoint of the world grow distorted conceptions of God and of ultimate things that compete with God's conception (2 Cor 10:5). According to Paul, God is determined to set aside these false conceptions, and by such means moreover as to demonstrate in the end their utter futility (1 Cor 1:19-21, 27-29; 3:19-21).

(2) There can be no question which of the two perspectives Paul espoused. Having been granted his own special glimpse into the other side (1 Cor 15:8; 2 Cor 3:6; 4:1, 6; 5:16; 12:1-10; cf. Gal 1:1-12), Paul now saw himself as a champion of God's perspective (2 Cor 5:20), engaged in open warfare with its alternative (2 Cor 10:3-5; cf. 1 Cor 15:34). He perceived temporal things as so partial as to be intrinsically misleading. From the world's congenitally truncated viewpoint, limited as it is to the merely apparent, reality is bound to be misunderstood. Only from God's perspective can one see ultimate things as they must be seen to be understood. Hence Paul counsels the Corinthians against understanding life merely as it appears from the vantage point τοῦ κόσμου. The Christian must not operate "by sight" (διὰ εἴδους, 2 Cor 5:7; cf. 5:12). To live on the level of "this life only" (τῇ ζωῇ ταύτῃ ... μόνον) meant for Paul only vanity and emptiness, a life devoid of ultimate significance (1 Cor 15:19, 32). The things seen (τὰ βλεπόμενα) are merely the temporal, the transient things; the things not seen (τὰ μὴ βλεπόμενα) constitute the eternal (2 Cor 4:18). By the yardstick of eternity the particulars humans can discover for themselves are not the ultimately important things. They are for the most part merely facets of the outward form of this world (τὸ σχῆμα τοῦ κόσμου τούτου, 1 Cor 7:31), which is passing away. Only from God's perspective can the true nature of ultimate things be grasped.

---

[2]Conzelmann (1975, p. 43).

(3) Paul maintained that it is impossible for humans to gain access to the other side, God's side, apart from revelation. Despite their best efforts, the limitedness of their worldly perspective is, in so far as they struggle on their own, without remedy. Ultimate things are hidden from them quite by design, says Paul (1 Cor 1:21, 27-29; Rom 11:33-36; cf. 2 Cor 4:3-4). In the end, all of their speculations leave them short, with a unidimensional and merely "this-sided" view that can never suffice. Only the Spirit of God knows fully the truth about God, and he is the only source from which an understanding of this truth can come (1 Cor 2:10-12). The world cannot construct this divine conception of things for itself (1 Cor 2:6-9); it must be willing simply to embrace the truth revealed by the Spirit (1 Cor 1:21-25; 2 Cor 3:14-18). Viewed strictly from the world's perspective, of course, this appears a foolish thing to do, an act of abdication or capitulation (1 Cor 2:14). But viewed in the full light of the other, divine perspective, such a capitulation becomes for Paul the ultimate act of wisdom for one who genuinely desires to find the truth (1 Cor 2:6-8; 3:18).

(4) Yet Paul did not maintain that any mortal could fully understand as God understands, even with the benefit of the Spirit's revelation. If the veil is lifted for one who turns to the Lord (2 Cor 3:16), it is not lifted entirely. The believer is given by the Spirit enough of a glimpse of God's perspective to know wherein the truth consists (1 Cor 1:23-24, 30), enough to provide a plumb line against which to order his own responses, but only just so. At best humans still understand only in part (ἐκ μέρους), says Paul, as if peering "in a mirror dimly" (δι' ἐσόπτρου ἐν αἰνίγματι, 1 Cor 13:12). To be sure, there will come a time in the future when the believer will discover a final knowledge of the truth, a time, says the Apostle, when we will know as we are presently known (ἐπιγνώσομαι καθὼς καὶ ἐπεγνώσθην, 1 Cor 13:12). It is in this same future, in fact, that all things will be made manifest, including "the things now hidden in darkness" (τὰ κρυπτὰ τοῦ σκότους) and "the purposes of the heart" (τὰς βουλὰς τῶν καρδιῶν, 1 Cor 4:5). Then will the ones who have operated in the light of "the things that are not seen"—and been ridiculed as foolish for it by those whose vision is limited to "the things that are seen"—then, after the full truth emerges, will the ones who were truly wise be vindicated (1 Cor 3:13; 4:5; cf. 2 Cor 10:18).

This contrast runs like a thread throughout the Corinthian epistles. For every place where we glimpse it there are many more where it has slipped out of sight but is working nonetheless to hold the fabric of Paul's thought together. It is in the light of this contrast that we must understand Paul's analysis of the Corinthian complaints and his consequent responses in 1 Corinthians 1–4.

1:1-3—Salutation

Paul begins his letter with a relatively expansive epistolary greeting that stresses not only his own position but, importantly, that of the Corinthians. He has been called by God to be an Apostle (1:1), but by the same token the Corinthians too are "called" (κλητοῖς, 1:2). Paul thus emphasizes the Corinthians' solidarity with him and with all other Christians: they constitute that branch of the "church of God" (τῇ ἐκκλησίᾳ τοῦ θεοῦ) that exists in Corinth; they are people who have already been sanctified (ἡγιασμένοις) by God in Christ Jesus; they are "saints by calling" (κλητοῖς ἁγίοις) who can be classed with all Christians everywhere who call on the name of Jesus Christ. Thus Paul speaks of Jesus as their Lord and of God as their Father.

The Apostle appears to go out of his way to stress here the genuineness of the Corinthians. By contrast, the theological integrity of the Galatians was under serious suspicion. Paul perceived them as in danger of abandoning the truth about Christ for a different or distorted gospel (Gal 1:6-7; 3:1; but cf. 5:10) and thus tersely addresses their letter merely to "the churches of Galatia" (ταῖς ἐκκλησίαις τῆς Γαλατίας, Gal 1:2). But Paul shows no such reticence with the Corinthians. On the contrary, just as the Galatian address is the most abrupt among Paul's letters, so this address is the most lavish.

1:4-9—The Thanksgiving

The proofs of the authenticity of the Corinthians' faith constitute the theme of Paul's thanksgiving. God in his grace had richly poured out on the Corinthians all of the gifts (χαρίσματι), so that they fell short in none (1:7). Paul interpreted the presence of these gifts as divine confirmation that the Corinthians had genuinely embraced "the testimony about Christ" (τὸ μαρτύριον τοῦ Χριστοῦ) he had preached to them (1:6). The presence of the gifts proved that God was truly working among them and confirmed the reality of their faith. Moreover Paul was confident that this process of confirmation would continue until the end (1:8). The divine purpose for the Corinthians was that, as a result of God's work in their lives, they might ultimately stand blameless at the final day of judgment. This is what the gospel promised, and the Corinthians could count on that promise being kept. Why? Because "God is faithful, by whom you were called" (πιστὸς ὁ θεὸς δι' οὗ ἐκλήθητε, 1:9).

It is noteworthy that throughout 1:4-9 God is portrayed as the initiator and the Corinthians as the recipients. The verbs indicate this clearly enough. In each case—"given" (4), "enriched" (5), "confirmed" (6), "will sustain" (8), "called" (9)—God is active, calling them, enriching them, confirming them until the end. The Corinthians are simply the locus of God's activity. Indeed, it was precisely for this spectacle—that is, God at work among the Corinthians—that Paul was so grateful (1:4).

We have in this introductory section, then, a preliminary indication of Paul's view of the Corinthians. It is only preliminary and must be measured against the remainder of the evidence, but it is worth noting the direction in which the details already point. Everything in this introduction suggests that Paul considered the Corinthians to be genuine and fundamentally sound theologically. The emphasis on their solidarity with him and with other believers, combined with the confident vision of God busily at work in their midst, gives no indication that Paul had discovered within their midst theological error of the most grievous sort.[3] There is not the slightest hint to suggest that the Corinthians had exchanged the gospel Paul had preached for another, or that they were somehow vitiating its efficacy by denying or distorting some of its central tenets. In fact this introduction would be an extraordinary way to begin if such serious theological problems did exist in Corinth. Again, in his letter to the Galatians Paul understandably omits the standard thanksgiving section and moves immediately to the issue: "I am astonished that you are so quickly deserting him who called you in the grace of Christ and are turning to a different gospel" (Gal 1:6). But there is nothing in the opening verses of 1 Corinthians to suggest similar problems in Corinth. To the extent that this introduction tells us anything about the Corinthians, it suggests the opposite. Paul seems to have considered the commitment of the Corinthians to his gospel to be basically sound and unchanged. The problems he is about to take up will lie elsewhere.

---

[3]The later denial of the resurrection in 1 Cor 15 might appear to contradict this. But upon closer inspection the contradiction proves illusory. First, among those who argue that a faulty Christology lay behind 1 Cor 1-4, none equate it with the denial of Christ's resurrection. Most see the Corinthian difficulties centered rather on the cross (cf. 1:17). Second, there is no indication in 1 Cor 15 that the Corinthians had denied Christ's resurrection. The problem was that "some" (15:12) had denied the resurrection of believers (see 15:12-13, 16, 18-23, 29, 35-58). The matter of Christ's resurrection as the "firstfruits" (15:20, 23) is introduced by the Apostle to prove the believer's resurrection. But third, and most important, Paul's argument in 1 Cor 15 actually depends on the fact that the Corinthians had *not* abandoned his gospel. The point of 15:1-2 is that they had embraced the full message Paul preached and that they yet held it fast. The conditional clause of 15:2 ("unless you believed in vain") assumes a positive answer. Paul reminds them that the gospel he had preached and that they held fast inherently includes Christ's resurrection. He then uses this to demonstrate the necessity of believing in the resurrection of the believer. This argument would be valid only if the Corinthians held to Paul's gospel. Hence 1 Cor 15 functions to reinforce our point rather than contradict it.

1:10-13—The Contentions

The most prominent difficulty in the Corinthian congregation was not theological but interpersonal, or so at least one would gather from the preeminence Paul gives to the matter of divisiveness. While as a Christian community (ἐκκλησία) the Corinthians ought to have been unified in mind and heart, focused on the oneness they enjoyed in Christ (1:10), the congregation was instead racked by contentions (ἔριδες, 1:11). Moreover, these ἔριδες centered on personalities. Some of the Corinthians associated themselves with Paul, others with Apollos and Cephas, and still others with Christ himself. But each of them (1:12) shared the responsibility for breaking the unity of Christ by proudly aligning himself with one against the others (cf. 1 Cor 3:21; 4:6). Their error lay in the sheer act of establishing such alignments, regardless of who the personality was. Paul viewed Christ's body as one (1 Cor 1:13; 12:12) and all such personality-centered factions—to the extent they divided Christian from Christian—as false and out of place in a church. This explains why Paul was as critical of those who aligned themselves with Christ and with himself as he was of the others; all were equally in error.

The second and third ironical questions of 1:13—"Was Paul crucified for you? Or were you baptized in the name of Paul?"—provide a useful insight into the nature of the Apostle's problem with the Corinthians. Paul plainly intends that the Corinthians should answer the questions in the negative and thereby be reminded of who in fact had been crucified for their salvation, and in whose name they had been baptized. He assumes that they accurately understand the cross and that they will be both able and willing to make the proper substitution on their own. In fact, his irony depends on it. In this way Paul shows that he did not perceive their problem to be that they had misunderstood, distorted or abandoned the cross and its salvific meaning. Rather, they had failed to see the implications of it in their conduct. Their soteriology was sound enough; it was their behavior that was lacking. They believed that Christ had been crucified on their behalf, and they had demonstrated that belief by being baptized in his name. But they were still unfortunately allowing ἔριδες to exist in the congregation. They lacked the spiritual insight and maturity to see that such wrangling was precluded by the very gospel they had embraced. Their problem was thus one of a serious breach between belief and behavior.

We can see this more clearly by observing A. E. Harvey's now widely embraced distinction between the two kinds of problems Paul faced in his letters.[4] Harvey differentiates between (1) theological controversies and (2) more behaviorally oriented "improprieties." First Corinthians 15 (denial of the believer's resurrection) represents the former, while 1 Corinthians 6 (litigiousness) and 1 Corinthians 11 (the Lord's table) illustrate the latter. According to Harvey, in the first instance Paul typically moves in to tackle the matter in straightforward theological terms; in the second, he addresses the practical issue by setting the behavioral matters in their theological context. In such cases, says Harvey, "Paul's theological treatment of the question is provoked, not by any arguments of the Corinthians, but by the fact that they clearly have not given it any serious thought at all." He continues,

> The Christians to whom Paul is writing have been behaving in a certain way which, to them, doubtless seemed harmless; but Paul sees the implications, and hastens to alert them to the seriousness of what they are doing. In both these cases [1 Cor 6 and 11] . . . , and in others like them in Paul's correspondence, it would be pointless to try to reconstruct arguments used by the other side. Paul's quarrel with them is precisely that they have no arguments—they have been acting unreflectively, without considering the implications, from a Christian point of view, of their conduct. Paul's arguments are not to be understood as answering the theological objections of his opponents but as awakening his correspondents from their theological thoughtlessness. This type of argument, therefore, needs to be distinguished from the other type, which starts from a clear difference of opinion on a theological issue, and to understand which it is necessary to look for the arguments of the other side.[5]

What were the "improprieties" that prompted the quarrels at Corinth? In other words, what sort of differences are represented by the slogans centering on Paul, Apollos, Cephas and Christ? Since the work of F. C. Baur this question has been debated hotly and at length, and the answers have been legion. Unfortunately, nothing approaching a consensus has emerged. In recent research it has increasingly been conceded that we lack the information necessary to specify with any certainty what the various slogans represented.

Yet our way is not altogether blocked by this lack of information. There is a route around the problem that may also in the end provide the perspective for solving it, at least in part. We need only observe that in the final analysis the

---

[4]Harvey (1968, pp. 319-21); cf. Grindheim's summary (2002, p. 689) of the contemporary consensus on this point.
[5]Harvey (1968, pp. 320-21).

Paul's Argument Introduced 169

specific content of the slogans regarding Apollos, Cephas and Christ may not be all that important. These slogans, after all, are never again mentioned in 1 Corinthians after chapter 4, and they make no appearance at all in 2 Corinthians.[6] And even in 1 Corinthians 1–4 they play only a limited and sporadic role, and not a determinative one at that. What is more important for our immediate purpose is that the apologetic nature of 1 Corinthians 1–4 be given due weight. In this light, the slogans can be seen to have a more certain, if also more general, meaning, and the differences between them become less important than what they hold in common: each represents a form of repudiation of Paul. This is Dahl's point when he says,

> Since the entire section contains an apology for Paul, and the strife at Corinth was linked up with opposition against him, it becomes fairly easy to interpret the slogans reported in 1:12. Those who said "I belong to Paul" were proud of him and held that his excellence surpassed that of Apollos or Cephas. The other slogans are all to be understood as declarations of independence from Paul.[7]

Thus we need not determine the peculiarities represented by each of the slogans—an endeavor that has been all but abandoned by New Testament scholars these days—in order to proceed. For the present it will be enough to conclude that in the broadest sense there were only two groups at Corinth: those who aligned themselves with Paul and those who aligned themselves with others against Paul. How those who aligned themselves with others may have differed among themselves is less important for understanding 1 Corinthians 1–4 than the fact that they chose not to align themselves with Paul. On this point, at least, all of the other groups—to the extent that actual groups existed at all; this point also continues to be disputed—were agreed. When it came time to choose sides, each of the proponents of these three slogans had chosen against Paul.

But we must still ask, what was the factor that prompted them to choose against Paul? On this negative question we have a great deal more to go on. We may be lacking the data that would allow us to understand how or why the opposition chose from among the Apollos, Cephas and Christ banners the one they preferred

---

[6]With the possible but dubious exception of the Christ party in 2 Cor 10:7. Winter (2003, p. 149) reads these parties into the later instances of conflict in Corinth, such as 1 Cor 6:1-8, but the texts there offer little warrant for doing so. The repetition of φυσιόω (passive: "to be puffed up") three times in 1 Cor 1–4 and three times in 5–16 certainly suggests that issues of pride infused all of the conflicts in Corinth, but it would take us beyond the evidence to argue that the later points of conflict were triggered by the same group alignments that were at work in the ἔριδες of 1–4.
[7]Dahl (1967, p. 322).

to rally behind, but we are not nearly so lacking in indicators of the ways in which they found Paul deficient. These deficiencies emerge with relative clarity in 1 Corinthians 1–4 as Paul attempts to defend himself against their complaints.

What is striking about these perceived deficiencies, however—and the difficulty of identifying what was behind the slogans lies just here—is that they seem to be highly unified and concentrated. There are not three sets of complaints corresponding to the views of three different groups. There is in 1 Corinthians 1–4 only one set of complaints and only one relatively integrated defense. In other words, it is as if Paul is not defending himself on three fronts but only one. But how then can this be correlated with several distinct opposing groups?

There are three plausible answers: either (1) there were no such groups in Corinth at all and the slogans are therefore a blind alley for exegetical purposes; (2) each of the three groups who declared their independence from Paul shared similar complaints about Paul, whatever their respective differences; or (3) one of the groups dominated the Corinthian dissidents, and Paul merely mentions the other two in passing for the sake of completeness. His actual defense, according to this last view, is for the most part directed toward the predominant group whose complaints about his ministry are by far the most influential and damaging.

For our purposes we can proceed without determining the precise identity of the three opposing groups or deciding among the above options. We will for now assume with Dahl no more than the negative conclusion that these three groups shared at least a declaration of independence from Paul. Beyond this we will leave their identity an open question. However, we propose to return to this question later to see if in the light of our study a more positive answer regarding the identity of these groups may not be forthcoming.

1:14-17—Paul's Commission

Paul's ironic question in 1 Corinthians 1:13, "You were not baptized in the name of Paul, were you?" affords him the opportunity to turn now to the subject that is the key topic of 1 Corinthians 1–4: his own ministry. For the first time in the epistle Paul explicitly brings up his activity in Corinth.[8]

It need hardly be said that Paul's disavowal of baptism in 1 Corinthians 1:14-16 constitutes no denigration of the sacrament as such. The reference to baptism functions largely as a foil to highlight the focus on proclamation within Paul's apostolic ministry. The matter of his preaching is plainly where Paul is heading,

---

[8] Unless one includes "the testimony about Christ" (τὸ μαρτύριον τοῦ Χριστοῦ, 1 Cor 1:6).

Paul's Argument Introduced

and these references to baptism are simply the means of arriving there. Hence from the ironical question of verse 13, which is designed to direct the reader not to baptism but to the centrality of Christ, to the forceful declaration about preaching in verse 17, which opens up the whole argument of chapters 1-4, Paul's references in verses 14-16 to his baptismal activity in Corinth form merely an effective literary springboard.

Some commentators attempt by reading between the lines to milk from these verses information about the Corinthians and their attitudes toward Paul and baptism. But such efforts are highly speculative and require elaborate assumptions about an alleged Corinthian theology.[9] Against such attempts it must be said that there is no indication here that the Corinthians initiated this topic or that erroneous views on their part had prompted Paul to bring it up. Indeed, the subject of water baptism plays no role whatsoever in the argument of either 1 or 2 Corinthians, much less in the apologetic of 1 Corinthians 1-4. Apart from the one enigmatic reference to the baptism for the dead in 1 Corinthians 15:29, Paul drops the subject entirely with the Corinthians after 1:17. Hence it is unlikely that these few nontheological verses legitimately reveal much about alleged Corinthian views of baptism.

How then may we understand the function of 1 Corinthians 1:14-16? The disavowal of baptism in verses 14-15, "so that no one may say that you were baptized in my name," may best be viewed as a sardonic rebuke of the Corinthians' proclivity to personality-centered ἔριδες.[10] The inescapable negative answer to Paul's question regarding baptism in 1:13—"Were you baptized in the name of Paul?"—rules out the possibility that he could have intended this disavowal as anything other than ironic. No one would actually have claimed such a thing, but the very absurdity of it is what heightens the irony. "You are so shamefully ready to divide up that I suppose you would have invented even this pretense had I given you the opportunity," Paul says. In reality, of course, they would not have gone this far, but it is the nature of irony to overstate the case.

In 1 Corinthians 1:17 Paul arrives at the nub of the issue. Verse 16 still reads

---

[9]E.g., Chester (2003, pp. 290-92).
[10]Pascuzzi (2009, pp. 826-27) speculates that this problem was due to the eloquence of Apollos: "In a city such as Corinth, characterized by competitiveness, boasting, and the constant pursuit of honor, Paul must have quickly become the object of humiliating comparisons with Apollos. Paul would have been seen as the loser in a contest whose conventions he never intended to follow, let alone be judged by (4:3-4). In such a context, it is not beyond imagining that denigrating assertions to the effect that Paul was a mere baptizer, while Apollos was the true preacher, circulated in the community in Corinth."

as if he regrets having brought up the matter of baptism, since it has bogged him down in the clarification of details. With 1:17, however, he shakes himself free of these details and leaps directly to what Rolf Baumann calls "the central question in Corinth."[11] In the light of the remainder of 1 Corinthians 1–4, one can see that this was where he was determined to arrive from the outset. He intends to speak of his preaching (εὐαγγελίζεσθαι), qualified with the as yet unexplained phrase "not in wisdom of words" (οὐκ ἐν σοφίᾳ λόγου, AT).[12]

Whatever other difficulties Paul faced in Corinth, perceived deficiencies in his preaching, when measured against Greco-Roman eloquence, presented the problem he had to address first. These were the deficiencies that prompted a section of the Corinthian congregation to complain about Paul's preaching and declare their independence from him. As we shall see, the existence of such complaints is what energizes Paul's argument in 1 Corinthians 1–4 and gives it coherence. For now, however, it will suffice to note how naturally this thesis explains Paul's apparently abrupt transition from the quarrels in Corinth (1 Cor 1:10-16) to a vigorous defense of his preaching (1 Cor 1:17–2:5). The simple answer is that in raising the subject of his preaching Paul has not left the Corinthian ἔριδες at all. On the contrary, he has moved to the heart of them.[13]

---

[11]Baumann (1968, p. 63).
[12]It should be noted that Paul has already used the word λόγος (along with γνώσει) in 1 Cor 1:5. It refers there to a spiritual gift granted by God to members of the congregation. In a similar context in 1 Cor 12:8 Paul refers again to the Spirit's having given various members of the congregation a "word of wisdom" (λόγος σοφίας) or a "word of knowledge" (λόγος γνώσεως). In both settings, 1:5 and 12:8, the references are entirely positive; they are both statements that emphasize the blessings of God on the Corinthian believers (see δοθείσῃ, 1 Cor 1:4; δίδοται, 1 Cor 12:8). By contrast, in 1 Cor 1:17 the reference to λόγος has nothing to do with spiritual gifts. It is here a negative reference ("*not* in wisdom of words"), unrelated to any notion of the Spirit's blessing. Paul's preaching is the topic, and the words σοφίᾳ λόγου represent its antithesis, precisely because of this phenomenon's potential to *displace* the work of the Spirit (1 Cor 2:4-5). It cannot be therefore that Paul has in mind the same phenomenon in both 1:5 and 1:17. The relative proximity of the two references is deceptive; the shift of thought in the intervening verses has been profound. In the two contexts Paul is referring to two different forms of verbal behavior, the one a charismatic gift of λόγος from the Spirit to be used freely for the edification of the church (1 Cor 14:26), the other a form of speech of human origin (1 Cor 2:13) that is to be avoided in the preaching of the gospel. The only thing the two phenomena have in common is that they are both verbal behavior and so can both be designated by the highly elastic and often ambiguous term λόγος—on which, see Kennedy (1963, p. 8). Thus the two uses of λόγος should not be used to interpret one another. Such a conflation of essentially different phenomena can only confuse the exegetical task and distract us from Paul's argument.
[13]In classical rhetorical terms, this issue constitutes the *causa* or *stasis* of that aspect of the rhetorical situation Paul is addressing in 1 Cor 1–4. Due to the bewildering thicket of issues surrounding the use of these and their related terms (see Troy Martin, 2010, pp. 78-93), I have chosen to avoid employing them here.

A COMMON BLIND SPOT

This is a crucial point many commentators appear to miss. See, for example, C. K. Robertson (2001), who argues for a complex understanding of the quarrels in Corinth, yet avoids the issue of Paul's preaching. Similarly, Lampe (1990) misses this dimension of Paul's argument entirely; see also Wanamaker (2003, p. 125); Frestadius (2011, p. 56). This sort of myopia consigns the discussion to needless turmoil. Smit (2002, p. 231) rightfully observes, "Scholars are unanimous in their opinion that 1 Corinthians 1:10–4:21 forms a rounded and coherent unit within the first letter of Paul to the church at Corinth," but he is also on target when he cites the inability of scholars to discern what it is that grants this passage its coherence: "Upon further consideration of the coherence of this much-discussed passage they all go their various ways." Why the disarray? Because of an inability or unwillingness to recognize the true organizing topic of the passage: Paul's defense of his *modus operandi* as a preacher. A failure to appreciate this point leads to confusion, of which Smit himself provides a useful example.

Smit cites the various sections and subthemes of 1 Corinthians 1–4 and then observes, "The question as to how these themes are interrelated and all together form a coherent unity, is apparently very difficult to answer. Widely divergent solutions are proposed." Smit then helpfully summarizes and documents these divergent proposals (pp. 233-34). Some scholars, he says, try to build the coherence around themes such as "party strength and wisdom; party strife and leadership; party strife, leadership and wisdom." Others focus on single themes such as "the crucified Christ as God's wisdom; the fight against factionalism; the fight against wisdom understood as the trade of sophists and rhetors; the example of Paul; right leadership." And to these options we must add the pursuit of "honor" (Finney, 2010). To what purpose does Paul address such themes? Smit (2002, p. 234) identifies three trends in the literature. The first "holds that in 1 Corinthians 1:10–4:21 Paul primarily fights factionalism in Corinth. A second trend contends that Paul proclaims the cross of Christ in order to fight an overestimation of wisdom among the Corinthians; a recent variant identifies this wisdom as classical rhetoric. A third trend asserts that this passage is apologetic in purport; Paul fights the depreciation which a number of believers at Corinth hold against his way of acting among them in order to reaffirm his authority; sometimes this underestimation of Paul is more in particular ascribed to the followers of Apollos."

Smit's summary of the confusing array of proposals on what it is that provides coherence to 1 Corinthians 1–4 is striking, not only for what it includes but for what it does not include. None apparently, according to Smit, view *the Apostle's vindication of his approach to preaching* as the unifying theme of 1 Corinthians 1–4. The closest Smit comes is his references to rhetoric and the sophists, an explanatory proposal he later dismisses as "untenable," not least because of the purported presence of "rhetoric" in these very verses (p. 245); on this issue, however, see below, p. 292-306. But what Smit misses—and in this he is scarcely alone—is the true unifying focus of 1 Corinthians 1–4: the Apostle's theological vindication of his preaching, which vindication, if successful, will have the effect of defusing the ἔριδες that were wracking the community. This overarching focus is what gives coherence to 1 Corinthians 1–4 and allows its "various themes [to] be related to each other in an unforced and satisfactory manner" (Smit, p. 233).

But if this proposal provides such a satisfactory answer to the question of the coherence of 1 Corinthians 1–4—a point on which readers of this book are invited to decide for themselves—why the scholarly confusion and lack of consensus? The reasons are complex and potential answers require speculation. Yet one issue that has certainly not helped the problem is the reluctance of the scholarly community to probe the significance of the determinedly non-rhetorical language Paul consistently uses to describe his preaching (on Paul's single exception, see "A Unique Exception" in chap. 13). The language of 1 Corinthians 1–4 has been minutely sifted for insight into the Apostle's argument, but one looks in vain, in treatment after treatment, for any detailed engagement with the language Paul uses to describe his preaching. Why this language? What is unique about what it denotes? In contrast to what? What is this language precluding? These and similar questions are crucial for grasping the argument of 1 Corinthians 1–4, but I have yet to find any thorough investigations of their contributions to this discussion. This curious blind spot, in a community that otherwise thrives on this sort of linguistic work, is something of a mystery. The failure to follow this trail to where it leads may be one of the reasons for the confusion cited by Smit.

According to 1 Corinthians 1:17, Paul viewed his preaching as an assignment from Christ himself. This preaching constituted the core of his apostolic calling. The qualifying phrase οὐκ ἐν σοφίᾳ λόγου specifies the manner in which this assignment was not to be conducted. In other words, Paul states that his assignment from Christ included not only the command that he should preach the gospel; it also involved some implicit or explicit indications regarding the *form* or *manner* of that preaching: "For Christ sent me . . . to gospelize, οὐκ ἐν σοφίᾳ λόγου" (AT). From the very beginning of this section, then, the matter of form plays an important role in Paul's argument. In fact it is the substance of this qualifying phrase, οὐκ ἐν σοφίᾳ λόγου, that governs the following argument.

It is tendentious to interpret οὐκ ἐν σοφίᾳ λόγου in verse 17 primarily in terms of content, as if Paul is merely asserting that the ideas he preaches must not be those of human wisdom. As we have seen (pp. 137-41), this phrase is but the first of ten related constructions in the Corinthian epistles that share a common emphasis on the form, appearance or manner of Paul's ministry, and especially his preaching ministry. Matters of content will arise soon enough in Paul's argument, but they are not yet in view here. So far Paul has merely stated that to be faithful to his assignment from the risen Christ his preaching must not take the form—contrary to the apparent desires of the Corinthians—of σοφία λόγου. And this, of course, brings us back to the most important exegetical question that confronts the interpreter of 1 Corinthians 1–4. What is the meaning here of the Corinthian use of σοφία?

In the earlier sections of this study we have traced at length the meaning of σοφία within the Greco-Roman rhetorical tradition. As we observed there, by the first century this rhetorical tradition lay at the core of over half a millennium of Greek cultural history. Moreover, during the lifetime of Paul this cultural tradition, with its profound emphasis on both λόγος and σοφία, was flourishing exuberantly in Greece and in Corinth in particular. It is only natural then that we should look first to this prominent tradition, which lays so readily to hand, when we confront references to σοφία λόγου in 1 Corinthians. Especially is this true when the subject matter that forms the context for these references is public speaking.[14]

What we discover when we look to this rhetorical tradition to unlock Paul's argument in 1 Corinthians 1–4 is that it is a remarkably illuminating thesis. Apparently bland arguments take on color, and otherwise enigmatic statements come clear. And in no case is this more apparent than the disputed clause of 1 Corinthians 1:17: "lest the cross of Christ be emptied" (ἵνα μὴ κενωθῇ ὁ σταυρὸς τοῦ Χριστοῦ). Since this clause encapsulates much of the theme of the section 1 Corinthians 1:18–2:5, we will in effect be exploring its meaning as we progress, but for now we must state at least the general thrust of it. When we have done so we will have discovered the essence of Paul's theology of preaching.

EMPTYING THE CROSS

The section 1 Corinthians 1:18–2:5 is bracketed by two crucial constructions. The close parallelism of these two statements is no accident. Johan Vos rightly calls 1 Corinthians 2:1-5 simply *eine Amplifikation* of 1:17.[15] The first looks forward, the second looks back; the first states the theme to be developed in 1:18–2:5, and the second restates the same theme, this time as a conclusion of what has just been

---

[14]But see also Barrett's discussions of the shifting meanings of σοφία in 1 Cor 1–4 (1982, pp. 6-11; idem, 1968, pp. 17-19, 67-68). As we shall see, the term σοφία flexes with the Apostle's needs and must not be treated simplistically.
[15]Vos (1996, p. 103).

developed. Thus the two statements form a commentary on one another and may be collated to help discover their meaning.

Table 12.2

1:17		
to preach the gospel	not in wisdom of words	lest the cross of Christ be emptied
2:4-5		
my λόγος and my κήρυγμα	not in persuasive words of wisdom	lest your faith (πίστις) rest on the σοφία of man and not the δύναμις of God

A comparison of the two statements sheds useful light on the meaning of the ἵνα clause of 1 Corinthians 1:17. In what sense would preaching the gospel in σοφίᾳ λόγου empty or make void the cross of Christ? A comparison of the two clauses suggests that the issue in 1:17 has nothing to do with an alleged Corinthian theology that vitiated the cross. The issue here, as in 2:4-5, is the form or manner of preaching.[16] Paul says that the form of preaching represented by the words ἐν σοφίᾳ λόγου must be avoided lest it engender an inappropriate (that is, false) response in the audience (1 Cor 2:5). It is in this sense that the cross may be emptied. The listeners may respond to the "wisdom of man" (σοφίᾳ ἀνθρώπων, AT) rather than the true object of response, the cross of Christ, which is the "power of God" (δυνάμει θεοῦ, 2:5; cf. 1 Cor 1:18, 24; Rom 1:16).

Commentators have sometimes puzzled over the way in which matters of form could void the power of the cross. But just here is where our earlier exploration of the relevant features of ancient rhetoric pays its dividends. To understand this point, and to prepare ourselves for grasping the full import of the argument that will follow, it will be useful to recall our summary of the dynamic on which the Greco-Roman orator depended.

Classical rhetoric assumed that the orator could do little to change the given aspects of the rhetorical situation. These aspects were merely there, "given" because they depended on who it was the orator faced, when, where and in what circumstances. They were not usually under the orator's control. In any case, changing these givens was not the point. Once the orator's goal was established, the point of the exercise was to manage these givens and work within their

---

[16]Cf. also 2 Cor 10:10. There it is Paul's λόγος, in contrast to his letters, that is considered weak and despicable. This would seem to throw the focus on matters of form, unless one is willing to argue that Paul had one "content" for his preaching and another for his letters, a dubious proposal. If it was the content the Corinthians objected to, they would surely have found Paul's letters as deficient as his preaching.

constraints so as to accomplish the predetermined result. Hence the orator's work was circumscribed in two important ways. Like an inventor attempting to build a machine out of makeshift parts, the orator found his efforts always bound and directed both by the nature of the available materials and the purpose of the thing. And the genius of the orator, like the genius of the inventor, lay in how well he could adapt to these constraints. Given this audience, given this subject, given this occasion, in the light of this goal, what are the various persuasive possibilities? Which of them would likely be most effective and in what arrangement? How might they be expressed and put across so as to achieve maximum impact? The ability to ask and answer these questions successfully, and then to execute the result before an audience, was what constituted an orator, and it was just this set of skills that ancient rhetoric was designed to teach.

It is crucial to underscore, then, the essential dynamic that lay behind Greco-Roman rhetoric. It was the dynamic of rhetorical adaptation, and the process in its entirety depended on the speaker. In the Grand Equation of ancient rhetoric the orator's efforts, incarnated in the message he finally delivered, were the variable required to make the equation work. If he could effectively analyze the demands of the rhetorical situation, devise a way of meeting them and then carry the whole thing off, he might be successful. The audience would be swayed, and the credit would accrue to him and his nimble rhetorical skills. If he was not up to the demands, to that degree he would fail. The audience would remain unmoved, and the orator would bear the onus. The entire process rested like an inverted pyramid on the orator's ability, in a wide variety of situations and sometimes on short notice, to discover arguments, organize them well, phrase them forcefully and then deliver the result with power.

All of this is relevant to our present discussion because it is precisely this human dynamic—the dynamic of Greco-Roman rhetoric—that Paul is here disavowing.[17] He is insisting that it would have been inappropriate for him to have depended on such a dynamic because in this way the results would have been rooted in his own facility as an orator, his own ability to adapt malleably to the rhetorical demands, his own capacity to manipulate the persuasive possibilities of the rhetorical situ-

---

[17]The term *dynamic* is perhaps the closest we can come to capturing the essence of δύναμις as it is used in the context of rhetoric; see, e.g., Aristotle, *Rhetoric* 1.2.1; Aristides, *To Plato* 302. The δύναμις λόγου represents the power or capacity to harness ideas and language to persuade, to create πίστις. This capacity to actualize the kinetic power of λόγοι is what is meant by the dynamic of rhetoric.

ation so as to engender πίστις in his audience.[18] Instead, Paul envisioned a wholly different dynamic, a dynamic that is inherent in the gospel itself. Paul considered the gospel of Christ crucified to be the δύναμις θεοῦ (1 Cor 1:18, 24; Rom 1:16) and as such to possess a persuasive dynamic all its own.[19] He does not explain here the workings of this divine dynamic; he merely asserts his determination to abide by it. He was simply an annunciator of this gospel. Only in this way could he be assured that the πίστις of his listeners would be the product of this divine dynamic rather than something of his own creation.[20]

---

[18] The semantics of the term πίστις are notoriously complex, shading in various contexts from "faith," "belief" or "conviction" to that which *generates* faith, belief or conviction—that is, "proof." Cf. p. 72 above, n. 20. But Winter's argument for rendering πίστις as "proof" in 1 Cor 2:5 (2002, pp. 159-60) is idiosyncratic and has gained no visible following. As Ong says, "*Pistis*, the Greek term for faith among the early Christians, which Paul says 'comes from hearing' (Romans 10:17), is the same word that occurs in rhetoric texts for the conviction that the public speaker undertakes to establish in his hearers" (1983, p. 5).

With Ljungman (1964, p. 106), we may best understand πίστις in Paul against a biblical and rabbinic background. Πίστις in Paul, says Ljungman, "is 'trust in' Christ. . . . [It] signifies man's 'believing' God, man acknowledges 'the truth' manifested through Christ. God, in his action . . . is acknowledged by man to be right; he is 'faithful' and 'righteous.' Man 'believes' him" (p. 107). Yet this point need not abrogate Ong's observation above, or Kinneavy's effort (1987) to demonstrate in the New Testament's use of πίστις nuances derived from its role in the context of rhetoric. For Paul πίστις was an unproblematic term, and he could use it in its customary sense without discomfort. This is because Paul was not focused in 1 Cor 1-4 on πίστις as the destination; his focus was the means used to generate πίστις within his listeners. It was not the herald's task to produce belief as it was the persuader's; so Barrett (1987, p. 14): "In the Gospel the voice of Christ himself is heard (Rom 10:14), and it is this that creates its contact with the hearer." Paul was determined to depend on the proclaimed word of the cross, so that in the end if the listener came to πίστις it would be the evident product of "the power of God" and not "the wisdom of man." Paul was confident of this divine power and was determined to avoid intruding upon it.

[19] Fitzmyer (1998, p. 153): Paul "views the gospel not merely as an abstract message of salvation or as a series of propositions about Christ (e.g., 'Jesus is Lord') which human beings are expected to apprehend and give assent to, but rather as a salvific force unleashed by God himself in human history through the person, ministry, passion, death, and resurrection of Jesus, bringing with it effects that human beings can appropriate by faith in him"; Betz (1986, pp. 35, 36): "The gospel is understood to exercise a certain authority over human beings, playing a normative role linked to its kerygmatic character. It accosts them, challenging them to conform to its proclamation"; "Wherein lies the power which makes Christian speech effective? . . . The power coming to expression in the Christian kerygma is a divine power supplied by the spirit of God." Cf. Hengel (1977a, pp. 23-28, 81).

[20] Some commentators avoid the force of Paul's point here, as when Barrett says of this "wisdom method of preaching" that Paul merely acknowledges that it was not his own without rejecting it outright. According to Barrett, the author of 1 Cor 2:6 and 12:8 could not have rejected it outright (1982, p. 11; cf. also Barrett, 1980, p. 103). But such views both ignore the plain statement of 1 Cor 1:17 and misconstrue 2:6 and 12:8. Neither 2:6 nor 12:8 is referring to what Paul rejects in 1:17. We have already noted that 12:8 does not belong to the present discussion; on 2:6 see below. In point of fact, Paul unreservedly rejects σοφία λόγου for the preaching of the gospel.

Witherington avoids Paul's point in a different way. In his book *New Testament Rhetoric*, for example, he argues strongly that Paul was a sophisticated user of Greco-Roman rhetoric, in both

Paul seemed to conceive of these two persuasive dynamics—that of the rhetor and that of the cross—as mutually exclusive. To embrace the one was to abandon the other. It was largely a question of which of the two one decided to trust. When Paul came to Corinth he apparently made (or, more likely, reinforced) a conscious decision (1 Cor 2:2) to depend as much as was in him on the power of the cross alone, lest the purely human element of persuasion interfere with the spiritual dynamic of the cross. Paul feared that operating according to the rhetor's dynamic would encroach upon the cross's Spirit-driven power to create belief. This is what he means when he asserts in 1 Corinthians 1:17 that he could not preach the gospel in σοφίᾳ λόγου lest the cross of Christ be emptied.

THE TWO DYNAMICS IN GALATIANS

In his commentary on Galatians, J. Louis Martyn provides an unusually insightful analysis of these contrasting dynamics, that of the rhetor and that of the cross. Echoing 1 Corinthians 1–4, Martyn shows the Apostle Paul in Galatians repudiating Greco-Roman rhetoric for the purposes of preaching. Yet, says Martyn, more is involved in this repudiation "than a negative portrait of a rhetorician." The Apostle "combines the assertion of gospel-mission with the denial of gospel-persuasion, and that combination causes one to ask what Paul is saying about *the gospel* God has called him to preach.... With theological rigor... we have to ask... what Paul can actually mean when he says that his gospel is preached apart from attempts to persuade." In other words, why does Paul feel the need to distance himself from the role of the persuader?

Regarding the rhetor's dynamic, we have documented in this book and summarized again in the preceding paragraphs the purely human psychological framework on which Greco-Roman persuasion was built. Martyn shows that this process of ferreting out the persuasive possibilities inherent in the rhetorical situation and then marshaling them to create πίστις in the hearer was precisely what, given his purposes, was unavailable to Paul. Why? Because Paul's gospel is not "what human beings normally

---

his speeches and his letters. Yet this book is devoid of any reference to 1 Cor 1:17, 1:21, or 2:1–5. As a well-known commentator on 1 Corinthians, Witherington was certainly aware of these passages, but he apparently would like it both ways. On the one hand, he says, during the first century preaching results were dependent on the application of powerful persuasive techniques: "How was one to change the cultural script so that truth was seen as the top value in the value hierarchy? This would take powerful rhetoric indeed" (2009a, p. 18). Yet he also insists that such persuasive prowess was not and is not sufficient: "According to Paul and others, it was not mere rhetorical skill that persuaded people but the divine content of the message" as applied by the Spirit (p. 240). Paul's concern about the potential incompatibility of these two things—that is, the ways human persuasive strategies can potentially usurp the work of the Spirit in creating πίστις—is left unaddressed.

have in mind when they speak of 'good news.'" Martyn argues that this problem "erects a clear roadblock to the normal use of rhetoric.... The rhetorician, knowing that both he and his hearers are human beings, builds his argument—to a large extent—on the basis of various cognitive and emotional elements that are already present in the minds and hearts of his hearers.... Were [Paul] to take these notions and ideas as his point of departure, he could indeed speak in a persuasive way, causing his auditors to say, 'Yes, that makes sense.' ... This, however, Paul cannot do, for the foundation of his message is something that is not already present in the minds and hearts of his hearers. He does not and cannot build his sermon on the basis of his hearers' notions and ideas, for ... what human beings have in mind when they speak of 'good news' is not the gospel. In short, what human beings already have in their minds cannot serve as the point of departure from which one can book a through train to the gospel. And that fact necessarily precludes one of the basic stratagems normally used in the art of persuasion." "In his initial proclamation, Paul cannot take as the foundation of his rhetoric substantive presuppositions he knows to be already present in the minds of his hearers." Paul's argument must start from an entirely different "non-rhetorical point of departure": "Christ's faithful death and resurrection in our behalf."

This brings Martyn to his second point, what we have called the dynamic of the cross. The issue here, he says, is "the genesis of faith," which is to say, what it is that generates authentic πίστις. "Although Paul is consistent in saying that God called him to preach the gospel to Gentiles (1:16), he is equally consistent in his certainty that it is not his powers of persuasion that elicit faith (1 Cor 2:4). The power to kindle faith resides solely with God's gospel (Gal 3:2; Rom 1:16-17), and that gospel does not make sense [to natural man]. It is, in fact, 'a stumbling block to Jews and foolishness to Gentiles' (1 Cor 1:23). But that means that the gospel Paul preaches—bringing its own criteria of perception and plausibility—is not and cannot be a message by which he seeks in the rhetorical sense to persuade.... [Thus] we begin to understand Paul's insistence that, in preaching the gospel, he is not a rhetorician."

According to Martyn, "the gospel has the effect of placing at issue the nature of argument itself. That is to say, since the gospel is God's own utterance, it is not and can never be subject to ratiocinative criteria that have been developed apart from it." Paul thus evinces a different "rhetoric," one that "presupposes God's action through Paul's words." This "Pauline rhetoric" involves taking the herald's rather than the persuader's stance. The distinction between these two rhetorics—Greco-Roman rhetoric and "Paul's rhetoric"—is "closely related to that between *an argument* and *an announcement*. To take an example, in writing this letter [to the Galatians] Paul is not at all formulating an argument designed to persuade the Galatians that faith is better than observance of the Law. He is constructing an announcement designed to wake the Galatians up to the real cosmos."

"The proclamation of Christ's faithful death is what has the power to elicit our trusting faith." "Paul is serious," of course, "when he allows human beings to be the subject of the verb 'to place one's trust.' Those who believe in Christ are not puppets. . . . But, just as these persons are not puppet believers, so they are not believers as a result of an act of their own autonomous wills, as though the gospel were an event in which two alternatives were placed before an autonomous decider, and faith were one of two decisions the human being could make autonomously. On the contrary, for Paul faith does not lie in the realm of human possibility. . . . For faith is not an option human beings can choose. Thus, when Paul speaks about placing one's trust in Christ, he is pointing to a deed that reflects not the freedom of the will, but rather God's freeing of the will. . . . The gospel is itself an invasive event, not merely the offering of a new option. . . . The act of trust does not have its origin in the human being. On the contrary, . . . that act springs from the proclamation of the risen Lord. It is incited by the preached message (Gal 3:2; Rom 10:17). It is empowered by the Spirit."

According to Martyn, then, Paul understood "himself to be a slave of Christ rather than a rhetorician who is seeking to persuade those to whom he speaks. For . . . the power to persuade—specifically the power to elicit faith—resides in the glad tidings of Christ's death in our behalf, and only in that glad tiding." "Paul does not suffer under the illusion that it is his rhetorical skill that elicits faith. He knows, on the contrary, that, when he first came to the Galatians, it was God who kindled their faith via the event of the oral gospel." Thus in Galatians 3:2, when Paul asks, "Did you receive the Spirit by works of the law or by hearing with faith?" the Apostle "is not asking the Galatians which of two human acts served as the generative locus in which they received the Spirit, a decision on their part to keep the Law or a decision on their part to hear with faith." "Faith is awakened by the gospel, the gospel has as its goal the awakening of faith." The question of Galatians 3:2 is thus "whether the Galatians received the Spirit as the result of their observance of the Law or as the result of God's message, . . . the gospel that has the power to elicit, to ignite, to kindle faith (*pistis*). . . . His focus lies on the apocalyptic event of God's action in Christ and—to say the same thing in other words—on the faith-eliciting message in which Christ is proclaimed. . . . The generative context in which the Spirit fell upon the Galatians was not their act of commencing observance of the Law; it was God's act in the revelatory proclamation of Jesus Christ suffering crucifixion, the act by which God kindled their faith" (1997, pp. 22-23, 146-48, 276-77, 288-89).

13

Paul's Argument Begun

1 Corinthians 1:17-20

The impetus for Paul's disavowal of σοφία λόγου in 1 Corinthians 1:17 arose primarily from a segment of the Corinthian congregation. They were the ones who so valued Greek eloquence and wisdom, not to mention the social status typically associated with them,[1] that they were critical when Paul failed to measure up. As Paul uses it here, the term σοφία therefore grows out of his understanding of their complaints about his ministry. What they missed in Paul was any semblance of that splendid confection of felicitous phrases, impressive argumentation and elegant presence they so applauded in the Greco-Roman orators who paraded before them. There is no indication here that they wanted Paul to modify the theological content of the gospel itself. At most they wanted him to clothe that message in the captivating λόγοι of Greek eloquence, a rhetorical form all would recognize as σοφός. But this, for theological reasons that were apparently lost on the Corinthians, Paul was unwilling to attempt. His task therefore was to spell out these theological reasons and show how they led inexorably not to Greek eloquence but to his own *modus operandi* as a herald.

1:18—The Word of the Cross

Essentially Paul will argue that his *modus operandi* as a preacher was not only justified by, but in fact required by, a fundamental principle of God's dealings with the world. In his wisdom God chooses to work through means that the world finds weak, foolish and unimpressive, so that there can be no question in

---

[1]As Pogoloff says of the term σοφία λόγου in 1 Cor 1:17, "When σοφία and λόγος are combined in ancient usage, they frequently imply far more than just technical skill at language. Rather, they imply a whole world of social status related to speech" (1992, p. 113; cf. pp. 114-19).

the end as to who has accomplished the result. At the most fundamental level, the cross itself illustrates this principle; the makeup of the Corinthian church also illustrates this principle; but third—and this is the goal of his immediate argument—so also does Paul's ministry. The Corinthians must see this so that they will cease measuring the Apostle against a false worldly standard, thereby giving occasion to divisions within the church.

Beyond the unique nuances of the verb εὐαγγελίζεσθαι (1 Cor 1:17), the phrase "the word of the cross" (ὁ λόγος . . . ὁ τοῦ σταυροῦ, 1 Cor 1:18) is the first description we find of Paul's preaching.[2] The term ὁ λόγος describes in the most general way the form of the preaching while the genitive τοῦ σταυροῦ supplies the content. It is important to note that the Apostle clearly wished to keep both elements in view here. This may be seen by setting "the cross" as the subject of the verb (as in the previous verse) and deleting ὁ λόγος altogether. Such a construction would have given perfect sense if Paul were only interested in matters of content, but it obviously leaves out an important ingredient in Paul's thought. That ingredient is the matter of form. The repeated article in the construction serves to prevent the focus from shifting away from form to content and balances the stress between the two: "The λόγος—namely, the 'regarding the cross' λόγος."[3]

Yet if ὁ λόγος retains Paul's focus on form, it is nevertheless a very bland term, which in itself tells us little about what the form might be. Since ὁ λόγος . . . ὁ τοῦ σταυροῦ is a reference to Paul's own preaching, we know that this must somehow stand in contrast to the form represented by the phrase ἐν σοφίᾳ λόγου, which he has just rejected. Thus we can begin to see what form ὁ λόγος is not. But we do not yet know positively what its form is. We must look to the remainder of Paul's argument to fill in the details.

In order to begin providing some substance to the meaning of ὁ λόγος . . . ὁ τοῦ σταυροῦ in 1 Corinthians 1:18, it may be useful to preview some of these details here. What we discover is that according to Paul the form of his preaching was determinedly straightforward and open. In contrast to the principles of Greco-Roman rhetoric, the persuasive efficacy of which was for the most part inversely proportional to the audience's awareness that such

---

[2] Unless one includes τὸ μαρτύριον τοῦ Χριστοῦ, 1 Cor 1:6. See below, pp. 187-88, on the significance of the term μαρτύριον to Paul's argument.

[3] Blass and Debrunner (1961, pp. 141-42): A substantive with an attributive genitive in the postposition and a repeated article is an unusual construction designed to stress the substantive (in this case, λόγος) rather than the adjectival element (in this case τοῦ σταυροῦ).

principles were being employed,[4] Paul's approach focused on the straightforward announcement of the gospel.

Among the clearest indicators of this contrast are the terms Paul uses to describe his own preaching. They are his standard terms, of course, employed consistently throughout his writings. But this only serves to reinforce the impression that Paul had from the outset given studied attention to the particular form of his preaching. In 1 Corinthians 1:18–2:5 we see the full implications of what he had chosen and why.[5]

It is too seldom recognized, much less appreciated, that the verbs Paul uses to describe his public speaking—such as εὐαγγελίζω, κηρύσσω, καταγγέλλω and μαρτυρέω—are decidedly non-rhetorical. No self-respecting orator used such verbs to describe his own *modus operandi*. Thus, even though they deal with the subject of human communication, such verbs play no significant role in the rhetorical literature. This is understandable because the essential form of communication they describe is very different from that of the orator; in fact, at its core it is the antithesis of rhetorical behavior.[6]

---

[4]See Aristotle, *Rhetoric* 3.2.4-5; Cicero, *Or. Brut.* 209; Tacitus, *Dial.* 19-20; cf. "Longinus" on the use of figures, *On the Sublime* 17.1-3. See also pp. 98-99, above.

[5]The failure to appreciate this point undermines Horrell's claim (1996, p. 122) that 1 Cor 1–4 constitutes, not an articulation of Paul's fundamental view of preaching, but merely an ad hoc response to the unique situation in Corinth. Horrell considers "Paul's formulation of the word of the cross and its implications" found in 1 Cor 1–4 to be "a specific and contextual attempt to confront the *hybris* and competitive pride of the prominent Corinthians." Thus, he says, "Such a polemical passage cannot be taken to reflect Paul's constant 'theory of preaching.'"

But two simple points count against this claim: (1) The "formulation of the word of the cross and its implications" that we find in 1 Cor 1–4 is Paul's standard formulation. The language he employs is his standard language, and the theological rationale, while fuller here than anywhere else, is nonetheless his standard rationale (on which see below on Rom 10, pp. 186-87). There is nothing in Paul's description of his preaching in 1 Cor 1–4 that is unique to Corinth; nor do the Corinthian specifics give it some new shape. On the contrary, Paul anchors his approach to preaching in God's own fundamental *modus operandi* in the world (1 Cor 1:27-29), thereby giving his argument universal relevance. (2) Horrell's conclusion is based on a mistaken premise: 1 Cor 1–4, he says, cannot be both "a specific and contextual" argument and a general "theory of preaching." But this is plainly a false choice. One of the key values of a general theory is its ability to inform specific situations. In this passage Paul is attempting to defuse the specific problems of the Corinthian church—in this instance, the ἔριδες reported by Chloe's people (1 Cor 1:11), at the core of which lay "the *hybris* and competitive pride" of the Corinthians that manifested itself in complaints about Paul's preaching (see above, pp. 132-41)—by laying out the theological rationale for why he had to operate as he did. Grasping and internalizing that rationale was the key to discrediting the worldly critique of Paul's preaching and healing the unfortunate quarrels. The argument of 1 Cor 1–4 is thus a both/and argument, not either/or.

[6]See, e.g., Nock (1933, p. 188). For a discussion of the "argumentation" inherent in rhetoric, in contrast to the "proclamation" inherent in these verbs, see Perelman and Olbrechts-Tyteca (1969, pp. 1-17).

The best examples of this antithesis are the terms associated with the ancient herald: κῆρυξ, κηρύσσειν and κήρυγμα. When describing his own ministry Paul typically used the language not of the orator or sophist but of this very different cultural figure. Paul's use of the herald motif was of course metaphorical; he obviously was not claiming that he literally belonged to the ancient Greco-Roman guild of κήρυκες or *praecones*.[7] His point was that his calling was *like* that of the herald. What was it about the herald that made this common figure such a useful analogue? We can appreciate the distinctiveness of the herald's role only by contrasting it with the role of those other voluble public speakers of the day, the orators.[8]

Unlike the orator, the herald's task was not to create a powerful message custom designed to generate belief (πίστις) or persuasion (πεισμονή) in the recipients. The herald's task was to convey as faithfully as possible the already-constituted message of another. He was simply an agent, a messenger.[9] As Jerome Murphy-O'Connor says, "The one idea that emerges with clarity" from an examination of the term κῆρυξ "is the subordinate character of the person it designated. He was a mouthpiece, devoid of all personal significance, without power to add to or subtract from the message entrusted to him. It was his message that was all important."[10] Thus the herald's task was essentially monological, a demonstration not of persuasive prowess but of faithfulness to the one who commissioned him. Says Furnish, "The herald was not expected to be 'original'—it was imperative that the message he brought *not* be his own, but that it be the message of another."[11] The herald was commissioned to declare, to make known, the message of the one he represented.

And so it was with Paul. His goal was to see that his listeners heard and understood the good news of Jesus Christ, and he surely willed them to embrace that good news. But unlike the orators, the use of rhetorical technique to generate that embrace—that is, to induce conviction or πίστις within his listeners—was beyond his commission. Such effects must be left to the Spirit working through the dynamic of the cross among the κλητοί. To enter into that realm armed with

---

[7]On which, see pp. 206-7 below.
[8]Cf. the juxtaposition of heraldry with rhetoric in Dio Chrysostom, *Discourses* 2.17-18; cf. also 75.9 and 77.39 with 76.4-5. As Plato observed in *The Statesman* (260D), "Heralds receive the purposes of others in the form of orders, and then give the orders a second time to others."
[9]Speaking of his initial preaching in Corinth (1 Cor 15:3): "I delivered (παραδίδωμι) to you as of first importance what I also received." On παραδίδωμι ("to transmit as a courier"), see Herodotus, *Histories* VIII.98.
[10]Murphy-O'Connor (1964, p. 50); see also Friedrich (1965, pp. 687-88).
[11]Furnish (1963, p. 55).

the techniques of human persuasion was to usurp the power of the cross and run the risk of false results (1 Cor 2:5). Hence the usefulness to the Apostle of the language of the herald for articulating his own approach to preaching.

THE SALVIFIC ROLE OF THE HERALD

Paul viewed the function of the herald as central not only to his own calling but to God's entire plan of redemption. This point is nowhere more clearly expressed than in Romans 10:12-17. Says Barrett (1987, p. 3) of this passage, "New Testament Christianity was a proclaimed faith. 'Faith comes as a result of hearing, and hearing comes through the word of Christ' (Rom 10:17). It is this that makes it distinctive among the cults of antiquity, and, it may be added, of the modern world also."

The focus of Romans 10 is the salvation (10:1, 9, 10, 13) God has provided his rebellious creatures. God has graciously provided this salvation through the life, death and resurrection of his Son, Jesus Christ. To appropriate this salvation, however, one must be willing to recognize and call on Jesus as Lord and Savior (10:13). But "how . . . will they call on him in whom they have not believed? And how are they to believe in him of whom they have never heard? And how are they to hear without someone preaching [κηρύσσοντος]? And how are they to preach [κηρύξωσιν] unless they are sent [ἀποσταλῶσιν]?" In this last term can be heard Paul's conception of his own commission as one "called by the will of God to be an ἀπόστολος of Christ Jesus" (e.g., 1 Cor 1:1; cf. Rom 1:1; 2 Cor 1:1; Gal 1:1). See Fee (2007, p. 136) and Dickson (2003, pp. 153-77) on the Old Testament, perhaps Isianic, roots of this calling.

The critical role of the commissioned *heralds* in God's plan of redemption becomes clear in Romans 10. First, God provides a way of salvation through the death and resurrection of his incarnate Son, Jesus Christ. Second, he commissions and dispatches messengers to declare this gracious provision to the world. Third, the messengers fulfill their commission by faithfully heralding (κηρύσσομεν, Rom 10:8) this good news to all. Finally, the listeners are called on to give this announcement the reception it deserves: that is, they must be willing to (1) open themselves to hearing it (as in Jesus' repeated invitation, "He who has ears to hear, let him hear"); (2) attend to what it says about God's salvific provision in Christ; (3) receive the message as true and welcome it as the good news it is; and consequently (4) recognize and embrace ("call on"; cf. "receive," Jn 1:12) as Lord and Savior this Jesus who stands at the message's center. Says Barrett (1987, pp. 12-13), "The hearer of the message accepts it, receives the word that he has heard. He repents; he puts his trust in Christ and accepts him as the redeeming and authoritative Lord."

Thus did Paul view the role of the commissioned herald. The herald served as a crucial link in this chain of salvific consequences. Paul gives no impression that it was God's plan to send out into the world a team of persuaders whose assignment it was to generate πίστις in their listeners. Instead God sent out announcers, so that when faith (πίστις) was the outcome, that faith would be the product not of human ingenuity but of the Spirit's convicting application of the messenger's word about Christ (διὰ ῥήματος Χριστοῦ, Rom 10:17) within τοῖς σῳζομένοις (1 Cor 1:18), that is, τοῖς κλητοῖς (1 Cor 1:24; cf. Rom 1:6).

A second motif, that of the μάρτυς ("witness"), reinforces the same point. The μάρτυς was unlike the κῆρυξ in that he did not speak for another; he spoke for himself. But what the μάρτυς held in common with the κῆρυξ was the absence of rhetorical adaptation for the sake of persuasion.

The ancient witness was not an orator. The role of the μάρτυς was to give testimony to something he knew or had seen. The verb μαρτυρέω describes the act of giving such testimony; the terms μαρτυρία or μαρτύριον refer to the substance of that testimony. The frequency of this language in Paul's letters (in 1 Cor alone, 1:6; 2:1; 15:15) suggests that he was partial to it, perhaps because of the instructions he himself had received in an earlier setting: "The Lord said, 'I am Jesus whom you are persecuting. But rise and stand upon your feet, for I have appeared to you for this purpose, to appoint you as a servant and witness [μάρτυς] to the things in which you have seen me and to those in which I will appear to you'" (Acts 26:15-16).

In the *Rhetoric* Aristotle claimed that the artfulness of rhetoric relates only to "proofs." These proofs constitute different forms of demonstration (ἀπόδειξις), "since we are most strongly convinced when we suppose anything to have been demonstrated."[12] But not all proofs, says Aristotle, are the same. Some "are inartificial [ἄτεχνοι] others artificial [ἔντεχνοι]."

> By the former I understand all those which have not been furnished by ourselves but were already in existence, such as witnesses [μάρτυρες], tortures [i.e., evidence obtained under duress], contracts and the like; by the latter, all that can be constructed by system and by our own efforts. Thus we have only to make use of the former, whereas we must invent the latter.[13]

The artfulness of the rhetor stands in contrast to the artless report of witnesses. The testimony of the μάρτυς, like a contract, simply is what it is. It can be used more or less artfully (cf. 1.15.1-33) by the rhetor, but the testimony itself is ἄτεχνοι. It is

---

[12]Aristotle, *Rhetoric* 1.1.11.
[13]Ibid., 1.1.2.

without its own artfulness. This is because it is not crafted according to the τέχνη of rhetoric.[14] It consists merely of someone reporting what he knows or has seen. Hence the usefulness of the image of the μάρτυς for Paul and his ministry.

According to Acts, Jesus' Pentecostal promise was that his followers would become his μάρτυρες throughout the world (Acts 1:8). This was the essence of the role to which Paul understood himself to have been commissioned. He was not in the business of persuasion, as were the orators; he was in the business of giving faithful witness or testimony (Acts 26:16; cf. Acts 22:15; 23:11), following God's own model (1 Jn 5:9-11). We see the same pattern in the Old Testament prophets, true and false (for example, Jon 1:2; Mic 3:5; cf. Acts 10:43), in the final prophet, John the Baptist (Mt 3:1; Jn 1:7, 34), in Jesus himself (Mt 4:7; Lk 4:18-19; Jn 18:37), in the Spirit (Jn 15:26) and in the commission of the other apostles (Mt 10:7; Mk 3:14; 16:15, 20; Jn 15:27; Acts 4:33; 8:25; 10:42; cf. 1 Jn 1:2; 4:14). Like the prophets, the apostles were conveyers of another's message; they were announcers: "What I tell you in the dark, say in the light, and what you hear whispered, proclaim [κηρύξατε] on the housetops" (Mt 10:27). And so, Jesus says, shall it be until the end of time (Mt 24:14).[15]

In just such terms did Paul view his ministry.[16] He perceived his public speaking in a different light from the orators so prominent in his day. He had been entrusted with a message and it was his task to declare it to all who would hear. What's more, he was under no illusions about the reception this an-

---

[14]See pp. 60-61 above.
[15]Hence D. Stanley's (1956) characterization of the preaching of the gospel "as testimony rather than proof.... The Bible is almost exclusively concerned with testimony.... The term proof has never formed part of the biblical vocabulary of salvation, whilst testimony is a key word in the soteriologies of both OT and NT. It is by testimony, ... not by proof, as Paul reminds us, 'that God has been pleased to save those who have faith (1 Cor 1,21).'"
[16]But not Paul alone. See the same terms (*proclaimer, testifier*) applied to the entire prophetic tradition (on which, see Costa, 2013) in Acts 10:36-43: "As for the word [τὸν λόγον] that he sent to Israel, preaching good news [εὐαγγελιζόμενος] of peace through Jesus Christ (he is Lord of all), you yourselves know what happened throughout all Judea, beginning from Galilee after the baptism that John proclaimed [ἐκήρυξεν]: how God anointed Jesus of Nazareth with the Holy Spirit and with power. He went about doing good and healing all who were oppressed by the devil, for God was with him. And we are witnesses [μάρτυρες] of all that he did both in the country of the Jews and in Jerusalem. They put him to death by hanging him on a tree, but God raised him on the third day and made him to appear, not to all the people but to us who had been chosen by God as witnesses [μάρτυσι], who ate and drank with him after he rose from the dead. And he commanded us to preach [κηρύξαι] to the people and to testify [διαμαρτύρασθαι] that he is the one appointed by God to be judge of the living and the dead. To him all the prophets bear witness [μαρτυροῦσιν] that everyone who believes in him receives forgiveness of sins through his name." For a discussion of the role of the apostle as a representative of Christ, and the consequent centrality of proclamation in contrast to any other form of discourse, see Rengstorf (1969, pp. 29-42, 85-96).

nouncing would receive. Yet adapting the message so as to render it more palatable and impressive to those who otherwise would find it scandalous or foolish was out of the question. That could only lead to false results. His assignment was simply to make Christ known, leaving it to the Spirit of God to take care of the rest.[17] Barrett helpfully expresses this non-rhetorical emphasis with the verb *to placard*.[18] Paul's mission was simply to placard Christ crucified. Perhaps his clearest statement of such placarding is found in Galatians 3:1: "O foolish Galatians! . . . It was before your eyes [οἷς κατ' ὀφθαλμοὺς] that Jesus Christ was publicly portrayed [προγράφω, "to set forth publicly"] as crucified."[19] Such an approach could scarcely have been in starker contrast to the kaleidoscopic, chameleon-like audience adaptation taught by Greco-Roman rhetoric.

A UNIQUE EXCEPTION

Among the scores of references to his own preaching, Paul's use of πείθειν ("to persuade") in 2 Corinthians 5:11 is the sole occurrence of a term that fits comfortably within the rhetorical tradition. Does this mean that Paul embraced the dynamic of Greco-Roman persuasion in his preaching? The evidence suggests otherwise. Though the rhetoricians spoke often of πείθειν, the verb was not merely a technical term that always and necessarily carried such implications. It was used more widely and popularly in settings that carried no such overtones. For instance, Philo can use πείθω when speaking of Abraham (*De Virtutibus* 217) without suggesting that Abraham was indebted in some way to Greco-Roman rhetoric. In such a context the verb specifies nothing more than the agent through whom listeners arrive at some conviction. In this less specific sense, of course, all of Paul's results were the product of πείθειν (on this point see below, pp. 292-306), which explains Luke's freedom in using πείθω of Paul's ministry of proclamation (Acts 13:43; 17:4; 18:4; 19:8; 28:23-24). For his own part, though, Paul typically avoids the verb, no doubt due to its rhetorical overtones (cf. Gal 1:10; 1 Cor 2:4). Even in the one instance where Paul does use πείθω of his preaching, the context indicates that he means nothing more by it than can be discerned in his standard terminology.

For insight into Paul's approach to "persuasion," in striking contrast to that of the rhetoricians, see Luke's description in Acts 28:23-24: "From morning till evening [Paul] expounded [ἐξετίθετο, "to set forth, declare, explain"] to them, testifying [διαμαρτυρόμενος] to the kingdom of God and trying to convince [πείθων] them about Jesus both from the Law of

---

[17]For varying expressions of this same thought, see 2 Cor 1:19; 5:20; Gal 1:6; 3:1; 5:8; 1 Thess 1:4-5; 2:13; 2 Thess 2:13-14.
[18]Barrett (1968, p. 51); see also Barrett (1982, p. 11).
[19]Cf. Fitzmyer (1998, p. 154) on evangelism as "re-presenting" Jesus to the listeners.

Moses and from the Prophets. And some were convinced [ἐπείθοντο] by what he said, but others disbelieved [ἠπίστουν]." Similarly, Acts 17:2-4: "And Paul went [into the synagogue], as was his custom, and on three Sabbath days he reasoned [διελέξατο] with them from the Scriptures, explaining [διανοίγων, "to open up, expound"] and proving [παρατιθέμενος, "to place before, to commend"] that it was necessary for the Christ to suffer and to rise from the dead, and saying, 'This Jesus, whom I proclaim [καταγγέλλω] to you, is the Christ.' And some of them were persuaded [ἐπείσθησαν] and joined Paul and Silas, as did a great many of the devout Greeks and not a few of the leading women"; see also 1 Corinthians 1:6, "the testimony (μαρτύριον) about Christ." According to Luke, Paul's rhetorical approach drew not on the orator's repertoire of persuasive strategies designed to engender πίστις, but on authoritative, Scripture-backed witness to the crucified Christ. Some were "persuaded" by this witness and turned to follow Jesus, but theirs, Paul would argue, was a response generated by the Spirit's application of the announced gospel (1 Cor 1:18; Rom 1:16), not by the messenger's rhetorical ingenuity (1 Cor 2:4-5). See also Galatians 5:8 where Paul insists that to be genuine, one's gospel "persuasion" (πεισμονὴ) must be engendered by "him who calls you" (ἐκ τοῦ καλοῦντος ὑμᾶς).

This straightforward, non-rhetorical approach to proclaiming the gospel is what is loosely summed up in the phrase "the word of the cross" in 1:18. It is precisely to this word, this placarding of Christ crucified, that listeners demonstrate different responses. To "those who are perishing" this λόγος is foolishness (μωρία; cf. 2 Cor 4:3-4). Its content, the cross, and its form, mere proclamation, both of which have by design been kept consistent with one another,[20] are alike unimpressive to the world. Neither is what the world recognizes as wise, powerful or grand. Consequently they are together dismissed as foolish. But to the ones "who are being saved"—that is, says Paul, "to us"—this same λόγος appears as the very power of God (δύναμις θεοῦ). These have been given by the Spirit the capacity to see through to the divine perspective and so have recognized in this placarded Christ the truth of salvation.

It is important to stress again that λόγος is the subject of both verbs (ἐστίν ... ἐστιν) in 1:18. It is not simply the cross that is μωρία or δύναμις, but ὁ λόγος, the simple *placarding* of the cross. Commentators sometimes lose sight of this point, as when E. Ellis says, "'Christ crucified' is set in opposition to the ... 'wisdom of

---

[20]Heinrici (1896, p. 84) titles the section 2:1-5, "The Procedure of Paul, How It Corresponds to the Nature of the Gospel (1:18-25) and Preserves Its Power." Says Gillespie (1990, p. 154), "Just as the social composition of the Corinthian church corresponds to 'the word of the cross,' so also the ministry of the apostle corresponds to his message."

word.'"[21] The content of the message may not here be extricated from its form, nor vice versa. Paul intentionally holds them together precisely because he wants the Corinthians to see the inextricable relation between the two. To have cast the gospel into σοφίᾳ λόγου would have undermined rather than enhanced its power; it would have injected an unwanted human element that would have obscured the cross's power rather than displayed it. Hence the simple form, the straightforward exhibition of Christ crucified, was crucial to the transaction.

THE DOUBLE FOOLISHNESS OF THE PREACHING

On the obvious "foolishness" of the content of the preaching, Adams (2008, p. 129) says, "That God could be crucified was inconceivable in the minds of the ancients. To them, a god was powerful and had honour and would never allow themselves to be subjected to crucifixion. It would have been mind-boggling to them and would have had the appearance of foolishness." Martin Hengel takes the point one step further. Following Justin (*Apology* I, 13.4), Hengel (1977b, p. 1) associates the μωρία of the cross not merely with "a purely intellectual defect nor a lack of transcendental wisdom" but with μανία ("madness"). "The heart of the Christian message, which Paul described as the 'word of the cross' . . . , ran counter not only to Roman political thinking, but to the whole ethos of religion in ancient times and in particular to the ideas of God held by educated people. . . . To believe that the one pre-existent Son of the one true God, the mediator at creation and the redeemer of the world, had appeared in very recent times in the out-of-the-way Galilee as a member of the obscure people of the Jews, and even worse, had died the death of a common criminal on the cross, could only be regarded as a sign of madness" (pp. 5-6). See also Breytenbach (2009, pp. 348-49).

On the additional "foolishness" of expecting listeners to embrace such a repellant message on the simple pronouncement of its herald—apart from a powerful persuasive case shaped to meet the audience's demands for proof—see Quintilian (*Inst. or.* 12.10.69) on the "sheer folly" (*stultissimus*) of not adapting rhetorically to your audience. As Dio Chrysostom observed, the man who failed to adapt himself to the rhetorical demands of the occasion was considered "an ignoramus and worth but little" (*Discourses* 71:1; cf. 42:1-2).

1:19-20—The Old Testament Roots of Paul's Approach

Paul was concerned to show that his conception of proclamation was not merely his own. Thus in 1 Corinthians 1:19-20 he places his argument in the context of

---

[21]Ellis (1978, p. 73); so also Scroggs (1967, p. 36).

revelation. Referring to Isaiah 29:14 Paul notes that God long ago promised to bypass the world's wisdom and thereby demonstrate its vanity. The repeated questions introduced by the interrogative ποῦ each require a similar answer: the wisest, the most knowledgeable and the most articulate figures of the world are "nowhere" when it comes to knowing God.[22] These may be the ones who are most admired by the world, but all their proud wisdom, knowledge and verbal skills have left them short. And this is just as God purposed. It was his wise design that the world would not by means of its own strivings come to know him. It pleased God to accomplish the salvation of the race after an entirely different fashion. He would work through the foolishness of the proclamation (διὰ τῆς μωρίας τοῦ κηρύγματος). Moreover, he would save, not those who everyone thought by their intellectual and verbal skills could scale the heights, but rather τοὺς πιστεύοντας, that is, the ones who are willing merely to receive and humbly embrace the announced word of the cross for what it actually is, the wisdom of God.

CHRYSOSTOM ON THE WISE AND FOOLISH

St. John Chrysostom's commentary on these two ways of coming to God—including his overstatement of Paul's views on human wisdom (on which, see chap. 16 below)—was typical of the early church:

"Since then by [its] wisdom the world was unwilling to discover God, He employed what seemed to be foolishness, the Gospel [κηρύγματος], to persuade [ἔπεισεν] men; not by reasoning [λογισμῶν], but by faith [πίστεως]. It remains that where God's wisdom is, there is no longer need of man's. For before, to infer that He who made the world such and so great, must in all reason be a God possessed of a certain uncontrollable, unspeakable power; and by these means to apprehend Him—this was the part of human wisdom. But now we need no more reasonings, but faith alone. For to believe in Him that was crucified and buried, and to be fully persuaded [πεπληροφορῆσθαι] that this Person Himself both rose again and sat down on high; this needs not wisdom, nor reasonings, but faith. For the Apostles themselves came in not by wisdom, but by faith, and surpassed the heathen wise men in wisdom and loftiness, and that so much the more, as to raise disputings is less than to receive by faith the things of God. For this transcends all human understanding.

"But how did He destroy wisdom? Being made known to us by Paul and others like

---

[22]We will not seek to specify more closely the identity of the σοφός, γραμματεύς and συζητητής. As Conzelmann says, "No subtle distinctions are to be sought between the three concepts" (1975, p. 43; cf. Best, 1980, p. 20). But for a useful discussion of the background against which Paul's inclusion of the scribe alongside the wise man and debater should be viewed, see McKane (1965).

him, He showed it to be unprofitable. For towards receiving the evangelical proclamation [τὸ κήρυγμα τὸ εὐαγγελικὸν], neither is the wise profited at all by wisdom, nor the unlearned injured at all by ignorance. But if one may speak somewhat even wonderful, ignorance rather than wisdom is a condition suitable for that impression, and more easily dealt with. For the shepherd and the rustic will more quickly receive this, once for all both repressing all doubting thoughts and delivering himself to the Lord. In this way then He destroyed wisdom. For since she first cast herself down, she is ever after useful for nothing. Thus when she ought to have displayed her proper powers, and by the works to have seen the Lord, she would not. Wherefore though she were now willing to introduce herself, she is not able. For the matter is not of that kind; this way [ὁδὸς] of knowing God [θεογνωσίας] being far greater than the other. You see then, faith and simplicity [of mind, ἀφελείας] are needed, and this we should seek every where, and prefer it before the wisdom which is from without. For *God*, says he, *has made wisdom foolish*" (*Homilies on First Corinthians* iv.4).

The crucial term κήρυγμα in 1 Corinthians 1:21 again preserves Paul's dual emphasis on form and content[23] and, in this sense, stands synonymous with ὁ λόγος... ὁ τοῦ σταυροῦ of 1 Corinthians 1:18. As in that first reference to μωρία, it is here not simply the cross that is foolish; the foolishness resides also in the *proclamation* of the cross. To substitute simply ὁ σταυρός for κήρυγμα in 1:21 would again deny the sentence an important aspect of its meaning. Yet this is the effect of interpreting κήρυγμα strictly in terms of content, as is commonly done. In using the word κήρυγμα Paul has intentionally chosen a term that collapses form and content into one. In fact, though it need hardly be said that by any objective standard the content of the gospel would be uppermost to Paul, in terms of his present argument matters of form take precedence.

The complaints against Paul had to do with the *manner* or *form* of his preaching, not its content. Hence the point of this passage is to justify that form. In the immediate context the issue of form introduces this section (ἐν σοφίᾳ λόγου, 1 Cor 1:17) and, as we shall see in 1 Corinthians 2:1-5, issues of form conclude it. Moreover, in the justification that lies between, matters of content function in the subsidiary role of providing a rationale for why the form of Paul's preaching was necessary. For all of these reasons it is critically important not to wash the issue of form out of κήρυγμα in 1 Corinthians 1:21. To do so not only ignores the obvious verbal origin and aspect of this substantive (on which, see

---

[23]On this important point, see the following chapter.

the following chapter); it also bypasses a crucial—in fact, *the* crucial—element in the Apostle's present argument.

In summary, then, throughout these verses it is the *placarded* cross that is μωρία, σοφία, σκάνδαλον, δύναμις or ἀσθενές, depending on the perspective of the recipient. Commentators typically—and rightly—give much attention to the content aspect of Paul's argument throughout this section, but seldom give sufficient attention to matters of form. Yet the question of form constitutes the *raison d'être* of this section and cannot be ignored without distorting the Apostle's argument.

Paul's goal is nothing less than to defend his *modus operandi* as a preacher. To do so he must demonstrate that it is theologically inspired.[24] Hence he argues that he could not have operated otherwise; he was locked into simple proclamation—in contrast to the eloquent argumentation and εὐγλωττία of the rhetors—by the demands of the gospel itself. According to Paul, God desires to save those he calls, not through the psychological ingenuity of human persuasion, but through the "weakness" of the announced word of the cross, the message of Christ crucified.

There was for the Apostle therefore no place in the proclamation of the gospel for those brilliant rhetorical moves that, depending on the genius of the one marshaling the means of persuasion, could mold the message into something so beguiling that the listener would find it more or less irresistible. The cross must simply be displayed. The world, or to be more specific, "those who are perishing" (τοῖς ἀπολλυμένοις, 1:18), will no doubt reject it. But "those who believe" (τοὺς πιστεύοντας, 1:21), "the called ones" (τοῖς κλητοῖς, 1:24), "those who are being saved" (τοῖς σῳζομένοις, 1:18), these will recognize it for what it is and embrace it. The matter of form was thus a critical link in the chain. A failure to grasp this point blinds us to a crucial dimension of Paul's argument.

---

[24] As Scroggs (1988, p. 24) says, "Paul never writes theology in the abstract, but uses his theology to support his practical judgments."

14

Paul's Argument Encapsulated

1 Corinthians 1:21

In 1 Corinthians 1:21 Paul continues his argument with these words: "For since in the wisdom of God the world did not know God through its wisdom, it pleased God through the folly of the *kerygma* [κηρύγματος] to save those who believe" (AT). If we are to understand Paul's theology of preaching, this verse deserves our closest attention, not least because it introduces into the discussion one of Paul's most iconic terms: *kerygma*. When we have grasped the significance of this verse, and the role of the term *kerygma* within it, we will have grasped the essence of Paul's theology of preaching.

The term *kerygma* has over the past seventy-five years taken on a life of its own in biblical studies. It has become virtually a technical term, used by countless scholars to refer to the essential apostolic gospel. Yet for playing such an important role in modern biblical studies, it is surprising how little formal attention this prominent Greek word has received. The focus of this chapter is to pause with this crucial term and consider its meaning.[1]

THE MEANING OF *KERYGMA*

There occasionally appear in every discipline books whose effects echo for decades thereafter. C. H. Dodd's *The Apostolic Preaching and Its Developments*, published in 1936, was one such book. In this seminal work Dodd stressed the New Testament distinction between *didache* (διδαχή) and *kerygma* (κήρυγμα)—that is, between teaching and preaching—and then attempted to distill from the New Testament the core content of that preaching. In doing so Dodd almost single-handedly raised the word *kerygma* to a technical term status

---

[1]The following is adapted from Litfin (2011).

and prompted a discussion that continues to this day.

The scholarly response to Dodd's work was at first positive. With time, however, a reaction set in as researchers began to question whether Dodd's strong distinction between *kerygma* and *didache* was warranted by the evidence.[2] More enduring was Dodd's outline of the content of the *kerygma*, but even that came under fire, with other scholars wading in with this or that addition, deletion, substitution or qualification.

What seems to have endured from Dodd's work untouched, however, is the use of the term *kerygma* as the "theologians' shorthand for merely 'the central message of the New Testament.'"[3] Scholars continue to speak as freely of the *kerygma* today as they did decades ago. We may doubt that the word was ever a technical term during the first century, since it occurs only eight times in the New Testament and six of those are from a single source, the Apostle Paul. Moreover, as Margaret Mitchell has demonstrated, *kerygma* is only one of several shorthand terms even Paul used for the gospel.[4] Still, there is no reason the term *kerygma* cannot continue to serve us usefully out into the future—provided, that is, that we understand the term *accurately*.

The Roman poet Martial famously complained about one Fidentinus who had been misquoting Martial's epigrams: "The work you are reciting, O Fidentinus, belongs to me. But when you recite it badly, it begins to belong to you."[5] If you are to quote me, Martial insists, you have an obligation to get it right. In a similar vein, we owe an obligation to *kerygma*'s original users. If we are to allow their merely transliterated word such a strategic role in our own discussions, it's important that we get it right. So we must ask: have Dodd, and a host of others following him, gotten *kerygma* right? Or is it possible that their grasp of this ancient term was so partial as to be seriously deficient?

The essential issue we must resolve is this: does the term *kerygma*, as it was used in the New Testament, refer to the *content* or the *form* of the apostolic preaching? Yet immediately upon posing this question we face a problem: to answer it we must first refine it. If we are asking of *kerygma* how it was used in the New Testament, we are for all practical purposes asking how Paul used the term, for as we have already noted, *kerygma* is essentially in the New Testament a Pauline term.

---

[2] See J. I. H. McDonald (1980, pp. 4-7).
[3] Doty (1972, p. 168). Cullmann (1950, p. 186), following Bultmann, calls the term a "kerygmatic summary of the faith."
[4] Mitchell (1994).
[5] Martial, *Epigrams* 1.38.

Matthew and Luke both place the word in the mouth of Jesus, but both writers are citing the same sentence: "The men of Nineveh," Jesus says in both Gospels, "will rise up at the judgment with this generation and condemn it, for they repented at the preaching [*kerygma*] of Jonah, and behold, something greater than Jonah is here" (Mt 12:41; Lk 11:32). These two references are jot and tittle duplicates of one another. So as it turns out, there is really only one non-Pauline use of *kerygma* in the New Testament, repeated twice. I will return to this single dominical reference and offer it as a helpful illustration of the fully nuanced meaning we will find in Paul. But first we must pick up our account with C. H. Dodd.

Dodd answered the form versus content question in the very first paragraph of his book. Quoting what is the *locus classicus* for determining the meaning of *kerygma*, our present passage, Dodd begins his book this way:

> "It pleased God," says Paul, "by the foolishness of the Preaching to save them that believe." The word here translated "preaching," *kerygma*, signifies not the action of the preacher, but that which he preaches, his "message," as we sometimes say.[6]

End of paragraph. And more importantly, end of argument. With no discussion whatsoever, much less any evidence, Dodd simply assumes what will constitute the working definition of *kerygma* throughout his influential work—namely, that the term *kerygma* refers only to the *content* of the preaching.

Dodd was not the first modern scholar to make this assumption. For example, J. B. Lightfoot had long before claimed that in 1 Corinthians 1:21 the foolishness of preaching refers "to the subject, not to the manner of preaching."[7] Similarly, Robertson and Plummer also limited the term to content, though they acknowledged "a slight emphasis upon the presentation."[8] But Dodd's work, focusing as it did entirely on delineating the content of the *kerygma*, solidified the trend, and there has followed ever since a train of commentators who without exploration or argumentation have merely assumed that *kerygma* in 1 Corinthians 1:21 refers exclusively to content.[9]

---

[6] Dodd (1936, p. 7).
[7] Lightfoot (1868, p. 161); see also Meyer (1870, p. 40).
[8] Robertson and Plummer (1911, p. 21).
[9] Further examples: G. G. Findlay, in *The Expositor's Greek Testament* (1900, p. 769), says the term *kerygma* "signifies not the act of proclamation . . . , but *the message proclaimed* by God's herald." In his commentary on 1 Corinthians, J. Moffatt (1938, p. 14; cf. pp. 15-16) put it this way: "It is the content rather than the form of utterance that engages [Paul's] . . . attention [in 1 Cor 1:21]." In 1943, A. M. Hunter (p. 21), while acknowledging that *kerygma* "may signify either the act of proclamation or the thing proclaimed," nonetheless asserted that for the most part in Paul, and in 1 Cor 1:21 in particular, "the emphasis falls on the *content* of the *kerygma*." F. W. Grosheide (1954,

Yet it is likely that such views, common though they may be, represent a serious truncating of the term *kerygma*. While *kerygma* certainly does refer to the content of Paul's preaching, it also delineates something important about its form, that is, about Paul's mode of communication. In fact, it appears that this term was specifically chosen by the Apostle to keep both content *and* form before his readers, stressing not only *what* Paul proclaims (his message), but also what he simply *proclaims* (its form).

But now, suppose for the moment that this dual focus of *kerygma* is correct. That would mean that this litany of experts who limit *kerygma* to content alone must be mistaken. How could so many eminent scholars have cut the term *kerygma* short? And does it really matter?

Importance of the Issue

The latter question is easier to answer than the first. This issue matters a great deal, for several reasons. First, if the term *kerygma* has any usefulness at all, it is useful as shorthand for something that lies at the core of the Christian faith. If we have left out significant elements of its meaning, we are not merely truncating an important term; we are likely truncating our understanding of what that term represents. Second, and more particularly, this term also stands at the center of, and in fact serves essentially as a distillation of, Paul's argument in 1 Corinthians 1:17–2:16, a passage that Gordon Fee describes as nothing less than "the key theological passage to the whole of the Corinthian correspondence, arguably to the whole of the Pauline corpus."[10] If we fail to get this term right, it

---

p. 47) later concurred, claiming that "the *foolishness of the preaching* represents the content of the preaching which God has commanded." In 1968 C. K. Barrett (p. 54) added his considerable weight to the discussion, asserting that *kerygma* "means not the act but the content of *preaching*." The following year, Hans Conzelmann (1969, p. 241) made the point even more strongly: "The folly," he said, "lies exclusively in the content of the preaching." More recent still, Gordon Fee (1987, p. 73) has written, "The word *kērygma* ... here means not the act of preaching itself, but the content of that proclamation." And with this Anthony Thiselton (2000, p. 167) agrees. He states flatly that in 1 Cor 1:21 *kerygma* refers to "*the substance of the preaching*" and has nothing to do with "the mode of communication." In fact, so well entrenched has this assumption become that Orr and Walther (1976, p. 155) can claim in their commentary on 1 Corinthians that the old King James translation "preaching" has been "superseded in almost all modern versions to indicate the content of the message"; hence the RSV, ESV, NIV: "what we preach." And apparently this trend is to continue. In the United Bible Society's *Translator's Handbook on Paul's First Letter to the Corinthians* (1985, p. 27), Ellingworth and Hatton instruct future translators of 1 Corinthians 1:21 that "the word which Paul uses here for 'preaching' means, not the act of preaching, but its content." So Inkelaar (2011, p. 44): "Κήρυγμα does not mean 'preaching' as activity but the content or message."

[10]Fee (1994, p. 122); similarly, Gorman (2004, p. 240) on 1 Cor 1:18–2:5: "one of the most important texts in all of Paul's letters."

will likely mean that we will not have gotten this passage right either. And those are high stakes indeed.

What's more, this issue also carries some large theoretical implications. Paul is working from fundamental theological presuppositions, which he here applies to his preaching. But these same presuppositions, once surfaced and understood, prove to have implications for other forms of ministry as well. It is not too much to say that an entire philosophy of ministry is at stake here. Thus the question of whether *kerygma* refers to content or form is not a trivial word game, and missing out on a key dimension of *kerygma*'s meaning is not a minor loss. Scholars who stress *kerygma* as content alone have bypassed a significant aspect of the Apostle's thought. Our goal here is to recover this crucial term's fuller significance.

REASONS FOR THE PROBLEM

As to the question of how so many first-rate scholars could be mistaken regarding this important aspect of Paul's thought, we may consider two related explanations. The first is a technical one: the nature of this primitive verbal substantive, *kerygma*, may have been misjudged. The following is for those who wish to consider the issues at stake.

GREEK WORD FORMATION

Greek primary substantives are nouns composed of a verbal root in combination with a formative suffix. There are two such substantives that concern us here: the first is our term κήρυγμα, and the second is a related word, κήρυξις. The root for both of these words is κηρυγ-, which stems from the verb κηρύσσειν, "to proclaim as a κῆρυξ (herald)."

While sharing the same root, κήρυγμα and κήρυξις obviously sport different suffixes, the one a -μα ending, the other a -ξις (-σις) ending. Of these two suffixes Blass and Debrunner (1961, p. 59) say: "Derivatives in –μα . . . specify the result of the action for the most part. . . . Abstracts are formed with [the -σις ending]." Thus κήρυγμα stresses the "result of the action" of the verb κηρύσσειν, while κήρυξις serves as an abstract of the verb, similar to what in Latin or English we call a gerund. It suggests not simply an action but a process. "Running," for example, is a gerund from the verb "to run." Like the Greek nouns ending in -σις, gerunds serve to abstract the verb, as in the sentence, "Running is my favorite exercise." Hence, κήρυξις gives us the abstract of κηρύσσω, which is to say, "proclaiming." Thus, for example, Dio Cassius (*Roman History,* VIII, 62.8.2) can use the term to speak of Nero crossing over into Greece where he spent his time with (translating very literally) "playings of the lyre, proclaimings (κηρύξει), and actings in tragedies."

Though I know of no example of the evidence being argued at any length, the grammatical case for the "content alone" view, to the extent it is mentioned at all, appears to run something like this: The -μα suffix on the word κήρυγμα means that term is referring to the "result" of the verb "to proclaim." This is therefore a reference to the content of the preaching. Had Paul wanted to stress the act of preaching, he would have used the verbal abstract κήρυξις; e.g., see Abbott-Smith (1921, p. 246); Findlay (1900, p. 769).

This argument, however, fails at two points. First, the reference to κήρυξις is misleading. The word never occurs in the New Testament and is rare even in the extrabiblical literature. We have no way of knowing whether it was even part of Paul's vocabulary. In any case, κήρυξις would have been unusable to Paul in this context because as a verbal abstract it would have focused too exclusively on the act or process of proclaiming. In speaking of the "foolishness of the preaching," Paul required a term that would allow both the content and the form of the preaching to remain in the frame. Thus the term κήρυξις, being merely an abstract of the verb κηρύσσειν, would not do.

Second, what also will not do is to conclude that the "result" of the verb κηρύσσειν is merely "content." As A. T. Robertson (1934, pp. 150-51) long ago warned, when dealing with Greek verbal substantives it is important to keep in mind the influence of both the suffix and the root verb. But this is what the "content alone" approach fails to do. If we are careful to maintain the balance between the meaning of the verb ("to proclaim as a herald") and the significance of the -μα suffix ("result"), we discover that the result of this particular verb is not merely content but content in a particular form, namely, proclamation. Says Collins (1999, p. 105), the term *kerygma* "evokes not only the content of Paul's preaching but also the manner in which it was preached." This is why a lexicographer such as Gerhard Friedrich, in his article on κήρυγμά in *TDNT* (1965, p. 714), concludes that the word "has a twofold sense . . . , signifying both the result of proclamation (what is proclaimed) and the actual proclaiming. In other words, it denotes both the act and the content. In many cases it is hard to say where the emphasis falls."

It is mistaken, then, to conclude that κήρυγμα inherently refers to content only. The combination of the root verb and the -μα suffix provides a balance to the term, so much so that if the Apostle wished to keep both the form and the content of his preaching before his readers, κήρυγμα was the only term available to him. It is the context that must determine which of the emphases, if either, predominates in any given passage. Better yet, it is probably safer to conclude that when κήρυγμα is used, neither emphasis ever completely disappears from the frame.

Finally, it is important to observe that in stressing that κήρυγμα refers to both the content and the *form* of Paul's preaching, our point is somewhat different from those early twentieth-century theologians—such as Karl Barth, Rudolf Otto and Rudolf Bultmann—who focused on both the content and the *act* of preaching. Our focus is on the external proclamatory *form* of Paul's preaching, while their focus is on the internal existential *encounter* that takes place each time the gospel is preached. In this encounter the preacher's witness to the past event of the cross becomes a "present recurrence" of that cross event as Christ addresses the listener anew in the proclaimed gospel; for a discussion of this movement, see J. M. Robinson (1959, pp. 40-47).

This existentialist emphasis was a needed reaction to the arid historicism of the so-called quest for the historical Jesus that had gone before, but it was a reaction that went too far in the opposite direction, "de-historicizing" the gospel by *overvaluing* its existential dimension at the expense of its historical facts. Thus Baird (1957, p. 191) observes that perhaps the two sides were "mutually corrective" and the truth is to be found somewhere in the middle; the historical facts of Christ's death and resurrection are indispensible to the gospel, but so is the Spirit's intent to infuse that message with the power to confront human hearts (Rom 1:16; 1 Cor 2:4).

In any case, our point here is that the emphasis of these theologians on the existential meaning of the always contemporary *act* of preaching should be recognized as something different from our emphasis on the proclamatory rather than persuasive *form* of Paul's preaching. Still, the two emphases can be brought together, as when Torrance (1950, p. 322) says, "God's testimony, *martyrion*, takes place through proclamation (κήρυγμα). . . . *Kerygma* may be defined as the straight-forward proclamation of this *martyrion* in such a way that the original *martyrion* actually takes place in the experience of the hearer. That is to say, the original event becomes event all over again through the power of the Spirit so that in *kerygma* a man encounters the living Christ, Christ crucified but risen. No doubt the *kerygma* in itself is mere speech . . . but it is not in the enticing words of man's wisdom nor with the excellence of speech, nor indeed by human or logical demonstration that the *martyrion* takes place, but in the demonstration of the Spirit and of power. . . . In other words, God bears witness to Himself as men proclaim the crucified and risen Christ."

A Blind Spot in New Testament Studies

Most competent New Testament scholars understand these technicalities, we may presume, and so we must ask why, given these options, so many still come down on the side of content alone in 1 Corinthians 1:21. Even Gerhard Friedrich, after acknowledging the dual possibilities inherent in the term κήρυγμα, along with the difficulty of deciding in any particular case which predominates, concludes that in 1 Corinthians 2:4 κήρυγμα refers to the *act* of preaching, while just thirteen verses back, in 1:21, the focus is on the *content* of preaching.[11] Why

---

[11]Friedrich (1965, p. 716, n. 15); cf. J. I. H. McDonald (1980, p. 2). C. F. Evans (1956, p. 26) rightly suggests that if, as is typically conceded, κήρυγμα in 1 Cor 2:4 involves the *act* of proclamation, "we should perhaps hesitate to require a change of meaning in the course of a few verses. In i.21

would so many call the issue in this way? To answer this question we must turn to the second and more important reason why scholars have cut κήρυγμα short.

In our introductory chapter we discussed the blind spot toward classical rhetoric that earlier in the twentieth century existed within New Testament scholarship. This problem was a modern one because for most of the church's history, students of the Scriptures, steeped as they were in classical studies, were fully aware of the Greco-Roman backgrounds of the New Testament. They were typically schooled in classical rhetoric and tended to understand its categories. But over the last century or two, as modern education broke free from its classicism and thus fewer scholars arrived at the New Testament with classical training, these backgrounds were sometimes eclipsed by more fashionable interests, such as Gnosticism, the Greek mystery religions or the syncretistic influences of the Hellenistic synagogue. The result was that for years the subject of Greco-Roman rhetoric not only fell into the shadows but was actively avoided by many New Testament scholars.

Part of the problem, of course, lay in what was happening within the field of rhetoric itself during this period. At its best in ancient times, rhetoric was about both thinking well and communicating effectively. But periodically political and social developments[12] would shear away its substance and leave rhetoric to deal mostly with issues of style and ornamentation, thus vindicating some of Plato's otherwise misguided criticisms. Unfortunately it was this diminished version of rhetoric, with its penchant for flowery elocution and its arid obsession with classification, that tended to dominate nineteenth-century teaching. One need only conjure up the name E. W. Bullinger to catch the point. In his 1898 book of seemingly endless classifications of figures of speech from the ancient period, Bullinger epitomized the limited definition of rhetoric with which he began his work: "Rhetoric is an adaptation of Figurative Language for the purposes of elocution."[13] This is a far cry from how Isocrates or Cicero or Quintilian viewed the art they taught, but it was just this cramped sort of thing against which many moderns were reacting. Hence we may be sympathetic to the demise of interest

---

> Paul may be saying that since through the activity of wisdom the world did not know God, it pleased God by the foolishness of the activity of preaching to save those who believe. The contrast will be between two methods or activities. The content of the activity corresponds with the activity itself, 'Christ crucified' being the apparently foolish content of the foolish activity of preaching." Disappointingly, however, Evans never identies, much less explores, the contrasting nature of these two methods or activities.

[12]For example, see Millar's study (1998) of these fluctuations.
[13]Bullinger (1898, p. ix).

in rhetoric witnessed during the earlier part of the twentieth century.

Today this problem has turned itself around. Rhetorical studies are now pervasive in New Testament circles. One can scarcely open a scholarly journal in biblical studies without coming upon another. Yet ironically, in some ways we have not risen very far beyond the old stereotypes. A passion for classification worthy of Bullinger himself remains heavy upon the field. Hundreds of rhetorical studies have appeared, but many appear to be bogged down in the task of demonstrating this or that rhetorical pattern in the text. Relatively few seem inclined to cut through to the essence of ancient rhetorical theory and contend with the deeper and more important ideas we discover there.

Unfortunately, this avoidance may have cost us something in our understanding of the verb κηρύσσειν, "to proclaim as a herald." A jeweler understands that her customer is much more likely to appreciate the exquisite features of a string of pearls if she displays them against a strong contrasting background. Similarly, we moderns may have missed some of this verb's underlying nuances, or at least failed to appreciate their significance, because we have not seen clearly enough what κηρύσσειν is semantically designed to stand over *against*. And if this is so, then we should not be surprised to discover that when we come to the verbal substantive κήρυγμα, we may have missed some of its nuances as well.

The Remedy

The remedy for this situation lies not in the discovery of new facts about the herald but rather in a fuller appreciation of the facts we already know. For that we require an appropriate contrast. All are agreed that κηρύσσειν means "to proclaim," and none dispute that the verb describes the behavior of the herald. But what is the significance of this observation? What is *peculiar* about the role of the herald? The answer emerges when we set that role against its alternative, the art of persuasion.

PAUL'S CORE CONCERN

In his book *St. Paul's Theology of Rhetorical Style* (1995), Michael Bullmore argues that in 1 Corinthians 2:1-5 Paul was challenging not the core of Greco-Roman rhetoric but a much more specific thing: namely, a "certain strain" (p. 209) of rhetoric, that "florid and voluble" style of oratory known as Asianism in which "the primary concern of rhetoric . . . shifted . . . from persuasion to expression" (p. 150). By the first century, Bullmore says, "oratory was predominantly an oratory of display and expression" (p. 151). If

Bullmore is right, the Apostle Paul's critique in 1 Corinthians 1–4 would prove to be far less sweeping. It would be reduced to a repudiation, not of the essential dynamic of human persuasion, but of self-promotion and verbal pyrotechnics in preaching.

But this argument (embraced by Thiselton, 2000, p. 205) falters on several counts: (1) While the so-called Asianist/Atticist debate was active during Paul's days, Bullmore fails to demonstrate his general conclusion that mere display had largely displaced persuasion. Indeed, this cannot be demonstrated. The evidence to the contrary is everywhere in the ancient literature (e.g., see Kennedy, 1972, pp. 428-552; Miller, 2013), not least in the extensive writings of the leading first-century Roman teacher of rhetoric, Quintilian. (2) But this point becomes moot, in any case, when Bullmore in his conclusion is forced by the Apostle's language in 1 Corinthians 2:1-5 to shift his focus back to the issue of persuasion. What Paul was concerned about, he concludes, was not simply a rhetoric that had given up persuasion for mere expression or display, but rather "the kind of persuasion . . . in which the power lay in the speaker and his stylistic virtuosity. It was particularly this kind of rhetoric . . . that posed a fundamental threat to the effective proclamation of the gospel" (222). But why the addition of "and his stylistic virtuosity"? Bullmore is certainly correct that Paul was concerned about "the kind of persuasion in which the power lay in the speaker," but why single out issues of style? Was Paul unconcerned about the nonstylistic aspects of human persuasion, aspects whose power also "lay in the speaker"? Bullmore never explains why it would only have been this "certain strain" of rhetoric that concerned the Apostle. Such an analysis badly understates the reach of Paul's critique. The fact is, persuasion as a goal was very much alive in first-century rhetoric, and Paul's critique struck to the core of the persuader's stance. As Judge (1983, pp. 11-12) says, "For Paul [the problem] was not simply a question of style"; rather, Paul "pin-points 'persuasiveness' as the particular excess he wishes to avoid." (3) Like most other writers, Bullmore leaves unaddressed Paul's language of the herald or witness. In attempting to describe the Apostle's "simple and unaffected style" (p. 225), Bullmore rightly refrains from equating it with "a conscious adoption of" Atticism's plain style, but he misses the significance of the Apostle's consistent and determined portrayal of his preaching as κήρυγμα and himself as a κῆρυξ, or simply a μάρτυς. As we have seen, a focus on the unique nuances of this Pauline language is crucial to appreciating what it was Paul was setting himself over against: the persuader's stance.

The persuader. Here is where our earlier material on Greco-Roman rhetoric proves so useful. As we have seen, training in Greco-Roman rhetoric formed the crown of a liberal education in the ancient world. The art was not about composing purple prose or dishonestly manipulating one's audience. At its best rhetoric was something powerful, even noble. It was that art that replaced violence and coercion in free societies: the art of persuasion through discourse.[14]

When we lay bare the essence of the thing, rhetoric was about the discovery, shaping and delivery of ideas so as to engender belief in one's listeners. At its core lay the kaleidoscopic ability of the persuader to mold all of his efforts, including form and content, to the demands of the given situation, with a view to winning a particular result from his listeners. Given *this* audience, *this* subject matter, on *this* occasion, how can I achieve the desired result? This was the question persuaders were trained to ask and answer, and the measure of their skill was the degree to which they could do so successfully, in whatever rhetorical situation they might be facing.

The herald. This is the backdrop against which to view the ancient herald. The role of the herald in the classical world is widely understood, and we need only cite some standard observations to see the important distinction. It was demanded of heralds, says Gerhard Friedrich, that they

> deliver their message as it is given to them. The essential point about the report which they give is that it does not originate with them. Behind it stands a higher power. The herald does not express his own views. He is the spokesman for his master. . . . Heralds adopt the mind of those who commission them, and act with the plenipotentiary authority of their masters. . . . Yet there is a distinction between the herald and the envoy. In general one may say that the latter acts more independently and that he is furnished with greater authority. It is unusual for a herald to act on his own initiative and without explicit instructions. In the main the herald simply gives short messages, puts questions, and brings answers. . . . He is bound by the precise instructions of the one who commissions him. . . . The good herald does not become involved in lengthy negotiations [sic] but returns at once when he has delivered his message. . . . In general he is simply an executive instrument. Being only the mouth of his master, he must not falsify the message entrusted to him by additions of his own. He must deliver it exactly as given to him. . . . He must keep strictly to the words and orders of his master.[15]

---

[14]Habinek summarizes the point well (2005, p. 15): "Political and social conditions changed dramatically from the founding of the Greek city-states to the fall of the Roman empire. But throughout that millennium of history, mastery of rhetorical speech united communities small and large, substituted for violent resolution of conflict and dispute, served as an identifying mark of political leadership, differentiated the free community from tyranny, and in time provided a medium for renewal of the leadership class and for communication across boundaries of space, time, and ethnicity."

[15]Friedrich (1965, pp. 687-88). Cf. Hunter (1943, pp. 24-26).

The herald's role was thus strikingly different from the persuader's. Like the persuader, the herald could not dictate who would make up his audience; he had to work with what he received. But beyond this the two roles are a study in contrasts. Far from being an ever-malleable variable, ingeniously adapted to the audience so as to win the desired response, the herald's message was set for him by another. It was not a variable at all but a *Constant*: the herald was given a message by the one he represented, and it was his assignment to deliver it faithfully. And the results? The herald could not maneuver rhetorically to achieve some particular effect; it was his fate to deliver his message and then watch the chips fall where they may. Upon completion of his assignment the herald might discover a variety of responses from his audience, but these were not his affair. Whatever he might desire for his audience, he was ever mindful that the responses of the audience were not in the end responses to himself but to the one he represented. It was not the herald's task to modulate his efforts so as to achieve this response or that, or to negotiate[16] the message with his audience, so to speak, in order to develop a word they might find maximally palatable, or better yet, wonderfully convincing, or best of all, simply irresistible. Unlike the persuader, the herald was not results driven; he was obedience driven. He was a man under assignment, methodologically obligated, restricted to the task of declaring or announcing. Instead of offering impressive arguments, he was a proclaimer; he testified, he notified, he reported. This is what it meant to be a κῆρυξ.

ROMAN HERALDS

The Latin counterpart to the Greek κῆρυξ was the Roman *praeco* (plural: *praecones*). The *praecones* became an important part of the system of communication required to organize and coordinate Rome's far-flung domain. Because the population of the empire was largely illiterate, the average Roman citizen received the bulk of his official information through oral proclamation. Thus "the proclamation of edicts or proposed laws . . . by praecones was fundamental to the basic awareness of the average Roman citizen" (Thorgerson, 1993, p. 20).

Like their Greek counterparts, Roman heralds were essentially proclaimers. "From

---

[16]On this point see Coenen (1990, 2:1277): "Der κῆρυξ . . . steht immer unter einer fremden. Autorität, deren Sprecher er ist; er übermittelt . . . die Botschaft und Meinung seiner Auftraggeber und hat deshalb . . . keinen eigenen Verhandlungsspielraum." ("The herald always stands under an outside authority, whose spokesman he is; he conveys the message and viewpoint of his client and does not therefore have his own room for negotiation.")

time immemorial," says Purcell (1983, p. 127), "[Roman] magistrates were served by scribes (*scribae*), messengers (*viatores*), lictors (*lictores*) and heralds (*praecones*)." All of these figures were in effect civil servants attached to those in authority (on which, see Jones, 1960). Scribes were the secretaries, *viatores* served as bailiffs and *lictores* were essentially body guards. But because "the form of communication which most magistrates needed to have provided by the state was not written but oral" (Harris 1989, p. 208), the *praecones* were the magistrates' public speaking proxies. Their role was variously to summon, call for silence, call to order, announce results, and read legislation aloud or make official pronouncements.

Some have argued that there were two types of *praecones*, those who served in the civil sphere (*praecones publici*) and those who operated for money in business affairs, particularly in auctioneering (*praecones privati*). Of the latter group Rauh (1989, p. 460) says, "They were flamboyant, loud, streetwise, and crass, relying upon obnoxious voices, crude remarks, and a willingness to say anything to lure in a buying public." Such figures were especially disdained by the literary elites, it seems, due in part to their lusty voices, a *praeco* requirement. The herald had to be able to gain an audience's attention and then be heard above the din. Thus Josephus speaks of one Euarestus Arruntius, "a public crier in the market place, and therefore of a strong and audible voice" (*Antiquities* 19.1.18). In any case, the Roman *praecones*, whether public or private, were typically of relatively low social status (Jones, 1960, pp. 154-55, 157). Their proximity to power and wealth made upward mobility possible for some, which typically required the abandonment of their profession. But most Roman heralds did not enjoy high social standing; cf. Juvenal, *Satires* VII.5. Nor did the Greek heralds before them. Plato (*The Statesman* 290A-B) classed heralds—along with laborers, clerks and others who are "only too glad to serve anybody for hire"—in the category of ὑπηρέτης ("underling, servant, helper").

That Paul was not hesitant to associate himself with such a low status/low power role is significant. But what is even more important for our purposes is the observation that, like their Greek counterparts, the central function of the Roman *praecones* was that of proclaimers/announcers. *Praecones* were relayers of messages. They were oral representatives of others. Indeed, according to Suetonius (*Life of Augustus* 84.2), even Augustus himself "sometimes because of weakness of the throat . . . addressed the people through a herald [*praeconis*]." When speaking in his official civic role, the *praeco* was always operating not from his own authority but on behalf of another.

THE FOOLISHNESS OF PROCLAMATION

With this contrast in mind, then, let us return to 1 Corinthians 1:21. Paul's assumption throughout 1 Corinthians 1–4—indeed, throughout all of his writings—

is that the human race is lost in its sin, and that it desperately needs to be saved from the judgment of the Creator against whom it has mutinied. What humans crave is life, meaning, significance and purpose. But left to themselves, what they face is the opposite: futility and death. Christ came to save the race from precisely this fate, but as always, human pride is the great barrier.

Humans are convinced that if only they apply themselves they can solve this dilemma for themselves. This was the notion Paul was eager to dispel. "Where is the one who is wise?" he asks. "Where is the scribe? Where is the debater of this age" (1 Cor 1:20) when it comes to solving this most pressing of all human needs? Whatever else their notable achievements, has not God made foolish their attempts to solve *this problem* apart from him? The world may be impressed by the prideful efforts of its best and brightest to scale the heights and achieve for themselves their own salvation. But God himself will have none of it. "As [Paul] will elaborate in Rom. 1:18-31, left to themselves mere creatures cannot find out the living God."[17] In his divine wisdom he has cut off their approach. Humans simply cannot and will not solve this dilemma in their own strength. If they are to find salvation, they must find it in God, says Paul, and they must do so on God's terms.

And his terms are these: God will provide the race with an avenue of salvation, but it will be available only through a means that runs profoundly contrary to human pride.[18] To discover this salvation, men and women will have to renounce their pretensions to self-sufficiency, acknowledge their helplessness and give up humanly striving to save themselves. Instead, they must humble themselves before God by acknowledging a crucified Jewish peasant to be Lord of the universe, and his death on a Roman cross as their only hope of salvation. They must trust him, and him alone, as their only means of salvation.

What's more, God will not tolerate any lingering pridefulness. Humans must be willing to place their faith in Christ solely on the basis of hearing and accepting God's *announced* word[19] on the subject, the gospel. He will not satisfy their pride in other ways. If in order to respond positively, they demand miraculous signs to

---

[17]Fee (1987, p. 72).
[18]See appendix three.
[19]Hays (1997, p. 30). Note how the only other use of κήρυγμα in the New Testament, Christ's reference to Jonah in Mt 12:41 and Lk 11:32, fits this pattern. Regarding Paul's emphasis on the foolishness of preaching in 1 Cor 1:21, Ciampa and Rosner (2010, p. 97) observe, "That knowing God *through* preaching is the solution to the problem of not knowing God *through* the wisdom of the world is signaled by the use of the same preposition in both clauses. One means of enjoying that relationship replaces another means, which has failed."

authenticate the announcement, they will be disappointed. If they insist on something more along the lines of what the Greeks required to be impressed—that is, "wisdom" in the form of convincing arguments designed to satisfy self-sufficient minds, eloquently dressed in winsomely impressive language—God will not provide this either. What they will receive is the simple declaration of the gospel by God's designated messenger, proclaiming "Jesus Christ and him crucified."[20] As Jesus himself often put it, "He who has ears to hear, let him hear."

BOTH ANCIENT AND MODERN

Grassi (1980, p. 103) describes the first mark of "sacred language" as follows: "a purely directive, revealing, or evangelical character (never a demonstrative or proving function), and it never arises out of a process of inference in order not to give up its original character or absolute undetermined character." This type of speech stands in "explicit contradistinction" to "rational speech," which claims "to be demonstrative and to offer proof because it gives the reasons for its assertions" (p. 104). This latter type of speech is the currency of our own times, says Grassi, because "today's situation is such that in our desacralized and demythologized world we believe in no annunciations, in no purely directive statements, in no evangelist, be it a God or a prophet. We turn to rational thought, to proofs and reasons in order to free ourselves from the subjectivity and relativity of appearances" (p. 104).

Grassi's assessment of our own times is no doubt correct, but it is important to see that this is no merely modern development. It speaks to the human condition and

---

[20]Cf. the interesting parallels in the realm of philosophical argumentation. Says Schouls (1969, p. 190), "The problem of philosophical communication derives from the presence of presuppositions in philosophy"—see Johnstone (1959, p. 33) on the distinction between "assumptions," "suppositions" and *pre*-suppositions. By definition, *pre*-suppositions cannot be "argued." Arguments supporting properly basic presuppositions are inevitably circular in that they must assume the truth of the presupposition they are attempting to support. Thus philosophers who hold common presuppositions can debate about what may follow from those presuppositions, but how is "argumentation" to proceed when their differences lie at the presuppositional level, where no noncircular "arguments" are available? This impasse prompts Schouls to introduce a form of communication different from "argumentation." Argumentation, says Rescher, is "the project of seeking to elicit the acceptance of certain contentions by means of explicitly adduced substantiating reasons" (2001, p. 77). When the differences lie at the level of competing presuppositions, where no such "substantiating reasons" can escape the problem of circularity, if communication is not to grind to a halt philosophical argument can only be replaced with a form of communication Schouls labels "proclamation," "advocacy or recommendation" (p. 194).

This technical discussion of philosophical communication lacks the obvious spiritual dimension (the role of the Holy Spirit) that was so prominent in Paul's thinking. But the Apostle would surely have understood and identified with the notion of a fundamental impasse that rules out "argumentation" as an available strategy, leading to the employment of "proclamation." For Paul's quite different—but in another sense, not altogether so—understanding of that fundamental impasse, see above, pp. 179-81, and appendix three.

in the end applies to the first century as well as the twenty-first. Grassi's contrast is precisely what lay behind 1 Corinthians 1:18-21: the contrast between the human (Jew and Greek) demand for proof versus the welcome given to the simply annunciated gospel (κήρυγμα) by the κλητοί. What was the difference? The presence of the Spirit's work among τοῖς σῳζομένοις (1 Cor 1:18). This work was the δύναμις θεοῦ Paul was determined to trust for his results. Hence his commitment to proclamation.

Kennedy (1984, p. 8) uses Grassi's distinction to make a similar point. The mark of what Kennedy calls "radical Christian rhetoric" is that it is "purely proclaimed," not argued. Kennedy (p. 6) cites Moses as an example: "The communications between God, Moses, Pharaoh, and the people in the first half of the book of Exodus will repay careful study by every student of the rhetoric of the Bible. Moses here does not persuade Pharaoh in the way a classical orator would appeal to him. He does not argue that to let his people go is in accordance with the common principles of justice and in the long-term best interests of Pharaoh himself. He speaks words God had given him and performs miracles, while God alternately hardens and softens Pharaoh's heart. The ultimate escape of the people is the result of God's action, not of Moses', or Aaron's, persuasive abilities." In the same way, "Jesus' message was essentially proclaimed, not argued on the basis of probability, and that is why it is often called by the Greek word for proclamation, *kerygma.*"

No doubt Paul understood that many in his audience, to the extent they were unwilling to renounce their pride, would find this announcement absurdly unsatisfying. The typical Jew, he says, will be scandalized by it, while the typical Greek will merely disdain it as foolish. In their vanity neither will be willing to identify themselves with such a low-status salvation because neither will be willing to accept the premise that they should be reduced to such a humble estate. But God knew from the beginning what he was doing. He might have come to the human race through their own striving, but he knew that in the end they would pridefully claim credit for their own salvation. Instead, God intentionally chose to make himself available through means the proud would find unacceptable; that is, through means that cast aside all human pretensions and allowed only the humble acceptance of a simply announced gospel, so that in the end it would be clear that God alone was responsible for salvation. No mortal could boast.[21]

---

[21]Cf. Polhill on 1 Cor 1–4 (1983, p. 329): "Paul establishes his basic premise that God has rendered worthless all human-centered attempts at salvation. Human wisdom has failed in its quest for God (1:21). Perhaps at this point Paul had in mind something like his argument in Romans 1:18ff. that humanity had distorted the divine revelation in nature, perverting it into idolatry and worshiping creation rather than creator. God did not merely reject the fruitless striving of human wisdom; He

This is the argument that forms the context for Paul's use of κήρυγμα in 1 Corinthians 1:21. It should not be difficult, therefore, to see that when he speaks of "the foolishness of the *kerygma*" he intends his reader to understand more than content alone. To be sure, the term refers to the content of Paul's preaching; by the standards of the world the account of "Christ crucified" is indeed a foolish message.[22] But it is important to see that this content is not the only thing that lacks standing in the eyes of the world. When an audience desires the persuasive argumentation and formal eloquence of the rhetor—in fact, *demands* them if they are to be impressed—the simple heralding of a declarative message will be greeted with derision. Along with the content, this form too will appear paltry and foolish,[23] so much so that it will insult them. It will offend the worldling's pride and seem demeaning to him that he should be expected simply to accept the message as announced, on the mere say-so of the messenger.[24]

It is just this point that we may find most difficult to digest. First-century audiences expected to be gratified by taking part in a transaction in which they held the upper hand. It was a buyer's market, so to speak, and they were in the happy position of being the buyers. Their role was to sit in judgment on the speakers who came before them and to decide whether they should be convinced or not. The occasion of listening to a speaker thus provided audiences not only amusement and entertainment but also immense ego satisfaction. Paul Corcoran captures this dimension of the ancient rhetorical transaction when he says:

> To be addressed by a speaker who wins you over, persuading you clearly of the good and the true position, is in itself gratifying. Doubt, hesitation, ignorance or ill-confidence are happily laid to rest. To fall under the sway of a learned and convincing orator is gratifying simply because of the coincidence of interest

---

chose a means of revelation actually contradictory to that wisdom—the foolish proclamation of a crucified Savior (1:21b). To the Greeks with their high standards of intellect, the idea was folly. The Jews were no better off, for their quest for signs scarcely differed from the Greek love of wisdom. The demand for a sign is a request for an observable proof from God which serves as a confirmation to reason. It too becomes an attempt at salvation by human achievement. God rejects both wisdom and sign and substitutes the foolish insignificance (by human standards) of the cross. Those, however who are set apart as God's own by their response in faith to the gospel are able in that faith to discern that Christ is the ultimate wisdom and power of God (1:24)."

[22]In fact, for many moderns, whose primary connection with the cross is a piece of attractive jewelry, the level of scandal, curse, shame, fear, intimidation, revulsion, humiliation, degradation and horror associated with ancient crucifixion, all of which served to offend and put off both Jew and Gentile alike, is difficult to grasp. See on this Chapman (2008); Adams (2008).

[23]See Goldammer (1957, pp. 80-81).

[24]See Alexander (1995, pp. 64-71) on this attitude in the ancient world, as seen in Galen.

between oneself and the speaker, who manifestly desires what you have to give: your attention and applause. The distance between oneself and the enlightened orator is no cause for pain, because in the very act of listening this gap is narrowed, and a community of interest expanded. It is gratifying, moreover, just to be the object of concern for the superior intellect, especially when one stands only to gain by it. Finally, it is highly rewarding to be, as an audience, with the strength of numbers and in a position to judge and evaluate the man of learning. It is not humiliating to fall under the sway of the orator, precisely because of the element of choice. If he were unconvincing, he could be ignored.[25]

This prideful stance, Paul argues, is what makes not only the content of the *kerygma* unpalatable but also its form. In hearing the message of God's herald, the audience is dethroned from its proud role as judge. Far from gratifying their pride, the audience is being called simply to accept the announced word of the cross as proffered. But this the prideful will be unwilling to do.[26] If the content of the gospel, Christ crucified, will be considered scandalous or foolish by the world's standards, so also will be its mere heralding. But this is very much by God's design. It pleased God, says Paul, through the foolishness of both the content and the form of the heralding to save τοὺς πιστεύοντας—those who simply "believe." This humble response is all God asks—indeed, all he will accept. But any such kneeling in repentance and submission is a tall order for the proud.[27]

Conclusion

When the Apostle referred to his own preaching as the *kerygma*, he was identifying his ministry explicitly with the figure of the κῆρυξ, the herald, and with all that term implies. The verb κηρύσσειν was not merely a generic term for public speaking; it carried a distinctive meaning, a meaning that can only be appreciated against the backdrop of the deft and splendidly adaptive eloquence of the persuader.

It was Paul's radically challenging argument that God is not in the business of gratifying prideful humans with the persuasive content and winsome forms they may demand. Faith, if we are thinking in biblical terms, means taking God at his word, and when it comes to the gospel, that word is what God is inclined to provide. That word, the word of the cross, is all that "those who are being

---

[25]Corcoran (1979, p. 46).
[26]On this natural human condition, see Perelman and Olbrechts-Tyteca (1969, p. 16).
[27]See St. Augustine on this point: *City of God* 10.28.

saved" (τοῖς σῳζομένοις, 1 Cor 1:18) require, and they receive it gladly. But to "those who are perishing" (τοῖς ἀπολλυμένοις) that same word appears to be folly. How can they be expected to be persuaded by the mere announcement of such a counterintuitive salvation? It is in this sense that the foolishness and inadequacy of the κήρυγμα applies as much to its form as to its content.[28]

---

[28]See Ciampa and Rosner (2010, pp. 96-98).

15

Paul's Argument Continued

1 Corinthians 1:22–2:5

1:22-25—The Foolishness of God

God's determination to accomplish his salvation through the exquisite foolishness of the κήρυγμα takes the world by surprise. Humans are not looking for the truth in this form: a crucified Jewish peasant portrayed before their eyes as Savior and Lord. The knowledge of God and of salvation is ostensibly what they seek, but they look for it elsewhere, along much more splendid avenues, and they expect it to take more appropriately convincing contours. For example, the Jews characteristically look for signs (σημεῖα) in their search for the truth—in fact require them to be impressed. The Greeks characteristically look for what they consider σοφία in their search for the truth—in fact require it to be impressed. "But we" (1:23), says Paul in sharp contrast, unresponsive to such demands for what the world finds convincing, simply herald (κηρύσσω) Christ crucified.

THE DEMAND FOR PROOF

In the light of the Greek tradition of wisdom we have traced, it is misleading for commentators to deny that Paul is suggesting here a genuine contrast between Greeks (not "Gentiles") and Jews. Why did Paul specify Jews and Greeks? Why not "other well-known people-groups such as the Phrygians, the Syrians, or even the Romans?" (C. Stanley, 2013, p. 178). It was due to the distinctive, identifiable mindsets of these two groups.

Paul's take on the Jewish tendency (on which, cf. Mk 15:32; Jn 20:25, 29) was his judgment after a lifetime of personal experience. But the same can be said for the Greek tendency. His observation about this Greek orientation was after all a commonplace of the Greco-Roman world. Ancient literature abounds with such assertions about the Greeks right up to and through the time of Paul. See Isocrates, *Panegyricus*

50; Cicero, *De or.* 2.153; Dio Chrysostom, *Discourses* 2.39; 37:26-27; Aristides, *Orations* (Dindorf) 10:69; 14:209; *Panathenaic Oration* 397. For a classic statement of the Greek attitude Paul had in mind, see Plutarch, *Moralia* 580A-C. On the Greek connection of knowing and seeing in general, see Kerényi (1962, p. 144).

As we have seen, the Greeks consistently associated σοφία with eloquence. Isocrates makes this explicit as early as the fourth century B.C. (*Antidosis* 293-96; *Paneg.* 45-50), and as late as Philostratus Ἕλληνες or Ἑλληνικός could still be used to mean, simply, students of rhetoric (*Lives* 571, 588, 613, 617). For a helpful analysis of this point, see Munck (1959, pp. 148-50). Yet Paul's assessment of the Greek tendency is broad enough to include its philosophical tendencies as well as the rhetorical. In fact, it's not at all clear that Paul would have been interested in overly distinguishing between the two. For example, even Johnstone's effort (1959, pp. 46-47; see also idem, 1965, p. 142), following in the footsteps of Plato, to distinguish pristine "bilateral" philosophical argumentation from its "unilateral" rhetorical counterpart does not manage to protect philosophers from the Apostle's critique. Even were Johnstone's distinctions to hold—in terms of the first century, however, they cannot; in actual Greco-Roman practice no such tight theoretical distinctions can work—the two forms of communication Johnstone describes remain instances of "argumentation," both of which leave humans enthroned as deciders about whether their demands for proof have been met. Perelman says, "All argumentation addresses itself to a mind which has to judge, to appraise" (1982a, p. 292; cf. ibid., p. 289, and Johnstone, 1982, p. 99; but cf. also Johnstone, 1982, p. 102, on "peremptory communication"), and so it was with Greek argumentation. What Paul apparently believed this Greek mindset, whether in its philosophical or rhetorical manifestations, held in common with the Jewish mindset was the human desire for "sight" or "proof" rather than a willingness to trust the announced word of the gospel (2 Cor 5:7).

The essence of the verb κηρύσσω again preserves Paul's emphasis on form along with the explicit statement of content, "Christ crucified." His point is that neither the form nor the content of the gospel feeds the world's appetite for what it deems impressive. Instead, the simple proclaiming of Christ crucified has the opposite effect on those who measure impressiveness by the world's standards. To such ones who are Jews the message is offensive (σκάνδαλον); to Greeks it is nonsense (μωρίαν). But these negative responses do not appear to worry Paul. He is braced for them, so to speak. More importantly, he is aware that among his listeners are a special group, the κλητοί, who will not find the message either scandalous or foolish. He knows that "to them . . . to the called ones," whether Jew or Greek, the straightforward proclamation of Christ crucified will have an altogether more elegant appearance. These will be able to see the simply proclaimed message of the cross for what it is, the power of God and the wisdom of God.[1] The κλητοί will not require to be impressed by what impresses the world.[2] They will see that even what the world may consider foolish is wiser than men, and what the world may consider weakness is stronger than men.

1:26-31—STATUS OF THE CORINTHIANS

In 1 Corinthians 1:26 Paul turns to the Corinthians themselves as evidence of his point. "Consider your calling, brothers" (Βλέπετε ... τὴν κλῆσιν ὑμῶν, ἀδελφοί), he says. Κλῆσις "is here the act of calling rather than the state of being called."[3] The emphasis is on the point at which the Corinthians heard and responded to Paul's proclamation (cf. 1 Cor 1:30).

Here again we find evidence of Paul's view of the Corinthians. He has already confidently assumed in 1 Corinthians 1:18 that they are not among "those who are perishing" but among "us who are being saved." Now he reiterates that confidence by mentioning again (cf. 1 Cor 1:2) that they are among the κλητοί. The tone of address is warmly fraternal (see also 1 Cor 2:1), standing in stark contrast to his address to the Galatians (Gal 3:1). There is not, nor has there been, any indication that they have abandoned or distorted the gospel. On the contrary, Paul explicitly asserts in 1 Corinthians 1:30 what is already implicit (in view of the argument of 1 Cor 1:18-25) in his observation that they are among the κλητοί, namely, that the Corinthians are "in Christ Jesus." They were among those who had perceived in the Jesus Paul preached the righteousness, sanctification and redemption of God, and they had therefore put their faith in him.

Paul's purpose in mentioning the makeup of the Corinthian congregation is to illustrate his central principle: God uses what the world considers unimpressive so that in the end there can be no question as to who has accomplished the result—no human being can boast. This is the principle he has used to justify his *modus operandi* as a preacher, and it is crucial that the Corinthians grasp it. The Corinthians themselves nicely illustrated this principle because for the most

---

[1] Cf. 1 Thess 2:13: "And we also thank God constantly for this, that when you received the word of God, which you heard from us, you accepted it not as the word of men [οὐ λόγον ἀνθρώπων] but as what it really is, the word of God [λόγον θεοῦ], which is at work in you believers [ἐν ὑμῖν τοῖς πιστεύουσιν]." Cf. 1 Thess 1:4-5.
[2] As Johannes Weiss (1909, p. 61) said of the Apostle himself, "Paul did not pass through the streets of Corinth with the cultural and enthusiastic self-complacency of a Greek brought up in an aesthetic atmosphere, but shut his eyes to much with which he met. All such splendor merely aroused in him the judgement that 'the things of this world pass away.'"
[3] Conzelmann (1975, p. 49).

part they were not by human standards an impressive lot.⁴ Some may have been counted among the wise, the powerful or the well-born of Corinth, but not many (1 Cor 1:26). The bulk of the congregation would not have been considered by the world to be among the aristocratic set of Corinthian society; they were not σοφοί, δυνατοί or εὐγενεῖς. In short, they lacked social standing in the community. Yet it was precisely such low-status people God had called, not the elite. This can only be explained by the principle under examination: God elects the low status—what the world find unimpressive—to bring to naught the high status—what the world considers impressive.

It is worth noting that these verses tell us as much about the social milieu of the Corinthians as they do about the Corinthians themselves, in both cases screened through the perception of the Apostle. Paul focuses on three primary dimensions by which social status was measured: wisdom, power and nobility. It may be significant that wisdom takes precedence. This was due in part, as we have already observed from external sources, to the importance of σοφία in Corinthian society. But it was also due to the intent of Paul's present argument. In any case, it is clear that in Paul's view, wisdom, power and nobility were what the Greco-Roman society honored. The perspective of the terminology in 1 Corinthians 1:26-28 is entirely that of the world.⁵ As Paul will argue later, God views things in the reverse, but the terms in this context define society's, not God's, concept of high and low status.

The contrast here of the world's versus God's perspective strikes to the heart of Paul's argument. The wise, the powerful, the noble—all the high-status figures the world so prizes—are in the process of being put to shame (καταισχύνω, 1 Cor 1:27), rendered null and void (καταργέω, 1 Cor 1:28; cf. 2:6) by God. To accomplish this, God has paradoxically chosen the very low-status means the world deems foolish,

---

⁴On the social status of the Corinthian congregation, see "The Social Stratification of the Corinthian Church" in chapter 11 above.

⁵Regarding the glorious things of Athens's history, Isocrates observes that it was not "those who did not stand out from the multitude who accomplished these things, but . . . it was men who were superior and pre-eminent, not only in birth and reputation, but in wisdom and eloquence, who have been the authors of all our blessings" (*Antidosis* 308). Pliny the Elder, a contemporary of the Apostle Paul, catalogued as follows "the ten greatest and highest objects in the pursuit of which wise men pass their lives": "To be a first-class warrior, a supreme orator and a very brave commander, to have the direction of operations of the highest importance, to enjoy the greatest honor, to be supremely wise, to be deemed the most eminent member of the senate, to obtain great wealth in an honorable way, to have many children, and to achieve supreme distinction in the state" (*Natural History* 7.43.139-40). Cf. Aristotle's similar list of the "goods" after which every man strives (*Rhetoric* 1.5.1–1.6.17). As Munck (1959, pp. 162-63) shows, the terms σοφοί, δυνατοί and εὐγενεῖς were commonly used of "those who are instructed in the sophist's art."

weak, base or "nothing."[6] And the reason for this is clear: so that no mortal can claim credit for salvation (1 Cor 1:29; cf. Rom 3:27). The Corinthians' own salvation, for example, was strictly "because of him" (ἐξ αὐτοῦ, 1 Cor 1:30). Hence, if there is to be any boasting it must only be boasting in the Lord (ἐν κυρίῳ, 1 Cor 1:31).

THE ROOT PROBLEM

Prior to the middle of the twentieth century, modern interpreters of 1 Corinthians invested prodigious efforts in trying to identify Paul's opponents in Corinth. F. C. Baur's nineteenth-century thesis that they were Judaizers was eventually eclipsed by a series of theories about other religious competitors: the Greek mystery religions, Gnosticism, or a Philonic synthesis of Greek and Jewish ideas being promulgated in the Hellenistic synagogues. Others claimed the opponents' errors were due to the philosophical influences of Stoicism, Cynicism and even Epicureanism. What these disparate interpretations typically held in common was the working assumption that baneful influences, whatever their source, generated theological differences between Paul and his opponents, differences that appeared to Paul to threaten the Corinthian congregation with serious theological error. Paul wrote 1 Corinthians in large measure to combat these opponents, counteract their theological influence and call the congregation back to his apostolic gospel.

During the second half of the twentieth century, however, the pendulum began to swing away from the assumption that there were Pauline opponents advocating an aberrant gospel in Corinth. See, for example, Munck's discussion (1959, pp. 135-67) of "The Church without Factions." Some argued that the problem in Corinth was more likely due to "pneumatic" enthusiasts or those mistakenly caught up in an over-realized eschatology. Based on new sociohistorical research, other scholars began to see more clearly that, unlike some of Paul's other epistles, 1 Corinthians does not seem to be directed against theological error. The root problem in Corinth was not a false gospel but a fractured congregation. Influential sociohistorical studies of the Corinthian situation began to emphasize the social stratification of the congregation. Disparities of wealth, education, social status and even politics created quarrels, parties and schisms (see "The Social Stratification of the Corinthian Church" in chap. 11 above). In one form or another, it was factionalism, not theological error, that constituted the root problem in Corinth. Hence, according to Mitchell (1991), the entirety of 1 Corinthians can be understood as a plea for reconciliation among the Corinthian believers.

Yet we must also exercise care in making generalizations about the overall situation in Corinth. The use of a catchall term such as "factionalism"—factions purportedly

---

[6]The phrase "the things that are not" (τὰ μὴ ὄντα) may be considered "a summary description of what is mentioned in all these constructions" (Munck, 1959, p. 163). Cf. Epictetus, *Discourses* 3.9.14, where Epictetus is judged to be "nothing at all" because of his verbal deficiencies.

generated by the social stratification of the Corinthian congregation—to sum up the several issues raised in 1 Corinthians must be qualified by the following observations.

First, we should probably view even the Corinthian factionalism as a symptom of something deeper: pride. At the end of a bewildering survey of the confused discussion of Paul's so-called opponents in Corinth over the past century and a half, Baird (1990, p. 131) helpfully concludes: "The most common feature of the Corinthian character . . . is pride. . . . This pride has fostered the factionalism that plagues the congregation."

Second, in any assessment of the social status of the Corinthians we must not lose sight of the fact that Paul explicitly says of them, "not many of you were wise according to worldly standards, not many were powerful, not many were of noble birth" (1 Cor 1:26). This is followed by an explanation of why God had nonetheless chosen *them*: God chose what is foolish in the world to shame the wise; God chose what is weak in the world to shame the strong; God chose what is low and despised in the world, even things that are not, to bring to nothing things that are, so that no human being might boast in the presence of God (1 Cor 1:27-29). Significantly, we have no later indication in the Corinthian correspondence that the Apostle's unflattering appraisal of the Corinthians' social status was met with howls of protest. However begrudgingly, the Corinthians apparently could not but acknowledge that Paul's assessment was essentially on target. In any case, the Corinthian congregation may not have been as "stratified" as some within the "new consensus" have concluded (see above, pp. 148-49).

Third, while the other cases of dissention in the Corinthian congregation (e.g., the σχίσματα of 1 Cor 11:18) may legitimately be cited alongside the ἔριδες of 1 Corinthians 1–4 as instances of a chronic "factionalism" in Corinth, in another sense they must also be differentiated. At one level every manifestation of disunity in Corinth may have reflected social disparities within the congregation. But on a more detailed level each such manifestation was unique in its own right and each must be understood in the context of its own location in the epistle. In the case of the party rivalries of 1 Corinthians 1–4 (1:13; 3:3), these are unique to these four chapters (a point referenced in 1 Clement 47:2-4), and they never surface again in the Corinthian correspondence. This is because of the Apostle's tight focus in these beginning chapters. The ἔριδες of 1 Corinthians 1–4 were uniquely prompted by the issues surrounding Paul's preaching.

Yet, as is now widely recognized, it was not the theological content of Paul's preaching that presented the difficulty; the Corinthians had not abandoned Paul's gospel. It was the form or manner of that preaching that created the problem. Paul's challenge to the ἔριδες of 1 Corinthians 1–4 and his defense of the form or manner of his preaching thus occupy the same space; indeed, they are one and the same. They constitute a single argument designed to address both problems simultaneously. This observation reinforces the notion that Paul's approach to preaching was the presenting issue in this, the first manifestation of disunity in the epistle. Paul's theological arguments in 1 Corinthians 1–2 play the focused role of providing the presuppositional foundation for his approach to preaching: proclamation. Paul anchors his arguments—both against the alternative preferred by some (σοφίᾳ λόγου, 1 Cor 1:17) and in defense of proclamation—in the gospel itself, the gospel he and the Corinthians continued to hold in common.

Fourth, Paul ascribes the Corinthians' divisive response to his preaching—that is, the party rivalries reflected in the ἔριδες of 1 Corinthians 1–4—not to theological error but to spiritual immaturity (νηπίοις, 1 Cor 3:1) and fleshliness (σαρκίνοις . . . σαρκικοί, 1 Cor 3:3-4). He could not treat them as spiritually mature (πνευματικοῖς) because their jealousy and strife (ζῆλος καὶ ἔρις, 1 Cor 3:3), demonstrated the opposite. Theirs was not a failure of allegiance to Paul's gospel, but rather a failure to appreciate that gospel's implications for their life together in the congregation.

It was this failure to grasp the gospel's implications that explained the Corinthians' worldly attitudes, values and judgments. In this they were "behaving only in a human way" (κατὰ ἄνθρωπον περιπατεῖτε, 1 Cor 3:3), that is, as those without the Spirit, the ψυχικὸς ἄνθρωπος of 1 Corinthians 2:14. They were operating uncritically on the value system of their surrounding culture and making their evaluations accordingly. Two of the symptoms of this failure were (1) their worldly infatuation with the eloquence of their society's vaunted σοφία λόγου and (2) their criticisms of Paul's more mundane—and therefore, by the standards of Greco-Roman eloquence, lackluster (cf. 2 Cor 4:7, "jars of clay")—practice as a mere herald.

Fifth, the concept of fleshliness or worldliness may thus be a more useful way of summing up the root problem in Corinth. Factionalism can take many forms, but it was the Apostle's assessment that all of them are symptoms of something deeper. When the Spirit is at work, says Paul to the Galatians, the result is love, joy, peace, patience, kindness, goodness, faithfulness, gentleness and self-control (Gal 5:22-23). But the marks of the flesh (σαρκός) are, among other things, enmity, strife (ἔρις), jealousy (ζῆλος), fits of anger, rivalries, dissensions, divisions and envy (Gal 5:20-21). In this sense, the factionalism of the Corinthians was the symptom, not the disease. The factionalism was the function of a more fundamental problem, the Corinthians' worldliness and fleshliness. As σαρκίνοις rather than πνευματικοῖς they were operating merely κατὰ ἄνθρωπον, a shortcoming that may help explain some of the other Corinthian faults (cf. the remaining entries in Paul's catalogue of the "deeds of the flesh": sexual immorality, impurity, sensuality, idolatry, sorcery, envy, drunkenness, orgies).

Sixth, the dual conclusion that Paul was not dealing with a false gospel in Corinth but rather with a serious problem of factionalism due to the social stratification of the congregation is thus relevant to our own study in two ways. It removes the older, misleading assumption that Paul's theological arguments in 1 Corinthians 1–4 were introduced to refute theological error, thus freeing them up to be seen for what they are: the presuppositional foundation, held in common by both Paul and the Corinthians, from which the Apostle will analyze the Corinthian criticisms and defend his approach to preaching. It secondly provides a useful context for understanding why some of the Corinthians found Paul's preaching deficient. In their carnality they were thinking, valuing and evaluating as "mere men"; that is, as ψυχικòι ἄνθρωποι rather than πνευματικòι (1 Cor 2:14-15). They were making their judgments, not as discerning, spiritually minded Christians, but as would those around them in their cultural setting who lacked the spiritual insight to do anything else (2:14). In other words, they were judging the ministers of Christ by the world's standards. This led in turn to the party rivalries of chapters 1–4. We lack sufficient information to pin down the precise claims of the various parties, but this much is clear: the upshot of their worldly judgments was the criticism of Paul's preaching. Paul's argument in 1 Corinthians 1–4 was designed to address this criticism by pinpointing its roots (their carnality) and calling them away from their ἔριδες and back to the gospel and its implications. These gospel implications bore relevance both for their life together as a congregation and for their appreciation of the Apostle's commission, not as a persuader but as a herald.

2:1-5—PAUL'S *MODUS OPERANDI*

The emphatic "And I" (Κἀγώ, 1 Cor 2:1; also 2:3) reaches back to Paul's instruction in 1 Corinthians 1:26: "Look to your own calling, brethren" (AT).[7] Just as the Corinthians demonstrated the principle that God chooses to work through unimpressive means, so also does Paul's ministry.[8] Thus Paul once again stresses his oneness with the Corinthians. The rebuke for the inconsistency of their behavior will emerge soon enough (1 Cor 3:1); for the present Paul is content to continue laying its foundation.

The strong focus on Paul's ministry in 1 Corinthians 2:1-5 provides the clearest and most detailed statement—both positive and negative—of the Apostle's manner of preaching to be found anywhere in his writings. We have already noted in 1 Corinthians 1:17 the form of communication Paul disavowed: σοφία λόγου. Here he reiterates that disavowal in two similar and essentially synonymous constructions:

2:1 οὐ καθ' ὑπεροχὴν λόγου ἢ σοφίας

2:4 οὐκ ἐν πειθοῖ[ς] σοφίας [λόγοις][9]

---

[7]Treating this section as a mere "digression" (e.g., Wuellner, 1970, p. 201) badly distorts Paul's emphasis. In point of fact, the sections dealing explicitly with Paul's preaching constitute the main thrust of the entire passage.
[8]As Wilckens notes, "1,26-31 und 2,1-5 parallele Argumentationen sind" (1979, p. 502; cf. p. 504).
[9]Regarding the textual choice between οὐκ ἐν πειθοῖ σοφίας and οὐκ ἐν πειθοῖς σοφίας λόγοις in 1 Cor 2:4, Bultmann (1965, p. 9) says: "As far as the interpretation of the sentence is concerned, it makes no difference which reading we accept. In either case Paul is stating that his preaching does not derive its power to convince from the rhetorical art of human wisdom."

Both of these constructions hold three important features in common with 1 Corinthians 1:17. First, in each case the subject is explicitly Paul's preaching;[10] second, each is a disavowal of a particular manner or form of that preaching; and third, in each disavowal σοφία and λόγος appear together.

On the other hand, the three constructions differ enough to indicate that they are not entirely synonymous. In 1:17 the genitive λόγου specifies what aspect of σοφία Paul has in mind: it is a wisdom having to do with speech. The phrase refers essentially to the Greco-Roman eloquence we have previously surveyed. But then with 1 Corinthians 1:18 Paul's argument widens and the use of σοφία widens with it. Paul moves temporarily away from the more narrow focus on his preaching to establish a general principle regarding divine versus human wisdom. Accordingly, in 1 Corinthians 1:18-31 σοφία, with its cognates and antonyms, occurs in a variety of more general positive and negative senses. In no case in these verses does it occur in tandem with λόγος. In fact, λόγος does not appear at all in 1 Corinthians 1:19-31. With Paul's return to his preaching[11] in 2:1, however, the two terms immediately appear together again. In 1 Corinthians 2:1 ὑπεροχὴν λόγου ἢ σοφίας appears to speak of an eloquent form and a wise content—both impressive to the world. In 1 Corinthians 2:4 the adjective πειθοῖς and the genitive σοφίας together define and delimit λόγοις.[12] It is specifically the form of words considered *by the world* to be "persuasive" and "wise" that Paul avoids.

While these three references thus differ slightly from one another, it nevertheless is clear enough that each refers in essence to the form of speech recommended by Greco-Roman rhetoric and practiced everywhere by the speakers of the day. This conclusion is strongly reinforced by a fourth construction found a few verses later in 1 Corinthians 2:13: "in words not taught by human wisdom" (οὐκ ἐν διδακτοῖς ἀνθρωπίνης σοφίας λόγοις). Again, the subject here is specifically Paul's speech, the construction represents a disavowal of a particular form or manner of speech, and λόγος and σοφία occur together. But the additional

---

[10] On the textual problem of μαρτύριον/μυστήριον (1 Cor 2:1), see Barrett (1968, pp. 62-63). While, as Barrett says, "the balance of probability favours *testimony*" (p. 62), for our purposes the choice makes little difference. The phrase should probably be read as an objective genitive.

[11] καταγγέλλων (2:1); ὁ λόγος μου καὶ τὸ κήρυγμά μου (2:4). The latter phrase represents a hendiadys referring to Paul's preaching. Given Paul's argument throughout this section, and given the fact that λόγος was a widely used rhetorical term and could thus be potentially misleading in the present context, Paul apparently added κήρυγμα, at once a more specific and more comfortable (to him) term, for the purpose of avoiding confusion. The two terms should probably not be interpreted here as distinguishing form from content.

[12] None of the textual variants within this phrase appreciably affect for our purposes the sense of this verse. All of the options give essentially the same meaning.

words help pin down Paul's meaning. What speech was "taught by human wisdom" for his readers? Certainly neither gnostic nor Hellenistic-Jewish Wisdom ideas would qualify, at least not in the minds of their proponents. Yet this is what Paul's argument requires; his readers must be willing to acknowledge the human origin of their ideas for Paul's plea to carry weight.

In the light of what we have observed about the Greco-Roman society of the first century, it is scarcely conceivable that this and its sister constructions could be anything other than a reference to the rhetorical teachings of the schools and the orators, whose task, we may remember, was from the beginning to produce students who were "wise in speech" (σοφωτέρους ἐν τοῖς λόγοις).[13] Paul rejected such teaching and the forms of wise discourse it produced as inappropriate for the preaching of the gospel. Unlike other critics of rhetoric, Paul nowhere suggests that Greco-Roman rhetoric was inherently unworthy or that it must be rejected in general. Philosophical discussions about the appropriateness of persuasive strategies for statesmen, orators or lawyers would likely have held little interest for Paul. His argument is merely that these strategies are inappropriate for the purposes of preaching the gospel.

This conclusion is still more firmly established by an examination of what it was that Paul set in the place of Greco-Roman rhetoric. First, Paul resolved, presumably before arriving in Corinth, that he would put aside all else[14] except the proclamation (καταγγέλλων) of Christ, and in particular, Christ "and him crucified" (1 Cor 2:2). He would eschew all λόγοι and σοφία calculated to impress (ὑπεροχὴν, 1 Cor 2:1), concentrating instead on the straightforward and therefore rhetorically unimpressive "announcing" of the gospel of the cross. Whether more or less elaborated (see "The Related Passages" in chap. 15 below), this announcing function would constitute the single, central, unchanging essence of his preaching.

PAUL'S CRUCICENTRIC PROCLAMATION

T. D. Still (2012) argues that Paul's concerted emphasis on "Christ crucified" in Corinth "was occasioned, at least in part, by the Thessalonians' fascination with, if not fixation upon, Christ's coming and the deleterious effects their preoccupation with the parou-

---

[13]Isocrates, *Antidosis* 200.

[14]Thurén (2002) is no doubt right to view as hyperbole Paul's statement in 1 Cor 2:2 that he had resolved to know "nothing" in Corinth except Jesus Christ and him crucified (p. 433), for as he says, a literal reading "would give rise to far-fetched conclusions" (p. 421). His inclusion of verse 3 in this assessment is, however, less certain.

sia was having upon that congregation" (p. 5). According to Still, "Paul thought it pastorally prudent, if not theologically necessary, to reshape his missionary message so as to place less stress on Christ's coming and more weight upon Christ's death." While Still's thesis presents no challenge to our reading of 1 Corinthians 1–4, it nonetheless represents a serious misunderstanding of Paul's proclamation. John's Gospel provides the conceptual framework needed to highlight the problem.

John records Jesus as saying to Nicodemus, "As Moses lifted up the serpent in the wilderness, so must the Son of Man be lifted up, that whoever believes in him may have eternal life" (Jn 3:14-15). The serpent reference, of course, was to Numbers 21:8-9, where Moses was instructed to lift the image of a serpent on a pole so that "everyone who is bitten, when he sees it, shall live." So it was that "Moses made a bronze serpent and set it on a pole. And if a serpent bit anyone, he would look at the bronze serpent and live."

Twice more in John's Gospel Jesus speaks of his being "lifted up." To those who oppose him he says, "When you have lifted up the Son of Man, then you will know that I am he" (Jn 8:28). And later, to a gathered crowd Jesus says, "The hour has come for the Son of Man to be glorified. . . . And I, when I am lifted up from the earth, will draw all people to myself" (Jn 12:23, 32). To this John adds the explanatory comment: "He said this to show by what kind of death he was going to die" (Jn 12:33).

Christ's "lifting up" thus carried a dual reference: a literal reference to his being brutally "lifted up" on a Roman cross, but still more profoundly, a figurative reference to his being "lifted up" in exaltation, the first stage of his return to glory (Jn 17:5). The hour of his "lifting up" on the cross was the very hour of his revelation and glorification, and it was from that highly visible position that he would "draw all people to myself." Like the lifted serpent in the wilderness, whoever raised their eyes in faith to the crucified Jesus would live. To look on that forsaken man lifted up on a cross, and yet to see there the exalted Son of God being lifted up to heaven in victory over death, is the avenue to salvation: "For this is the will of my Father, that everyone who looks on the Son and believes in him should have eternal life" (Jn 6:40).

Against this backdrop it becomes clear that Jesus' crucifixion was scarcely something Paul decided to emphasize in Corinth in contrast to Thessalonica; it was central to *all* of Paul's proclamation. "The death of Christ matters so much to Paul because it is the only way of salvation" (Inkelaar, 2011, p. 304). Since Paul was Christ's commissioned herald, Jesus' death was the consistent centerpiece of his apostolic message (Rom 10:9-13), wherever and to whomever he preached it—including the Thessalonians (1 Thess 1:10; Acts 17:1-3).

The herald was not a persuader; he was a proclaimer, and Jesus' words help to explain why. The herald's calling was, on each new occasion, to "lift up" the crucified Christ before his listeners so that they too might look on him in faith and live. This is, in fact, precisely how Paul described his missionary preaching to the Galatians: "It was before your eyes [οἷς κατ' ὀφθαλμοὺς] that Jesus Christ was publicly portrayed [προεγράφη] as crucified" (Gal 3:1). The verb προγράφω denotes the announcing or giving public notice of something. Paul was determined to depend on the simple proclamation of the herald, confident that the power of his message did not lie in his prowess as a speaker but in the exalted Christ's intent to use his "lifting up"—the public setting forth of "Christ and him crucified"—to draw the listeners to himself.

Second, and closely related, Paul would depend on the power of the Spirit working through the proclaimed gospel to produce results in the listeners. He would avoid the use of the psychological dynamic of persuasion to engineer πίστις. Instead he would count solely on the dynamic of the cross. The hendiadys "Spirit and power" (πνεύματος καὶ δυνάμεως, 1 Cor 2:4) emphasizes what Barrett calls "the supernatural conviction and force" with which the demonstration or "proof" (ἀπόδειξις) of the gospel is driven home where the δύναμις θεοῦ is at work (1 Cor 2:4-5).[15] Paul was determined to depend on this power alone for results in his preaching.[16]

The affirmations of 1 Corinthians 2:1-5 constitute a repudiation of the dynamic of rhetoric for the purposes of preaching. This becomes clear when we compare the approach Paul is proposing with the persuasive strategies we have already observed. Unlike for the persuaders, for Paul the message was not a manipulated variable; it was a sturdy, unchanging *Constant*—Christ crucified, simply proclaimed. The wavering variable was the matter of *results*. Instead of determining at the outset what results he would accomplish, Paul insisted on leaving the outcome to the Spirit. We need only summarize the often repeated datives in Paul's argument to catch this point:

1 Corinthians 1:18

    to the perishing . . . foolishness

    to the ones being saved . . . the power of God

---

[15]Barrett (1968, p. 65). These two terms (πνεύματος καὶ δυνάμεως) may best be taken as objective genitives. Wilckens (1979, p. 505; cf. also Chevallier, 1966, pp. 108-9) seeks to make them subjective genitives, but this is unlikely given the second member. Wilckens's attempt to circumvent the difficulty by labeling δυνάμεως epexegetical is unpersuasive.

[16]Paul's preaching in Corinth may or may not have been accompanied by signs and wonders. But even if so, these do not play a large role in the argument of 1 Cor and are not the significance of ἀπόδειξις here. Cf. Paul's similar dependence on the convicting work of the Spirit, in contrast to his own efforts, in 1 Thess 1:5 (NIV): "Our gospel came to you not simply with words [οὐκ . . . ἐν λόγῳ μόνον] but also with power [ἐν δυνάμει], with the Holy Spirit and deep conviction [ἐν πνεύματι ἁγίῳ καὶ πληροφορίᾳ πολλῇ]." See also 1 Thess 2:13 (NIV): "When you received the word of God, which you heard from us, you accepted [δέχομαι, "to receive something offered"] it not as a human word [οὐ λόγον ἀνθρώπων], but as it actually [ἀληθῶς] is, the word of God, which is indeed at work [ἐνεργεῖται] in you who believe."

1 Corinthians 1:23-24
> to the Jews . . . a stumbling block
>
> to the Greeks . . . foolishness
>
> to the called ones, Jew or Greek . . . the power of God and the wisdom of God

1 Corinthians 1:30
> to us . . . wisdom from God, righteousness, sanctification, redemption[17]

When Paul stood before an audience, he could not know who among them were the "the perishing" or who were "the called." He could only herald the message of Christ crucified and leave the distinction to the Spirit. As a steward of the gospel it was his task to proclaim it faithfully, but it was not his responsibility, as it was the persuader's, to produce πίστις in the listeners. That was something that must remain contingent on the power of God, not on his facility as an orator. As Paul himself put it in 2 Corinthians 2:14-17:

> But thanks be to God, who in Christ always leads us in triumphal procession, and through us spreads the fragrance of the knowledge of him everywhere. For we are the aroma of Christ to God among those who are being saved and among those who are perishing [ἐν τοῖς σῳζομένοις καὶ ἐν τοῖς ἀπολλυμένοις], to one a fragrance from death to death, to the other a fragrance from life to life. Who is sufficient for these things? For we are not, like so many, peddlers of God's word, but as men of sincerity, as commissioned by God, in the sight of God we speak in Christ.

Paul reckoned the stakes in his preaching to be momentous. Eternal destinies hung in the balance; hence the question, who is sufficient for these things? This much is certain: Paul believed that he as a preacher was not competent to bear such a burden. His confidence lay elsewhere.

PAUL'S WEAKNESS AND FEAR

It is sometimes asked whether Paul could have measured up to the standards of Greco-Roman eloquence had he been so inclined. The answer depends on what we mean by eloquence. Many commentators seem to want to answer this question in the affirmative on the basis of the obvious effectiveness of Paul's letters. This approach, however, requires

---

[17]Though Christ is the subject of ἐγενήθη in 1 Cor 1:30, the change took place in the Corinthians. Whereas previously something else had been σοφία to them, when they heard the gospel, Christ "became to us wisdom from God." The emphasis falls on their change of perception.

us to brush aside the plainly stated distinction between Paul's letters (ἐπιστολαί), which according to his critics were "weighty and strong," and his missionary preaching (λόγοι), which according to the same critics was deemed "of no account" (ἐξουθενημένος, 2 Cor 10:10). Further, this approach also fails to appreciate what ancient Greco-Roman audiences considered eloquent. As Mitchell (2002, p. 242) says, "Classical *paideia* constituted instruction in grammatics and rhetoric. . . . Such *paideia*—training in proper speech and in the literary classics—was limited in the Imperial period to small numbers of elites and those they supported. Its attainment maintained from generation to generation an upper social class who would know one another on sight, anywhere in the empire, just as those without *paideia* would give themselves away the moment they open their mouths." By the exacting standards of this sort of rhetorical education and practice, the critics were no doubt right about Paul; in fact he concedes as much in 2 Corinthians 11:6. Compared to the cultured orators the Corinthians so appreciated, Paul's proclamation did indeed give the appearance of being rhetorically unimpressive.

In this light, Paul's language in 1 Corinthians 2:3 ("I was with you in weakness and in fear and much trembling") should probably be read as something more than the renouncing of an otherwise available option (cf. 1 Thess 2:3-6). We may recall our earlier discussion of the hazards speakers of the day faced: "Judgement is passing upon us as often as we speak" (Cicero, *De or.* 1.123-25; see chap. 6 above). Significantly, according to Acts 18:9 it was at Corinth that Paul teetered on the brink of abandoning his preaching, prompting a message from the Lord: "Do not be afraid, but go on speaking and do not be silent." We may lack the basis for defining too closely the nature of this fear, but the problem was clearly related to his role as a preacher. His expression of weakness, fear and trembling in 1 Corinthians 2:3 occurs as part of a contrast with "lofty speech or wisdom" (1 Cor 2:1). Thus, however one understands it, the weakness is of the sort that may be juxtaposed with rhetorical skill and power. See Black (1984, pp. 100-104).

Perhaps the best way to think of Paul's fearfulness and weakness may be to view them as normal human responses to a combination of (1) the overt hostility Paul's preaching consistently engendered, not least in Corinth (Acts 18:1-17), and (2) the weightiness of the issues at stake (2 Cor 2:14-17); see on this second point Quintilian: "I am not unwilling that the man who has got to make a speech should show signs of nervousness when he rises to his feet, should change colour and make it clear that he feels the risks of his position" (*Inst. or.* 12.5.1). Bouyer (1990, p. 6) brings out this nuance in his summary of 1 Corinthians 2:3-5 when he says, "So the contrast from which everything begins is clear: On one side, a wisdom of the Greek kind, with high-flown ideas beautifully expressed; on the other, an announcement, like that of a herald who is himself of no account—hence this consciousness of personal weakness, this fear and trembling of a representative, not so much before those whom he addresses as before him whom he represents: God." Finally, (3) the awareness of his own inadequacies as a messenger ("earthen vessels," 2 Cor 4:7 AT; cf. 2 Cor 10:10).

ELOQUENCE AND SELF-ASSURANCE

The Apostle's sense of inadequacy in his preaching placed him in stark contrast to the popular orators of the day. For their part, Greco-Roman speakers stepped before audiences with a wondrous, if not always justified, confidence. The immensely popular first-century orator Scopelian, for instance, was the very model of the assured orator, one who appeared before his audiences, according to Philostratus, not "with the bearing of a timid speaker, but as befitted one who was entering the lists to win glory for himself and was confident that he could not fail."[18] Scopelian's confidence was typical of the orators of Paul's day.

The much earlier Isocrates might be adduced as an exception here, but Isocrates was in fact an exception that reinforces the rule. According to Cicero, ancient scholarship generally agreed that Isocrates was a consummate orator. Yet Cicero himself, though he respected Isocrates, felt that Isocrates lacked completeness because "his oratory does not take part in the battle nor use steel, but plays with a wooden sword."[19] This was a reference to the fact that, though he was a renowned speech writer and teacher of rhetoric, Isocrates himself shrank from actually standing before an audience. Why did Isocrates avoid the crowds, devoting himself, as Aristotle says, "wholly to the composition of theory and models of oratory"?[20] "I have abstained from . . . practicing oratory," Isocrates said, because "my voice was inadequate and I lacked assurance" (τόλμα).[21]

Isocrates's reference to a lack of τόλμα before an audience is striking, for this sort of self-assurance was the one thing without which no orator could succeed. Comparing the relative advantages of rhetorical education, native ability and practice, Isocrates said,

> [Education's] powers are not equal nor comparable to [the other two]. For if one should take lessons in all the principles of oratory and master them with the greatest thoroughness, he might, perhaps become a more pleasing speaker than most, but let him stand up before the crowd and lack one thing only, namely, assurance (τόλμα), and he would not be able to utter a word.[22]

Reticence and fearfulness were simply incompatible with Greek eloquence. When it came to oratory, a strong speaking voice and a self-confident bearing

---

[18]Philostratus, *Lives* 519.
[19]Cicero, *Opt. gen.* 17; cf. Philostratus, *Lives* 505.
[20]Quoted by Cicero, *Brutus* 48.
[21]Isocrates, *Epistles* 8.7; cf. Isocrates, *To Philip* 81.
[22]Isocrates, *Antidosis* 192. See also the data cited on θάρσος ("courage") by Munck (1959, pp. 158-59).

were the very things "which have the greatest power" (μεγίστην δύναμιν).[23] As Dionysius put it, Isocrates "lacked the first and most important qualities of a public speaker . . . without which it is impossible to address a crowd."[24]

But this sort of self-assurance is precisely what Paul disavows to the Corinthians. He reminds them that he had come before them "in weakness and in fear and much trembling" (1 Cor 2:3).[25] Paul by no means lacked confidence in the effectiveness of his preaching; on the contrary, he was supremely confident of its power. But this confidence was based on the fact that in both form and content his preaching was dependent on the power of the gospel.[26] Hence, unlike the orators, Paul's confidence was not in his own ability to create πίστις through the σοφία ἀνθρώπων. His was a confidence in the δυνάμις θεοῦ working through the announced gospel (1 Cor 2:5). As John Calvin put it, paraphrasing the Apostle, "The reason why I lacked embellishments of speech, and did not argue with more refinement and subtlety, was because I did not strive after those things, in fact I rather disdained them, because only one thing mattered to me—to proclaim Christ with simplicity."[27]

EXPERIENTIAL PROOF OF THE GOSPEL

"The ideas expressed by Paul and the terms he uses must lead us to the conclusion that Paul deliberately rejects Greek rhetoric in his preaching of the gospel" (Marshall, 1987a, p. 389.) That Paul is using the technical language of rhetorical discourse here is acknowledged even by Wilckens (1979, p. 505). But on Paul's use of the term ἀπόδειξις in particular, contrast 1 Corinthians 2:4 and 4:9 (and 2 Cor 4:2) with Aristotle, *Rhetoric* 1.1.11; Plutarch, *Moralia* 387A, 422C. For a somewhat too finely distinguished but nevertheless useful discussion of ἀπόδειξις in 1 Corinthians 2:4, see Oke (1956).

Of what did the ἀπόδειξις Paul refers to in 1 Corinthians 2:4 consist? As Witherington (1995, p. 125) says, the term ἀπόδειξις was "a technical rhetorical term that Quintilian says refers to 'a clear proof,' 'a means of proving what is not certain by means of what is certain' (*Inst. or.* 5.10.7). Cicero defines it as a 'logical proof' (*Academia* 2.8). If we bear in mind that the standard definition of rhetoric in Quintilian's day was the *dyna-*

---

[23]Isocrates, *Panathenaicus* 9.
[24]Dionysius, *Critical Essays*, Isocrates 1.
[25]See Drake Williams (2001, pp. 149-56) on Zech 4:6 as the background to Paul's weakness.
[26]Cf. 2 Cor 12:9-10: "But [God] said to me, 'My grace is sufficient for you, for my power is made perfect in weakness.' Therefore I will boast all the more gladly of my weaknesses, so that the power of Christ may rest upon me. For the sake of Christ, then, I am content with weaknesses, insults, hardships, persecutions, and calamities. For when I am weak, then I am strong."
[27]Calvin (1960, p. 49).

mis ('power') of persuasion (*Inst. or.* 2.15.2-4) and that Dio Chrysostom refers to the gift of eloquence simply as *dynamis* (33.3), this passage becomes clearer. Paul says that the 'proof' he offered of the truth of the gospel about Christ crucified was not in the form of formal rhetorical proofs, but came from the experiential proof that the powerful Spirit had changed the Corinthians' lives when he preached. Because of this their faith would not be in the power of human rhetoric or wisdom but in the power of God (2 Cor 12:12)."

But what was this "experiential proof" of which Witherington speaks? Witherington's reference to 2 Corinthians 12:12—where Paul says, "The signs of a true apostle were performed among you with utmost patience, with signs and wonders and mighty works"—points to miraculous signs. Others, such as Barrett (1968, p. 66), argue that the ἀπόδειξις was simply that "divine power" that gripped some of the hearers when Paul preached Christ and "constrained them to penitence and faith; this was the work of the Holy Spirit." Collins (1999, p. 117) says, "The source of [the proclamation's] demonstrative power is not the eloquence of the human rhetor, Paul, but the Spirit and power of God. . . . The power of the Spirit contrasts with Paul's weakness and trembling. The demonstrative power that comes from the Spirit contrasts with the persuasive words of merely human wisdom."

In his *Homilies on 1 Corinthians*, Chrysostom argued at length for this latter view. "If without signs [the apostles] wrought conviction, far greater does the wonder appear." When observers are convinced by miracles and wonders (in contrast to "discourse being the only instrument of conviction"), "necessity has done this, and the evidence of the things seen, and it is not of choice, but by the vastness of the spectacle the powers of the mind are dragged along. It follows that by how much the more evident and overpowering the course of events, by so much is the part of faith abridged." Chrysostom's point is that genuine faith rests on "the unseen" (the truth of the gospel), not "the seen" (signs and wonders). This was why, Chrysostom says, despite the fact that the Apostles did sometimes work miracles, the ἀπόδειξις of which Paul speaks in 1 Corinthians 2:4 was a "spiritual" demonstration—and why, he goes on to argue, "miracles are not done now" (IV.4-5). See also Thomas Aquinas's similar argument, citing both Ambrose and Gregory, regarding the question of "whether Christ should have manifested the truth of his resurrection by proofs" (*Summa Theologiae*, III.55.5).

THE RELATED PASSAGES

At this juncture we are in a position to grasp more fully the arguments encased in each of the statements noted in chapter eleven regarding the manner or form of Paul's ministry. We have already seen the first five statements in 1 Corinthians 1–2. The remaining five are found in 2 Corinthians. These five passages inevitably reflect further developments in Paul's relationship to the Corinthians.

However one understands these developments, we know they were complicated and difficult for all involved. The background to the following passages thus reflects developments several painful stages beyond that of 1 Corinthians 1–4. Yet for our purposes the important point is this: each passage significantly reinforces essentially the same understanding of the Apostle's approach to preaching that we discover in 1 Corinthians 1–4.

2 Corinthians 1:12. Paul could claim that he had a clear conscience before God (cf. 1 Cor 4:4).[28] The reason his conscience was clear was that he had consistently conducted himself "in the world"—but especially before the Corinthians—in a manner that was characterized by simplicity (ἁπλότητι;[29] cf. 2 Cor 11:3 and context), sincerity (εἰλικρινείᾳ) and the grace of God. By contrast, he had not conducted himself "in fleshly wisdom" (ἐν σοφίᾳ σαρκικῇ, NASB; cf. 1 Cor 3:3). While this statement reaches beyond Paul's preaching to include other aspects of his behavior, the reference to fleshly wisdom in contrast to simplicity and sincerity (cf. also 2 Cor 2:17 below) suggests that this passage may best be understood against the background of the issues treated in 1 Corinthians 1–4. Paul was eager that his open and transparent approach in proclamation be viewed by the Corinthians as something to be proud rather than ashamed of (2 Cor 1:14; cf. also 5:12; 12:11).

THE APOSTLE AS DECEIVER

Some are disinclined to trust Paul's claims to sincerity. For example, consider Given's thesis (2001, p. 3): "Paul's rhetorical strategies, both according to the historical novel called Acts and his own epistles, display such a degree of intentional ambiguity, cunning, and deception as to make him justifiably vulnerable to the polemical charge of perpetrating sophistries." Given's argument is that Paul deliberately used misleading rhetoric because he *had to* in order to accomplish his purposes "in an apocalyptic world filled with deception" (p. 4).

With regard in particular to Paul's disavowal of eloquence, DeWitt (1954, pp. 107-8) says of his "beguilements" in 1 Corinthians 1:17–2:5, "It is part of his artfulness to conceal his art." Hence, when Paul disavows "all knowledge of rhetoric and philosophy" his words are to be understood as rhetorical sleight of hand: "This is mere literary irony and its purpose is to forestall any impression that might diminish the acceptability of the

---

[28]Cf. Patrick and Scult (1999, pp. 79-80) on "God as Universal Audience" in rhetoric.
[29]The reading ἁπλότητι in Nestle-Aland (26th and subsequent eds.) represents a change from earlier editions, which preferred ἁγιότητι. The manuscript evidence is balanced, but the fact that Paul never elsewhere uses ἁγιότητι and the good sense made by ἁπλότητι favor the latter.

message. In point of fact he is about to do the very thing he disavows; he will be writing artfully and in this very same second chapter he will set up a canon of truth; which is a concept of sheer philosophy." Later DeWitt says, "Paul, in spite of his disavowals of eloquence, exhibits abundant knowledge of the rules. . . . He is a practical rhetorician." Marshall (1987b, p. 371; cf. p. 372) considers Paul's self-deprecation regarding eloquence to be "shameful," going "well beyond the rules for this device of rhetoric as well as offending other social customs"; Shaw (1982, p. 65) views this passage as "devious and unrelenting." See Mussies's comparisons (1972, pp. 154-55); and Brockriede (1955, pp. 380-81) on Bentham's criticisms of Paul. See also Judge (1968, pp. 37-40, 44).

Such criticisms ignore the obvious question raised by Martyn (1997, p. 147): "One might suggest," he says, "that Paul distinguishes an initial and nonrhetorical proclamation of the gospel from a later and rhetorically sophisticated formulation of a written argument addressed to persons who are already Christians. In short, does Paul consider rhetoric to be both useful and appropriate when the communication is being carried out within the bosom of the church?" Though it is typically ignored by Paul's accusers, Martyn's distinction between (1) "a nonrhetorical proclamation of the gospel" to unbelievers and (2) "a later and rhetorically sophisticated formulation of a written argument addressed to persons who are already Christians" is potentially an important one. See appendix three (also above, pp. 179-81) on the profound epistemological differences between these two audiences, differences that would certainly have justified or even required contrasting communicational approaches. But this observation must be coupled with a second, equally important point: we require a much more careful and nuanced understanding of what it was Paul was, and was not, disavowing; see the analysis in chapter seventeen below. The accusations of deceitfulness betray a tin ear on the part of the critics to both of these points, revealing a certain obliviousness to Paul's essential argument and the deeper epistemological issues it reflects.

---

2 Corinthians 2:17. In this passage Paul once again establishes a contrast. He is not like the "many" who adulterate and peddle (καπηλεύω) the word of God. Instead he speaks with sincerity (εἰλικρινείᾳ) as one whose preaching is both "commissioned by God" (cf. 1 Thess 1:5, 8; 2:2, 4, 8, 9, 13) and conducted "in the sight of God." Paul does not explain who "the many"[30] were, nor what he means by adulterating the word of God. Yet the verb καπηλεύω was sometimes used critically of rhetoricians; Socrates, for instance, disparaged the ancient sophists as "those who take their doctrines the round of our cities, hawking them about [καπηλεύω] to any odd purchaser who desires them."[31]

---

[30]Or "the rest" if one prefers the alternate reading, λοιποί.
[31]Plato, *Protagoras* 313D; cf. Philostratus, *Life of Apollonius* 1.13. See Wilken (2003, pp. 72-77)

In view of Paul's contrast with the sincerity and heavenward orientation of his own approach (cf. the same contrast in 4:2 below), it seems reasonable to conclude that the corruption of the word of God Paul has in mind was related to the employment of σοφία λόγου.

2 Corinthians 4:2. Paul has stressed the straightforwardness and transparency (παρρησία) of his approach since 2 Corinthians 3:12. Here he emphasizes his renouncement of hidden agendas or strategies.[32] He does not practice "deception,"[33] nor does he "handle deceitfully"[34] the word of God. Instead, he is determined to stand or fall by the simple exhibition[35] of the truth. It is only by this open proclamation that he strives to commend himself "to everyone's conscience in the sight of God" (cf. 1 Thess 2:4). This passage thus shares with 1 Corinthians 1–4 Paul's portrayal of his preaching: the direct, non-rhetorical announcement of the gospel (cf. 1 Cor 4:5). Where it differs is in its emphasis (in concert with 2 Cor 2:17 above) on the issue of trickery and deceit. No such emphasis appears in 1 Corinthians 1–4.

2 Corinthians 4:7. This statement represents a cryptic metaphorical summary of the abstract principle that undergirds 1 Corinthians 1:18–2:5. The context indicates that the treasure is the gospel (4:2-6). The picture of the earthenware vessel portrays the unimpressive appearance of its external form to the world. Though the metaphor is broader than Paul's preaching, it just as certainly includes his preaching, a subject that is an integral part of the immediate context (2 Cor 3:12; 4:2, 5, 13).[36] The ἵνα clause is virtually a mirror image of the ἵνα

---

for a discussion of this phenomenon in the Roman world; cf. Dio Chrysostom, *Discourses* 8.9, for a vivid description of a late first-century Corinthian example during the Isthmian games.

[32] τὰ κρυπτὰ τῆς αἰσχύνης; on this phrase, see Glover (1945, p. 190).

[33] πανουργίᾳ, "trickery"; cf. Galen, *De placitis Hippocratis et Platonis* 1.6.17; 2.5.49.

[34] δολόω, "to disguise, make false through deception"; cf. οὐδὲ ἐν δόλῳ, 1 Thess 2:3. The rhetorician Lucian (*Hermotimus* 59) compared philosophers to tavern keepers (τοῖς καπήλοις) because both cheat and give false measure by adulterating (δολόω) their wares.

[35] φανερώσει, "to manifest, make clear."

[36] Origen interestingly applies Paul's metaphor not just to Paul but to all of the apostles and the Scriptures too. All of the apostles, he says, would have admitted with Paul to being "rude in speech but not in knowledge." "Then there is the passage, 'But we have this treasure in earthen vessels, that the exceeding greatness of the power may be of God, and not from ourselves'; which we interpret of the treasure elsewhere described as the treasure of knowledge and hidden wisdom, and we take the 'earthen vessels' in the sense of the ordinary, and, in Greek estimation, contemptible diction of the Scriptures, wherein the exceeding greatness of the power of God is really seen. For the mysteries of the truth and the force of what was said, in spite of the ordinary language, were strong enough to reach the ends of the earth, and bring into subjection to the word of Christ, not only the foolish things of the world, but sometimes also its wise ones" (*Philocalia* 4.2; G. Lewis, 1911, p. 35).

clause in 1 Corinthians 2:5 (cf. also 1 Cor 1:31). Thus this statement contributes to the broad perspective within which the specifics of Paul's view of his preaching must be seen. "The worthlessness of the vessels is evidence that the transcendent power which attends the preaching of the gospel, the change which it effects in human lives, is God's and not the apostle's."[37]

2 Corinthians 10:3-4. Some in Corinth reckoned Paul strictly by human standards, as if his ministry were conducted merely "according to the flesh" (κατὰ σάρκα). But Paul replies that while he is indeed a mortal man, his ministry is not to be measured merely by human standards. His ministry is a spiritual battle, and the weapons of that battle—that is, the means by which he conducts his ministry—are not merely human but are divinely powerful (οὐ σαρκικὰ ἀλλὰ δυνατὰ τῷ θεῷ). As such they are powerful enough to overthrow "arguments" (λογισμοὺς, "the product of a cognitive process . . . reasoning") and every towering thing that rises up against the knowledge of God. Paul's central "weapon" was of course the κήρυγμά, the proclaimed gospel. The phrase οὐ σαρκικὰ ἀλλὰ δυνατὰ τῷ θεῷ can only be fully appreciated in the light of the above passages, and 1 Corinthians 1–4 in particular. Paul was supremely confident that the placarded cross was powerful enough to triumph over even the most impressive human competitors.

A summary of what the apostle embraces and rejects in these five passages shows how plainly they echo the ideas we have observed in 1 Corinthians 1:17–2:5. According to Paul, his ministry was not characterized by human wisdom or hidden strategies. He neither operated "according to the flesh" nor depended on human persuasive strategies. On the contrary, he says, his straightforward ministry was characterized by simplicity, innocence, sincerity and transparency (cf. 1 Thess 2:3). Paul understood that the message he preached would remain veiled to "those who are perishing" (2 Cor 4:3-4), but eschewing any human attempt to impress (cf. 2 Cor 4:5; 10:12; 1 Thess 2:6), he focused on simply placarding the truth of Christ before the consciences of his listeners. His ministry was not only from God; it was conducted with an open face before God. While such a ministry may have given a humble, earthenware appearance to the world, it nevertheless possessed the divine power to bring down whatever impressive opposition might be raised against it.

---

[37] Bruce (1971, p. 197); cf. in this regard Ballard's argument (2014), based on 2 Cor 5:13, that Paul's shortcomings extended beyond his rhetorical deficiencies to his leadership in general.

AN EARLY CHURCH ECHO

Origen (ca. A.D. 185–254), an early Christian scholar and theologian, on the power at work in the preaching of the gospel:

"I [affirm] that to people who can study the question about Jesus' apostles intelligently and reasonably it will appear that these men taught Christianity and succeeded in bringing many to obey the word of God by divine power. For in them there was no power of speaking or of giving an ordered narrative by the standards of Greek dialectical or rhetorical arts which convinced their hearers. It seems to me that if Jesus had chosen some men who were wise in the eyes of the multitude, and who were capable of thinking and speaking acceptably to crowds, and if he had used them as the means of propagating his teaching, he might on very good grounds have been suspected of making use of a method similar to that of the philosophers who are leaders of some particular sect. The truth of the claim that his teaching is divine would no longer have been self evident, in that the gospel and the preaching were in persuasive words of the wisdom that consisted in literary style and composition. And the faith, like the faith of the philosophers of this world in their doctrines, would have been in the wisdom of men, and not in the power of God. If anyone saw fisherfolk and tax-collectors *who had not had even a primary education* . . . and who with great courage not only spoke to Jews about faith in Jesus but also preached him among the other nations with success, would he not try to find out the source of their persuasive power? For it is not that which is popularly supposed to be power. Who would not say that Jesus had fulfilled the saying, 'Come follow me, and I will make you fishers of men,' by a certain divine power in his apostles? Paul also . . . says: 'And my word and my preaching were not in persuasive words of man's wisdom, but in demonstration of the spirit and of power, that our faith may not be in the wisdom of men but in the power of God.' . . . [Jesus' saying about becoming "fishers of men"] is relevant; for it shows both the foreknowledge of our Savior about the preaching of the gospel, which is obviously divine, and the strength of the Word which without teachers conquers those who believe by the divine power of its persuasion" (Origen, *Contra Celsum* 1.62; Chadwick, 1953, pp. 57-58).

16

Paul's Argument Completed

1 Corinthians 2:6–4:21

We have now observed the essential features of Paul's view of proclamation. Because this has been the object of our investigation from the beginning, it might be possible to conclude here and turn to the implications of Paul's argument. But it would be premature to do so for two reasons: First, we would be leaving our treatment open to the suspicion of undue selectivity. While setting limits is always necessary, too much selectivity can lead to distortion. Hence we must examine, albeit more briefly now, at least the remainder of our literary unit, chapters 1–4. Second, the above treatment of 1 Corinthians 1:10–2:5 will help with some of the interpretational issues found in the remaining chapters.

It will be useful, therefore, to trace Paul's ideas through to the end. Our goal will be to highlight those aspects of Paul's argument that gain added, deeper or different meanings in the light of what we have discovered in 1:10–2:5.

1 Corinthians 2:6-16—Perspective of the Mature

The transition at 1 Corinthians 2:6 is a major one, marking Paul's passage into the next movement in his thought. Karl Prümm is correct in emphasizing that this verse is "not a break" from the previous section, but simply "the transition" into the next section.[1] The paragraph 2:6-16 represents a continuation of Paul's argument regarding his preaching, not a termination of it.

Yet at 2:6 there does occur a significant shift in the Apostle's argument. Whereas the perspective of the world has governed the first movement (1 Cor 1:18–2:5), the divine perspective will govern the second (1 Cor 2:6-16).[2] This is

---

[1] Prümm (1963, p. 90).
[2] On these two perspectives, see pp. 161-64 above. Says Hays (1997, p. 28): "As the word of God breaks into the world, it divides all humanity in two": *those who are perishing* and *those who are*

immediately apparent in 1 Corinthians 2:6-7 in the shift Paul introduces regarding the term σοφία. In 1 Corinthians 1:17-2:5 the terms σοφία, μωρία or their cognates occur twenty-one times. In seventeen of these occurrences the perspective of the term is that of the world: something is wise or foolish as the world views it. In 2:6-7, Paul signals a shift away from this worldly frame of reference to its counterpoint, the divine perspective. Wisdom here is not wisdom as the world measures it, but wisdom as God measures it.

It is important for the interpretation of this passage to note, however, that the notion of "the wisdom of God" is not introduced in 1 Corinthians 2:6 for the first time. It has already appeared in 1:24 and 1:30, where it refers to the message of the cross, that is, the gospel. In both instances the dative constructions (τοῖς κλητοῖς, 1 Cor 1:24; ἡμῖν, 1 Cor 1:30) underline the issue of perspective. The proclamation of the gospel may have appeared differently to others, but "to the called," "to us," it appeared to be wisdom of God. In 2:6 the dative ἐν τοῖς τελείοις ("among the mature") represents a parallel construction with a similar emphasis on perception.[3] To the "mature," Paul says, his preaching appears for what it in fact is, the wisdom of God. Indeed, it is the defining trait of the τέλειοι that they view the matter from just this perspective. The τέλειοι are those who grasp things from God's point of view, not the world's.[4]

---

being saved. "This apocalyptic sundering of humankind creates a sharp epistemological division as well: The whole world is now perceived differently by those who are being saved." These are those who "recognize the cross for what it is, the power of God, and this changes the way they understand everything else as well."

[3] Note the interesting parallel between Paul's argument and language throughout 1 Cor 1:17-2:6 and Plato's proof that the madness of the poet "is given by the gods for our greatest happiness." Says Plato, "Our proof (ἀπόδειξις) will not be believed by the merely clever, but will be accepted by the truly wise (σοφοῖς . . . πιστή)" (*Phaedrus* 245C). The terminology (ἀπόδειξις, σοφός, πίστις), the grammatical construction (contrasting datives) and the ideas (the contrast of those who are truly wise with those who only think they are) each mirrors the Apostle's argument in 1 Cor 1-2. Cf. also *Phaedrus* 275B; *Republic* 516C; and especially *Apology* 22D-23B.

[4] Some interpreters, though fewer today than in the past, treat the term τέλειος in 1 Cor 2:6 as a technical term referring to the initiates of the mystery religions; e.g., see Bauer (1979, p. 809); Wilckens (1959, p. 53). Against this, however, is (1) the fact that "complete," "perfect" or "mature" is the predominant meaning throughout the literature; (2) the lexical treatments of both Bauer himself and Delling (1972, vol. 8, p. 76) support "mature" here; (3) in 1 Cor 14:20 it must mean "mature"; (4) the argument of 2:6-3:2 seems plainly to be dealing with the idea of maturation: τέλειοι=πνευματικοί vs. νήπιοι; cf. the clear parallels in Heb 5:11-14. In addition, as Pearson (1973, p. 28) points out, "The term τέλειος is not the usual term used for one who has been initiated into the mysteries." Both Pearson and Davis (1984) argue that the background of this term is much more likely to be Jewish. Hence Barrett (1968, p. 69) says, "There is no need to see in Paul's use of this word a direct allusion to, or a borrowing from, the mystery cults." On this see also Moffatt (1938, pp. 27-28); R. E. Brown (1958, p. 438); Masson (1957, p. 104); and especially the full treatment by Baird (1959).

Commentators frequently struggle with the shift that takes place in Paul's argument in 1 Corinthians 2:6 because they construe the dative construction ἐν τοῖς τελείοις in such a way as to suggest that Paul had another message, a message of σοφία that he reserved for an elite group, the τέλειοι.[5] Stressing a contrast with ἐν ὑμῖν (1 Cor 2:2), this is an old interpretation, reaching back at least to the Valentinian Gnostics of the second century. But such a reading misconstrues the Apostle's point and leads to exegetical confusion; hence B. E. Gärtner's observation that the section 1 Corinthians 2:6-16 is often mistaken as a *Fremdkörper* ("foreign body") in Paul's argument.[6] A better reading of this verse, given the context of Paul's argument[7] and the parallel passage in Colossians 1:28, suggests that Paul is speaking only of how his single message, the message of Christ (1 Cor 1:30; 2:2), is perceived. While the world considers Paul's proclamation foolish, the τέλειοι perceive that same proclamation for the godly wisdom it is. In other words, as far as the τέλειοι are concerned, Paul speaks σοφία. Says Gerhard Delling, "The mature are those who understand the message of the cross . . . as the wisdom of God, and who embrace it in faith."[8] Any attempt on the basis of this passage to distinguish Paul's κήρυγμα from his σοφία thus becomes vain;[9] they are one and the same (1 Cor 1:24, 30), a *Constant* for Paul. Only the responses of his listeners vary.

In this light Paul's argument becomes elegantly simple and easy to follow. He has been speaking of how foolish his proclamation appears from the world's perspective. Here he shifts to God's perspective. From this vantage point his proclamation appears to be the very essence of wisdom, something every mature believer understands. What then does this imply about the Corinthians who found Paul's preaching deficient? It forms an indictment of their worldly

---

[5]On which struggle, see Gillespie (1990, p. 156).
[6]Gärtner (1968, pp. 216, 221).
[7]Not only the general argument we have traced from 1 Cor 1:17, but specifically the datives through 1 Cor 1:18, 23-24, 30; 2:6, 10, 14-15. See especially in this connection two parallel passages in 2 Cor 2:14-17 and 4:3-4, where the ἐν τοῖς construction is used to express the idea of perspective (see also 1 Cor 14:11). On 2 Cor 2:14-17 in particular, see Provence (1982, pp. 54-56).
[8]Delling (1972, vol. 8, p. 76); cf. Hays (1997, pp. 39-41).
[9]As part of his argument that "Paul must have had an esoteric wisdom teaching entirely separate from his kerygma" (p. 35), Scroggs (1967, p. 37) says of 1 Cor 2:6-16, "The language remains extremely veiled. Paul does not disclose a single example of the content of wisdom. Despite the carefulness and consistency of the section it surprises because Paul nowhere else in his extant correspondence suggests he has such a teaching, nor are several words and phrases that appear here repeated elsewhere by Paul. One could deduce from this either that he is copying his detractors or that he has just for this time and purpose constructed a wisdom teaching to combat that of the Corinthians." Or, alternatively, one could deduce that such an interpretation has missed the Apostle's point.

attitudes and values, an indictment Paul will make explicit in 1 Corinthians 3:1.

The identity of the rulers (ἄρχοντες) of 1 Corinthians 2:6 and 2:8 has engendered much debate. We need not join that debate here. Whatever else the ἄρχοντες may be, the group certainly includes that class of high-status figures that so occupied the Apostle in chapter 1. The verb καταργέω ("to render inoperative") is a reference to Paul's claim in 1 Corinthians 1:28 that those who so impress the world—in contrast to those who are considered "nothing"—are being nullified by God so that no "flesh" will have any basis for boasting. Hence the least speculative interpretation, and the one that will serve for our purposes, is to view the ἄρχοντες as the chief leaders of society, that class of prominent figures who wield the reins of social, political and economic influence.[10] We need not specify here whether these ἄρχοντες are Gentile or Jewish. The term is generic enough to include both, as in Romans 13:3. Nevertheless, of special significance to this reference may be Paul's experiences with the prominent figures in Athens (Acts 17:16-34), and in Corinth in particular (Acts 18:12-17). In a similar experience in Philippi (Acts 16:19), Luke describes Paul and Silas being dragged "into the marketplace before the rulers" (ἄρχοντες). In any case, the τέλειοι are those who do not measure Paul by the standards of this age, the standards of these apparently powerful and influential figures who in fact are being brought to nothing. Instead, the mature are those who measure Paul by God's standards and thus perceive his proclamation as the σοφία θεοῦ.

Paul has emphasized from 1 Corinthians 1:18 that the world perceives his proclamation as foolishness rather than wisdom. He has also explained that this is very much by God's design (1 Cor 1:21). Here he further clarifies the reasons for the world's misapprehension of his preaching. What Paul preaches is hidden "in mystery" (ἐν μυστηρίῳ); that is, it is something unavailable to humans (1 Cor 2:9) except through divine revelation. In fact, Paul says, God foreordained this hiddenness "for our glory" (εἰς δόξαν ἡμῶν, 1 Cor 2:7), for though none of the human ἄρχοντες perceived the hidden things of God's wisdom—which is obvious from the fact that they crucified Christ (1 Cor 2:8-9; cf. Acts 3:17; 13:27; Lk 23:13, 34)—God has revealed these hidden things "to us" (ἡμῖν in the emphatic position, 1 Cor 2:10) "through the Spirit." The Spirit is the one—indeed, the only one—who knows "the deep things of God" (1 Cor 2:10-11 AT; cf. Rom 11:33-36), and it is precisely this Spirit, in contrast to "the spirit of the world," that *we*

---

[10]Hays (1997, p. 44).

(emphatic ἡμεῖς, 1 Cor 2:12) have received. Why was God's Spirit given to us? So that we might know "the things freely given us by God" (2:12).[11]

So far in this section, then, Paul's emphasis has been largely on the content of his preaching. We are immediately alerted to this by the accusatives in 1 Corinthians 2:6-7. For the first time (and twice at that) Paul uses σοφία as the direct object of a verb of speaking: wisdom is *what* he speaks. In 1 Corinthians 2:7 the dative ἐν μυστηρίῳ indicates not the outward form of this content but its essential character, which prompts a further series of accusatives of content:

Table 16.1

2:9	The things which God has prepared for those who love him, but which no one has ever conceived.
2:10	The deep things of God.
2:11	The things of God.
2:12	The things freely given to us by God.

It is not until we arrive at 1 Corinthians 2:13, however, that we pick up again the continuing thread of Paul's argument. It is the same argument about the form of his preaching he has been pressing from the outset: οὐκ ἐν σοφίᾳ λόγου (1 Cor 1:17). All of the previous accusatives of content are summed up now in the article when Paul says, "which things we ... speak" (ἅ ... λαλοῦμεν, NASB). Then follows the dative construction specifying form, which we have already examined: "words not taught by human wisdom but [words] taught by the Spirit" (οὐκ ἐν διδακτοῖς ἀνθρωπίνης σοφίας λόγοις, ἀλλ' ἐν διδακτοῖς πνεύματος). In this way form and content once again converge in Paul's argument, and the difficulty of interpreting the much debated phrase "combining spiritual with spiritual" (πνευματικοῖς πνευματικὰ συγκρίνοντες NASB) in 2:13 practically eliminates itself. Taking πνευματικοῖς as neuter and συγκρίνω in its most straightforward meaning, "to combine, to bring into combination," Paul makes explicit what we have already seen. In choosing to avoid σοφία λόγου and opting instead for the simple plac-

---

[11]Regarding the content of the mystery, in Rom 16:25-26 Paul equates the mystery (μυστήριον), the secret that has now been revealed, with "my gospel and the preaching of Jesus Christ." Similarly, in Col 1:26-28 the μυστήριον is equated with the message of Christ Paul proclaims (καταγγέλλω) to "everyone" with all godly σοφία in order that he might present every person "mature in Christ" (τέλειον ἐν Χριστῷ). The parallels with 1 Cor 2:6-7 and 4:1 are plain enough. The term *mystery* in these passages refers to the previously hidden but now revealed (1 Cor 2:7-10) gospel of Christ (including all its many entailments and ramifications), which Paul has already twice called the "wisdom of God" (1:24, 30); on this point see Grindheim (2002, pp. 696-701). The τέλειοι are by definition those who are mature enough to grasp, to a relatively high degree, the full divine wisdom of this message. This wisdom remains hidden, however, to the world (1 Cor 2:8, 14; 2 Cor 4:3-4).

arding of Christ, Paul is combining spiritual things (content) with spiritual things (forms).[12] In other words, the proverbial "like with like." Says B. E. Gärtner, "In the whole *corpus paulinum* 1 Corinthians 2:6-16 is the only passage where it is evident that the principle 'like by like' is used."[13]

The exact meaning of the phrase "taught by the Spirit" (διδακτοῖς πνεύματος, 1 Cor 2:13) is difficult to ascertain. Does Paul intend some such thought as we find in Jesus' instruction to the Twelve that they should have no worry about how or what they would speak, since the Spirit will give them appropriate words at the right moment (Mt 10:19-20; Lk 12:11-12)? This would make sense, and it is a possibility. Yet against it is the fact that διδακτοῖς is not quite right—though its use might be explained by the opposite member of the contrast. More important, the subject of Jesus' instructions in both Matthew and Luke is the speech of self-defense before hostile authorities, while Paul is discussing here the proclamation of the gospel in general. Moreover, nowhere else in Paul's writings do we find a similar thought expressed. Hence reading Jesus' words into Paul's here may in the end be misleading.

A preferable interpretation is to view διδακτοῖς πνεύματος as a subjective genitive[14] (the Spirit is the one doing the teaching) by which Paul meant no more than what he has already argued at length. The λόγοι represent the external form, even metaphorically the "container" (2 Cor 4:7) of the content. The question is, where may one learn the most appropriate form, from man or from God? Paul has been assigned the form of his preaching from God: he is to serve as a κῆρυξ. We need not assume that Paul has in mind here some special inspiration. The question remains one of proclamation versus persuasion. Paul has asserted that it was his

---

[12] A. T. Robertson (1934, p. 654): "In 1 Cor 2:13 ... the presence of [λόγοις] inclines one to the notion that Paul is here combining spiritual ideas with spiritual words." For a helpful discussion of this construction, see Lightfoot (1904, pp. 180-81). The sometime blindness of some New Testament scholars to the rhetorical aspects of Paul's argument is nowhere more clearly illustrated than in Hanson's abrupt rejection (1980, p. 73) of this reading because "it has little to be said for it." Indeed, Hanson rejects even the similar translation "explaining things of the Spirit in the words of the Spirit," with these observations: "It is doubtful whether in Paul's thought the adjective *pneumatikos* could properly apply to *logos* or *logoi*. Could one envisage the opposite, *logoi psychikoi* or *sarkinoi*? It hardly makes sense in a Pauline context." Hanson's inability to conceive of Paul's contrast here is a sobering instance of myopia. At any rate, in 2 Cor 1:12 Paul speaks of "fleshly wisdom" (σοφίᾳ σαρκικῇ). Why should λόγοι σαρκικοί be unimaginable, particularly in the light of what we know of classical rhetoric in general and the obvious association of λόγοι and σοφία in 1 Cor 1:17, 2:1 and 2:4-5?

[13] Gärtner (1968, p. 215). See Thiselton (2000, pp. 264-67) on the complexities of interpreting this phrase. The above appears to do the best service to the various lexical, grammatical and contextual considerations.

[14] So Moule (1959, p. 40).

commission from Christ simply to proclaim the gospel without depending on σοφίᾳ λόγου (1 Cor 1:17). Here he attributes this instruction to the Spirit. For Paul this was, of course, no contradiction; to him the phrases "we have received . . . the Spirit who is from God" (1 Cor 2:12) and "we have the mind of Christ" (1 Cor 2:16) were synonymous. The Apostle's point is that both the form (straightforward proclamation) and the content (the crucified Christ) were for him divinely directed.

Paul can thus define both form and content alike as πνευματικὰ, "spiritual things." Needless to say, there is nothing inherently spiritual about proclamation as such. Simple proclamation is a "spiritual" thing only in the sense that in the communication of the gospel it is a form that consciously and determinedly depends for its results on the δύναμις θεοῦ rather than the psychological strategies of human persuasion (1 Cor 2:4-5). Hence both the form and content are among "the things of the Spirit of God" which the "natural man"—the ψυχικός, "the human being with a normal physical life and natural human faculties, but without the Holy Spirit"[15]—does not understand (1 Cor 2:14). He perceives such spiritual things as folly. Lacking the Spirit, he has no option but to render his evaluations from the perspective of the world, since God's perspective is unavailable to him. Hence it is not surprising that such a man should find the form and content of Paul's preaching foolish. Neither meets the world's standards of what is impressive.

But the one with the Spirit (ὁ πνευματικὸς) is of a different order. As Eduard Schweizer put it, "The miraculous power of the Spirit determines both the content and the form of the preaching, and is for that reason only perceptible to those who are 'spiritual.'"[16] These πνευματικοί both possess and obey the Spirit and therefore hold the capacity to discern all such things (1 Cor 2:15).[17] The ones without the Spirit may not understand ὁ πνευματικὸς and his ways, but he understands them and their ways, for he possesses the νοῦς of Christ (1 Cor 2:16). Unlike the one without the Spirit, he has the ability to grasp "the things of the Spirit of God" (τὰ τοῦ πνεύματος τοῦ θεοῦ, 1 Cor 2:14) and to see

---

[15]Witherington (1995, p. 128).
[16]Schweizer (1960, p. 68).
[17]"All things" (τὰ πάντα, 1 Cor 2:15) is the culmination of the series of accusatives begun in 1 Cor 2:6: σοφίαν, 2:6; σοφίαν, 2:7; ἅ, 2:9; τὰ, 2:10; τὰ, 2:11; τὰ, 2:12; ἅ, 2:13; τὰ, 2:14. As such it refers to "all such *spiritual* things," not simply all things in general. On the relationship of "the spiritual person" (ὁ πνευματικὸς, 2:15; the one who has received the Spirit, 2:12) to spiritual perception, Schweizer (1960, p. 66) says: "I Cor ii 13—iii 3 calls *pneumatikoi* not a group of 'ecstatics,' but those who understand the gospel of the cross." And later: "In I Cor ii 13-15 *pneumatikos* means the man who in the power of God's Spirit acknowledges God's saving work, . . . while the *psychikos* is blind to it" (p. 87; cf. also pp. 68-69).

that such things are not folly but wisdom. To him, Paul suggests, both the form and the content of the proclamation will make perfect sense.

Yet, as will soon become apparent, things are not quite this simple. If the ψυχικός represents for Paul a clear-cut category—the one without the Spirit—the same cannot be said for the one *with* the Spirit. The possession of the Spirit does not automatically place one among the τέλειοι or πνευματικοί. The "mature" or "spiritual" person in 1 Corinthians 2:6-16 (the terms appear to be synonymous here; cf. Gal 6:1) represents for Paul the ideal Christian, the Christian as he can and should be, the one who can and does discern the wisdom of God with all its implications due to the presence of the Spirit within him. In practice, however, the Christian's capacity for spiritual discernment may remain only partially appropriated, leading to the introduction of a third term,[18] a hybrid category that Paul will introduce in the following section: the one who, though he possesses the Spirit, nonetheless continues to view things, at least in part, as if he does not. It is in this unfortunate category that Paul will place the Corinthians.

1 Corinthians 3:1-4—The Contentions Again

Paul has shown the Corinthians that there was nothing deficient about his *modus operandi* as a proclaimer. Viewed from the world's perspective it may appear deficient, but viewed from God's perspective, as it patently must be by Christians, it is wholly justified—indeed, required—by God's own *modus operandi* in the world. This is something that truly mature Christians understand. Thus if there was nothing wrong with Paul's preaching, the problems in Corinth must lie elsewhere. And so they did. They lay within the Corinthians themselves. The church's contentions thus said more about the congregation than they did about their ostensible object, Paul and his preaching. This object has been weighed by God's standards and found worthy. The real deficiencies, Paul now shows, are to be found within the critics themselves.

The τέλειοι or πνευματικοί[19] understand the wisdom of Paul's proclamation

---

[18]This is the point Grindheim appears to miss. His argument (2002, pp. 704-9) that Paul uses the term τέλειοι to refer to all believers, so that those who fall short of it are in danger of "forfeiting the divine gift" or "jeopardizing their salvation" (p. 709), is unpersuasive. Grindheim's citation of the contrary evidence—to the effect that (1) τέλειος "usually refers to a state that is seen as a goal for believers," and (2) "Paul's use of the term τέλειος in other contexts . . . seems to militate against taking the term as a referent for the Corinthians" (p. 706)—makes a strong case against his own reading and in favor of the above.

[19]Paul introduced the term πνευματικοί as a positive one (1 Cor 2:15; cf. Gal 5:16–6:1) and would like to apply it to his readers. But he cannot. There is nothing in this passage, however, to indicate

even if the ψυχικοί do not. Unfortunately, the personality-centered divisions proved that a number of the Corinthians, though they were Christians, were nonetheless thinking and behaving more like ψυχικοί than πνευματικοί. When he first preached to them, Paul was forced to treat the Corinthians as immature Christians; that is, "as infants in Christ" (ὡς νηπίοις ἐν Χριστῷ, 1 Cor 3:1) who in their immaturity still reckoned things according to the flesh (cf. 1 Cor 14:20). This was understandable at the time because they were new believers. But their contentions (ἔριδες, 1 Cor 1:11) proved that there had been little maturation since; they were still operating "like mere men" (κατὰ ἄνθρωπον, 1 Cor 3:3 NASB; cf. Gal 5:19-21)—that is, like those without the Spirit. For when they said, "I follow Paul," or, "I follow Apollos," did this not indicate that they were viewing things from the limited human perspective alone (1 Cor 3:4)?

It is important here to observe that Paul apparently adjusted the weight of his instruction to the maturity of his pupils, as is indicated by the contrast between "milk" (γάλα) and "meat" (βρῶμα) in 1 Corinthians 3:2. But this pedagogical point should not be used to obscure the notion of perspective in 1 Corinthians 2:6. Paul does not indicate that he had two messages, the gospel for some and then a hidden σοφία or γνῶσις for an inner elite. More accurately, once we arrive at 3:2 we see that Paul had a single message that he expounded with more or less depth according to the maturity of his listeners.[20]

Yet even here the notion of perspective remains crucial to Paul's thought. The "natural" person views Paul's preaching as foolishness (1 Cor 2:14); the "mature"

---

that the Corinthians claimed the term for themselves. This common assumption is the primary weakness, e.g., of Painter (1982), who refers repeatedly to the "self-styled pneumatikoi" without ever defending from the text the validity of such a term. He also assumes without warrant that πνευματικῶν in 1 Cor 12:1 is masculine (p. 242), and glosses over much of the substance of 1 Cor 1-4 so as to be able to conflate these chapters with chapters 12-14 and claim that they are dealing with the same topic: Paul's response to "pneumatic wisdom" at Corinth (p. 240). We may only note in response that much of Paul's argument in 1 Cor 1-4 against the wisdom of the world would have been considered irrelevant by the Corinthians had they styled themselves as πνευματικοί; cf. Wilckens (1979, p. 520). Or, if Painter is right, such a situation would have required Paul to debate the definition of πνευματικὸς, which he does not do. A more satisfying approach is to understand πνευματικοί as Paul's own term representing an ideal of which the Corinthians fall short. In this light, Paul's inability in 1 Cor 3:1 to treat the Corinthians as πνευματικοί is to be viewed in contrast to his desire to do so (cf. 1 Cor 4:14-16), rather than against any purported claims on their part.

[20]Cf. St. Augustine's interesting comment on this point: "For even in the very food that we take, so far is there from being any contrariety between milk and solid food, that the latter itself becomes milk, in order to make it suitable to babes, whom it reaches through the medium of the mother's or the nurse's body.... Christ crucified is both milk to sucklings and meat to the more advanced" (*Tractates on the Gospel of John* 98.6). On the Jewish background of this pedagogy, see R. E. Brown (1958, pp. 438-39).

or "spiritual" person views it as wisdom (1 Cor 2:6, 14-16). In which category do the Corinthians belong? Paul wants to grant that they are Christians but also to rebuke them for their ἔριδες and their worldly evaluation of his proclamation—that is, for valuing and behaving like non-Christians. So he places them in the middle ground. He must treat them, he says, "as people of the flesh, as infants in Christ" (ὡς σαρκίνοις, ὡς νηπίοις ἐν Χριστῷ).[21] These νήπιοι or σάρκινοι are not therefore to be confused with the ψυχικοί, those without the Spirit. The νήπιοι or σάρκινοι are Christians who nonetheless are still immaturely looking at things from their old worldly point of view. Hence the issue in 1 Corinthians 3:1-4, as in 2:6, remains one of the world's perspective versus God's perspective, only now on the part of Christians.

It is important to stress again, however, that Paul never equates the βρῶμα with σοφία, and it is misleading for commentators to conflate 1 Corinthians 3:2 with 2:6 in such a way as to make it appear that he does. Paul's entire message, whether proffered at the level of milk or meat, is the more or less fully elaborated message of Christ (1 Cor 2:2; cf. Col 1:9, 28; 2:3), a message that is σοφία to those who are able to discern it as such (1 Cor 1:24, 30; 2:6, 10, 12, 15). It was precisely this wisdom, says Paul, that he had preached to the entire Corinthian church at the outset—though apparently not in its fullest detail—and it was this wisdom the Corinthian Christians as a whole had embraced (1 Cor 1:24, 30; cf. 15:1-2).

Nevertheless, if the βρῶμα represents not an esoteric σοφία distinct from Paul's κήρυγμα but merely a fuller elaboration of the truth about Christ, it is fair to ask of what sorts of things this fuller elaboration might have consisted. In other words, what kinds of things about Christ might Paul have expected mature Christians to be able to assimilate (cf. 1 Cor 13:11; see also Eph 4:13-15; 1 Pet 2:2) but not immature Christians?

In 1 Corinthians 15:3-8 Paul provided a sketch of the gospel he had preached (εὐηγγελισάμην, 1 Cor 15:1-2; cf. παρέδωκα, 15:3) to the Corinthians and which they had received. But this summary provides only the merest, if also the most essential, distillation of the full content of the gospel. We have neither the space nor the need to launch out into an elaboration of the full range of that content, both because Paul's epistles do that well enough and because so many others

---

[21]Cf. Carson (1984, p. 91) on Paul's claim to possess "knowledge" rather than rhetorical prowess in 2 Cor 11:6: "It appears . . . that the Corinthians were in danger of being seduced by a certain delectable [rhetorical] form. Stylized rhetoric mattered more than truth. An infant might be more intrigued by the wrapping paper than the parcel it envelops; but no one else should be. Paul is not inferior as a preacher after all—provided the right criteria are used!"

have addressed the subject. But we may be certain that the apostolic message of "good news" in its fullest form was broad enough to encompass God's entire plan of redemption, from Genesis to its crescendo in the incarnation, life, death, resurrection, ascension and exaltation of the Son of God. This crescendo in turn carried apocalyptic implications that changed everything for everyone, in both the "already" and the "not yet" of God's kingdom. The gospel included all of this and could be explored variously depending on the setting.

When the occasion called for it, Paul could obviously distill this full account to its most critical features. At the other extreme, the story told at its fullest encompasses the minutest of details. One thinks of Jesus' comment about the woman who had anointed him with expensive perfume: "Truly, I say to you, wherever the gospel is proclaimed in the whole world, what she has done will be told in memory of her" (Mk 14:9). Similarly, this redemptive story could be told in such a way that even νήπιοι could grasp it. Or, in the right setting and with those mature enough to assimilate them, this same story could be plumbed for its most mysterious and cryptic meanings. The obvious parallels in Hebrews 5:11-14 suggest that the Melchizedekian priesthood of Christ may serve as an example of this sort of instruction. The writer to the Hebrews says that this teaching, though of great importance, was difficult for his readers to comprehend, not inherently but due to their immaturity. Though they had had enough time to mature as Christians, they had not done so and thus remained νήπιοι who needed milk rather than solid food. Solid food such as the teaching of the Melchizedekian priesthood of Christ is for the τέλειοι, he says. Perhaps this is as instructive an example as any of those types of things regarding Christ that Paul himself might have refrained from expounding to the immature Corinthians.

1 Corinthians 3:5-9—Paul and Apollos

Having again denounced their personality-centered divisions—divisions focused at their core on the now-defused issue of Paul's preaching—the Apostle begins in 1 Corinthians 3:5 a concerted effort to help the Corinthians to a more healthy way of viewing the various ministers of Christ.[22] Paul and Apollos are simply the ones "through whom (δι' ὧν) you believed." In other words, "We were merely agents of God; he is the one who prompted your πίστις." Hence all boasting must be "in the Lord" (1 Cor 1:31), not "in men" (1 Cor 3:21). The emphasis of the agricultural metaphor in 1 Corinthians 3:6-7 is the pure instrumentality of the agents: God

---

[22]See appendix one on the role of Apollos in Corinth; see also appendix two on Acts 18.

alone is the one causing growth. In 1 Corinthians 3:8-9 Paul stresses the unity of the two agents and their joint role as fellow workers in God's service. The reference to the reward that each will receive "according to his labor" is a reminder that it is God's evaluation Paul must be concerned about and not the Corinthians'. The utter inappropriateness of their worldly evaluations is thus highlighted. The Corinthians constitute the locus of God's work—God's field, God's building—while Paul and Apollos are merely fellow workers (συνεργοί, 3:9) therein.

1 Corinthians 3:10-17 — A Warning

Paul's reference to the future judgment of a Christian's work prompts a warning to the other ministers. Having relinquished the agricultural metaphor, Paul takes up the figure of God's building (1 Cor 3:9). As a wise master-builder (σοφὸς ἀρχιτέκτων), says Paul, I laid the only foundation one can lay, Jesus Christ. Someone else (ἄλλος) now builds on it. Each one should give attention to how he builds (1 Cor 3:10). In the day of judgment God's fire will test the work of each minister to show of what sort it is (1 Cor 3:13). Work that passes God's test will receive its reward, but the one whose work fails God's test will lose his reward, though not his salvation (1 Cor 3:15). The reason for such a severe judgment is that the edifice in question is not just any building; it is the temple of God where his Spirit dwells. If any man ruins this temple, Paul says, God will ruin him, for the temple of God is holy—"and you are that temple" (1 Cor 3:17).

Two things stand out in these verses. First, there is no indication that the poor workmanship Paul has in mind is theological in nature. It is the manner (πῶς, 3:10) of building, the sort or kind (ὁποῖόν, 3:13) of work (ἔργον) that is at stake here. There is apparently a proper way to work and an improper way. The former meets God's approval while the latter does not.

Second, it is difficult to avoid seeing here a veiled criticism of Apollos. Commentators are virtually unanimous in emphasizing the cordial relationship between Paul and Apollos, and rightly so since Paul all but says as much himself (cf. especially 1 Cor 16:12).[23] But who is the ἄλλος of 1 Corinthians 3:10? In the light of 1 Corinthians 3:6-9 Apollos seems the obvious, indeed, the inevitable, answer. Paul in fact acknowledges this in 1 Corinthians 4:6. Yet the present tense of ἐποικοδομεῖ ("is building") in 3:10 begins to deflect attention away from Apollos—he is with

---

[23]Significantly, 1 Clement, a letter written to the Corinthian church from the church in Rome sometime during the last two decades of the first century, speaks of Paul, Peter and then Apollos as "highly reputed apostles and a man [Apollos] approved by them" (47:4).

Paul in Ephesus now rather than in Corinth (see 1 Cor 16:12). Moreover, the vague but emphatic ἕκαστος ("each one") further spreads the focus to include any ministers to whom Paul's warning might apply. But has Apollos ever quite disappeared from the frame? Paul's warning, unlike the material surrounding it, is directed to ministers who had worked within the congregation, and it is difficult to avoid seeing here at least an implied question about the very prominent and successful ministry of Apollos. To be sure, if there is criticism here, it is circumspect criticism. Yet the close proximity of Paul's remarks about the follow-up ministry of Apollos (1 Cor 3:5-9) to his warning to ministers in general about the manner of their follow-up ministry (1 Cor 3:10-15) must at least have appeared as a hint to the Corinthians of something Paul preferred not to say explicitly. Says J. C. Hurd, "Perhaps we are justified in saying that Paul's feelings toward Apollos were ambivalent."[24]

1 Corinthians 3:18-23—Worldly Wisdom Again

Yet the essential problem was not Apollos or any other of the ministers. The problem was within the congregation itself. Paul returns to this theme, and the echoes of his argument regarding the manner of his preaching become apparent. Some of the Corinthians were deceived. Instead of viewing things from God's perspective, they considered themselves wise by the world's standards (σοφὸς ... ἐν ὑμῖν ἐν τῷ αἰῶνι τούτῳ, 1 Cor 3:18). Never mind that they were no such thing; Paul exhorts them to give up their worldly perspective and embrace God's perspective instead. In doing so they may appear foolish in the world's eyes but they will be wise in God's estimation. God has turned the tables on the world's wisdom. Citing the Old Testament, Paul points out (again; cf. 1 Cor 1:19, 27-38) that God has caught the σοφοί in their own craftiness (πανουργία; cf. Job 5:13); he knows the vanity of their "reasoning" (διαλογισμοί, 1 Cor 3:20; cf. Rom 1:21-22).

In each of these references the condemnation of cleverness and of subtlety of persuasive discourse can be discerned. Compare, for example, in 2 Corinthians 4:2 the association of πανουργία with adulterating the word of God in contrast to the straightforwardness and transparency of Paul's own manner. Sophists, orators and philosophers alike were known for precisely this sort of cleverness—in fact, it was just such cleverness that won them their reputations. The Corinthians were caught up in this cultural feature and mistakenly applied these worldly standards to Paul

---

[24]Hurd (1965, p. 207). On the use of covert allusions throughout 1 Cor 1–4, see Fiore (1985, pp. 85-102). See also Pickett's claim (1997, p. 57) that "wisdom was regarded primarily as rhetorical eloquence by the followers of Apollos in Corinth, and that wisdom construed in this way was the basis not only of their attack on Paul but also of an exalted self-consciousness."

and his fellow ministers, giving rise to slogans that centered on personalities. Thus, in 1 Corinthians 3:21 Paul prohibits this divisive boasting "in men." You need not choose among Christ's ministers, Paul says. From God's perspective all of them belong to you, you belong to Christ and Christ belongs to God (1 Cor 3:23).

1 Corinthians 4:1-5—Evaluation of Paul

The contentions in Corinth stemmed from the way the Corinthians viewed the various ministers of Christ, and Paul in particular. They had regarded the ministers as those whose measure could and should be taken according to human standards. But Paul seeks to shift the paradigm. He wants them to reckon (λογιζέσθω) the various ministers as mere servants of Christ, mere stewards (οἰκονόμους) of the now-revealed mysteries of God (1 Cor 4:1; cf. 2 Cor 6:4). When the ministers are viewed as such, the yardstick must be revised. They are not to be measured by the world's standards; they are only required to be faithful to their commission (1 Cor 4:2). It was because Paul realized this that he claimed to find the Corinthians' negative evaluation (ἀνακρίνω, "to examine so as to judge") of his preaching insignificant. No human evaluation—neither theirs, nor any other's, nor ultimately even his own—matters in the end. It is only God's ἀνακρίνειν that counts (1 Cor 4:4; cf. 2 Cor 5:9-10; 10:18; 1 Thess 2:3-6). Thus the Corinthians should cease their premature judging (κρίνειν, "to pass judgment on"). The appropriate time for judgment will be when the Lord returns. At that time God will bring to light all the unknown factors no one in their meager human judgments can possibly weigh: the hidden things one cannot see, such as the inner motives of a person's heart. Then will a true judgment be rendered and each receive whatever praise he is due from God (1 Cor 4:5; cf. 2 Cor 5:9-12).

We should note here that it is Paul who has raised and maintained the eschatological element in the argument (1 Cor 3:8, 13-15; 4:3-5).[25] These verses give no indication that the Corinthians saw any eschatological implications in their judgments. In fact the sheer worldliness of their values and attitudes works against such a notion. An eschatological framework is by definition a way of viewing things from God's perspective; that is, in the light of "the age to come." But such a per-

---

[25]It is crucial, however, to remember how closely this eschatological focus is bound up with Paul's heralding of the "word of the cross." See Dickson (2003, pp. 153-77). As Engberg-Pedersen (2008, p. 259) rightly says, "In Paul's thought the whole world is on the move toward a single event." But this eschatological *telos* is bookended for Paul by the cross: "A corresponding event has already occurred that constitutes a single fact about the world that also operates as the one and only criterion of value, thereby dividing the world up completely between good and evil."

spective is precisely what was lacking in the Corinthians. They considered themselves wise "in this age" (1 Cor 3:18).²⁶ Their judging of Paul by worldly standards of eloquence and wisdom indicated not a mistaken eschatological perspective but the lack of an eschatological awareness altogether. In their worldliness they were behaving "only in a human way" (1 Cor 3:1-4). Hence Paul links their ἀνακρίνειν with the judgment of a "human court" (ἀνθρωπίνης ἡμέρας, 1 Cor 4:3) and dismisses it as premature (πρὸ καιροῦ, 1 Cor 4:5). His claim that such judgments are πρὸ καιροῦ is thus a product of his own way of looking at things, not theirs. Because they were enamored by the cultural values of their own time and place, the Corinthians' criticisms of Paul's preaching were devoid of the relevant "now-then" distinctions. Hence the eschatological reference point must be imported into the discussion by Paul. He raises it as a means of rebuking the Corinthians for their worldliness and reminding them that ἀνακρίνειν is something that belongs to the future judgment of God and is therefore inappropriate for Christians in the present. Keeping this in mind proves helpful when we come to the following section.

1 Corinthians 4:6-13—A Contrast

The "these things" (ταῦτα) of 1 Corinthians 4:6 refers to the arguments Paul has adduced since the ἔριδες, and the name of Apollos in particular, were brought up again (1 Cor 3:4). Paul has intended in the intervening remarks that he and Apollos should be uppermost in the reader's mind. Yet his underlying concern was the Corinthians. Paul's discussion of himself and Apollos was designed to teach the Corinthians to avoid personality-centered contentions. Whether this sudden twist in Paul's argument could eradicate or countermand any underlying implied criticism of Apollos is difficult to determine. What is clear, however, is that Paul wanted to deflect the thrust of the admonition away from Apollos to the Corinthians themselves. They were the ones who had lined up "in favor of one against another" (1 Cor 4:6), presumably without prompting from Apollos, and it is this problem Paul wishes to address.²⁷

The rhetorical questions of 1 Corinthians 4:7 are designed to deflate the pretensions of the Corinthians. Their being "puffed up" on behalf of one against the

---

[26] See Barclay (1992, p. 65) for a contrast between the eschatological orientation of the Thessalonians and the Corinthians. Says he, "Unlike the Thessalonians, the Corinthians did not regard their Christian experience as an eager anticipation of a glory ready to be revealed at the coming of Christ."

[27] I leave aside here the disputed meaning of the phrase "not to go beyond what is written" (1 Cor 4:6). For our purposes we need not decide among the options. But for an interesting take on the meaning of these words, see Welborn (1997, pp. 43-75).

other apparently involved more than simply championing their favorite. It was tied to a false estimate of themselves and a false boasting in their own achievements. They viewed themselves as σοφοί (1 Cor 3:18), distinguished from—and obviously, above—the less cultured (1 Cor 4:7). These pretensions were no doubt prior to their partisanship and the cause of it. Unlike the erudite Apollos (see appendix one), Paul did not suit their inflated image of themselves. But the Apostle punctures their pride by pointing out again their lack of distinction, and then adding that even if they could claim any such distinctions, these were ultimately gifts of God and thus no excuse for boasting.

In this light Paul's ironic statements—or rhetorical questions, whichever—of 1 Corinthians 4:8 require careful interpretation. The enigmatic assertions that the Corinthians are already satiated, rich and ruling without him have often been examined for detailed information about how the Corinthians viewed themselves, as if this verse reflected their own terminology. In this way the language is used to argue for the well-known "over-realized eschatology" in which the "already" has overwhelmed the "not yet."

This view is based in large measure on a correlation of 2 Timothy 2:18 and 1 Corinthians 4:8, combined with the presence of similar ideas in later Gnosticism and arguably in 1 Corinthians 15. Such an interpretation is possible but by no means necessary. In fact, its speculative character and its need to read so much between the lines serves to make one wary. A more straightforward possibility is that 4:8 tells us little about the Corinthians beyond what we have already observed of their unwarranted adulation of and identification with the σοφοί, δυνατοί and εὐγενεῖς of society. Once again the eschatological element in the verse is purely the importation of the Apostle, and it functions as a rebuke of their attempt to emulate such a worldly elite.

As we have seen, the association of wisdom, power, wealth, nobility and eloquence were pervasive in the Greco-Roman society of Paul's day. For example, consider Plutarch, a Greek historian of the Roman emperors and a late contemporary of the Apostle Paul, on the Stoics: "In their sect the wise man is termed not only prudent and just and brave, but also an orator (ῥήτωρ), a poet, a general, a rich man, a king."[28] This interlocking of wisdom, prominence, honor, wealth and eloquence had long been common. A century earlier Cicero could speak to Cato of "those brief maxims that you propounded, that the Wise Man alone is

---

[28]Plutarch, *Moralia* 472A.

King, dictator, millionaire—neatly rounded off no doubt as you put them; of course, for you learnt them from professors of rhetoric."[29]

It is simply a matter of historical record that in the ancient Greco-Roman world training in rhetoric "formed a peculiarly conspicuous social dividing line between those who belonged to the leisured circles for whom such education was possible and those who could only afford the common literacy necessary to earning one's living."[30] In this world wisdom, eloquence and wealth, along with social and political influence, tended to travel together. From kings and emperors to the local aristocracy, these features were the defining characteristics of social status. Others lusted after these qualities and, in select cases, by gaining them joined the honored elite of society.

Some of the Corinthians were apparently among those who longed to be counted a part of, or who at least much admired, this elite. Thus it requires an unnecessary degree of exegetical strain to stretch beyond this obvious cultural context and interpret Paul's language in terms of some spiritual elite, whether on the basis of purported gnostic ideas or on the basis of Philo and his alleged influence on the Corinthians via Apollos.[31] The popular Greek rhetorical-philosophical tradition we have examined provides more than enough basis for a nonspiritual interpretation. This straightforward understanding of the status terminology of 1 Corinthians 4:8-10 keeps us on firm exegetical ground and well within the confines of Paul's argument.

In 1 Corinthians 4 Paul rebukes the Corinthians for their misplaced values. To rebuke the Corinthians for their prideful boasting and to show the utter worldliness of it, Paul sets their pretensions in contrast to the apostles, and especially to himself. In doing so he once more casts the issue in the light of God's eternal perspective. The ironic and reproachful "already" of 1 Corinthians 4:8 is thus the product of Paul's eschatological frame of reference (cf. 1 Cor 10:11),[32] not the Corinthians'. Paul attributes no eschatological views, mistaken or otherwise, to the Corinthians. Their error is far more prosaic and natural. They have looked on the high-status figures of this world and, in a typically human fashion, coveted that status. As a result they have falsely and futilely attempted to model themselves after these figures.

---

[29]Cicero, *De fin.* 4.3.
[30]Judge (1960, p. 44).
[31]See appendix one.
[32]See Furnish (2009) on the radically Christ-centered eschatology that shaped Paul's entire perspective; cf. also Gupta (2009), Dickson (2003, pp. 153-77).

In their attempts at emulation these Corinthians apparently longed to be numbered among the wise, strong and distinguished, satiated with wealth and power. The shamefulness of such a worldly set of values within Christians is highlighted in the contrasts with the Apostle's own experience in 1 Corinthians 4:9-13.[33] The other-worldly image of the apostles in this age being exhibited as weak and despised, a spectacle (θέατρον, 1 Cor 4:9) to angels and men, demonstrates again Paul's determination to shift the framework to the divine perspective. Membership in a ruling class may be the future hope of the Christian, but not the present. In the first chapter Paul had emphasized that, for the present, the Christian should expect to be characterized in the world's eyes as weak and unimpressive. Hence it is with sarcasm that Paul, not the Corinthians, suggests the ridiculous image of the Corinthians somehow "already" having attained their eschatological destiny, while he has been left behind in weakness. This thought was all the more ironic because the Corinthians were anything but a distinguished ruling class.

The resulting picture is absurd, and Paul takes it down immediately. "I wish your inflated pretensions were actually true," he says, "for then it would be time for all of us to rule" (1 Cor 4:8). But instead, Paul's life is characterized by the opposite of satiation, wealth and power. In contrast to the Corinthians, who yearned, though they belonged to Christ, nevertheless also to be considered wise, strong and distinguished, Paul was "on account of Christ" an embarrassing spectacle to the world—foolish, weak and without honor. The catalogue of suffering in 1 Corinthians 4:11-13 is designed to spell out in concrete terms what it means to be foolish, weak and without honor in the world (cf. Rom 8:17). All of this Paul relates in order to admonish the Corinthians (1 Cor 4:14), not for an alleged misguided eschatology, but for their misplaced values and false aspirations. They must follow Paul's example instead and reconcile themselves to—indeed, learn to glory in—their lack of worldly impressiveness (1 Cor 4:16; 2 Cor 12:9-10).

1 Corinthians 4:14-21—A Final Exhortation

Realizing the shame these contrasts might engender within the Corinthians, Paul seeks to shift his emphasis. It is not humiliation he's after; he wants them to abandon their worldly ways and adopt the values evident in his own life (for example, 2 Cor 11:30; 12:5, 9-10). He does not wish to hurt them; he wants to admonish them "as my beloved children" (1 Cor 4:14). They may have many Christian

---

[33]Cf. also 2 Cor 4:7-12; 6:4-10; 11:23-29; 12:9. On Paul's irony in this contrast, see Plank (1987, pp. 33-69).

"guides," but only Paul is their spiritual father (1 Cor 4:15). His relationship to them therefore is (or ought to be) uniquely significant and authoritative. Hence they should give up their worldly pretensions and become "imitators" of him (1 Cor 4:16). In fact, it was precisely for this that Paul had sent Timothy to them—so that Timothy might remind them of Paul's "ways" (ὁδοί, 4:17).

We should observe three things about these "ways" of Paul. First, it seems plain enough that the ὁδοί refer loosely to the catalogue of Paul's experiences in 1 Corinthians 4:9-13, and still more importantly to the values and attitudes— each rooted in God's, not the world's perspective—that undergird them, as spelled out in 1 Corinthians 1:10-4:13. Second, these were the same ὁδοί Paul had practiced and taught everywhere, presumably including Corinth (1 Cor 4:17). Third, the Corinthians had abandoned, or more likely, never fully assimilated, Paul's ὁδοί. With regard to Paul's formal doctrines (the παραδόσεις), the Corinthians held fast all that Paul had delivered to them (see 1 Cor 11:23; 15:1, 3; cf. Rom 6:17; 2 Thess 2:15; 3:6). But the more subtle matter of Paul's ὁδοί had never quite taken among them.

This observation once again reinforces the view that Paul is not refuting theological error in 1 Corinthians 1-4, much less something so serious as a different gospel. The problem had to do with the contrast of ὁδοί as seen in 1 Corinthians 4:6-13. The Corinthians had become puffed up in their worldly values, which after Paul's departure had led to personality-centered ἔριδες. Such contentions were unlikely to have occurred while Paul was in Corinth; his personal presence would have stifled the critics' criticisms of his ministry. They erupted only when the Corinthians thought Paul might not be coming back (1 Cor 4:18). But Paul warns that he is ready to return to Corinth to deal with those who are causing the problem. When that occurs he will discover not the word (λόγος) of those who are puffed up but their power (δύναμις), for the kingdom of God is not in λόγος but in δύναμις (1 Cor 4:19-20).[34] The only question was how they preferred him to come—with discipline or in a spirit of gentleness.

This represents Paul's final word on the ἔριδες in Corinth. The subject never emerges again in the Corinthian correspondence, perhaps because 1 Corinthians 1-4 proved potent enough to eliminate, or at least dampen, this specific facet of the church's factionalism.[35] At any rate, it is significant for the interpre-

---

[34]See Spencer (1989, pp. 51-61).
[35]Given the goal of our investigation—Paul's theology/philosophy of preaching/rhetoric—we have focused on those chapters where Paul addresses this subject, 1 Cor 1-4. For a broader focus on the

tation of chapters 1–4 as a whole that Paul comes full circle to a concluding reference to λόγος, which surely must be translated here "eloquence."[36] A concern for eloquence was central to the pride of the Corinthians and thus to their ἔριδες (1 Cor 4:6). The issue of their love of human eloquence and their consequent criticism of Paul's preaching—the issue that dominates 1 Corinthians 1–2—has never been lost sight of. He reiterates it here in his parting word. The emphasis on λόγοι instead of the power of God among those who are arrogant (τῶν πεφυσιωμένων), contrasted with an opposite emphasis in God's kingdom (1 Cor 4:19-20), ties together the main threads of Paul's entire argument thus far in the epistle. The pride of the Corinthians leading to contentions, the centrality (in 1 Cor 1–4) of eloquence to this pride, the contrast of this eloquence to the power of God, the antithesis between the worldly framework of the Corinthians and the divine perspective of Paul—all come together in Paul's final comments on the ἔριδες in Corinth.

---

underlying issue of status-oriented factionalism in Corinth, of which the problems in chapters 1–4 are simply the first example, see Pogoloff (1992).
[36]Barrett (1968, p. 118).

Part Three

Summary and Analysis

17

Paul's Ministry Model

We are now in a position to give final shape to the Pauline insight that informed his view of preaching. We discover this principle at work throughout Paul's ministry and writings, but it comes to its fullest expression in the passage we have explored at length: 1 Corinthians 1–4, and 1:17–2:5 in particular.

In 1 Corinthians 1:17–2:5 the Apostle Paul contrasts his own approach to preaching with a very different type of discourse, one that was much appreciated by the Corinthians. It is safe to say that we will not fully understand the former until we have grasped something of the latter. Without this alternative as a background, important details of Paul's view of preaching remain obscure, hidden for lack of contrast.[1] But against the appropriate backdrop the outlines of Paul's approach to preaching vividly emerge.

The most appropriate backdrop against which to see Paul's statements about his *modus operandi* as a preacher is that broad and pervasive rhetorical tradition that played such an important role in first-century society. At each point where Paul refers to what he must disavow, his language directs our attention to this rhetorical tradition: his preaching was not to be in σοφία λόγου (1 Cor 1:17); he had come to them proclaiming the testimony of God, but not with superiority of speech or of wisdom (1 Cor 2:1); his λόγος and κήρυγμα were not in persuasive words of wisdom, but in the demonstration (ἀπόδειξις) of the Spirit and power (1 Cor 2:4); his speaking was not in words taught by human wisdom but in those taught by the Spirit (1 Cor 2:13). The most plausible background for such

---

[1] E.g., in their *Translator's Handbook on Paul's First Letter to the Corinthians* (1985, p. 27), Ellingworth and Hatton promote a faulty understanding of κήρυγμα in 1 Cor 1:21 (as "not the act of preaching, but its content"—on which mistake, see above, chap. 13) due to their inability to grasp the contrast Paul had in mind. They rightly, but also irrelevantly, observe, "Paul is not contrasting the 'use of words' and some other kind of action." Hence, they erroneously conclude, the problem must be the "content" of the κήρυγμα.

language lies, not in the Hellenistic synagogues, the gnostic mystery religions or the over-enthusiastic displays of Corinthian charismatics, but in the ubiquitous if also more prosaic realm of Greco-Roman rhetoric. Indeed, the great German classicist Eduard Norden put the matter bluntly when he observed that we will simply fail to grasp the import of 1 Corinthians 1:17–2:5 unless we remember that Paul wrote it during a time when the art of speech was considered everything. Indeed, says Norden, we must above all remember that Paul wrote these words to the Corinthians, that is, to citizens of a city that was known for its high estimation of rhetoric.[2]

Because we cannot fully appreciate what Paul is affirming unless we reconstruct the opposite member of the contrast, we have taken pains to describe the relevant aspects of the Greco-Roman rhetorical tradition. Such an approach is necessary so as to avoid setting up a straw man for the Apostle to knock down. It is simply too facile to stereotype classical rhetoric in overly negative terms as a bag of oratorical tricks for manipulating an audience, or to trivialize it as little more than the technique of verbal embellishment, bombast or purple prose. This does a disservice not only to classical rhetoric but to Paul's argument in 1 Corinthians 1–4. The truth is that, for all its shortcomings, ancient rhetoric was something far more substantial than such superficial assessments allow. At its core lay the power of language and ideas to sway minds and generate πίστις. Unless we are prepared to grasp this crucial point, we will understand neither ancient rhetoric nor the contrast Paul establishes with his own preaching.

GOOD RHETORIC VERSUS BAD RHETORIC.2

Thiselton's treatment of rhetoric in his shorter commentary on 1 Corinthians (2006) is a classic instance of blunting the Apostle's argument by setting up the sort of straw man described in the above paragraph. Thiselton reduces Paul's concern to "the rhetoric of 'display' associated with the Second Sophistic movement in provincial cities." Says he, "Paul does not oppose the use of honest, 'good' rhetoric, for he uses its forms in this epistle. . . . Nevertheless, he utterly rejects *manipulative* and *audience-dominated* rhetoric. This was frequently attention seeking and aimed simply to persuade people, regardless of the truth of the matter at hand. 'Good' classical Roman rhetoricians, most notably Cicero and Quintilian, would have endorsed Paul's disdain

---

[2]Norden (1909, vol. 2, p. 493).

for those in Corinth who regarded rhetoric as a competitive 'performance' designed to elicit applause, approval, and status from audiences" (pp. 51-52).

But this sort of analysis fails on several fronts. First, its simplistic division of classical rhetoric into good and bad is far too facile. See our earlier treatment of this mistake (pp. 150-53). To argue that the "good" rhetoric of Aristotle, Cicero and Quintilian was interested in the "effective communication of truth," while the "bad" rhetoric of "some provincial centers" was concerned only with winning, display and self-aggrandizement (pp. 14-15), badly overstates the case. First-century rhetorical practice (and practitioners) cannot be reduced to such easy moral categories. Second, even if such a division were possible, the historical information available to us, whether biblical or extrabiblical, simply will not justify the conclusion that the Corinthians were enamored only by the "bad" rhetoric. Third, the rhetorical tradition we have traced in this book—and still more thoroughly in *SPTOP*—is precisely the "good" Ciceronian tradition that reached back to Isocrates and Aristotle and was represented in the first century by Rome's leading teacher of rhetoric, Quintilian. Yet it is just here, in this mainstream tradition, that we find the issues that most exercised the Apostle in 1 Corinthians 1–4. Fourth, and most importantly, these troublesome (to Paul) issues are not the ones Thiselton ascribes to "bad" rhetoric. Paul does not disclaim the vaunted σοφία λόγου of the Corinthians because it was manipulative and self-aggrandizing. He repudiates it for the purposes of preaching the gospel for a much more substantial reason: its potential for producing false results, generating πίστις that is based on the wisdom of human beings rather than the power of God (1 Cor 2:5). In his fuller commentary on 1 Corinthians (2000, p. 209), Thiselton accurately identifies Paul's chief concern: "If the audience assents to certain claims for the wrong reason, this may not constitute a lasting work of God's Holy Spirit." The use of human persuasive strategies to generate such "assent" was precisely what the best of the rhetorical tradition was about. On the inadequacy of this good/bad rhetoric distinction as an explanation for Paul's own use of rhetoric, see "Good Rhetoric Versus Bad Rhetoric.3" below (pp. 294-97).

THE ESSENCE OF GRECO-ROMAN RHETORIC

When all the minutiae of Greco-Roman rhetorical theory are pared away and the essence of the thing lies open before us, we discover the dynamic of rhetorical adaptation.[3] It is this fundamental dynamic, rather than the myriad of details required to implement it, that must be grasped if we are to strike to the heart of the rhetorical tradition. To see this clearly, let us return to what we have earlier called the Grand Equation of Rhetoric.

Modern theorists tend to insist on a more inclusive framework for thinking

---

[3]On this, see Perelman and Olbrechts-Tyteca (1969, pp. 23-26).

about rhetoric,[4] but for the ancients the equation remained relatively simple.[5] Their emphasis focused on the efforts of the speaker, so that the elements in the equation may for our purposes be reduced to three (see fig. 17.1).

Audience + Speaker's Effort ⟶ Results

Figure 17.1. The Grand Equation of Rhetoric

The orator began with his audience. They were for him a *Given*. He could not choose them; his task was simply to understand them and to work with what he received. Moving to the other end of the equation, the orator determined what results he wished to accomplish within the audience.[6] In primary rhetoric these results took the form of some kind of πίστις.[7] It was πείθειν, the calling forth of some particular judgment or verdict or conviction from the audience, that fired classical rhetoric. Hence, the orator's goal functions in our equation as an *Independent Variable*—namely, that which, once set, has the effect of shaping the *Dependent Variable*.

Most important of all, then, the orator's efforts constituted that *Dependent Variable*. They were dependent in the sense that all of the speaker's strategies were contingent on the other elements in the equation: the audience and the preset goal. Everything—arguments, arrangement, word choice, delivery—was weighed in the light of whether it would help accomplish *this* goal with *this* audience. To be fair, for the majority of ancient rhetors this was not the sole consideration; a genuine rhetorical stance also involves a certain faithfulness to one's subject matter—in so many words, honesty—and this was a not uncommon theme of ancient rhetorical theory. Yet classical rhetoric was explicitly utilitarian and goal oriented.[8] Within the confines of a more or less honest treatment of his subject, the ancient orator worked to discover the persuasive possibilities inherent in his rhetorical situation. He then shaped his efforts accordingly, toward the goal of winning the desired result from his listeners—or at least, to cite Aristotle's qualification, to come as close to this goal as possible. Everything hung on the speaker's insight into the audience, his knowledge of

---

[4]See, e.g., the encyclopedic treatments by Jasinski (2001); Sloane (2001); Enos (1996).
[5]See, e.g., Lausberg (1998, pp. 460-64) on the *aptum* of the speech.
[6]Bryant (1974, p. 210): "What makes a situation rhetorical is the focus upon accomplishing something predetermined and directional with an audience."
[7]Cf. Kinneavy (1987, pp. 33-48).
[8]See on this point Crouch (1996, p. 333).

the subject matter, and his ability to discover and forcefully put across λόγοι that would be persuasive to his hearers—that is, arguments that would demonstrate to the audience in one way or another the worthiness of his point, thereby providing sufficient grounds for their belief or acceptance. This was the orator's role, and the success of the rhetorical equation hinged on his ability to fulfill it. He it was who must adapt himself and his discourse to the exigencies of each rhetorical situation, and he it was who, by doing so successfully, generated πίστις in his listeners. The entire complex of ancient rhetorical theory, technique, teaching and writing was designed so as to train the orator in how to do precisely this. For Greco-Roman rhetoric, then, the Grand Equation looked like this (see fig. 17.2).

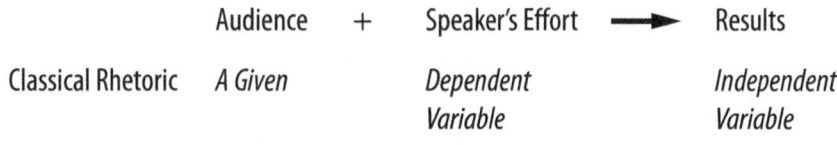

Figure 17.2. The Grand Equation in Greco-Roman rhetoric

Paul's Contrasting View

The Apostle Paul's view of the role of a preacher contrasted sharply with that of the Greco-Roman orator. To be sure, Paul also viewed the audience as a *Given*. But unlike the orator, Paul disavowed the task of inducing belief in his listeners. He insisted that creating πίστις was the sole province of the Spirit of God working through the cross of Christ. This Spirit-powered creation of faith in the saving efficacy of the crucified Christ constituted for Paul the persuasive dynamic of the cross.

Paul plainly wanted his listeners to embrace Christ in faith, but he eschewed the use of persuasive technique designed to move them to do so. To use such techniques, Paul held, would have raised the specter of the listener's πίστις resting on the preacher's facility as a rhetor and, therefore, of the preacher thereby usurping the Spirit's role in creating πίστις. In other words, it would have replaced the divine dynamic of the cross with the human, merely psychological dynamic of rhetoric, thereby preempting the saving power of the cross. While such an approach might achieve a certain type of results, they were not the results Paul craved. Indeed, Paul found the prospect of such illegitimate results repugnant and took steps to avoid them.

The *modus operandi* Paul adopted in order to avoid usurping the power of the cross is summed up in the term *proclamation*—the straightforward placarding of the cross, a notion well captured by the German equivalent *Bekanntmachung* (lit. "known-making"). The essential difference between proclamation and the approach of the persuader focuses on the process of adaptation. Whereas the genius of the rhetorical dynamic was its emphasis on adaptation with a view to inducing πίστις, the emphasis of the herald's proclamation lay elsewhere. The herald was one who carried the message of another. It was not the herald's task to persuade but to convey. He was a declarer, a testifier, a messenger, an announcer.[9] In contrast to the shrewd and ingenious modulations of the rhetor, each calculated to achieve its effect, the proclaimer took essentially the same message with him from audience to audience. If he fulfilled his role faithfully, this message remained a *Constant*. It was the proclaimer's function to make certain that the recipients heard and understood, but it was not the proclaimer's role to engage his rhetorical skills so as to induce his listeners to yield to the message, however much he might desire them to do so. Their response to the message was a matter between them and the originator of the message. The herald was simply the messenger.[10]

In one sense this reduced role made for a more humble stance than that of the persuader. In another, however, Paul's determination to limit himself to the role of a herald, proclaiming a divine message that was not open to negotiation, had the opposite effect: it constituted an offence to human pride. Perelman and Olbrechts-Tyteca rightly observe that for the persuader, the desire

> to convince someone always implies a certain modesty on the part of the initiator of the argument; what he says is not "Gospel truth," he does not possess that authority which would place his words beyond question so that they would carry immediate conviction. He acknowledges that he must use persuasion, think of arguments capable of acting on his interlocutor, show some concern for him, and be interested in his state of mind.[11]

---

[9]Thus Nock (1933, p. 188): "*Kerygma*, heralding, implies an activity like that of the town-crier."
[10]Barrett (1987, p. 3): "It is of the essence of the New Testament proclamation that it must be made; response is a secondary matter. Peter and John declare, 'We cannot but speak the things that we have seen and heard' (Acts 4:20). That is (they are speaking to the Council), You may believe what we say, ignore it, or kill us for saying it; that does not concern us. We must say it. The theme is repeated throughout the New Testament.... To say this is not to say that the New Testament preachers were indifferent to the results of their work; it means that the proclamation has an objectivity which makes it independent of both preacher and response, and that the response that occurs is not wholly dependent on either preacher or hearer."
[11]Perelman and Olbrechts-Tyteca (1969, p. 16).

But the opposite was true for Paul. He did not view it as his business to accommodate these common human expectations by providing impressive arguments "capable of acting on his interlocutor[s]." He was in the business, precisely, of announcing "Gospel truth,"[12] confident that by the power of the Spirit this divine message would "carry immediate conviction" to those "who are being saved" (1 Cor 1:18); that is, to "those who are called" (1 Cor 1:24).

In just such terms did Paul view his preaching ministry. His argument in 1 Corinthians 1:17–2:5, not to mention his terminology and imagery elsewhere, is unmistakable. By limiting himself to the role of the herald, Paul could be confident that the results he saw were not based on his own power as a persuader but on the πίστις-inducing work of the Spirit. The crucified Christ would be his constant, unchanging, inexhaustible theme, simply placarded before all. He would avoid artful argumentation with a view to engendering belief by rendering the message somehow impressive and compelling, indeed, irresistible. The matter of the listener's πίστις must be left to the Spirit alone. Thus the herald's proclamation would constitute the essence of Paul's *modus operandi* as a preacher.

Demonstrating the Truth of the Gospel

It is important to observe that the contrast Paul has in mind here is not between reason and irrationality. It is rather between two different ways of bringing listeners to see the truth of the gospel. As Günther Bornkamm has pointed out in his influential essays on faith and reason in Paul,[13] the Apostle nowhere advocates the abandonment of human reason—the so-called *sacrificium intellectus*—and this is certainly not the argument of 1 Corinthians 1–4.[14] The contrast in

---

[12]Perelman and Olbrechts-Tyteca's distinction between the persuader's stance and that of the announcer of "Gospel truth" is echoed throughout the literature on philosophical and rhetorical argumentation. E.g., in his discussion of the differences between persuasive and philosophical forms of argumentation, Johnstone (1959, p. 46) introduces in passing a third option, that of the "prophet": "The man who wishes to persuade usually cannot hope to do so merely by making a statement.... Unless he is regarded as a prophet, he must be willing to discuss it with others and defend it against their objections." Wallace (1963) famously, and rightly in my view, argued that the very "substance" of rhetoric, old and new, is "good reasons," providing listeners convincing reasons, of whatever sort, to believe the speaker's message. This is the essential function Paul, in his role as a herald, eschewed.

[13]Bornkamm (1958; 1969). Bornkamm (e.g., see 1969, p. 35) emphasizes the important distinction between the function of reason in "those who are perishing" becoming "those who believe," and the role of reason in the life of "those who believe" thereafter. The points Paul makes in 1 Cor 1:17–2:5 are essentially addressed to the former; see below, pp. 304-6.

[14]This point was well understood by Augustine, who answered the anti-Christian philosopher Por-

1 Corinthians 1–4 is focused on the preacher's method in the propagation of the gospel. Paul believed that the gospel made eminently good sense, but he was also convinced that only the Spirit of God should, or in the end could, demonstrate this to the listener.

This was fundamentally for Paul an issue of epistemology, that is, of his theory of knowledge. Paul's problem was not with human reason per se, but rather with the sinful and idolatrous tendencies that inevitably blight the human exercise of reason, tendencies only the Spirit of God can remedy. In his extended study of "Paul's way of knowing," Ian Scott demonstrates that Paul viewed human rationality as "corrupted by endemic moral failure so that the human mind consistently resists interpreting the world in the terms which the Gospel requires." Paul's problem, Scott argues, was not with reason itself but with "reason which has been hijacked by human vices":

> The Spirit's role . . . seems to be a moral restoration of believers which allows them to move into a new system of values within which the Gospel is rational and plausible. Here too there is reason to believe that Paul understood the Spirit to *renew* human reason, rather than to displace it. [C. K.] Barrett points to Paul's statement in [1 Cor] 2:15 that the spiritual "discern all things" and suggests that Paul understands the believer to gain a new ability to "consider and appraise" things in the world, because the Gospel has provided "a moral standard by which all things may be measured." [Thomas W.] Gillespie goes further and points out the consistent reference to cognitive activities in 2:6-16. The apprehension of divine wisdom does not seem to suppress rational thought, but rather involves "understanding" (εἰδέναι, 2:12) and enables the mature to "interpret" (συγκρίνειν, 2:13) and "judge" (ἀνακρίνεσθαι, 2:14, 15). At the end of the passage the "spiritual" believer is left with "the mind of Christ (νοῦς Χριστοῦ)," a new way of thinking and reasoning. This seems to confirm

---

phyry by drawing on Paul's point in 1 Cor 1: "You despise [Christ] on account of the body He took of a woman and the shame of the cross; for your lofty wisdom spurns such low and contemptible things, and soars to more exalted regions. But He fulfills what the holy prophets truly predicted regarding Him: 'I will destroy the wisdom of the wise, and bring to nought the prudence of the prudent.' For *He does not destroy and bring to nought His own gift in them*, but what they arrogate to themselves, and do not hold of Him. And hence the apostle, having quoted this testimony from the prophet, adds, 'Where is the wise? Where is the scribe? Where is the disputer of this world? Hath not God made foolish the wisdom of this world? For after that, in the wisdom of God, the world by wisdom knew not God, it pleased God by the foolishness of preaching to save them that believe. . . . ' This is despised as a weak and foolish thing by those who are wise and strong in themselves; yet this is the grace which heals the weak, who do not proudly boast a blessedness of their own, but rather humbly acknowledge their real misery" (*City of God* 10.28; italics added).

at least that the Gospel is itself comprehensible (even if some cannot accept it) and that the one who, under the Spirit's impulse, has accepted that message gains a new ability to reason about the world.[15]

It was his task, Paul believed, to announce the gospel, but it was the Spirit's role to show "those who are called" the divine reasonableness of this gospel from God's point of view. "Those who are perishing" (τοῖς ἀπολλυμένοις) would continue to find the placarded Savior ridiculous. As ψυχικόι (those without the Spirit) they would be unable to perceive in the crucified Christ the wisdom of God. But to the "called ones" (κλητοί) the Spirit of God would allow this same κήρυγμα to appear as profoundly right and true and worthy of belief (cf. Acts 13:48; 16:14; see also Lk 24:45; 1 Jn 5:20). Indeed, through the Spirit's illumination this κήρυγμα would appear for them to be the very power of God and the wisdom of God, reasonable not in the sense that they now understood all the ins and outs of *how* God was in Christ saving them, but rather in the sense that they now understood *that* God was in Christ saving them. As F. L. Godet put it, when Paul speaks in 1 Corinthians 2:4 of the demonstration (ἀπόδειξις) of the Spirit and of power, the term ἀπόδειξις "indicates a clearness which is produced in the hearer's mind, as by a sudden lifting of the veil; a conviction mastering him with the sovereign force of moral evidence."[16]

THE HUMAN FACTOR IN SALVATION

Margaret Thrall produced a detailed analysis of "the various motives that may have impelled individuals to convert to Christianity" in Corinth (2002, p. 69). The analysis is highly speculative, but this is not its chief shortcoming. The larger issue is that her study is focused entirely on the merely human factors (religious, cultural, sociological) that may have attracted Paul's converts.

Such a focus is not inherently problematic. In insisting that God had called him to preach the gospel, Paul is *ipso facto* asserting that there are legitimate human elements at work in salvation. "I planted, Apollos watered, but God gave the growth," Paul said (1 Cor 3:6). If only God can give the increase, it nonetheless remains that God chooses to work through human agencies for the planting and watering. Thus, the recognition

---

[15] Scott (2006, p. 34); cf. Bornkamm (1969, pp. 33-34); Gillespie (1990, pp. 156-60). Scott's topic is the Apostle's epistemological stance, but his findings strongly support and further explicate our argument about Paul's resistance to the use of persuasive strategies in preaching. See appendix three for a summary of Scott's important treatment of Rom 1:18-32 and 1 Cor 1:17–2:16.
[16] Godet (1886, vol. 1, p. 129).

of legitimate human factors in the process of conversion was axiomatic for the Apostle.

Yet Paul would surely also have found such a human focus, if not wrong, yet profoundly inadequate as an explanation of the Corinthians' conversion. Paul attributed the faith of the Corinthians to a very different source: the δύναμις θεοῦ at work in the proclaimed gospel (1 Cor 1:18-24). While Paul nowhere called for a denial of human factors in salvation, he nonetheless emphasized the limitations God places on the means he chooses to use. According to Paul, God chooses "what is foolish in the world to shame the wise; . . . what is weak in the world to shame the strong; . . . what is low and despised in the world, even things that are not, to bring to nothing things that are," all "so that no human being might boast in the presence of God" (1 Cor 1:27-29). A focus on human factors alone thus falls far short of what Paul believed was at work in the conversion of the Corinthian believers.

Our modern tendency to focus solely on human explanations of the motives that may have impelled individuals to convert to Christianity stands in striking contrast to the practice of the early church, which tended to argue the opposite. For example, echoing what had long become a stock argument of his predecessors, Chrysostom claimed that the relevant *human* factors actually worked against such horizontal explanations: "When the one preaching is unskilled and poor and undistinguished, and the message preached not alluring, but even scandalous, and the ones hearing it poor and weak and nobodies, and the dangers continuous and unremitting for both teachers and disciples, and the one being proclaimed a victim of crucifixion, what caused it to conquer? Is it not clear that it was some divine and ineffable power?" (*De laudibus sancti Pauli apostolic* 4:13, Mitchell, 2002, p. 463. Cf. Chrysostom's famous contrast between Paul and Nero in *Homilies on Timothy*, Hom. 4, on 2 Tim 2:10).

In this argument Chrysostom was echoing Paul's own. Whatever the human factors, they were deficient as explanations of the conversion of the Corinthians. The Gospel of John records Jesus as saying to some of those who had both seen his works and heard his words, "You do not believe because you are not among my sheep. My sheep hear my voice, and I know them, and they follow me" (Jn 10:26-27). In Paul's view, it was the voice of this Shepherd that his sheep—"the called ones"—by the power of the Spirit heard in the gospel he proclaimed. Recognizing this voice is what rendered his κήρυγμα an ἀποδείξει πνεύματος καὶ δυνάμεως (1 Cor 2:4) in the minds and hearts of "those who believed." For Paul, this voice was the prime factor that "impelled individuals to convert to Christianity" in Corinth.

Means of Demonstration

The true contrast in Paul's argument, then, is between two different ways of demonstrating the truthfulness of the gospel, and therefore between two different bases of belief. On the one hand, the rhetorical approach produced the unacceptable result wherein the listener's belief was the product of the speaker's ability to induce πίστις by employing the ingenious rhetorical strategies so effectively wielded by the orators. Perelman and Olbrechts-Tyteca rightly capture the essence of this process when they define rhetoric, old and new, as "the study of the discursive techniques allowing us *to induce or to increase the mind's adherence to the theses presented for its assent.*"[17] It is fundamentally a human approach, applying human strategies, with predictably human results. On the other hand, his calling as a herald meant for Paul that all such human strategies must be abandoned to the conviction that it was only the Spirit who could or should be responsible for the πίστις of "those who believe."

This also meant, of course, that Paul was required to leave the matter of results to the Spirit. The orators determined at the outset the results they wished to accomplish and then shaped their strategies accordingly. As Plato taught (according to Aristides), "Oratory is the maker of persuasion"; it "aims at things and guides its words, according to its aim."[18] Paul's determination, by contrast, was to hold his preaching constant (1 Cor 2:2). This threw the variability in the equation to the end. For Paul the results became the equation's *Dependent Variable*, a factor that could scarcely be addressed until after the fact.

Each time Paul preached the gospel, he perceived himself to be introducing the *Constant*, the message of Christ crucified. But it was the Spirit who would use this message to distinguish between "those who are perishing" and "those who are being saved." The former would find the simply proclaimed gospel foolish or even offensive, but the latter would come to view it, through the supernatural force of the Spirit's conviction, as the truth of their own salvation.[19] In this way Paul's unchanging message of the cross carried the stench of death to the one but the fragrance of life to the other, depending on the work of the Spirit. Paul could not know beforehand which listeners were which, of course; it was only afterward as he observed and assessed the consequences of the preaching that he could reach any such conclusions (cf. 1 Thess 1:4-5; 2:13). We

---

[17]Perelman and Olbrechts-Tyteca (1969, p. 4). Their book, *The New Rhetoric*, represents a rigorous modern discussion of this human process and is highly recommended. Following in the train of their ancient predecessors, Perelman and Olbrechts-Tyteca demonstrate the indispensability of rhetoric in human affairs. Their treatment serves as a healthy reminder that the Apostle Paul nowhere denigrates the art of persuasion as such. His reservations have to do only with the potential for false results when its powers are harnessed for the promulgation of the gospel.

[18]Aristides, *To Plato in Defence of Oratory* 138.

[19]See appendix three for a detailed discussion of this contrasting response.

may therefore contrast the approach of Greco-Roman rhetoric with Paul's *modus operandi* as a preacher as follows (see fig. 17.3).

	Audience +	Speaker's Effort ⟶	Results
Classical Rhetoric	A Given	Dependent Variable	Independent Variable
Paul	A Given	A Constant	Dependent Variable

Figure 17.3. Paul's approach vs. Greco-Roman rhetoric

The most striking aspect of this contrast is the clarity with which it illuminates the key issue of 1 Corinthians 1:17–2:5. If we examine the two approaches—asking of each the question, Where does the contingency lie?—the fundamental difference emerges clearly. In the first, the contingency lies with the orator's efforts. The process at work is from first to last a human psychological one. In the second, that upon which the process is contingent lies *outside* the equation. There is a *Dependent Variable* (the results), but it does not in the end "depend" on the human dimensions of the equation (that is, Paul's rhetorical ingenuity). It hinges on the sovereign working of the Spirit in commending "the word of the cross" (the *Constant*) to human hearts. In effect, then, the equation, representing as it does the purely human plane, is incapable of capturing the dynamic on which Paul was determined to depend. But this is, of course, just as Paul would have it, for he claimed to be operating according to a divine dynamic, not a human one.

As Paul saw it, his *modus operandi* as a herald was required by his theological presuppositions. The most important theological presupposition that undergirds 1 Corinthians 1:17–2:5 relates to God's own *modus operandi* in the world: God uses what the world considers unimpressive to accomplish his purposes so that in the end there can be no question about who has achieved the result. God has achieved it so that no human can boast. According to Paul, this is a principle that transcends the cultural setting in Corinth; indeed, it transcends all cultural settings. It is nothing less than a fundamental pattern of how God chooses to operate in the world.

Paul uses this pattern to explain and defend his own *modus operandi* as a preacher. The Corinthians were critical because Paul's preaching was, by their customary standards of eloquence, unimpressive. But Paul responds by showing that such a criticism is inconsistent with the Corinthians' own theological beliefs. In other words, Paul cites the gospel—to which the Corinthians remained committed, despite their inadequate grasp of its implications—as the premise on which his defense must stand. By reminding the immature Corinthians of the merely human framework of their esteemed σοφία λόγου on the one hand, and pointing out the consonance of his own approach with the fundamental pattern of God's method in the world on the other, Paul hoped to defuse their criticisms, squelch the quarrels and mature the Corinthians' own theological understanding.

This explains, then, why Paul emphasizes the nature of the gospel so strongly in 1 Corinthians 1:17–2:5. At no point does he imply that the Corinthians had abandoned or distorted the gospel itself. His treatment is not corrective in this sense at all. Paul stresses the gospel because he is dealing with what Maurice Natanson calls the *philosophy of rhetoric*, or more appropriately in Paul's case, his *theology of preaching*. Paul is here exploring "the underlying assumptions" of Christian proclamation. Thus he rejects the rhetorical approach to discourse urged by the Corinthians by pointing out its theoretical roots—it is the outworking of a purely human and worldly system of thinking and as such is inappropriate for the purposes of preaching the gospel. By the same token, he defends his own approach by pointing out its working assumption: God's preferred method of working in the world as seen preeminently in the cross. In both cases, what occupies Paul in this passage is the relationship between an approach to discourse and the philosophical/theological presuppositions that give shape to it.

THE KEY CONTRAST

In our introductory chapter we sketched a distinction between two models of behavior: the *natural paradigm* and the *Pauline paradigm*. Now we are in a position to give more specificity to our terms. The herald's stance we have just described constitutes the centerpiece of the Pauline paradigm. The persuader's stance, by contrast, constitutes the centerpiece of the natural paradigm. What sets these two models apart are the engines that drive them. The natural paradigm/persuader's stance is *results* driven, while the Pauline paradigm/herald's stance is *obedience* driven.

The persuader's stance begins at the far right of the equation by determining the desired result, then selects its strategies so as to achieve that result. In this way the desired result drives the strategy: How can I achieve *this* result with *this* audience on *this* occasion? Skill in answering this question and then successfully implementing the chosen strategies constituted the genius of the rhetorical art. The persuader's stance is inherently results oriented.

The herald's stance starts at a very different place in the equation. It focuses on the speaker's efforts. The question it asks of those efforts is not, *What must I do to achieve some predetermined result?* The herald's question is, *What is God calling me to be and to do?* The herald then bends every effort toward being that and doing that. It is in this sense that the herald's stance is obedience driven rather than results driven. The herald is uniquely focused on fulfilling the calling of God, which in turn requires a willingness to leave the matter of results to the Spirit.

These two models mark the essential difference between proclamation and persuasion. Success in the former is measured by God's approval of one's faithfulness, while success in the latter is measured by the results achieved. Paul viewed himself as a herald called by God to proclaim the word of the cross. Some of his listeners would, by the power of the Spirit, recognize in this proclamation the wisdom of God and power of God. Others would turn away, finding that same message to be nonsense or scandalous. Yet these mixed results were not Paul's measure of success. It is required of a steward, he says, to be found faithful to his commission (1 Cor 4:2). Thus did Paul measure his own ministry.

REFINING THE CONTRAST

We have employed the term *stance* to describe the two contrasting approaches to discourse. This use of the term was popularized in a famous essay by University of Chicago professor Wayne Booth titled "The Rhetorical Stance."[20] This essay is worth pausing with for two reasons. First, it is a winsome and nicely readable modern treatment of the ancient rhetorical tradition. It expresses the noblest aspects of that tradition, what we may think of as "rhetoric at its best." But second, this essay also provides a framework for refining our understanding of the differences between the herald's stance and the persuader's stance.

"Rhetoric," says Booth, echoing the ancients, especially Aristotle, "is the art of finding and employing the most effective means of persuasion on any subject." This task involves taking what Booth calls a "rhetorical stance"; that is,

---

[20]Booth (1963). The following quotations are from pp. 139-45. Booth composed this essay for an audience of writing teachers, but he addresses his subject at a level that renders the writing/speaking distinction largely unimportant. The essay is especially useful for our present discussion.

> a stance which depends on discovering and maintaining in any [rhetorical] situation a proper balance among three elements that are at work in any communicative effort: the available arguments about the subject itself, the interests and peculiarities of the audience, and the voice, the implied character, of the speaker. I should like to suggest that it is this balance, this rhetorical stance . . . that is our main goal as teachers of rhetoric.

To clarify what he means by a rhetorical stance, Booth contrasts it with several of its corruptions, that is, "unbalanced stances often assumed by people who think they are practicing the arts of persuasion." The first he calls the "pedant's stance." The pedant's stance depends "entirely on statements about a subject," while "the notion of a job to be done for a particular audience is left out." This perversion of a truly rhetorical stance "springs from ignoring the audience" and reflects "an over-reliance on the pure subject."

The second corruption is the "advertiser's stance." This stems from "*under*valuing the subject and overvaluing pure effect." Here the goal is to produce a particular effect in an audience "even if the truth of the subject is honed off in the process."

> Having told [students] that good writers always to some degree accommodate their arguments to the audience, it is hard to explain the difference between justified accommodation—say changing *point one* to the final position—and the kind of accommodation that fills our popular magazines, in which the very substance of what is said is accommodated to some preconception of what will sell.

A third corruption is the "entertainer's stance"—"the willingness to sacrifice substance to personality and charm." And Booth suggests there are other corruptions. But what he is primarily after is the balance found in the classical rhetorical stance.

> Balance itself is always harder to describe than the clumsy poses that result when it is destroyed. But we all experience the balance whenever we find an author who succeeds in changing our minds. He can do so only if he knows more about the subject than we do, and if he then engages us in the process of thinking—and feeling—it through.

This sort of balance, says Booth, is what made first-rate communicators such as John Milton, Edmund Burke and Winston Churchill so effective.

> Each presents us with the spectacle of a man passionately involved in thinking an important question through, in the company of an audience. Though each

of them did everything in his power to make his point persuasive, including a pervasive use of . . . emotional appeals . . . , none would have allowed himself the advertiser's stance; none would have polled the audience in advance to discover which position would get the votes. Nor is the highly individual personality that springs out at us from their speeches and essays present for the sake of itself. The rhetorical balance among speakers, audience, and argument is with all three habitual.

Booth here puts into words the finest tradition of rhetoric. It is the rhetoric of Isocrates, Aristotle, Cicero and Quintilian. It is the rhetoric of Western history's greatest orators and writers. From the beginning there were those who perverted this tradition into the corrupted stances Booth describes; but in the same way there have always been—at least where social and political conditions permitted it—those who practiced the art in the balanced and principled way Booth describes. All the more striking, then, to discover that *it is not just the corruptions of this tradition that Paul calls into question for the purposes of preaching; it is the essence of the tradition itself.*

On what basis must the Apostle judge as inappropriate for preaching not merely its perversions but even the most high-minded expression of this rhetorical tradition? Paul certainly did reject the various corruptions, as when he repudiated any dependence on "disgraceful, underhanded ways" or "cunning" in his dealings with the Corinthians (2 Cor 4:2). But in 1 Corinthians 1–4 the Apostle's scalpel cuts deeper still. His argument there is not that a rhetorical stance is somehow unethical. By Paul's standards it need be no such thing. In the hands of a skilled and ethical persuader, it can be a principled and socially useful thing. As its ancient proponents often argued, the art of persuasion, exercised in a free society, was a crucial skill and far to be preferred over the coercion of tyranny or the art of war,[21] and we have no grounds for concluding that the Apostle Paul would have quibbled with their argument. But that is because Paul's concerns lay elsewhere. For Paul, the inadequacy of the rhetorical approach, even at its best, consisted not in its being inherently dishonest but in

---

[21]E.g., Plutarch (*Moralia* 802C-E) on Pericles: "The government [of Athens] in Pericles' time was 'in name,' as Thucydides says, 'a democracy, but in fact the rule of the foremost man,' because of his power of speech. . . . [When Thucydides] was asked by Archidamus King of the Spartans whether he or Pericles was the better wrestler, he replied 'Nobody can tell; for whenever I throw him in wrestling, he says he was not thrown and wins by persuading the onlookers. . . . The wolf, they say, cannot be held by the ears; but one must lead a people or a State chiefly by the ears. . . . For leadership of a people is leadership of those who are persuaded by speech."

the fact that it is so quintessentially *human*.²² It is a *natural* psychological process that produces predictably *natural* results. And this for Paul was its fatal flaw when it came to preaching.

Just here is where we moderns find it most difficult to follow the Apostle's lead. What Paul is rejecting is the natural paradigm we described in our introductory chapter. It is one that is familiar to us all. It is a common, useful and quintessentially human approach that works in concert with our native inclinations. Countless individuals function unreflectively within its framework every day. This widespread use in turn reinforces its dominant status.

> Every businessman decides what he wants to accomplish and then builds his business plan to achieve it. Every lawyer determines what decision she wants from the jury and then organizes her case accordingly. Every advertiser decides what he wants the customer to do and then shapes his message so as to achieve that aim. Every politician judges how she wants the voters to think and vote and then designs her communication strategy appropriately. In the same way those in ministry may strategize so as to accomplish their preset goals. The wisdom of this approach is self-evident. It is universally employed, patently effective, glaringly obvious. What could be more natural? (pp. 47-48 above)

To all of which Paul's might respond, "Precisely," for it is that very naturalness that constitutes the problem. It is on these grounds that the Apostle calls the persuader's stance into question. However useful it may be elsewhere, its very *naturalness* renders it fundamentally flawed as an approach to Christian ministry.

Listen again to Booth's expression of the best of the rhetorical tradition: Rhetoric, he rightly says, is "the art of finding and employing the most effective means of persuasion on any subject." A speaker can "succeed in changing our minds" only "if he knows more about the subject than we do, and if he then engages us in the process of thinking—and feeling—it through"; the greatest persuaders have been those who were "passionately involved in thinking an important question through, in the company of an audience," each one doing "everything in his power to make his point persuasive."²³ Here, fairly stated, is the natural paradigm at work.

Now consider Paul's expression of its alternative, that of the itinerant tentmaker who was called by Christ, not to discover and employ persuasive strategies,

---

²²Cavadini, citing Augustine: "The art of rhetoric is useful . . . precisely because it embodies a science of human motivation and therefore helps us to learn what will make the truth not only true but *moving*. The fact that it is true is not, normally, enough" (1995, pp. 164-65).
²³Booth (1963, pp. 139-45).

but simply to *announce* the good news (εὐαγγελίζω, 1 Cor 1:17); that is, to proclaim as a herald (κηρύσσω) the "word of the cross," knowing full well that this core message would be heard as foolishness by "those who are perishing," but also as the power and wisdom of God by those "who are being saved" (1 Cor 1:18). When he arrived in Corinth, Paul said to the Corinthians, his preaching was scarcely marked by rhetorical power and finesse. Instead, "I decided to know nothing among you except Jesus Christ and him crucified" (1 Cor 2:2). As Christ's herald, it was not his task to change their minds about the gospel through ingenious arguments clothed in artfully crafted language, doing "everything in his power to make his point persuasive." The widespread effectiveness of the orators was proof enough that the employment of such human cleverness was a virtual prescription for engendering human results; that is, results based on "the wisdom of men" rather than "the power of God" (1 Cor 2:5). Instead, Paul determined to restrict himself to the ministry to which he had been called, that of the herald. He would faithfully fulfill his commission to placard the crucified Christ and then look to the Spirit's application of that proclaimed gospel for the results.

The Issue of Audience Adaption

Booth's analysis of the rhetorical stance and its several corruptions provides a helpful continuum, with pure subject at one extreme and pure effect at the other. The pedant's stance hovers at the pure subject end of the continuum, while both the advertiser's stance and the entertainer's stance skew toward pure effect. Booth wants to place the classical rhetorical stance somewhere in the middle, reflecting a balance between the two poles. What Booth does not address is the location of the herald on this continuum.

Where would we place the herald's stance on Booth's continuum? We have said that the rhetorical stance (and even more so its corruptions) is results driven, while the herald's stance is obedience driven. Booth's continuum enables a further refinement of this point. The rhetorical stance and two of its corruptions are located away from the pure-subject extreme precisely because of their willingness to take the audience into consideration in shaping their message. While the corruptions go too far in this direction, the rhetorical stance maintains an ideal balance between the two poles. But what about the herald's stance? Does not this stance also adjust its message to its audience?

As we shall see momentarily, it does. Thus the difference between the persuader's stance and the herald's stance cannot be the presence or absence of audience adaptation. The difference lies deeper. Both of these stances adapt themselves to their audiences, but our more specific question must be: audience adaptation, yes, but for what *purpose*?

An Ancient Debate

To answer this question, we may be tempted to turn to an ancient debate for help. But for our purposes that debate will lead us astray.

Cicero famously defined the three functions of oratory as *docere* ("to instruct"), *delectare* ("to delight") and *movere* ("to move"): "The orator is duty bound to instruct; giving pleasure is a free gift to the audience, to move them is indispensable."[24] On this point Quintilian and other major rhetoricians agreed.[25] Yet there were also those who disagreed. These were the proponents of the Stoic theory of style called Ἑλληνισμός in Greek or *Latinitas* in Latin.[26] In English the most common term for this movement is Atticism.

The Attic theory of style was grounded on several philosophical premises. The most important for our purposes was the Stoic principle of ἀπάθεια, that is, detachment, freedom from emotions, mastery over the passions. On this view, the role of an orator was merely to address the reason of the listener through instruction (*docere*). *Delectare* and *movere* appealed to what were considered lesser elements in the listener and were designed only to cloud his reason. Such tactics were viewed by the Stoics as unworthy of the orator. This led to a spare, unadorned classical style that repudiated emotion in favor of linguistic purity, clarity, precision and conciseness.[27]

This struggle between Atticism and the dominant Ciceronian tradition was in full swing during the first century, and we may be tempted to conclude that this was what was at stake in Corinth.[28] According to this line of thinking, the

---

[24]Cicero, *Opt. gen.* 4.
[25]E.g., see Quintilian, *Inst. or.* 3.5.2, 8; *Prooemium* 7, 32; 12.10.43.
[26]See Smiley (1906).
[27]E.g., Pliny on one such austere orator: "One of our contemporary orators is a sound and sober speaker while lacking in grandeur and eloquence, so that I think my comment on him has point: his only fault is that he is faultless." Pliny preferred those orators who were "roused and heated, sometimes even to boiling-point" (*Letters* 9.25.1). In their emphasis on austerity, the Atticists— or those Quintilian calls the "dries" (*aridos, Inst. or.* 8; *Prooemium* 17)—were critical of the "copiousness" of the Ciceronian tradition. But as Quintilian observes, "Copiousness . . . is of two kinds: one rich, one ornate and flowery" (*Inst. or.* 8.3.87). Following Cicero, Quintilian advocated the first and disavowed the second.
[28]For a discussion of these two styles, the plain versus adorned, see Dionysius of Halicarnassus, *Isocrates* 11; *Demosthenes* 4-5; *Pompeius* 2.

problem in Corinth was that the Corinthians enjoyed the fuller Ciceronian style involving *delectare* and *movere* as well as *docere*, while the Apostle Paul insisted on limiting himself merely to *docere*. But this analysis is unhelpful in several ways.

First, it turns the Apostle Paul into an advocate of the Atticist theory of style, a style grounded in Stoic philosophy. But this is highly unlikely. Paul grounds his approach to discourse not on Stoic philosophical principles but on a radically different foundation: his own Christ-centered theology.

Second, the Stoic theory's insistence on linguistic purity and precision involved the careful search for precisely the right word. The speaker's language was to be drawn from the ancients under the assumption that their vocabulary was nearer to a primitive and more natural, uncorrupted manner of speaking. Every word to be uttered was to be tested, eliminating all solecisms and barbarisms. Concision was critical. By such standards the ample κοινή ("common") Greek of the Apostle Paul was utterly deficient. The Apostle was neither an advocate nor a practitioner of the Atticism of his day.

Third, the distinction between *docere* and *delectare/movere* is simply not the one we need if we are to understand Paul's concerns. As a herald, Paul certainly wished to instruct his hearers, but the Stoic doctrine of ἀπάθεια held little interest for him. His view of the human person was more holistic than the Stoics'— which is to say, it was more Semitic than Greek. Paul would have been far less inclined than his Greek counterparts to think in terms of separating out reason from the other dimensions of his listeners.[29] The argument between the Atticists and the broader Ciceronian rhetorical tradition is thus inadequate for clarifying the distinction Paul is after in 1 Corinthians 1–4.

ATTENTION, COMPREHENSION AND YIELDING

A more useful approach may be found in a modern source. In an extended article on attitude change in the *Handbook of Social Psychology*, psychologist William McGuire explains that human persuasion may be broken down into at least five steps or levels: *attention, comprehension, yielding, retention* and *action*. The hearer must "go through each of these steps if communication is to have ultimate persuasive impact," says McGuire, "and each depends on the occurrence of the preceding steps."[30] To be said to have been persuaded, a listener must give attention

---

[29]In fact, note the important contrast between Paul and Hellenistic philosophy in general: "The agent of self-mastery for Paul is the Spirit (Gal. 5:23), not human reason" (Aune, 2008, p. 232).
[30]McGuire (1969, p. 173).

to a message, comprehend it, yield to it, retain it and act on it. McGuire's analysis is a useful reminder that human persuasion is typically less an event than a process. His "stepwise analysis of the persuasion process" makes possible the necessary distinctions between the persuader's stance and the herald's stance.[31]

All five steps of the persuasion process are the legitimate focus of the rhetorical stance. Without sacrificing an honest treatment (ideally) of its subject, the rhetorical stance bends its strategies toward achieving each of the steps. Yet because the final two steps, *retention* and *action*, are the aftereffects of the first three, these can occur only when the speaker's efforts are finished. Thus a rhetorical stance typically focuses its efforts on the first three steps, recognizing that if it can succeed here, the fourth and fifth steps will tend to take care of themselves. It is therefore the first three steps of the persuasion process that are important for our purposes. This is where we will discover the difference that proves so useful in setting the persuader apart from the herald.

The herald's stance is focused on the first two steps in the process—*attention* and *comprehension*. The herald is not only willing but is required to adapt his message to his audience for just these purposes. To fulfill his assignment he must gain his audience's attention and couch the commissioned message in such a way that his listeners can comprehend it. In this way, *attention* and *comprehension* constitute the essence of the herald's role. Rhetorical strategies designed to accomplish these first two steps not only do not compromise the herald's role; they help fulfill it.

Strategies focused on yielding, on the other hand, do overreach the herald's role. It was not the herald's assignment to induce the audience to yield to the com-

---

[31]Ibid., p. 174. McGuire offers this "commonsense sequence of steps" as "a generally applicable convenience." This sort of analysis is needful, he says, due to the complexity of the persuasion process. "In order to reduce the vast literature on communication-induced attitude change to manageable size, it is useful to analyze into classes the antecedent and the consequent variables. The antecedent (the verbal communication) can be analyzed into its components . . . ; and the consequent (the attitude change behavior) can be analyzed into its components. . . . In this way we can place any of the communication-persuasion relationships within the framework provided by this matrix" (p. 172).

Yet McGuire also warns of the potential for oversimplification is such analyses. The categories are helpful at the theoretical level (e.g., for our present purpose), but the interaction of what he calls the antecedent and consequent variables (a speech act, and its effects on a recipient) in any given instance is highly complex. Theorists have recognized this challenge from the beginning (see, e.g., Aristotle's treatment of *ethos, pathos* and *logos* in the *Rhetoric*), but the extended treatments of the process of persuasion by modern theories only reinforce the point. Thus we will use McGuire's five-step sequence only in the most basic way. Both Paul's preaching and the Greco-Roman orator's speech were instances of what McGuire calls "antecedent" verbal communications. Yet Paul insisted on distinguishing between the two. What was the difference? McGuire's "commonsense sequence of steps" is useful in sorting out an answer.

missioned message. The audience's response remained an issue between them and the one who dispatched the herald. The herald was a messenger whose success or failure was measured by the faithfulness with which he fulfilled his assignment. The success of the herald cannot therefore be determined by measuring the listener's acceptance of (*yielding to*) the message. It can only be measured by the degree to which the herald has satisfied the commissioner's instructions.

The persuader's stance, by contrast, involves no such limitation. In fact it *permits* no such limitation. As we have seen, the response of the audience is very much the responsibility of the persuader. The ultimate focus of the rhetorical stance—again, assuming a more or less honest treatment of the subject—is persuasion, and the persuader's audience adaptation is driven toward this goal. The persuader is free to employ the full panoply of rhetorical strategies designed to engender not only *attention* and *comprehension* but also *yielding*. Indeed, the rhetor's skill in doing so will largely determine the result.

The effectiveness of the persuader was thus measured by the degree to which his audience "yielded" to his rhetorical efforts. Just here, said Quintilian, "lie the task and the toil" of the persuader.[32] The focus of the art of rhetoric is precisely on those techniques designed "*to induce or to increase the mind's adherence to the theses presented for its assent.*"[33] The persuader's expressed purpose is to see to it that the audience embraces his arguments, and falling short of this goal is what calls his efforts into question. As Aristotle observed, "Rhetoric is useful, because the true and the just are naturally superior to their opposites, so that, if decisions are improperly made, they must owe their defeat to their own advocates; which is reprehensible."[34]

Two Important Implications

The ambiguity of "persuasion." McGuire's distinctions are useful for our discussion in two ways. First, they constitute a warning about the inherent ambiguity of the notion of "persuasion." The observation that Paul was clearly "persuasive," in the sense of seeing some of his listeners navigate all five of McGuire's steps, is both true and, for our purposes, uninformative. Paul clearly wished his listeners to be "persuaded" by his preaching, and on one occasion was willing to speak of himself as the one doing the persuading (ἀνθρώπους πείθομεν, 2 Cor

---

[32]Quintilian, *Inst. or.* 6.2.7.
[33]Perelman and Olbrechts-Tyteca (1969, p. 4).
[34]Aristotle, *Rhetoric* 1.1.12.

5:11; cf. Acts 18:4; 28:23-24). Yet the deeper question we must ask is this: What limited role did the Apostle aspire to play *within* that persuasion process?

Suppose that Paul restricted himself to the role of the herald in preaching the gospel, focusing his efforts on the *attention* and *comprehension* steps, and then some of his listeners were moved by the Spirit to yield to that gospel—for example, Lydia: "The Lord opened her heart to respond to [προσέχω] Paul's message" (Acts 16:14 NIV; cf. 13:48)—retain it and act on it. Could it be said that Paul had "persuaded" them? The answer must certainly be yes. As with any herald, at a purely horizontal level the Apostle was the human agent whose message the audience had heard, embraced, retained and acted on. In Acts 17:3-4, for instance, Paul's proclamation (καταγγέλλω) is followed immediately by, "And some of them were persuaded" (ἐπείσθησαν NASB; cf. Acts 28:23-24). But this observation, while accurate, obscures the essential issue. McGuire's five-step process provides the finer distinctions required to appreciate the crucial if also more subtle concerns of the Apostle.

The persuader's stance orients its strategies toward achieving not only *attention* and *comprehension* but also *yielding*, whereas the herald's stance is focused on the first two. Thus, while the herald's and the persuader's efforts may both result in a form of πίστις in the listeners, the bases of those two convictions will potentially differ. In the former, the listeners' belief may be the result of the Spirit's application of the herald's announcement; in the latter, it will be the result of the persuader's strategies designed to promote *yielding*. Paul gives no indication that he would have pressed this distinction in society at large, but when the subject was his preaching, the latter result was precisely his concern. The Apostle was determined that when his listeners were "persuaded" by his preaching, their πίστις would be genuine, a product of the Spirit's application of the "word of the cross" rather than of rhetorical prowess on his part.

This is precisely the issue—Paul's rationale for playing a limited role *within* the persuasion process—that Augustine failed to discern in his famous treatment of preaching in Book IV of *De Doctrina Christiana*. In the introduction we noted that Augustine agreed with Paul—indeed, drew upon the Apostle to support his argument—that left to themselves the preacher's efforts cannot accomplish anything of lasting value.[35] Thus the preacher must bathe his preaching in prayer, recognizing that he will accomplish "more through the piety of his

---

[35]Cf. 1 Cor 3:7 and Augustine, *Doctr. chr.* 4.16.33.

prayers than through his orator's skill." The sacred orator, says Augustine, must be "a petitioner before a speaker."

> At the very time … when he is going to preach, before he loosens his tongue to speak, he should lift up his thirsting soul to God, in order to give forth what he will drink in, and to pour out what he will be filled with. For although on every topic which can be treated according to faith and love, there is much that may be said, and many ways in which it may be said by those versed therein, who knows either what is best for us on a special occasion to say, or what is best that others should hear from us, if it be not He who sees the hearts of all? And who can make us say what we ought, and in the manner we ought to say it, if not He in whose hands are both ourselves and our words?[36]

Thus far Paul and St. Augustine were in concert. The crucial final step in Paul's thought, however, was where Augustine fell away. Both the Apostle and Augustine grasped the fact that God deigned to use human instruments to accomplish his purposes in the world, but for Paul this was not the final word. When it came to the vital process of generating πίστις in his listeners, the Apostle was concerned about the potential for producing false results. Hence Paul's determination to restrict himself *within* the persuasion process to the more limited role of the herald, leaving the issue of producing πίστις to the Spirit. Augustine, by contrast, saw no need for any such reticence.

As we observed earlier, the pages of *De Doctrina Christiana*, Book IV, reveal little awareness of Paul's argument in 1 Corinthians 1–4. The brilliant bishop of Hippo, so insightful in so many other ways, seems oblivious to the Apostle's concern about the potential for false results. Hence he gives no thought to the need for restricting one's role in the process of persuasion. For Augustine, the full panoply of Ciceronian (see 4.17.34) rhetorical strategies—the subdued style, the moderate style, the grand style; informing, charming, convincing—are not only available to the preacher; it is incumbent on the preacher to put them all to their fullest possible use.[37]

> Because of those whom by reason of their prejudice truth does not satisfy if it is put in any other way than that whereby the speaker's words are attractive, no small place has been given in oratory even to the art of pleasing. And still, when this is added, it is not enough for hardened natures who reap no profit

---

[36] Augustine, *Doctr. chr.* 4.15.32; Sullivan (1930, pp. 115-17).
[37] Sullivan (1930, pp. 102-3).

from having understood and having enjoyed the [preacher's] speech. For what do these two things avail a person who both owns the truth and praises eloquence, but who does not give his assent.... It is necessary, therefore that the sacred orator, when urging that something be done, should not only teach in order to instruct, and please in order to hold, but also move in order to win. For indeed, it is only by the heights of eloquence that that man is to be moved to agreement who has not been brought to it by truth, though demonstrated to his own acknowledgment, even when joined with a charming style.[38]

Augustine saw the "sacred orator" as responsible for all five of McGuire's steps to persuasion and was dismissive toward those who disagreed. Paul's theological argument in favor of the more limited role of the herald was apparently lost on him.[39]

Paul's audience adaptation. This analysis of the distinction between the roles of the persuader and the herald is also useful in helping us understand how the Apostle viewed his own audience adaptation. As we have noted, in discussing his preaching Paul consistently employed the language of the herald or witness. In 1 Corinthians 1–4 he spells out why. Christ did not call him to preach with persuasive words of wisdom, he says, but rather to declare, to announce and to give testimony to "Christ and him crucified." This was his constant message, a message that typically engendered mixed results. Yet these varied results did not deter Paul, nor did the criticisms of those who insisted on measuring his preaching by a worldly yardstick. As a commissioned steward of the gospel, Paul was accountable to God alone and would stand or fall with his approval. It was Paul's goal merely to be found faithful as a herald of Christ.

Should Paul's argument, then, be construed to mean that as a herald, accountable only to the one who commissioned him, he was required to embrace the pedant's stance, eschewing all efforts to adapt his message to his audience?

---

[38] Augustine, *Doctr. chr.* 4.13.29; Sullivan (1930, pp. 107-9).
[39] According to James Murphy (2008), *De Doctrina Christiana* is marked by Augustine's "insistence upon the folly of abandoning a useful tool [rhetoric] to the enemy" (p. 218). Murphy portrays Augustine as trying to avoid two opposing "rhetorical heresies": "The sin of the sophist is that he denies the necessity of subject matter and believes that *forma* alone is desirable. An opposite vice ... depends upon the belief that the man possessed of truth will *ipso facto* be able to communicate the truth to others. It is a dependence upon *materia* alone." This Murphy calls the "Platonic rhetorical heresy" (p. 217). Murphy's overly simple distinction probably does a disservice to both the sophists and Plato, but for our purposes the more important observation is that Paul's position is certainly not to be identified with the latter option. Paul was determined to depend, not merely on the *materia* (content) of the gospel to do its work, but rather on the Spirit's powerful use of that simply proclaimed message to do God's work, namely, the creation of genuine πίστις within those "who are being saved" (1 Cor 1:18).

Clearly not. By his own testimony Paul was radically sensitive to his audience and adapted himself accordingly. But again, the more specific question we require is this one: audience adaptation for what *purpose*?

McGuire's distinctions help answer this question. Paul adapted his communication to his audience in the way every herald must: for the sake of gaining a hearing (*attention*) and communicating his commissioned message (*comprehension*).

> For though I am free from all, I have made myself a servant to all, that I might win [κερδαίνω] more of them. To the Jews I became as a Jew, in order to win Jews. To those under the law I became as one under the law (though not being myself under the law) that I might win those under the law. To those outside the law I became as one outside the law (not being outside the law of God but under the law of Christ) that I might win those outside the law. To the weak I became weak, that I might win the weak. I have become all things to all people, that by all means I might save [σῴζω] some. I do it all for the sake of the gospel, that I may share with them in its blessings. (1 Cor 9:19-23; cf. 1 Cor 3:1-2)

In this important passage we discover Paul's awareness of both of the points discussed above. Paul recognized, first, that his placarding of Christ constituted the human occasion the Spirit was using to prompt "those who are being saved" to yield to Christ. It is in this secondary sense that Paul can say that he himself is "gaining" or "saving" some. But second, Paul also perceived that his role as a herald required radical feats of audience adaptation, without which he would be unable to fulfill his assigned role.

- To the Jews I became as a Jew
- To those under the Law, as under the Law
- To those without law, as without law
- To the weak I became weak
- I have become all things to all people
- I do all things for the sake of the gospel

Paul understood and embraced the responsibility of the herald to adapt himself to his audience so as to gain their hearing and communicate his commissioned message.

18

Important Questions

Paul's view of preaching as proclamation rather than persuasion raises two tangential questions. First, what were the origins of this view of preaching? And second, how did Paul's thinking about preaching correlate with his practice? We cannot do either of these questions full justice here, but we can at least offer some tentative directions in which we might search for answers.

The Origins of Paul's View of Preaching

In one sense, of course, we have argued at length that the origin of Paul's view of preaching lay in his theological presuppositions. But this answer begs our present question. What we are asking here has to do with the historical rather than the theological antecedents of Paul's understanding of preaching.

Almost inevitably these historical antecedents will be found in Paul's Old Testament background and in the ministry of Jesus. In fact, George Kennedy suggests as much in his work *Classical Rhetoric and Its Christian and Secular Tradition*. In an all-too-brief section of twelve pages, Kennedy traces the tradition in which Paul stood—which he calls "Judeo-Christian rhetoric"—from Moses through the prophets to Jesus and the apostles.[1] According to Kennedy, this tradition, running from the Old Testament to the New, stressed revelation, authority and grace through its emphasis on simple enunciation rather than persuasion. In this prophetic tradition God is the one who is at work; the speaker is merely a messenger. Even Jesus followed this pattern,[2] says Kennedy, and so did the other apostles.

---

[1] Kennedy (1980, pp. 120-32). Cf. Costa (2013); and see Rengstorf (1952, pp. 25-31) on the Old Testament background of the term ἀπόστολος.

[2] E.g., Mk 1:14, 38: "After John was arrested, Jesus came into Galilee, proclaiming the gospel of God [κηρύσσων τὸ εὐαγγέλιον τοῦ θεοῦ].... 'Let us go on to the next towns, that I may preach [κηρύξω] there also, for that is why I came out.'" Cf. Mt 4:17.

Kennedy's treatment is too cursory and anecdotal to do more than whet the appetite for a thorough investigation into the antecedents of Paul's view of preaching. Yet Kennedy is undoubtedly on the right track. Paul's rejection of the psychological dynamic of Greco-Roman rhetoric and his emphasis on straightforward proclamation cannot in the end be viewed in isolation. They must be understood against the background of the preaching of Jesus and the Old Testament messengers.[3] In each of these cases revelation played a key role in the theological system, and there is intriguing evidence to suggest that whenever this is the case, proclamation comes to the fore. Socrates, for example, suggested that if only divine revelation were available, human wisdom might be dispensed with.[4] In Dio Chrysostom a divinely inspired message—which Dio may be ridiculed "as a traveling vagabond" for transmitting—is contrasted with "the words of men and all their rhetorical artifices" (σοφίσματα).[5] Similarly, Plutarch defends the straightforward simplicity of the divine oracles against those who complained that such messages ought to be put across more grandiloquently.[6] In each case, when divine revelation enters the picture, the persuasive wisdom of men may be seen to give way to the straightforward enunciation of the revelatory message.

The Relation Between Paul's Theory and Practice

This is a far more difficult question, due in large measure to the confusion that reigns in the discussion of the relevant issues. Three of the more significant problems are as follows.

(1) As we have noted, there is a large potential for semantic confusion in the use of the term *rhetoric*.[7] The term is commonly applied to at least four distinguishable aspects of rhetoric. At its most fundamental level, *rhetorical* is used broadly of any communication that is intentional, any communication in which

---

[3] See Ross Wagner (2002); Aernie (2012).
[4] Plato, *Phaedo* 85D, 99C; *Phaedrus* 274C; cf. Xenophon, *Memorabilia*, bk. 4, 7.10. Cf. on this phenomenon Kennedy (1984, pp. 6-7).
[5] Dio Chrysostom, *Discourses* 1.53-57.
[6] Plutarch, *Moralia* 408D-409D.
[7] The problem is pervasive in New Testament studies. E.g., Witherington is known for his claims that Paul was trained in and a sophisticated user of Greco-Roman "rhetoric." But then consider a sentence such as this: "The rhetoric of Jesus and Paul about marriage and singleness was radical" (2009b, p. 4). Is Witherington suggesting that Jesus also was trained and experienced in Greco-Roman rhetoric? Surely not; he's using the word differently here. But these sorts of semantic shifts, without warning or explanation, are what render the term *rhetoric* so slippery for the average reader. They tend to muddle the underlying issues rather than clarify them.

the communicator hopes somehow to influence the receiver.⁸ In this broader "universal" sense—a sense that is characteristic of what is often called the New Rhetoric—all of Paul's communication was rhetorical. Indeed, in this sense virtually all of human communication is rhetorical since all communication is in some sense intentional. Even the briefest greeting is designed to make some difference, however slight, in the recipient. Thus, in this broadest sense it is entirely proper to speak of "Paul's rhetoric" or his "philosophy of rhetoric."⁹ On the other hand, this is not to be confused with the more specific claim that Paul embraced and freely employed the persuasive strategies of Greco-Roman oratory in his preaching. This claim is a much more focused thing, related to the historical context of Paul's life and ministry. If confusion is to be avoided, it is crucial when discussing alleged rhetorical qualities in Paul to avoid this sort of equivocation.

(2) Even if certain linguistic features discussed by the ancient rhetoricians appear in Paul's letters, it does not follow that Paul embraced Greco-Roman persuasive strategies for his own use. As classicist C. J. Classen observes, the issues are more complex.

> In any speech or piece of writing, elements or features occur which we know from handbooks of rhetoric and which we are inclined to classify and designate accordingly. They may originate from four sources: from rhetorical theory (and its deliberate application); from a successful imitation of written or spoken practice; from unconscious borrowing from the practice of others; or from a natural gift for effective speaking or writing.¹⁰

This is an important point that deserves to be emphasized. Ancient rhetoric was first descriptive and only secondarily prescriptive. In this it was much like medicine, which in fact often crops up as an analogy in ancient discussions of rhetoric. First the theorist observed what worked "in nature," then he systematized this knowledge for prescription.¹¹ As a result, the rules of rhetoric were largely descriptive of what effective communicators did anyway, only stated now

---

⁸See Perelman and Olbrechts-Tyteca (1969, pp. 1-17); cf. also Kennedy (2001, p. 6).
⁹As when Kennedy (1990, p. 200) says that in 1 Cor 2:3-4 Paul "described his own rhetoric: 'I was with you in weakness and in much fear and trembling; and my speech and my message were not in plausible words of wisdom, but in demonstration of the Spirit and of power.'"
¹⁰Classen (1992, pp. 322-23).
¹¹Cf. Plato, *Phaedrus* 270B-271B; Quintilian, *Inst. or.* 2.17.9; Augustine, *Doctr. chr.* 4.7.21, 16.33. Says Antoinette Wire, "Just as a child can speak her native tongue correctly without schooling, so a man can sell a horse or a conviction very persuasively without reflecting upon how he does it" (1991, p. 2).

as principles and systemized for the purposes of teaching. Hence, to discover in Paul general features of communicational practice that were also discussed by the rhetoricians (features sometimes called *micro-rhetoric*,[12] such as metaphor, rhetorical questions and antithesis) is no indication that the Apostle embraced Greco-Roman oratorical practice in general or without reservation.[13] Many such common features would have been a matter of indifference to Paul. His misgivings were more focused.

(3) Then there is the foundational question of how much direct knowledge we have of Paul's practice as a missionary preacher. Do the speeches in Acts provide verbatim transcripts—the so-called *ipsissima verba*, "the very words"—of Paul's missionary messages? Apparently not; they are far too short. They are condensed speeches, abridged by Luke, and may (or may not) reflect elements of Luke's skills and function as a chronicler mixed with Paul's practice as a preacher.[14] This leaves the discussion dependent on whatever evidence of Paul's missionary proclamation we may discern in his epistles.

But how much evidence is there? Paul's epistles were uniformly written to believers. Their didactic purpose and their epistolary form thus distinguish them from Paul's oral discourse in the declaring of the gospel to his missionary audiences. According to 2 Corinthians 10:10, even Paul's critics saw a strong contrast between these two dimensions of Paul's communication. How legitimate then is the assumption that we may discern in Paul's letters the practice of his missionary proclamation?

PAUL'S PREACHING AND PAUL'S LETTERS

In his commentary on Galatians, J. Louis Martyn (1997, p. 145) offers an interesting discussion of this question. Martyn portrays Paul in Galatians as repudiating rhetoric for the purposes of his missionary preaching: "In Gal 1:10, using an expression that is virtually a definition of rhetoric, Paul denies with great emphasis that, in preaching the gospel, he is seeking to persuade human beings." Yet Martyn also argues that in numerous places Galatians "shows us an author who is a rather sophisticated rhetori-

---

[12] See Witherington (2009a, pp. 7, 230).
[13] As, e.g., Du Toit (1989, pp. 193-94).
[14] E.g., Paul carefully avoids rhetorical verbs such as πείθω in describing his preaching (see above, pp. 189-90, on the one exception), while Luke's descriptions in Acts show no such reticence (cf. appendix two). On the use of Paul's speeches in Acts in this discussion, see Porter (1999a, pp. 234-48; 2013, pp. 344-47).

cian." This prompts Martyn to ask, "How are we to explain the presence in the letter of rhetorical forms?" It is the same question posed by Paul's repudiation of rhetoric in 1 Corinthians 1–4, in a letter that is considered by some to be a rhetorical tour de force.

One way to answer this question, Martyn suggests, might be to distinguish between Paul's initial missionary proclamation to those who lack the Spirit and his subsequent letters to those who possess the Spirit, that is, believers. "One might suggest," says Martyn, "that Paul distinguishes an initial and nonrhetorical proclamation of the gospel from a later and rhetorically sophisticated formulation of a written argument addressed to persons who are already Christians. In short, does Paul consider rhetoric to be both useful and appropriate when the communication is being carried out within the bosom of the church?" (p. 147).

In addressing this question earlier (chap. 16), we suggested that for Paul, the epistemological differences between these two audiences—those without the Spirit, the ψυχικοὶ (1 Cor 2:14), and those with the Spirit, the πνευματικοὶ (1 Cor 2:15)—are profound (see appendix three, and above, pp. 179-81). These differences, combined with the following refinements in our understanding of what Paul was and was not disavowing in 1 Corinthians 1–4, suggest that it is a mistake to assume that Paul's letters and his missionary preaching were essentially similar in their communicational approach; see "Paul's Inconsistency" below.

But let us suppose for the moment that it has been established that Paul regularly took recourse to Greco-Roman persuasive techniques in his missionary preaching. How might such a thing be squared with his disavowal of such strategies in 1 Corinthians 1–4?

One common approach is to suppose that Paul's disavowals in 1 Corinthians 1–4 were merely a rhetorical ploy, the typical denial of eloquence by a speaker who wished to put his audience off guard. But as noted early in our study (preface, "Critical Theories"), this suggestion fails to grasp the weight and passion of Paul's argument in 1 Corinthians 1–4. Paul grounds his disavowal in his deepest convictions about God, the Spirit and the cross of Christ. To view this as merely a persuasive stratagem badly underestimates the argument of 1 Corinthians 1–4. It also calls into question Paul's integrity.

PAUL'S INSINCERITY

This assessment appears unavoidable, despite the fact that some would like to avoid it. To view Paul's disavowals as merely a rhetorical ploy is inevitably to treat them as lacking in candor, sincerity or authenticity. It is to view them as concealing hidden agendas and strategies, focused less on transparency than on offering an appearance or portrayal designed to achieve a particular rhetorical goal.

According to Aristotle, because the object of rhetoric is to win a particular result from an audience, "It is not only necessary to consider how to make the speech itself demonstrative [ἀποδεικτικός] and convincing [πιστός], but also that the speaker should show himself to be of a certain character and should know how to put the [audience] into a certain frame of mind. For it makes a great difference with regard to producing conviction [πίστις] . . . that the speaker should show himself to be possessed of certain qualities and that his hearers should think that he is disposed in a certain way towards them; and further, that they themselves should be disposed in a certain way towards him. . . . For the orator to produce conviction [εἶναι πιστούς] three qualities are necessary; for, independently of demonstrations [ἀποδείξεις], the things which induce belief [πιστεύω] are three in number. These qualities are good sense, virtue, and goodwill. . . . These qualities are all that are necessary, so that the speaker who appears to possess all three will necessarily convince his hearers" (*Rhetoric* 21.1.3-7).

Aristotle here illustrates why reducing Paul's arguments to merely a rhetorical ploy is so unsatisfying. It suggests that Paul cared mainly about appearances, which casts an unnecessary shadow over the Apostle's motives and sincerity. Worse yet, it undermines Paul's entire argument. For example, Dunn (2004, p. 307) says, "Paul was quite capable of composing a rhetorically pleasing phrase. Indeed, he was quite capable of using the rhetorical techniques that he here [1 Cor 2:1-5] played down. Such recognition of a *rhetorical* 'put-down' of *rhetoric* should at once alert us to the danger of reading passages like [1 Cor] 1.18-2.5 simply at face value. The ear that is not attuned to irony and wordplay will miss significant dimensions of the text." Similarly, see Levison (1991, pp. 36-40).

To reduce Paul's argument in 1 Corinthians 1:18–2:5 to a rhetorical "put-down" of rhetoric is inevitably to slight that argument's theological motivation and gravity. Dunn is no doubt right that it is possible to flatten out a text by unduly limiting it ("simply") to its "face value." But that is only one way to hear a text with a tin ear. Another is to nullify the substance of a writer's argument by dismissing it as irony and wordplay. Paul was certainly willing to employ irony (e.g., in our passage, 1 Cor 1:13; 4:8), but there is little in the deeply cruciform argument of 1:18–2:5 to suggest that he did not intend this section to be read as an impassioned but also straightforward theological rationale, first on behalf of his own approach to preaching (cf. Hays, 1997, p. 36), and second against its popular alternative.

Nor should Paul's own purported use of rhetoric be thrown onto the scale against such a reading. That Paul was capable of composing a winsome Greek phrase, or using common linguistic conventions, or arguing a strong theological case against the Corinthian infatuation with σοφία λόγου, is incontrovertible. But this point counts for little against his disavowals in 1 Corinthians 1:18–2:5. Once again, the confusing semantics of the term *rhetoric* let us down. Given the right definition of the term, Paul unquestionably does demonstrate "rhetorical skills," including the "rhetorical character" of 1 Corinthians 1–2. But put thusly such a claim is both unhelpful and potentially misleading. What we require are the finer distinctions discussed below. This more nuanced treatment demonstrates why the presence in Paul of some of the common features of Greco-Roman communicational practice is less telling than is often supposed. These features would have presented no contradiction to Paul's more pointed concerns in 1 Corinthians 1–4, either in Paul's mind or in that of the Corinthians.

More likely than the rhetorical ploy argument is the possibility that Paul was, so to speak, unwittingly inconsistent. According to this view, the argument of 1 Corinthians 1–4 is sincere enough, but Greco-Roman rhetorical techniques crept into the Apostle's communication nonetheless.[15] This was, in fact, a common occurrence among those who criticized rhetoric in antiquity. For instance, the very writings Plato composed to disparage the rhetoric of the sophists were used ever after by the rhetoricians as models of Greek eloquence. Said Cicero of Plato's *Gorgias*, "It was when making fun of orators that he himself seemed to me to be the consummate orator."[16] Quintilian complained bitterly that "some are in the habit of denouncing rhetoric most violently and of shamelessly employing the powers of oratory to accuse oratory itself."[17] Similarly, in Tacitus's *Dialogus*, Maternus chides Aper, who has just finished an attack on the ancient Greek orators, for "borrowing from their own armory the very weapons which he was afterwards to turn against themselves!"[18] These examples could be multiplied many times over.[19] Paul would have been neither the first nor the last to use rhetoric even while rejecting rhetoric.

But perhaps the most useful solution, in the sense of its ability to do justice

---

[15]Smit (2003, p. 201) argues for an unusual version of this view. According to Smit, Paul's original missionary preaching in Corinth was indeed rhetorically wanting. But Paul apparently regretted leaving the Corinthians with the impression that he was rhetorically inept. Thus he wrote 1 Cor 1–4, itself a sterling example of Greco-Roman epideictic rhetoric, to demonstrate his rhetorical expertise and present himself after all "as a competent speaker to restore thereby his status and authority" (cf. also idem, 2002). Needless to say, the notion that in the end Paul *wanted* the Corinthians to base their measure of his "status and authority" on his rhetorical prowess manages to turn the Apostle's concerns in 1 Cor 1–4 on their head.
[16]Cicero, *De or.* 1.11.47.
[17]Quintilian, *Inst. or.* 2.16.1.
[18]Tacitus, *Dial.* 24.1.
[19]E.g., see C. T. Murphy (1938, p. 69) on Aristophanes; Usher (1969, p. 371) on Marcus Cato; Gwynn (1926, p. 179) on Seneca; Sider (1971) on Tertullian.

to all of the data, may be found in McGuire's more nuanced analysis of the concept of persuasion we have already examined.

The persuasion process can be parsed into five distinguishable steps or levels: (1) *attention*, (2) *comprehension*, (3) *yielding*, (4) *retention*, (5) *action*. The hearer must negotiate all five steps if the communication is to be persuasive. This framework is, of course, a modern one. Yet in another sense it is timelessly basic because it deals with a familiar psychological process that is fundamentally human. It is a framework the ancients would have readily grasped. This is why, directly or indirectly and in varying degrees, we can observe the persuasive strategies of Greco-Roman rhetoric addressing all five of McGuire's steps.

Yet it must also be said that these five steps do not receive equal attention in the ancient literature. When the subject was *persuasion*, classical rhetoric placed a particularly heavy premium on step three, yielding. Whether the speaker's subject matter was trivial or weighty, attention and comprehension were never enough. In *epideictic* as well as *deliberative* and *forensic* oratory, the ancient orators were intent on having their way with their listeners.[20] In this sense their goal was always, to use Plato's and Aristotle's terms, to engender some form of conviction or belief in the listener. Seeing their audience yield to their rhetorical efforts—or to put it the other way around, when finished, leaving their audience having been "persuaded" by those efforts—was the expressed goal of the ancient orator. Indeed, his measure as a rhetor was taken by how effectively he could marshal the persuasive possibilities to make this happen.

By contrast, the approach Paul advocated did not focus on *yielding*. It focused on steps one and two: *attention* and *comprehension*. The business of the audience's yielding belonged to the Spirit and Paul was determined to avoid encroaching on it. His calling from Christ was to serve as a proclaimer, an announcer to the world of the many-faceted message of "Christ and him crucified." Only by limiting himself thus could he be confident that the consequent πίστις engendered in his listeners was the product of the Spirit's working and not of his own ingenuity as a rhetor.

This distinction serves as a warning about the pitfalls inherent in the debate about whether Paul employed "rhetoric," or engaged in "persuasive" preaching. Such debates too easily gloss over and thereby obscure the key issues. For example, as noted above, one may confidently affirm that Paul's letters are, in the

---

[20]See Perelman (1982b, pp. 19-20) on this point.

broadest sense of the term, genuinely "rhetorical." Paul wrote with a purpose, and as Stephen Pogoloff says, quoting George Kennedy, "Purposeful words are rhetorical, for rhetoric is 'that quality in discourse by which a speaker or writer seeks to accomplish his purposes.'"[21] In this broadest sense virtually all human communication is "rhetorical," including Paul's.

Furthermore, and more particularly, we may assume that Paul certainly did employ in his missionary preaching some of the common communicational features (for example, metaphor, rhetorical questions, analogies, contrasts) discussed by the rhetoricians. Given the all-inclusiveness of their discussions he could scarcely have composed an intelligible sentence without doing so. To use language was inevitably to place oneself in the purview of the rhetorical theorists.

LANGUE AND *PAROLE*

It is helpful on this point to recall Saussure's (1959) distinction between *la langue* and *la parole*. Saussure used the term *langue* to refer to language in general; that is, the abstract system of words, rules and conventions that are potentially available to users of a language. *Parole* refers to actual uses of that linguistic system by a signifier (say, a writer or speaker). *La langue* thus preexists and, so to speak, is inherited by actual users. It stands independent from them. Yet users who wish to communicate with other users must do so within the stock of possibilities their shared *langue* provides. Otherwise no meaningful communication can take place.

The possibilities inherent within the *langue* of the Greco-Roman world were the home turf of the ancient rhetoricians, and they left few of its stones unturned. What's more, this same *langue* was Paul's *langue*, and all of his actual efforts to communicate (*parole*) were necessarily conducted within its boundaries. Inevitably, then, it should not surprise us to find occurring in Paul's *parole* features of the common *langue*, features that were also discussed at length by the rhetoricians.

Further yet, we may be certain that Paul wanted his missionary audience to be "persuaded" by his message; that is, he wished as fervently as did any of the orators that his listeners might proceed through all five steps of the persuasion process. And further still, when his listeners did cover all five steps, Paul's proclamation could legitimately be said to have "persuaded" them. He was the human agent through whom they came to faith. So in this sense Paul was clearly a "persuader."

---

[21]Pogoloff (1991, p. 348); Kennedy (1984, p. 3).

None of these claims is problematic. Yet if our goal is to appreciate Paul's theology of preaching, neither are they particularly helpful. In fact, they are potentially misleading. Their shortcoming lies in their capacity to obscure rather than clarify the key issue; that is, the issue that highlights rather than muddles the difference Paul is after between his own approach and that of the persuaders. Paul's focus is the role the speaker fulfills *within* the process of generating πίστις and, hence, whether the resulting πίστις is genuine or counterfeit. To this question Greco-Roman rhetoric provided one answer, while the Apostle insisted on a quite different one. Focusing on this difference helps explain, as noted above, some of the features of Greco-Roman rhetorical practice we may find in Paul's practice, despite his strong disavowals.

GOOD RHETORIC VERSUS BAD RHETORIC.3

The apparent discrepancy between Paul's disavowals of rhetoric in 1 Corinthians 1–4 and the presence of recognizable features of Greco-Roman rhetoric in his letters has long been observed. But as modern critics have increasingly scoured his writings, finding "rhetoric" there at every turn, this discrepancy has gained more attention. This in turn has given rise to several approaches to resolving the disparity.

Some New Testament scholars observe no such disparity because they do not read 1 Corinthians 1–4 as a repudiation of rhetoric. But as we have already observed, among those who do emphasize this disparity three explanations have become common. Some argue that Paul's disavowals in 1 Corinthians 1–4 are not to be taken seriously; instead they should be viewed as insincere, even deceitful, examples of rhetorical sleight of hand—the intentional use of rhetoric to disavow rhetoric. Second, more generous scholars view the disparity as unwitting; Paul genuinely meant what he said in 1 Corinthians 1–4 but could not consistently live it out. A third option employs a "good" rhetoric versus "bad" rhetoric distinction to narrow the focus of what Paul seems to be disavowing in 1 Corinthians 1–4.

Of these three approaches, this last option has in recent years gained increased support. We have already examined two instances of this approach (see above, pp. 150-53 and 260-61), but Lampe (2010) provides a third example that is particularly instructive. Given the increasing prevalence of this view, it may be useful to give Lampe's argument some attention.

Lampe begins by acknowledging the "discrepancy between Paul's expressed distancing of himself from rhetoric (e.g., 1 Corinthians 2:1, 4) and his actual practice of using rhetorical means" (here and following, p. 18). His proposed solution to the problem is immediately signaled by his citation of F. Siegert (1985) to the effect that what

Paul is distancing himself from is an approach to preaching "that assimilates to the standards of the rhetorical guild and to the stylistic criteria of the educated," standards that involve "manipulating the audience by means of emotions without respect to the truth." Paul never rejected rhetoric in general, Lampe says, only a certain kind of oratory. What kind? The bad kind, the kind that "specifically tries to invoke *pistis* in Christ by means of bedazzling and seductive rhetoric." This is the sort of thing Paul was determined to avoid, replacing it with his own more "modest and humble" approach, so that "if the gospel, when clothed in modest and humble rhetorical attire, reaches the people and nonetheless awakens *pistis* in them, then Christians may be confident that God's own power, and not human persuasion, is at work here (1 Cor 2:5)."

For Lampe, the contrast Paul embodies "mirrors a discrepancy within the ancient rhetorical world at large." It is a contrast between *bad* rhetoric and *good* rhetoric, between "the rhetoric of the sophists, on the one hand, and the Platonic and Aristotelian rhetoric, on the other." The latter presented no difficulties for Paul; in fact, it became the model for his own practice. What Paul rejected was "a sophistic complacency that manipulatively aimed at quick success in the listeners' minds and was uninterested in the quest for truth. With radical skepticism, sophists even denied in principle that truth can be found. For them, only subjective opinions standing side by side existed, and whoever was able to pump a weak position into a strong one was the better orator. This attitude, which is still used in today's advertising industry, alienated platonically or peripatetically oriented rhetoricians. Ancient rhetoric, with its different camps, was divided, and this furnishes the background for understanding the Pauline discrepancy at stake."

Lampe's argument here is accurate on at least two counts. First, the debate between sophists and philosophers reaches back at least to Plato, and is yet with us today; see Kimball's survey of this debate in his book *Orators and Philosophers: A History of the Idea of Liberal Education*. Today's postmodern thinkers are in many ways the successors of the ancient sophists. The complex of ideas the term *postmodern* typically conjures up, with a radical perspectivalism at its center, is as old as the early sophistic movement, against which in one way or another virtually all of Plato's dialogues were written. Reading an account of these ancient thinkers—for example, W. K. C. Guthrie's *The Sophists* (e.g., see pp. 4-13, 50; cf. Plato, *Cratylus* 385E)—is like reading a *fin de siècle* account of our own academic environment, including its fascination with rhetoric. See on this sophistic connection McComiskey (2002); Olson (2002); and see Vos (2010, pp. 172-79) on the "(Neo-)sophistic perspective" in Pauline studies in particular. Krentz (2003, p. 285) rightly argues against R. Dean Anderson's claims (1998, p. 65) that the age-old dispute between the rhetoricians and philosophers had subsided by the first century. This debate certainly waxed and waned over the centuries, but it was very much alive during the early centuries of the Christian era.

Second, we can also agree that Paul had little regard for the kind of rhetoric Lampe describes. If his dramatic references to seducing and manipulating the audience with no concern for truth—Plato's old criticism, well deserved in some cases, very undeserved in others, but echoed nonetheless by many subsequent philosophers; see, e.g., Locke (1894, vol. 2, 3.10.34); Kant (1952, sec. 53)—overly prejudice the issues, we may nevertheless agree that this sort of behavior would have been "abhorrent" to the Apostle (see "The Related Passages" in chap. 15 above). In this regard Lampe rightly observes that "1 Thessalonians 2:5 rejects very clearly the sophistic *kolakeia* [κολακεία, "flattery, fawning," on which, see chap. 5 above], which Plato also criticized, using the same term (*Gorgias* 463B)."

Yet we must still ask, is Lampe's good rhetoric/bad rhetoric distinction the one that best informs Paul's disavowals in 1 Corinthians 1–4? Succinctly, the answer is no. Raising the specter of *bad* rhetoric serves as a convenient straw man, but it is misleading when it comes to understanding Paul's concerns in 1 Corinthians 1–4. What worries Paul there is not merely sophistry but the human art of persuasion in general.

Lampe's argument that it was only the *bad* rhetoric of the sophists that concerned the Apostle flies in the face of Paul's own language. What the Apostle disavows in 1 Corinthians 1–2 (σοφίᾳ λόγου, 1:17; ὑπεροχὴν λόγου ἢ σοφίας, 2:1; πειθοῖ[ς] σοφίας, 2:4) says nothing about underhanded means. Contrast, for example, this language with Paul's emotionally loaded terms in 2 Corinthians 1:12; 2:17; 4:2. Paul is concerned in 1 Corinthians 1–2 about a broader issue: avoiding that πίστις which is generated simply through the σοφίᾳ ἀνθρώπων (1 Cor 2:5). Paul nowhere here raises the issue of manipulation and dishonesty; he is exercised about the use of ἐν διδακτοῖς ἀνθρωπίνης σοφίας λόγοις (1 Cor 2:13) in general. This concern encompasses the entire rhetorical tradition.

What's more, Lampe's attempt to recruit Paul to the *good* rhetoric of Plato and Aristotle also fails. If Paul's concern, as Lampe says, was to ensure by his more modest and humble form of presentation that when πίστις was awakened in his listeners he might "be confident that God's own power, and not human persuasion, is at work," how would the rhetoric of Plato and Aristotle help? It was precisely their rhetoric, embraced, elaborated and taught by the best of the rhetorical tradition after them, that was designed to teach rhetors the most ingenious techniques for awakening πίστις in their listeners. The goal of every rhetor, said Plato, is "to produce conviction in the soul" (*Phaedrus* 271A; cf. 271C; *Gorgias* 452D-453A). Aristotle taught the same thing (*Rhetoric* 1.2.8; cf. 2.1.1-7), and his handbook on the subject is the shrewdest of treatises on how to do so. It is precisely the tradition of this "good" rhetoric that we have traced in this book, from its beginnings in ancient Athens to the first century and beyond. And as we have seen, this tradition consistently focused on human psychological strategies for creating πίστις in one's listeners. In this way the language of this broader tradition, unlike sophistry, corresponds exactly with Paul's expressed concerns in 1 Corinthians 1–2. Thus the conclusion that this *good* rhetoric tradition is not only *not* what Paul is calling into question, but what he actually *valorizes* and *embraces* for his own use, is dramatically wide of the mark.

In the end, attempts such as Lampe's to recruit the age-old debate between rhetoric and philosophy to explain Paul's concerns simply do not work. Betz (1986, p. 36) notes that "Paul clearly takes the side of the philosopher over against the orator." But he also observes that the Apostle's "concerns are still different from those of the philosopher." This is because in its own way the "rhetoric" of the philosopher is just as problematic for Paul as the rhetoric of the orator. Both share the same problem: a dependence on human ingenuity. In his work *Philosophical Rhetoric*, Mason (1989, p. x) rightly observes, "Philosophy is written for an audience and its main point is to bring this audience around to the way of thinking and looking at the world advocated by the text. To bring this about the writing aims to persuade the audience of the truth of its central claims. It is idle to suppose that philosophical writing is free of persuasive force. . . . Philosophical arguments, their premises, conclusions, and the logic connecting them, are in fact part of the overall persuasive force of philosophical writings." Neither the orator nor the philosopher was Paul's model.

So what was Paul's model? Lampe refers to the "modest and humble rhetorical attire" of the Apostle. But like so many other commentators he simply ignores the Apostle's own description of that attire. Paul's careful choice of non-rhetorical language—the language of the herald, testifier or witness—to describe his preaching is left pristinely untouched. A modicum of attention to the significance of this language might have signaled that Paul's preferred rhetorical attire fits as poorly within the good rhetoric tradition as it does the bad.

In the end, the good/bad rhetoric distinction fails as an explanation of the disparity between Paul's argument in 1 Corinthians 1–4 and his practice as a letter writer. A better resolution is the nuanced distinction between the roles of the persuader and the herald we are exploring here.

It is important here to remember when discussing the question of Paul's practice that *classical rhetoric* is our term, not Paul's, nor even the first century's.[22] What we refer to as classical rhetoric was for Paul simply a pervasive, amorphous aspect of the Hellenistic culture in which he lived. The notion of a wholesale renouncing of such a thing would have made little sense to Paul, and, stated this baldly, this certainly is not the argument of 1 Corinthians 1–4. The Apostle had no such general term as "classical rhetoric" to work with; his concerns were more focused.

In any case, as we have already observed, it would have been impossible for Paul to abandon the Greco-Roman rhetorical tradition and remain a participant in the world he inhabited, even had he wished to do so. As George Kennedy says,

---

[22]"Neither 'rhetoric' nor 'history' are [sic] part of Paul's vocabulary; they are 'our' approximations or translations of things he thought of differently" (Kennedy, 1990, p. 197).

even for the Apostle who "pointedly rejected the 'wisdom of the world,'" if he was intent on communicating with his contemporaries there still had to be "some overlap between the content and form of what he said and the expectations of his audience."[23] The all-encompassing Greco-Roman rhetorical tradition was too ubiquitous to be avoided. Rhetoric was not present in the Greco-Roman world as colored marbles are present in a glass of water, easily distinguishable and separable; it was more like the ink that tinted the cultural and linguistic water in which Paul and the people of his missionary world swam. It touched all of life and language for the inhabitants of the first century. Given its cultural scope, the full range of what we study under the rubric of *classical rhetoric* was simply inescapable for Paul.

What's more, much of that rhetorical tradition would not have required the Apostle's escape. It was simply neutral and mundane with regard to the issues that troubled Paul and so would have been unproblematic for him. Even heralds, after all, benefitted from aspects of rhetorical training; they too were required to be effective communicators, and much of ancient rhetorical education would have been, and was, relevant to their task. The question of whether Paul used "rhetoric"—or stated differently, whether aspects of what the rhetoricians discussed can be found in Paul—is thus too broad and undiscerning to be helpful. What we require is a finer set of distinctions.

AN ANCIENT QUEST

The quest for such distinctions is as old as the Christian church. For example, during the late fourth century John Chrysostom, a former teacher of rhetoric and an ardent admirer and defender of the Apostle Paul, provided his own analysis of the issues.

In his fictional dialogue with Basil recounted in *On the Priesthood*, Chrysostom emphasized the need for strong preaching in the churches. But if this is so important, Basil asks, "Why then was not Paul eager to attain perfection in this quality? He is not ashamed of his poverty of speech, but expressly confesses that he is inexpert (ἰδιώτην) in it. And he says this when writing to the Corinthians who were admired for their eloquence and [greatly] prided themselves on it" (4.6; Neville, 1964, p. 119).

---

[23]Kennedy (1984, p. 10). Says the German classicist C. J. Classen, "Anyone who could write Greek as effectively as Saint Paul did must have read a good deal of works written in Greek, thus imbibing applied rhetoric from others, even if he never heard of any rules of rhetorical theory; so even if one could prove that Saint Paul was not familiar with the rhetorical theory of the Greeks, it can hardly be denied that he knew it in its applied form" (1992, p. 323).

This argument irritated Chrysostom because he had heard it used to defend indolence and passivity among the priests. Thus he responds with some vehemence: "This is the very excuse that has ruined most men and made them more casual about true doctrine. Being unable to examine accurately [ἀκριβῶς] the depth [βάθος] of the Apostle's thought or to comprehend the meaning of his words [ῥημάτων, "expressions"], they have spent all their time nodding and yawning, and prizing, not the form of unlearnedness [ἀμαθής] which Paul acknowledged, but a form from which no man under heaven was ever as free" (pp. 119-20).

The Apostle Paul, Chrysostom insisted (here, and everywhere else in his writings), was an extremely strong apologist for the truth. Yet, unlike Augustine, Chrysostom refused to dodge Paul's disavowals of eloquence. How to reconcile these two things? Chrysostom found his solution in 2 Corinthians 11:6: "Even if I am unskilled in speaking, I am not so in knowledge." By "unskilled in speaking" Chrysostom understood Paul to be disavowing expertise in the rhetorical arts; but by claiming to be strong in "knowledge" he took Paul to be acknowledging great power in contending (μάχεσθαι) "for the doctrines of the Truth" (p. 121).

This is the distinction Chrysostom uses to explain his insistence on strong preaching despite the Apostle's disavowals in 1 and 2 Corinthians. Says he, "Now if I were demanding the polish of Isocrates and the grandeur of Demosthenes and the dignity of Thucydides and the sublimity of Plato, it would be right to confront me with the testimony of Paul. But in fact I pass over all those qualities and the superfluous embellishments of pagan writers. I take no account of diction or style. Let a man's language be lacking and his verbal composition simple and artless, but do not let him be inexpert [ἰδιώτης] in the knowledge and careful statement of doctrine" (pp. 121-22). Paul may have been lacking in "the external subtlety of words," Chrysostom says, but he was without peer in doing verbal battle for the truth. This latter virtue constituted for Chrysostom its own form of eloquence.

Chrysostom had studied rhetoric under the tutelage of the pagan rhetorician Libanius and was himself an expert in the Greco-Roman rhetorical tradition. Moreover, his admiration for the Apostle Paul knew no bounds. Thus his assessment that by the standards of that tradition Paul was indeed unskilled in speech should be seen as carrying no little weight. Chrysostom would certainly have found it bizarre to hear Paul hailed today as a master of that rhetorical tradition and his letters portrayed as exemplars of the persuasive arts it taught. Chrysostom viewed Paul, his preaching and his letters as very powerful indeed, but he considered the source of their strength to lie elsewhere. By what power, he asks in *De laudibus sancti Pauli apostoli*, could a man "who did not demonstrate the power of eloquence, but, to the utter contrary, was unlearned, to the lowest degree of poor learning" (4.10), make such a profound impact on the world? Not through his own power but only through the divine power of the gospel: "When the one preaching is unskilled [ἰδιώτης] and poor and undistinguished, and the message preached not alluring, but even scandalous, and the ones hearing it poor and weak and nobodies, and the dangers continuous and unremitting for both teachers and disciples, and the one being proclaimed [καταγγελλόμενος] a victim of crucifixion, what caused it to conquer? Is it not clear that it was some divine and ineffable power?" (4.13). This is the only possible explanation, Chrysostom says. The astonishing power of the gospel was due not to "human power" (ἀνθρωπίνης δυνάμεως) but to "the power of the man who was crucified" (4.14).

In her detailed treatment of Chrysostom and Paul (2002), from which the above *De laudibus* quotations are taken (pp. 458-67), Margaret Mitchell places Chrysostom's argument in its necessary historical context (pp. 242-45). By Chrysostom's time his had become something of a stock argument, used regularly by earlier church defenders. Their repeated employment of this argument for rhetorical purposes does not mean that these early Christians did not genuinely believe it. On the contrary, the reason they cited it so often was that (1) they found it first "in the biblical record" (Mitchell, p. 242), and (2) they themselves found it convincing.

More pertinent to our purposes, however, is Mitchell's additional claim that Chrysostom overstated Paul's lack of education in order to enhance the argument's rhetorical effect. She supports this assessment by citing all the various ways Chrysostom contradicted himself by valorizing Paul's verbal power (pp. 278-82). Chrysostom no doubt did overdramatize Paul's lack of education, as when he says that Paul not only lacked verbal power (λόγων ἰσχὺν) but was in fact "the most ignorant of the ignorant" (τὴν ἐσχάτην ἀμαθίαν ἀμαθὴς ὤν, 4.10). Yet even accounting for such hyperbole, the discrepancy in Chrysostom remains. How could he affirm so strongly both Paul's lack of rhetorical skill and his awesome verbal power?

Mitchell may be right in suspecting that behind Chrysostom's inconsistency there lurked conflicted feelings about his own use of rhetoric. Yet Chrysostom may not have been as inconsistent as Mitchell claims. At any rate, it is difficult to imagine him owning up to such a glaring contradiction. It may well be that a more focused analysis of both the verbal power Chrysostom says Paul lacked and the verbal power he says Paul demonstrated would take us back to his distinction, based on 2 Corinthians 11:6, between, on the one hand, Paul's being by Greco-Roman rhetorical standards ἰδιώτης τῷ λόγῳ, while yet on the other hand being strong in "contending for the doctrines of the Truth." How would Chrysostom have analyzed the difference? Was it simply a matter of style (cf. Mitchell, p. 287), or something deeper? Chrysostom would surely have argued it was something deeper. Citing 1 Corinthians 2:2, 4, he dismisses the notion that Paul's power could be explained by the persuasive skills of the messenger; he states that "though he was unskilled and uneducated," Paul nonetheless was "in some ways a persuasive [πιθανὸς] speaker" (4.11). The answer was not to be found in the messenger, however. The answer, Chrysostom says, could only be found in the power of God: first, in the "marvelous and incredible power of the gospel message" itself (4.15; Mitchell, p. 464); and second, in the fact that "into this tentmaker Christ breathed such a large measure of power" (4.10; p. 462). The blessings to the world may have come "through Paul's tongue" (διὰ τῆς Παύλου γλώττης), but they were in the end due to the grace (χάριτος) God implanted within him (4.20; p. 467. Cf. Chrysostom's similar take on the Apostle John, *Homilies on St. John* 2.1-6). Thus did Chrysostom's assessment of the Apostle's ministry echo Paul's own: "But we have this treasure in jars of clay, to show that the surpassing power belongs to God and not to us" (2 Cor 4:7).

Is the distinction Chrysostom derived from 2 Corinthians 11:6 in the end sufficient to illuminate Paul's concerns in 1 Corinthians 1–4? Not entirely, for it fails to grapple with the theological issues at work in Paul's choice of the herald's stance. For that discussion we must look elsewhere in Chrysostom, preeminently his *Homilies on First Corinthians* (see especially 4.4-6). But Chrysostom is pointing us in the right direction. Paul neither looked nor sounded like those eloquent persuaders so prized by the Corinthians. Instead he modeled himself after a very different image: that of a commissioned herald, dependent for his results on the Spirit's application of the gospel he proclaimed. The essential distinction between these two approaches is what we are after.

This is where McGuire's analysis proves useful. It helpfully informs the very distinction Paul seemed to be after in contrasting his heraldic announcing or his testimony about the crucified Christ with that "superiority of speech or wisdom" (1 Cor 2:1) and "persuasive words of wisdom" (1 Cor 2:4) preferred by the Corinthians. The herald's role focused on the *attention* and *comprehension* of the listener, while the persuader was explicitly responsible for the listener's *yielding* as well. Thus it may have been only those dimensions of the orator's art that required the preacher to tread beyond the herald's role into psychological strategies designed to promote *yielding* (the inducing of πειθώ or πίστις in the listener) that Paul found problematic. This sort of humanly engendered faith was the result Paul was determined to avoid. To enter that πίστις-inducing realm was to tread where only the Spirit belonged.

Again, we scarcely need to rehearse here the strategies we have in mind; we have discussed them at length in our earlier chapters. They showed themselves, as Cicero says, in that "kind of eloquence which rushes along with the roar of a mighty stream, which all look up to and admire, and which they despair of attaining."[24] Behind such displays lay the shrewd psychological calculations that make this sort of rhetorical power possible. We may recall, for example, Socrates's astute three-stage analysis: First, if a persuader is "to proceed in a

---

[24]Cicero, *Or. Brut.* 97.

scientific manner" to use "proper discourses [λόγοι] and training" to produce "the desired belief [πειθώ] and virtue" in someone, he must understand that person's fundamental psychological makeup, what Socrates calls their "soul" (ψυχή, "the conscious self or personality, the center of emotions, desires and affections"). Second, he must understand the person's consequent inclinations; that is, he must peer into that soul and "say what its action is and toward what it is directed, or how it is acted upon and by what." Then, third, he must "classify the speeches and the souls and adapt each to the other showing the causes of the effects produced and why one kind of soul is necessarily persuaded [πείθεται] by certain classes of speeches, and another is not [ἀπειθεῖ]."[25] Only then could the persuader hope to achieve the results he was after.

These were the sort of penetrating calculations taught by Greco-Roman rhetoric. They were designed to enable the speaker to discover and then exploit the persuasive possibilities inherent in any rhetorical situation. Such calculations required the very shrewdness Socrates describes, but they were necessary if the orator was intent on persuading his audience.

This is what the Apostle Paul understood about ancient rhetoric, and why he so forcefully called it into question in 1 Corinthians 1–4. To fully appreciate Paul's complaint, however, it is equally important to underline what it was not. Paul nowhere argues that there was something inherently immoral or manipulative about this persuasion process. At its best the art of persuasion could be a noble and worthy thing. The ancients regularly emphasized a truth that is important to us all: persuasion is what replaces tyranny and coercion in free societies.[26] If now, as then, there are those who use this art dishonorably, like the ancients we must not allow that to blind us to its importance. The democratic marketplace of ideas depends on persuasion's free exercise and rightly honors those who do it well and honestly. Thus it is important to recognize that Paul's complaint was not that the art of persuasion is inherently unworthy. It was that the art of persuasion is so quintessentially *human*—that is, so thoroughly dependent on ingenious psychological calculations in even its noblest forms. This is what rendered it unsuitable for the purposes of preaching the gospel.[27]

---

[25]Plato, *Phaedrus* 270B-271B.
[26]See, e.g., Isocrates's eloquent defense of the art of persuasion, *Nicocles* 5-9.
[27]Gooch (1987, p. 48) conflates the two arguments that must here be kept distinct: (1) the argument that rhetoric is inherently manipulative and dishonest, and therefore evil; and (2) the argument that rhetoric's human techniques of persuasion render it inappropriate for the purposes of preaching the gospel. Of the first Gooch says, "Commentators, of course, wish to resist the implication

In Paul's day as in ours, the persuader's arguments and style were to be so craftily adapted to the audience, occasion, subject matter and purpose of the speech as to win the desired response, and teaching speakers how to make and then execute these canny calculations lay at the core of the rhetorical tradition. These were the sorts of calculations the Apostle Paul, in his role as a herald, disavowed. To engage in the business of creating πίστις through the application of human psychological ingenuity was, according to Paul, to court counterfeit results; that is, results engendered by skillful strategies of the persuader rather than the Spirit-driven power of the gospel. It was apparently this dimension of the broad rhetorical tradition that Paul found inappropriate for the purposes of his preaching.[28] Rhetorical techniques focused on enhancing the attention or comprehension of the listener may have seemed unproblematic to Paul, for these would have carried no moral or theological implications. Aristotle taught that "it does make a difference, for the purpose of making a thing clear, to speak in this or that manner."[29] In fact, Paul explicitly claims to have adapted his approach to his various audiences in just this sense (1 Cor 3:1-2; 9:19-23); that is, in order to win a hearing and accommodate the comprehension of his listeners. As Günther Bornkamm says, this adaptation "certainly must not be seen as an easing of the σκάνδαλον-character of [Paul's] message, but as an appropriate clarification of it."[30] Perhaps it was only those psychological dimensions of ancient rhetoric that Paul viewed as designed to induce *yielding* that would have appeared out of bounds to him, for it was only in this realm that one began to tread beyond the role of the herald and impinge on the work of the Spirit.[31]

---

of a general critique, that rhetoric is inherently evil." Then he cites C. K. Barrett in support. But the lines he quotes from Barrett ([1968] 1971, pp. 67-68) do not speak to Gooch's point (argument 1). Barrett is addressing argument 2, as follows: "Wisdom is used in a bad sense when it denotes simply the skilled marshalling of human arguments, employed with a view to convincing the hearer. This process is by no means evil in itself, and becomes evil only when it is employed as a substitute for true Christian preaching, and veils the power of the Spirit by its show of human persuasiveness." As noted above, ours (and Barrett's) is the second argument, not the first, a point Gooch finally comes to when he says of Barrett's "notion of substitution" that it "might suggest that rhetoric is acceptable in 'human' arguments—say, about politics—but not in proclamation where the preacher should never aim to convince."

[28]Judge (1983, pp. 11-12): "Paul disclaims any 'excessive' reliance upon speech or wisdom, and pin-points 'persuasiveness' as the particular excess he wishes to avoid."
[29]Aristotle, *Rhetoric* 3.1.6.
[30]Bornkamm (1966, p. 197); cf. Norden's discussion of Augustine on this point (1909, vol. 2, pp. 503-4); see also Weiss (1959, vol. 1, p. 242).
[31]This is the key insight missing in Forbes's otherwise useful summary (2010, p. 160). According to Forbes, Paul both used rhetoric and disowned it; he employed rhetoric, but not always and not in all ways. Some aspects of the rhetorical tradition were unobjectionable, while others were deemed

In this light, the fact that certain identifiable features of Greco-Roman rhetorical practice are found in Paul's letters—or even, if it were possible to determine it, in his missionary preaching—is unsurprising, and certainly does not imply a contradiction with the disavowals of 1 Corinthians 1–4. Paul may have been working with conscious or semiconscious distinctions considerably more subtle than many modern commentators have appreciated, distinctions easily missed in simplistic debates about whether Paul used "rhetoric." Many of the general features we associate with the classical tradition would have been theologically inconsequential and a matter of indifference to the Apostle. In fact, some of those features (for example, those valued by the Greek or Roman heralds) may conceivably have appeared useful to him. It was only those core aspects of the persuader's art—that is, those human psychological strategies focused on marshaling logical, emotional and ethical proofs so as to engender πειθώ or πίστις[32]—that presented a threshold Paul was unwilling to cross.

PAUL'S INCONSISTENCY

This more limited understanding of what it was Paul rejected goes a long way toward alleviating a common criticism of the Apostle. As we have seen, critics sometimes accuse Paul of inconsistently, or even shamelessly, employing "rhetoric" in his letters, even while claiming to disavow "rhetoric" (e.g., see "The Apostle as Deceiver" in chap. 15). But not all such accusations deserve to be taken seriously. First, critics are not always clear about what they mean when using the terms *rhetoric* or *rhetorical* to describe what Paul is disavowing in 1 Corinthians 1–4, or what he is practicing in his letters. As we have noted, employing these multilayered terms without sufficient definition can be confusing. Second, by failing to appreciate the narrower focus of Paul's concerns in 1 Corinthians 1–4, critics often wind up overstating Paul's supposed inconsistencies. Understanding the tighter focus of Paul's disavowals has the effect of reducing the potential for conflict with the more general "rhetorical" features of Paul's letters.

What's more, these two observations must be coupled with a third. Critics who emphasize the purported inconsistency between Paul's disavowals and his epistolary practice often ignore or minimize the differences between his dual audiences. The dis-

---

incompatible with the godly values that must govern the *ekklesia*. So which were which? Which aspects of the art of rhetoric were a matter of indifference to Paul, freely usable, and which did he feel compelled for theological reasons to disown, and why? These would seem to be crucial questions for Forbes's analysis, but he offers no help in answering them. McGuire's five-step process helps supply the distinctions we need to generate the answers Forbes omits.

[32]Cf. Aristotle, *Rhetoric* 1.2.1-6.

avowals of 1 Corinthians 1–4 are directed toward Paul's missionary preaching to *unbelieving* audiences, while his letters are uniformly addressed to *believers*; cf. Bornkamm (1969, p. 35). The profound epistemological differences between these two audiences (see appendix three) tend to work against the claims of inconsistency on Paul's part.

What Paul disavows in 1 Corinthians 1–4 is the approach—which he summarizes under the heading "wisdom of the world" (1 Cor 1:20)—that Greco-Roman audiences demanded if they were to be convinced. Working within the confines of their listeners' belief systems and psychological inclinations, persuaders strove to provide eloquently expressed and forcefully delivered arguments—logical, emotional, ethical—designed to engender belief. Upon these arguments the listeners would then pass judgment, deciding whether the persuader's efforts were worthy of acceptance. If the arguments satisfied the audience's demands for proof or demonstration, they would embrace them; if not, they could be dismissed. This was the way the wisdom of the world worked.

But for Paul, when it comes to finding God and the salvation he has provided, this worldly approach is fatally flawed. It is the approach that comes naturally to those without the Spirit (the ψυχικὸι, 1 Cor 2:14), but its very naturalness is its prime defect. It is so tainted by humanity's moral rebellion and failure that it becomes an exercise in hubris; it consists of the ψυχικὸι striving on their own to save themselves. But God will have none of it. He has rendered foolish all such prideful human striving, substituting instead the simple announcement of his gracious provision of salvation through the cross of Christ. Salvation is to be found, not through the exercise of worldly wisdom (cf. Martyn's discussion above, pp. 179-81), but simply by receiving the gospel message and embracing the crucified Christ it proclaims. "For since in the wisdom of God the world did not know God through its wisdom, it pleased God through the folly of the heralded gospel [τοῦ κηρύγματος] to save those who believe" (1 Cor 1:21 AT).

It is crucial, then, to recognize the role of Paul's epistemology in this discussion. The disavowals of 1 Corinthians 1–4 are due precisely to the epistemological status of his missionary audience. To use the Apostle's categories, all of his listeners at the outset are ψυχικὸι. Yet Paul also knows a deeper truth about them. All of these ψυχικὸι belong to one or the other of two subcategories: those "who are perishing" and those "who are being saved" (1 Cor 1:18). Paul's proclamation of the gospel was designed specifically to bring this invisible difference to the surface. "Those who are perishing" will find his proclamation of the cross to be nonsense or scandalous, but to those "who are being saved," that same word of the cross will appear as "the power of God and the wisdom of God." "For we are the aroma of Christ to God among those who are being saved and among those who are perishing," says Paul, "to one a fragrance from death to death, to the other a fragrance from life to life" (2 Cor 2:15-16).

But now, what happens when Paul's audience changes? His letters are not addressed to ψυχικὸι, those without the Spirit; they are uniformly addressed to πνευματικὸι, those who possess the Spirit. Some of these may indeed be fleshly and immature (1 Cor 3:1), but the indwelling Spirit is at work even in them. This represents a profound difference in how Paul can approach them: "The natural person [ψυχικὸς] does not accept the things of the Spirit of God, for they are folly to him, and he is not able to understand them because they are spiritually discerned" (1 Cor 2:14). But by contrast, the πνευματικὸι *are* able to accept the things of the Spirit of God. Such things do not appear as folly to them; they are able to understand them because they are spiritually discerned (1 Cor 2:15), and they possess the Spirit.

Paul's communication with believers can therefore be different from his communication with unbelievers. With πνευματικὸι Paul is not limited to simple proclamation; he can venture into precisely the kind of teaching, exhortation, correction and elaboration we discover in his epistles. He is not worried with this audience about generating false πίστις; they have already come to πίστις. His pastoral concern is to deepen their faith and help them live it out more completely. Because they possess the Spirit—and the discernment the indwelling Spirit bestows—Paul can appeal to them accordingly. He can present them with spiritually minded *arguments* he hopes they will find persuasive. Yet his arguments are of a very different sort from those demanded by the ψυχικὸι. His is a type of argumentation—of which 1 Corinthians 1–4 is a textbook example—that depends for its persuasiveness on the authority of revelation, the truth of the gospel and its entailments, his own apostolic insight and authority, and ultimately the inner working of the Spirit in the πνευματικὸι.

Critics who find Paul's disavowals and practice inconsistent typically ignore or minimize the epistemological shift that distinguishes Paul's two audiences. Stated as baldly as possible, the accusation is as follows: rhetoric involves persuasive argumentation and tactics; Paul disavows rhetoric; yet Paul engages in persuasive argumentation and tactics. Hence Paul is inconsistent, or even dishonest. But for all of the above reasons, this sort of complaint requires much more nuance than is often provided. What do we mean by "rhetoric"? Which aspects of this "rhetoric" did Paul disavow, and why? Which aspects were matters of indifference to him? Which aspects did he practice? Which did he avoid? For which audience, and for what reasons? How did Paul's "argumentation" differ from the persuaders' "argumentation"? These are the sorts of questions that must be finessed if we are not to do a disservice to Paul and his letters.

19

Appropriate Strategies

The important distinction between the herald's stance and the persuader's stance raises the obvious question of which rhetorical strategies are which. McGuire's five-step process is useful at a theoretical level, but what does it mean in practice? What does the herald actually do, or, equally important, not do? In other words, which rhetorical tactics are legitimate for the herald, in the sense that they are focused on the *attention* and *comprehension* of the listeners, depending on the Spirit to accomplish genuine *yielding*, and which are to be avoided because in their dependence on typically human means of persuasion they may generate false, merely human results—a counterfeit form of *yielding* or πίστις that is the product of the σοφία ἀνθρώπων but not of the δύναμις θεοῦ?

What Belongs

The Apostle Paul is obviously the best measure of what he regarded as the herald's appropriate or inappropriate practices. His letters, unfortunately, written as they were to believers, are of only limited use as a model. Despite the efforts of some to collapse the distinction between Paul's missionary preaching and his letters, the Apostle's opponents in Corinth apparently discerned a clear difference between the two (2 Cor 10:10), and Paul made no attempt to set them straight. My own inclination is to trust Paul's judgment in the matter and treat his letters as examples of his apostolic ἐπιστολαί addressed to the πνευματικοί, not his missionary preaching addressed to the ψυχικοί.[1] But then this leaves us without a model of Paul's missionary preaching. The closest we can come is the secondary record presented in the book of Acts. For the broader relevance of Acts to our discussion, the reader may consult appendix two, but to gain a brief glimpse of what Paul may have considered

---

[1] See "On Letters Versus Speeches" in chapter 11 for a discussion of this subject.

legitimate practice, let us consider the evidence from a single but directly relevant chapter: Acts 17.

The contribution of Acts 17. In Acts 17 we find Paul in Thessalonica, Berea and Athens, immediately prior to his arrival in Corinth. In each of these locations he followed his normal practice (Acts 17:2) of taking the gospel to the Jews of the community first, then to the Gentiles. In Thessalonica Paul spent three sabbaths reasoning from the Scriptures (διελέξατο . . . ἀπὸ τῶν γραφῶν) in the Jewish synagogue, explaining (διανοίγω) and setting forth (παρατίθημι, lit. "to set before") that "it was necessary for the Christ to suffer and to rise from the dead." This was the essence of Paul's message: "This Jesus, whom I proclaim [καταγγέλλω] to you, is the Christ" (Acts 17:3). And to this message Paul received the customary positive and negative responses. Some were persuaded (ἐπείσθησαν) by it and embraced Christ (Acts 17:4), while others were so enraged that they managed to drive the Apostle from the city (Acts 17:5-9).

A similar experience awaited Paul in Berea. The response of the Bereans to Paul's proclamation of "the word of God" (ὁ λόγος τοῦ θεοῦ) was famously more positive (Acts 17:11, 13), but the hostile opponents from Thessalonica eventually discovered Paul in Berea and drove him from that city as well. This sent Paul to Athens where he once again interacted with (διελέγετο) those in the synagogue and those he came across in the marketplace (Acts 17:17). There,

> some of the Epicurean and Stoic philosophers . . . conversed with him. And some said, "What does this babbler [σπερμολόγος, "one who picks up and retails scraps of knowledge"] wish to say?" Others said, "He seems to be a preacher [καταγγελεύς] of foreign divinities"—because he was preaching [εὐαγγελίζομαι] Jesus and the resurrection. And they took him and brought him to the Areopagus, saying, "May we know what this new teaching is that you are presenting [λαλέω]? For you bring some strange things to our ears. We wish to know therefore what these things mean." (Acts 17:18-20)

This inquiry prompted Paul's famous Areopagus speech. For our purposes the primary feature we need to observe about this speech is how dramatically it differs from what Paul did in the synagogues. The speech contains no references to Scripture or to anything Jewish. Its appeals are to general rather than special revelation and its points of contact are with the philosophical issues of his Gentile listeners. The main thrust of the speech was to fill in the identity of the Athenians' "unknown" God: "What therefore you worship as unknown," Paul says, "this I proclaim [καταγγέλλω] to you" (Acts 17:23). Thus the speech contains only the most cursory reference to Christ: God "has fixed a day on which he will judge the world in righteousness by a man whom he has appointed; and of this he has given assurance to all by raising him from the dead" (Acts 17:31). But, as reported by Luke, Paul's speech provides no indication of who this appointed person might be or where and when his resurrection took place.

Three observations. This brief snapshot of Paul's missionary efforts in Greece reinforces three points. First, whether before a Jewish or Gentile audience, Paul functioned as a herald. In both settings his business is not Greco-Roman persuasion but the announcement or declaration (καταγγέλλειν) of a message (Acts 17:3, 18). This was not only, as we have seen, how Paul—and now Luke—characterized his missionary preaching; the Epicurean and Stoic philosophers of Athens also perceived him to be not a philosopher or another of the orators, but a καταγγελεύς ("one who proclaims, a herald") of a religious message.

Second, Acts 17 provides within the span of a single chapter a striking example of Paul's willingness to adapt his message to his audience. To the Jews Paul's καταγγέλλειν was Scripture oriented. Paul's case in the synagogues was composed of thus-says-the-Lord arguments from Scripture rather than the type of argumentation taught by Greco-Roman rhetoric; but to the Gentiles there was not a hint of Scripture. With the members of the synagogue, both Jews and proselytes, Paul could assume a certain depth of pre-understanding, and his message was correspondingly more advanced and complete; with the Gentiles he could assume no such pre-understanding, and his message was kept preliminary and preparatory. Thus did the Apostle adjust his καταγγέλλειν to his audience's capacity to receive and comprehend his message.

Third, Acts 17 offers insight into not only the substance of Paul's καταγγέλλειν but also its presentation. That is, the dominant verb καταγγέλλω is buttressed in this passage by a series of other verbs that enrich our understanding of what Paul, in his role as a καταγγελεύς, actually did. The semantics of καταγγέλλειν ("to announce, proclaim, declare") are lexically well attested and speak for themselves, but the companion verbs in Acts 17 help to flesh this verb out. The terms διαλέγω ("to discourse, lecture"), διανοίγω ("to reveal, explain"), παρατίθημι ("to set forth in teaching") and εὐαγγελίζομαι ("to proclaim as good news") all portray a speaker focused on the *attention* and *comprehension* of his audience. They offer no hint of the typical Greco-Roman persuader's argumentative strategies designed to promote *yielding*.

What Doesn't Belong

If we can fairly easily discern the shape of what Paul considered legitimate activity for a herald, the same cannot be said for those tactics Paul appeared to consider out of bounds. The Apostle clearly disavowed dishonest or underhanded tactics, but what about those rhetorical strategies that are no such thing? What about those dimensions of the persuader's stance that, while not inherently unethical, are nonetheless focused squarely on the audience's *yielding*?

That there were a variety of such dimensions is plain. Our earlier survey of the rhetorical tradition reveals this clearly enough. Plato defined rhetoric as the art that "leads the soul by means of words," the purpose of which is to mold the listener's convictions. Rhetoric, said Gorgias, is "the ability to persuade with speeches." With this Socrates agrees: Rhetoric is "a producer of persuasion [πειθοῦς δημιουργός], and has therein its whole business and main consummation." Rhetoric is about nothing other than "effecting persuasion in the minds of an audience."[2]

Cicero, speaking through Brutus, argued that the "ability to influence the minds of his hearers and to turn them in whatever direction the case demands" was the most essential requirement of the orator, his "chief source of power (*vis maxima*)."[3] It was this skill, Quintilian says, that was built into the very definition of rhetoric: rhetoric is, simply, the *vis persuadendi*.[4] "There is to my mind no more excellent thing," said Cicero,

> than the power, by means of oratory, to get a hold on assemblies of men, win their good will, direct their inclinations wherever the speaker wishes, or divert them from whatever he wishes.... [What is] so pleasing to the understanding and the ear as a speech adorned and polished with wise reflections and dignified language? Or what achievement so mighty and glorious as that the impulses of the crowd, the consciences of the judges, the austerity of the Senate, should suffer transformation through eloquence of one man?[5]

It is important here not to underestimate the power and effectiveness of the persuasive strategies of the orators. We have widespread evidence that the Greco-Roman speakers and audiences concurred on the matter. Cicero, as we have seen, put it this way: "This eloquence has the power to sway men's minds

---

[2]Plato, *Gorgias* 452D-453A. But see the ensuing discussion between Gorgias and Socrates for Plato's epistemological reservations about this fact.
[3]Cicero, *Brutus* 276-79.
[4]Quintilian, *Inst. or.* 2.15.3.
[5]Cicero, *De or.* 1:30-32.

and move them in every possible way. Now it storms the feelings, now it creeps in; it implants new ideas and uproots the old."[6] He cites one "excellent poet" to the effect that such eloquence is the "soul-bending sovereign of all things."[7] Thus the true orator is able to move his audience as he wishes, "laughter when he wills it, or if he wills, tears."[8]

> When one hears a real orator he believes what is said, thinks it true, assents and approves; the orator's words win conviction.... The listening throng is delighted, is carried along by his words, is in a sense bathed deep in delight.... They feel now joy now sorrow, are moved now to laughter now to tears; they show approbation detestation, scorn aversion; they are drawn to pity to shame to regret; are stirred to anger wonder, hope fear; and all these come to pass just as the hearer's minds are played upon by [the orator's] word and thought and action.[9]

Without this sort of rhetorical power, says Quintilian, "all else is bare and meager, weak and devoid of charm. For it is in its power over the emotions that the life and soul of oratory is to be found."[10] This is the art of rhetoric at work, says Dio Chrysostom, the "power of persuasion that is keener and truly formidable, ... a power that holds sway both in the forum and on the rostrum."[11]

What were the tactics the orators employed that proved so effective in bending audiences to their will, which is to say, in achieving the *yielding* they were after? For a shorthand summary of the key issues, we can scarcely do better than to look again to Aristotle's *Rhetoric*. There he reminds us that persuasion always rests on some form of demonstration (ἀπόδειξις): "We are most strongly convinced when we suppose anything to have been demonstrated."[12] We believe what we see, or think we see. Hence, to persuade the speaker must cause his listeners to *see* by demonstrating his point through the various means of persuasion: λόγος, πάθος and ἔθος. Belief is something the speaker generates in the audience through the use of logical, emotional and ethical arguments. Says Aristotle, "Persuasion is produced ... when we establish the true or apparently true from the means of persuasion applicable to each subject." The purpose of Aristotle's *Rhetoric* was to spell out how to go about it.

---

[6]Cicero, *Or. Brut.* 97.
[7]Cicero, *De or.* 3.187.
[8]Cicero, *Brutus* 290.
[9]Ibid., 188.
[10]Quintilian, *Inst. or.* 6.2.3-5, 7.
[11]Dio Chrysostom, *Discourses* 33.1.
[12]Aristotle, *Rhetoric* 1.2.7.

This is not the place for a full-scale exploration of the *Rhetoric*'s recommended strategies, but even a casual reading of this ancient document suffices to make the point. Aristotle spends the bulk of his treatise dealing with the fundamental psychology of persuasion. What is it that motivates people? How can we appeal to these motives so as to achieve our persuasive goals? Which kinds of proofs work best with which kinds of audiences, on which kinds of occasions? Which decisions regarding not only our arguments but even such details as our choice of words, the arrangement of the parts of the speech and our delivery will most likely produce the desired effects? These are the kinds of practical questions every persuader must answer, and the ancients never had a better teacher than Aristotle. His is a classic work on how effective persuaders go about producing *yielding* in an audience—or come as close to it as humanly possible.

A classic instance of the kinds of rhetorical choices the ancient orators faced had to do with the overall style of their speech. Victory depended on their ability to match the right styles with the right audiences and occasions. "The man of eloquence whom we seek," said Cicero,

> will be one who is able to speak in court or in deliberative bodies so as to prove, to please and to sway or persuade. . . . For these three functions of the orator there are three styles, the plain style for proof, the middle style for pleasure, the vigorous style for persuasion; and in this last is summed up the entire virtue of the orator. Now the man who controls and combines these three varied styles needs rare judgment and great endowment; for he will decide what is needed at any point, and will be able to speak in any way which the case requires.[13]

Each of these styles must be under the orator's control. Yet which style to use, as Quintilian wisely observed, did not in the end "depend upon the orator. For he will use all styles, as circumstances may demand,"[14] a point with which Tacitus's Messala concurred:

> Whether he has to address himself to a hostile or a prejudiced or a grudging audience, whether his hearers are ill-humoured or apprehensive, [the orator] will feel their pulse, and will handle them in every case as their character requires, and will give the right tone to what he has to say, keeping the various implements of his craft lying ready to hand for any and every purpose. There are some with whom a concise, succinct style carries most conviction, one

---

[13] Cicero, *Or. Brut.* 69-70.
[14] Quintilian, *Inst. or.* 12.10.69.

that makes the several lines of proof yield a rapid conclusion; with such it will be an advantage to have paid attention to dialectic. Others are more taken with a smooth and steady flow of speech, drawn from the fountain-head of universal experience.[15]

In just such terms did the ancient rhetoricians instruct one another in how best to generate *yielding* within their audiences. And what of the audiences themselves? To the irritation of Dio Chrysostom, they were often complicit in the process. The evidence indicates that ancient listeners typically enjoyed being persuaded every bit as much as the orators enjoyed persuading them. Dio analyzed the audience's all-too-eager tendency to give the persuaders what they wanted:

> The speaker . . . pours forth a steady and copious flood of speech, like some abundant river that has been dammed up within him. Then, as you listen, the thought of testing his several statements or of disturbing such a learned man seems to you to be shabby treatment and inopportune, nay, you are heedlessly elated by the power and the speed of his delivery and are very happy, as, without a pause for breath, he strings together such a multitude of phrases, and you are affected very much as are those who gaze at horses running at a gallop—though not at all benefited by the experience, still you are full of admiration and exclaim, "What a marvelous thing to own!"[16]

How *marvelous* indeed. The ancient rhetorical literature abounds with descriptions of audiences bending to the will of the orators—and even more so, with practical instructions unapologetically focused on how to make it happen. That Paul understood how effectively such persuasive tactics could be employed to generate merely human results is indicated by the attention he gave to avoiding them.

The five steps in the process of persuasion are useful in helping us differentiate the roles of the herald and the persuader, but this analysis can only take us so far in specifying which rhetorical strategies may be appropriate or inappropriate for the herald. Many such strategies do not fit neatly into these theoretical boxes. Any given strategy may contribute to more than one of the steps, or might contribute mainly to one step in one listener and to a different step in another listener. Mixed strategies aimed at achieving combined goals in diverse audiences make for exceedingly complex results, as difficult to unravel as the

---

[15]Tacitus, *Dial.* 31:4-7.
[16]Dio Chrysostom, *Discourses* 33.5.

proverbial Gordian Knot. The subtlety and indeterminate qualities of human persuasion are often too elusive to be parsed out so tidily.

On the other hand, this reality need not render the five steps valueless. Its distinctions are important for understanding even what we mean by persuasion. They provide the taxonomy we require to appreciate the multiple dimensions of what is taking place on any persuasive occasion. For the practitioner, the steps may function not as rules but as beacons. What is it, the communicator may usefully ask on any given occasion, that I'm trying to accomplish here? If the goal is persuasion, the five-step process may serve as a useful framework for thinking through the best tactics to use with a given audience on a given occasion. In the same way, one who wishes, as did the Apostle Paul, to restrict himself to the role of the herald may also use the steps as beacons. *This* is my appropriate role, the herald may decide, and *this* is not my role; and the appropriate rhetorical choices can be made accordingly. In this way the distinctions between *attention, comprehension* and *yielding* may help the herald think through his or her own rhetorical decisions.

Yet beneath these specifics there lies an even deeper and more important ministry insight. Here we return to our earlier and more general observation that the persuader's stance is *results* driven while the herald's stance is *obedience* driven. This fundamental distinction, summarized in our concluding chapter, may be the most important difference of all.

20

Conclusion

The Pauline Model

The persuader's stance is inherently focused on results. In what we have called the Grand Equation of rhetoric, the desired results drive the equation. The ancient persuader's decisions about what to do and say were from the beginning shaped by the results he wished to achieve. This observation need not, as we have said, automatically render a persuader's efforts unworthy. The ancients understood the distinctions between worthy and unworthy goals and means and often worked to maintain them. When Aristotle, for example, said, "What makes the sophist is not the faculty [δύναμις] but the moral purpose [προαίρεσις],"[1] he was making the point that the capacity to persuade need not render a speaker suspect; it is the moral purpose that determines whether the effort should be considered "sophistical" (σοφιστικός). Persuasive efforts may be entirely ethical, depending on the moral purpose and method of the persuader. Our point here, however, is the broader one: either way, whether the results and means are or are not worthy, the persuader's stance is inherently results driven. It is utilitarian, focused on bending the audience to the persuader's predetermined purposes.

The herald's stance, by contrast, is obedience driven. We may recall Gerhard Friedrich's lexical discussion of the κῆρυξ. It was expected of heralds, Friedrich says, that they

> deliver their message as it is given to them. The essential point about the report which they give is that it does not originate with them. Behind it stands a higher power. The herald does not express his own views. He is the spokesman for his master. . . . He is bound by the precise instructions of the

---

[1] Aristotle, *Rhetoric* 1.1.14.

one who commissions him.... In general he is simply an executive instrument. Being only the mouth of his master, he must not falsify the message entrusted to him by additions of his own. He must deliver it exactly as given to him.... He must keep strictly to the words and orders of his master.[2]

As a Christian herald Paul viewed his role as very different from that of the persuader. The herald was a commissioned messenger. He had received an assignment, one that involved faithfully delivering the commissioner's message to the designated audience. It was not Paul's assignment to engineer the response he desired from his audience. Success for Paul was measured not by the audience's response but by the degree to which he faithfully executed his commission.

It is in this sense that Paul's model is obedience driven rather than results driven. Both the persuader and the herald must set and reach for goals, but their respective goals are dramatically different. The persuader determined the result he was after and then ordered his efforts accordingly. Paul, by contrast, was determined to be faithful to his calling and then leave the matter of results to God. This dramatic paradigm shift, from *results driven* to *obedience driven*, is the fundamental difference between the *persuader's stance* and the *herald's stance*, between the *natural paradigm* and the *Pauline paradigm*. It is this difference that constitutes the centerpiece of a Pauline model for ministry. To embrace the herald's stance by implementing an obedience-driven instead of results-driven approach to ministry is to follow the Pauline model.

From Specifics to Principle

Throughout 1 Corinthians 1–4 Paul is intent on defending his approach to preaching. To do so he places his approach in the context of a much larger and more general principle, one broad enough to encompass all Christian ministry. This broader principle thus undergirds, informs and is implied throughout Paul's argument in chapters 1–4, but it comes to explicit expression in 1 Corinthians 4:1-5:

> This is how one should regard us, as servants [ὑπηρέτας] of Christ and stewards [οἰκονόμους] of the mysteries of God. Moreover, it is required of stewards that they be found faithful [πιστός]. But with me it is a very small thing that I should be judged by you or by any human court. In fact, I do not even judge myself. For I am not aware of anything against myself, but I am not thereby acquitted. It is the Lord who judges me. Therefore do not pro-

---
[2]Friedrich (1965, 3.687-88).

nounce judgment before the time, before the Lord comes, who will bring to light the things now hidden in darkness and will disclose the purposes of the heart. Then each one will receive his commendation from God.

In this passage Paul describes how he viewed his own ministry, and how he wished the Corinthians to view it. In this description his language rises to the *principial* level. He expresses the broader premise of which he considers his calling as a preacher to be a specific instance: *Faithfulness is the essential requirement of stewards.* This principle entails the following points, each of which Paul has in 1 Corinthians 1–4 applied to his calling as a proclaimer of the gospel.

1. God delights in employing humble means to accomplish his purposes.

2. Those who do God's work are to be viewed accordingly: they are simply Christ's servants fulfilling his calling.

3. Such servants are required above all to be obedient to what the risen Christ has called them to be and do; their highest priority must be the fulfillment of their divine commission.

4. Because they are Christ's servants obeying his call, only his approval matters. No other assessment is relevant, not even their own. Success can only be measured by faithfulness to what the Master has called the servant to be and to do.

Implications for Ministry

A consideration of these features prompts four general observations.[3]

First, it is important to appreciate how radically these features depart from the natural paradigm. In the following formulation,

Audience + Servant's Efforts → Results

the natural paradigm begins with the results; it is in this sense *results driven*. Having predetermined what results it desires, the natural paradigm then designs its strategies—hopefully within ethically acceptable boundaries—so as to achieve those results. The Pauline paradigm, by contrast, enters the equation at a different place: the servant's efforts. It asks not *How can I achieve some preset result?* but, *What is Christ is calling me to be, and what is he calling me to do?* Its intentional focus on discovering and fulfilling the answers to these questions is what distinguishes the Pauline paradigm. It is in this sense that the Pauline model is *obedience driven*.

---

[3] See appendices four and five for more focused applications. These appendices may be suggestive of other potential applications of the Pauline model.

Grasping this contrast is the key to understanding why Paul was so unwilling to replace the *herald's stance* with the *persuader's stance*. He was focused on obeying Christ's instructions. This required that he be willing to leave the results to God: "For Christ did not send me to baptize but to proclaim the gospel [εὐαγγελίζεσθαι]. . . . [Hence] we herald [κηρύσσομεν] Christ crucified, a stumbling block to Jews and folly to Gentiles, but to those who are called, both Jews and Greeks, Christ the power of God and the wisdom of God" (1 Cor 1:17, 23-24 AT).

Second, this shift from *results driven* to *obedience driven* transfers a good deal of weight onto the issue one's calling. What is Christ calling me to be? What is he calling me to do? The Pauline model is dependent on the ability to answer these questions. How or where does one discover such answers?

It would take us too far afield to address this complex issue in anything but the most summary fashion. But I do not regret that the Pauline model forces the issue upon us. I am convinced that the issue of one's *calling* receives too little attention in Christian circles.[4] I do not refer here to the servant's initial call to faith (as in 1 Cor 1:26) but rather Christ's call upon his servants thereafter.

This latter calling takes at least two forms. The first is the general calling of every follower of Jesus. The Scriptures and the historical teaching of the church provide extensive and profound content to this general calling. It's a calling that touches every dimension of the servant's existence: personal life, family life, life in the community of believers, in society at large and in the natural world. Every legitimate aspect of this biblical and ecclesiastical instruction constitutes a calling from Christ himself: "If you love me," Jesus said, "you will keep my commandments" (Jn 14:15).

Then there is also the unique calling of the individual Christian. As Paul said to the Corinthians, every follower of Christ has been appointed to unique service: "For just as the body is one and has many members, and all the members of the body, though many, are one body, so it is with Christ" (1 Cor 12:12). The believer's calling may be to a profession, or a particular role, or some specific area of service, or any of a wide range of other possibilities. It may be permanent or temporary; it may be singly focused or multifaceted. The permutations are endless. Each calling is uniquely tailored to the individual. But every follower of Jesus Christ bears a calling and, as Paul instructs the Corinthians, none is insignificant.

Third, these same observations apply to churches or other Christian organiza-

---

[4]But see Labberton (2014) for a helpful discussion of the Christian's calling, including (as below) its twofold nature, or what Labberton calls the "first calling" and the "next calling."

tions. If the risen Christ, the Head of his church, has called that organization into existence—and if not, what, from a Christian point of view, is its warrant for considering itself a *Christian* organization?—he did so for a purpose. That organization thus bears, like the individual Christian, both the general calling inherent in serving Jesus and an individual calling unique to itself. Why are we here? Why did Christ raise up this organization? What is he calling us to be? What is he calling us to do? Prayerful answers to such complex questions are not always easy to come by, but they are crucial to the ability of the organization to fulfill its God-given calling.

Fourth, while the Pauline model's shift from a *results orientation* to an *obedience orientation* is both countercultural and, for most of us, counterintuitive, in the end it is wonderfully liberating.[5] It frees us from obsessing over results and enables us to redefine what we consider success. We gain a different and much superior yardstick by which to measure our efforts: the prospect of a "Well done, good and faithful servant" assessment by the glorified Christ (Mt 25:21, 23; Lk 19:17). Such a yardstick requires a dramatic reorientation of our thinking and planning. Our focus becomes not results but the far healthier issue of faithfulness (1 Cor 4:2). *If it is required of a servant to be found "faithful," what is Jesus, our exalted Head, calling us to be and do? How can we be that and do that to the fullest?* These are the liberating questions that drive the Pauline model.

Paul's model is also liberating in a different way. To illustrate, the Old Testament figure of Nehemiah may be useful. Nehemiah faced a daunting task, one that appeared beyond his reach. He had to build a massive defensive wall around Jerusalem within a short period of time. It seemed impossible. Yet to everyone's surprise the wall went up. Nehemiah assigned families, clans and individuals their own sections of the wall (Neh 3). When each party fulfilled their particular assignment, the wall became a reality (Neh 6:15).

Nehemiah's approach suggests a useful analogy for Christ's servants as well. While none can do everything, all can do, and are indeed called to do, *something*. So the servant's question must be: What is the *something* Christ is calling me to do? What is my part of the wall? Only God can manage the whole, and we must leave that to him; he calls us to tackle only the part he has assigned to us. Thus the servant must always ask: What part of the task is Jesus calling me to fulfill?

This approach is deeply liberating because it involves the crucial recognition that Christ does not expect his servants to respond every time they discover a

---

[5]See Litfin (2012, pp. 203-5).

need. *A need is not a call.* The needs of the world will always far outstrip our ability to meet them. Thus only God can bear such a burden. Attempting to respond to every worthy need—and then inevitably experiencing guilt and disappointment when our efforts prove so inadequate—is a prescription for failure and burnout. We are trying to do what only God can do.

Far better is to make our decisions on the basis of Christ's call. We cannot do everything, but we can do *something.* Of the seemingly limitless needs in the world, which is God calling *me* to address? What is my part of the wall? Answering this question can prevent us from throwing up our hands in frustration and defeat when the world's needs vastly exceed our ability to meet them. We must let God be God, and then apply ourselves to the sacrificial tasks to which he has called us.

The term *sacrificial* here is an important one. The above is not an approach designed to relieve Christ's servants from costly service. On the contrary, as we spend ourselves and our resources in building our part of the wall, we must be willing to do so sacrificially, for Christ's sake and for the sake of those to whom he calls us. Learning to respond to call rather than need is not a technique for releasing ourselves from costly service; it's a plan for avoiding false guilt. False guilt is what we experience when we try to operate unreflectively on the unspoken premise that every need is automatically a call. This is a presumptuous idea, one that assumes we possess God-like capacities rather than creaturely limitations. Treating every need as a call is a surefire prescription for the futility that arises when we inevitably fall short in our efforts to accomplish what God never expected, enabled or called us to do.

In our day of instant worldwide communication, we are constantly witness to more human need than any previous generation could have imagined. Yet we can never do *everything* even in one situation of need, much less in all such situations. We will quickly be overwhelmed if we try to respond to it all. We must learn, instead, to follow Paul's lead. What is Christ calling us to be? What is Christ calling us to do? Let us be that and do that to the best of our ability, and then leave the results up to him. This is a far healthier way for Christians to live, wooed by the call of Christ and driven only by their determination to fulfill it.

Conclusion

As we said at the outset, this book constitutes an exploration of the origins of a crucial Pauline insight for ministry. This ancient insight is woven throughout the apostle's writings, and if we are alert enough to catch them, we can hear its echoes down through church history to the present day. But this insight receives its fullest biblical exploration in 1 Corinthians 1–4. What is this insight? Why is it important? What are its implications? These are the issues that have occupied us in this book.

We began our study by observing that every theory of discourse is anchored in the soil of its author's philosophical or theological presuppositions, and that the Apostle Paul's approach to preaching is a particularly clear expression of this relationship. This is the premise that informs the argument of 1 Corinthians 1–4. In these unparalleled chapters Paul was determined to defend his preaching against a cultural alternative preferred by some of the Corinthians. To do so he contrasts his approach with their alternative and takes recourse to his theological presuppositions to explain and defend why he must practice the one and not the other. Whatever else 1 Corinthians 1–4 may be, this argument is what renders this passage unique in Paul's writings. These pivotal chapters constitute a singular study in the Apostle Paul's own theology of preaching.

To grasp the distinctive features of Paul's theology of preaching, we devoted the first section of this book to the exploration of the alternative preferred by some of the Corinthians: the art of persuasion as taught and widely practiced in the Greco-Roman world. It is not until we have grasped the central features of the persuader's approach that we are in a position to discern, first, Paul's concerns about it, and second, the distinctive features of his preferred alternative, the herald's approach. Our study has therefore focused on recovering this aspect of the Greco-Roman background and then displaying the apostle's argument against it. We then turned to summarizing the issues and analyzing some of their relevance for contemporary practice.

This book, then, has been largely a study in the Apostle Paul's theology of preaching. But even this theology of preaching must be viewed as an expression of something deeper: Paul's underlying philosophy of ministry in general. In 1 Corinthians 1–4 Paul is challenging not simply an alternative theory of discourse but the entire way of looking at things—what we have called the *natural paradigm*—that undergirds it. In its place Paul lays out his own contrasting view of things, the *Pauline paradigm*. This contrast represents a fundamental shift, from a *results*-driven to an *obedience*-driven approach to ministry. For those who take Paul's argument seriously, this insight requires a profound reorientation of one's focus, not only in one's approach to preaching, but in one's approach to Christian ministry in general.

Appendix One

Paul, Apollos and Philo

Why did Paul choose Apollos as his counterpart in 1 Corinthians 3:4–4:6 and not the much more important figures of Cephas or Christ? The answer becomes clear if we retrace the section and attempt to substitute in the argument either Christ or Peter for Apollos. With Christ the argument becomes grotesque, while with Peter it becomes merely incomprehensible. For example, the section 1 Corinthians 3:18-21 is an encapsulated, even redundant, version of the argument in 1 Corinthians 1:18–2:5 where Paul repudiates Greco-Roman wisdom and eloquence. As such it fits comfortably within a larger section (1 Cor 3:4–4:5) designed to rebuke Corinthian parties lined up for (ὑπὲρ) Apollos, the learned, eloquent and presumably Greek-educated Alexandrian,[1] and against (κατὰ) Paul (1 Cor 4:6), the weak and trembling (1 Cor 2:3) apostle who is lowly, undistinguished (ταπεινὸς, 2 Cor 10:1) and unskilled in speech (ἰδιώτης τῷ λόγῳ, 2 Cor 11:6). But the function of 3:18-21, with all its overtones of 1:18–2:5, would be unintelligible if it appeared in a section that centered on a contrast between Paul and the former Jewish fisherman, Cephas. The conclusion seems clear: in the argument of 1 Corinthians 3:4–4:5 as it stands, Apollos was the only plausible option.

This is an important point because it directs us toward a potentially useful observation. We have earlier noted the apologetic unity of 1 Corinthians 1–4. Paul appears to be defending himself on a single united front. Here we have seen that in a large and relatively typical (even to the point of redundancy) subsection of chapters 1–4, Paul expressly directs his arguments to the "I am of Apollos" group, so much so that neither of the other two slogans could be substituted. What then does this tell us about chapters 1–4 in general? We are led to suspect that what is expressly true of the representative subsection (1 Cor 3:4–4:6) is also true of the whole (1 Cor 1–4): it is virtually all directed to the Apollos group and

---

[1] See the discussion on Acts 18 in appendix two.

is peculiar to their complaints. This would explain why the figure of Apollos and the "I am of Apollos" slogan play such a prominent role in chapters 1–4,[2] while the Cephas group is mentioned again only once after 1 Corinthians 1:12, and that only obliquely, in 1 Corinthians 3:22, and the Christ group still more obliquely, if at all, only in 1 Corinthians 3:23.

But if chapters 1–4 are addressed largely to the concerns of an Apollos group, why does Paul mention the Cephas and Christ slogans at all in 1 Corinthians 1:12? There are no conclusive answers to this question. Perhaps if we understood more about what was behind such slogans, we could see that there are elements within chapters 1–4 that do address their concerns. Without this background, however, identifying such elements becomes an exercise in speculation, prohibitively so. The subsection 1 Corinthians 3:4–4:5 affords us enough of a glimpse of an argument addressed explicitly to an "I am of Apollos" group to gain some insight into their concerns, and to conclude that much of the rest of chapters 1–4 may be addressed to them as well. But we lack any such hints for the other two slogans.

Perhaps the most plausible explanation for why Paul mentions the other two groups, therefore, is as follows. When Chloe's people reported the "contentions" (ἔριδες, 1 Cor 1:11) to Paul, the picture they painted was one in which the congregation was divided into two vaguely defined camps, the partisans for Paul and the partisans against Paul. But this latter camp was not entirely homogenous. To be sure, dominant among them were those who had found Paul's preaching deficient and who were partial to the eloquent Apollos. This was a crucial issue in the ἔριδες in Corinth, the one that most needed to be rectified. But there were also two lesser elements in this group. They shared with the dominant Apollos element their reservations toward Paul but for different reasons, about which we can only guess. In the final analysis, however, the problems posed by these two smaller elements appeared at this time minor compared to the more damaging (to the church, cf. 1 Cor 3:17) partisanship of the "I am of Apollos" group. It was their worldly attitudes and behavior that were causing the most serious difficulties for Paul.[3] Hence it is this group and their criticisms that receive the bulk of the Apostle's attention. Paul mentions

---

[2] Six of the ten references to Apollos in the New Testament occur in 1 Cor 1–4 (1:12; 3:4, 5, 6, 22; 4:6). Significantly, three of the other references explicitly relate Apollos to the Corinthian congregation (Acts 18:24-28; 19:1; 1 Cor 16:12). Only the passing mention of Apollos in Titus 3:13 fails to show a Corinthian connection.

[3] This would also explain Apollos's reluctance to return to Corinth (1 Cor 16:12); he did not want to exacerbate the problem.

the other two groups for the sake of completeness—since it is partisanship itself that is wrong and they too are guilty—but the specific refutations in the Apostle's argument are addressed to the dominant "I am of Apollos" group.

This scenario does justice to the data regarding the ἔριδες in a way that other theories regarding Apollos do not. For example, R. M. Grant holds that Apollos was the key to the party strife in Corinth but sees him as merely a source of Stoic-Cynic doctrine.[4] Grant fails altogether to explore the role of Greek eloquence in the dispute. By contrast, Horsley provides in his treatment of wisdom in Corinth strong support for the conclusion that both the issue of eloquence and the person of Apollos were central to the problem in 1 Corinthians 1–4.[5] Unfortunately, Horsley without warrant also makes Apollos a mouthpiece for Philo and views the Corinthians as espousing a love not only for Greek eloquence but also for a Philonic type of σοφία as a means of salvation.[6] But as we have seen, Paul nowhere affirms this. Moreover, the easy relationship between Paul and Apollos would have been inconceivable if Apollos had taught Philonic doctrines to the Corinthians and thereby become the source of Paul's problems there. At any rate, Horsley must stretch Philo's views on eloquence to fit the Corinthian situation.[7] If anything, Philo's repeated criticism of the Greco-Roman sophists aligns him with Paul rather than with what Paul is disavowing.[8] To be sure, Philo begrudgingly tolerated rhetoric as a base-born handmaiden to philosophy.[9] Philo considered rhetoric a skill that was needed

---

[4]Grant (1951, p. 55).
[5]Horsley (1977, pp. 224-39); cf. also Pearson (1975).
[6]Horsley (1977, p. 232). Similarly, Weiss (1959, vol. 1, p. 334); Sellin (1982, pp. 71ff).
[7]Davis's attempt (1984), following Horsley, to document a similar emphasis on eloquence in other Hellenistic-Jewish literature is exceedingly weak. Indeed, Horsley appears to be stretching even on Philo's view of wisdom. As W. L. Knox (1937, p. 68) points out, the abstract philosophical term λόγος was of far more importance to Philo than σοφία; cf. Knox (1939, pp. 81, 114).
[8]E.g., Philo, *The Worse Attacks the Better*, 1, 28, 33-35, 38, 41, 71-74; *The Posterity and Exile of Cain* 101; *Confusion of Tongues* 33-35, 39; *Who Is the Heir* 246; *Preliminary Studies* 18, 64-67; *On Dreams* 1, 107. Significantly, though her thesis requires her to contrast Paul and Philo, which she does on numerous other counts, M. E. Andrews (1934, p. 154) is forced to note the similarities between Paul and Philo in their "distaste for fine language" and "disapproval of the sophists." In this connection, Chadwick's curious statement (1965-1966, p. 296), despite the many other evidences he cites that Paul and Philo had "fished from the same pool" (p. 292), that "no close analogies occur in Philo for the Apostle's sarcastic attack on clever phrase-makers in 1 Corinthians 1," is puzzling, especially since Chadwick himself acknowledges the existence of many passages in Philo that "express hostility and scorn" for the sophists; cf. Winter (2002, pp. 17-112).
[9]See Philo, *On Drunkenness* 49-51; *Preliminary Studies* 9-11, 24, 27-31, 35, 72-78. Philo's description of rhetoric in the abstract is, however, surprisingly balanced and positive: "Rhetoric, sharpening the mind to the observation of facts, and training and welding thought to expression, will make the man a true master of words and thoughts, thus taking into its charge the peculiar and special

by the proponents of the truth as a means of offsetting the erroneous plausibilities of the sophists.[10] But he undoubtedly preferred the speech that was prompted by God.[11] The fact is, Philo might have written 1 Corinthians 2:13 almost as comfortably as the Apostle Paul.[12]

Finally, we may note that by no reading of Philo can the matter of speech be considered one of his prime doctrines. For example, in his classic *Introduction to Philo Judaeus*, E. R. Goodenough provides an exceptionally useful analysis of Philo's ideas without even mentioning the theme of rhetoric. Thus, even if one were to grant that Apollos taught Philonic ideas in Corinth (and however briefly at that), it would still be impossible to account for the prominence of the issue of σοφία λόγου in Corinth by looking to Philo.

---

gift which nature has not bestowed on any other living creature" (*Preliminary Studies* 17). Such a statement might as easily have been written by Isocrates, Cicero or Quintilian as Philo. But this is only because Philo has in mind not simply rhetoric, but rhetoric in the hands of a certain kind of person. In any case, such school subjects were at best for Philo merely the "preliminary studies" to philosophy: "Observe ... that our body is not nourished in the earlier states with solid and costly foods. The simple and milky foods of infancy come first. Just so you may consider that the school subjects and the lore which belongs to each of them stand ready to nourish the childhood of the soul, while the virtues are grown-up food, suited for those who are really men" (19).

[10]See Philo, *The Worse Attacks the Better* 35-36, 39, 41-42; *Confusion of Tongues* 32-34.

[11]Like Paul, Philo did not disparage speech per se. He viewed speech as the brother of mind (*The Posterity and Exile in Cain* 100, 107-9; *The Worse Attacks the Better* 40, 126). Both content and expression were important to Philo (*Preliminary Studies* 17-18, 29, 33; *The Worse Attacks the Better* 43, 74). Mind is the fountain, speech the outlet (*The Worse Attacks the Better* 40, 126; *Preliminary Studies* 33). Hence, speech can be either good or bad, depending on the user: "Now speech is an ally employed by those who hate virtue and love the passions to inculcate their untenable tenets, and also by men of worth for the destruction of such doctrines and to set up beyond resistance the sovereignty of those that are better, those in whose goodness there is no deceit" (*The Confusion of Tongues* 34).

[12]According to Philo, those who are equipped with practical wisdom but who lack formal study in expression (Moses vs. Aaron) "must be content to wait, until God shall have equipped in addition the most perfect interpreter, pouring out and making manifest to him the fountains of utterance" (*The Worse Attacks the Better* 44). God is the one who shows and perfects "all the qualities which are essential to expression of thought" (ibid., 39). "Never may the speech of a worthless man essay to interpret Divine ordinances. He disgraces their beauty by his own pollutions. On the other hand, let base and licentious ideas never be set forth by the lips of a man of worth, but let holy things always be expounded by sacred and holy speech" (ibid., 133; cf. 127). In this light, Paul's disavowal in 1 Cor 2:13 of words taught by *human* wisdom would have totally missed the mark if Philonic doctrines were at issue. Followers of Philo would have quite agreed with Paul. Only if the Corinthians must concede that the wisdom they were so eager for was of expressly *human* origin (as would be the case with Greco-Roman rhetoric) could Paul's disavowal make sense.

Appendix Two

The Book of Acts

In this book we have founded our treatment on Paul's epistles, and this for methodological reasons. In the investigation of Paul's ideas, his own writings must always be viewed as the primary sources, with all else, including Acts, considered secondary. J. C. Hurd discussed this principle at length in his article "Pauline Chronology and Pauline Theology," and N. A. Dahl applied it directly to 1 Corinthians 1–4 in speaking of the "strict method" that must govern the study of this passage "if the result is not going to add to a chaos which is already bad enough":

> In so far as they do not directly serve the purpose of philological exegesis, but provide materials for a more general, historical and theological understanding, information from other Pauline epistles, Acts, and other early Christian, Jewish, Greek, or Gnostic documents should not be brought in until the epistolary situation has been clarified as far as possible on the basis of internal evidence.[1]

This is sound exegetical counsel. But now that we have examined the internal evidence of the Corinthian epistles, it's appropriate that we survey the contribution of the book of Acts to our investigation. Acts is an important historical source, and as such we must ask to what degree it confirms or contradicts the picture of the Corinthian situation we have gleaned from Paul's epistles. We need not here enter into the seemingly endless debates over the authorship, date, purpose or historical reliability of Acts—and in particular, those debates surrounding the Areopagus speech of Acts 17[2]—but we can at least summarize the ways in which Acts contributes to our treatment of 1 Corinthians 1–4.

---

[1] Dahl (1967, p. 318).
[2] For an extended discussion of these issues, see Porter (1999b).

The Ministry of Paul

We may begin by noting the centrality of public speaking to Paul's ministry in Acts. Immediately upon his conversion (Acts 9:1-19) Paul begins to preach (Acts 9:20, κηρύσσω). When Barnabas commends him to the Jerusalem apostles, it is for his bold speaking (παρρησιάζομαι, Acts 9:27), which the new convert enthusiastically continues (Acts 9:28). After Paul is sent out on his initial missionary journey by the Holy Spirit in Acts 13:4, the first reference to the activity of proclamation (καταγγέλλω) occurs immediately (Acts 13:5). From this point on proclamation is the most persistent element in the account of Paul's missionary activity. Whether the term is εὐαγγελίζω, κηρύσσω, καταγγέλλω, πείθω, παρρησιάζομαι, διαλέγω, μαρτυρέω, διαμαρτύρομαι, παραδίδωμι or διδάσκω, and whether the audience is large or small, formal or informal, indoors or out of doors, preaching remains at the center of Paul's ministry. Hence we are unsurprised when the final verse of Acts leaves Paul "proclaiming [κηρύσσω] the kingdom of God and teaching [διδάσκω] about the Lord Jesus Christ with all boldness" (Acts 28;31).

This emphasis on preaching is especially apparent during the second missionary journey. Having completed his first journey and returned to Antioch for a period of local teaching and preaching (διδάσκω, εὐαγγελίζω, Acts 15:35), Paul decided to set out again (with Barnabas) for the cities wherein he had previously proclaimed the word (καταγγέλλω, Acts 15:36). But upon being forbidden by the Spirit to speak (λαλέω, Acts 16:6) the word in Asia, Paul (with Silas now) was called by God in a specific vision to travel west and preach the gospel (εὐαγγελίζω, Acts 16:10) in Greece. Hence Paul wound up proclaiming Christ in Philippi (Acts 16:13-14, 17, 21, 32), Thessalonica (Acts 17:2-3), Berea (Acts 17:11, 13), Athens (Acts 17:17-34) and from there in Corinth (Acts 18:1-18).

Before considering Paul's experiences in Athens and Corinth more closely, it is worth noting the brief description Luke provides, in his discussion of Thessalonica, of Paul's customary approach (κατὰ . . . τὸ εἰωθὸς, Acts 17:2) to preaching. Seeking out an audience in the synagogue, Paul discoursed from the Scriptures (διελέξατο αὐτοῖς ἀπὸ τῶν γραφῶν, 17:2), explaining (διανοίγω) and setting before (παρατίθημι) them the message that "this Jesus, whom I proclaim [καταγγέλλω] to you, is the Christ" (Acts 17:3). In response to this proclaiming "some of them were persuaded" (ἐπείσθησαν), both Greeks and Jews, and threw in their lot with Paul and Silas (Acts 17:3-4). In a similar way, many also "believed" (ἐπίστευσαν) in Berea (Acts 17:12).

In regard to Athens we must limit our remarks severely. Especially must we avoid drawing any conclusions based on alleged characteristics of the Areopagus speech of Acts 17:22-31. The estimates of this speech are so varied as to suggest that the debate is anything but an objective one. The data are apparently open to an array of more or less subjective interpretations. Hence we will avoid drawing in our own brief space any conclusions based on alleged Greek or non-Greek qualities of the speech itself. Instead we will limit ourselves to the straightforward statements of the text.[3]

According to Luke, Paul was struck by the idolatry of Athens (Acts 17:16). Yet he went about his customary business of spreading the gospel in both the synagogue and the marketplace (Acts 17:17). In the latter context Paul encountered some Epicurean and Stoic philosophers whose response to the Apostle's message ranged from disdain (they called him a σπερμολόγος, "one who peddles scraps of knowledge picked up from others") to curiosity.[4] Significantly, Luke says that some of them considered Paul a καταγγελεύς of foreign deities because of his "proclaiming" (εὐαγγελίζω) of the resurrection (17:17). Wishing to know more of this teaching, the philosophers took him to the Areopagus where Paul delivered his famous speech.

As we have said, we will not attempt to analyze this address. Suffice it to say that within the address itself the Apostle describes his activity as announcing (καταγγέλλω, Acts 17:23) and sets it in the context of God's own announcing (παραγγέλλω, Acts 17:30). And once again the response is the same: a mixture of derision and curiosity (Acts 17:32). Even in the midst of this less than satisfying reaction, however, "some," including Dionysius, Damaris and others, believed (ἐπίστευσαν) and followed Paul (Acts 17:34).

In light of the willingness of some of the Areopagites to hear Paul again (Acts

---

[3]On the relationship between Paul's experience in Athens and his behavior in Corinth, we need not conclude, as do some (see Still's documentation, 2012, pp. 6-7), that Paul tried (and failed in) using an unfamiliar Greek rhetorical approach in Athens that he subsequently jettisoned before arriving at Corinth. On the other hand, perhaps we should not totally disassociate Paul's experiences in Corinth from those in Athens. Conzelmann (1973, p. 97), for example, understands 1 Cor 2:3 as a comment on Paul's condition in Athens as well as in Corinth.

[4]According to Luke, some saw Paul as a plagiarist of old ideas (Acts 17:18), while others were struck by the newness of his ideas (Acts 17:19-21). On this contrast see Isocrates's analysis of the dilemma faced by orators: "If they repeat the same things which have been said in the past, they will be regarded as shameless babblers, and if they seek for what is new, they will have great difficulty in finding it" (*Antidosis* 83). On the subject of the plagiarizer, or one who goes about picking up bits and pieces of wisdom from others, see the parallels in Dio Chrysostom, *Discourses* 32.9, 42.4-5.

17:32), the abrupt departure of the Apostle for Corinth in Acts 18:1 is startling. There had been fruit with even this elite and hostile audience. Why would Paul not have followed his address with further efforts? Luke does not explain. Athens is one of the few cities Paul departed without leaving even a fledgling church behind.

From Athens Paul traveled to Corinth. There he made contact with Aquila and Priscilla. Using their home as his base, he discoursed (διαλέγω) every sabbath in the synagogue, seeking to persuade (πείθω) both Jews and Greeks (Acts 18:4). When Silas and Timothy joined him from Macedonia, moreover, Paul was "confined to the word," an elliptical expression that apparently refers to Paul's redoubled and concentrated efforts at preaching the gospel, solemnly proclaiming (διαμαρτύρομαι) to the Jews in particular the message that Jesus is the Christ (Acts 18:5). When these Jews resisted his message and blasphemed, Paul turned to the Gentiles (cf. Acts 13:44-48; 28:25-28) and set up shop next door to the synagogue in the house of one Titius Justus (Acts 18:6-7). Yet even in the midst of this negative reaction from the Jews, there were again a few who believed, most notably Crispus, the leader of the synagogue, with his entire household. Furthermore, among the citizens of Corinth in general, "many" who heard the preaching believed (ἐπίστευον) and were baptized (Acts 18:8).

All the more surprising, then, is the vision Luke reports in Acts 18:9-10. There has been no hint of fearfulness in the Apostle regarding his speaking. Yet in the night the Lord comes to Paul and tells him: "Do not be afraid, but go on speaking [λαλέω] and do not be silent, for I am with you, and no one will attack you to harm you, for I have many in this city who are my people." With this divine encouragement Paul continued to minister among the Corinthians for eighteen months (Acts 18:11).

The final episode in Corinth reported by Luke is Paul's appearance before the Roman proconsul Gallio. Incensed at Paul's continued preaching, the Jews hauled Paul before the βῆμα and accused him of persuading (ἀναπείθω) people to worship contrary to the Jewish law (Acts 18:13). But Gallio would hear none of it and refused even to allow Paul to speak in his own defense. He dismissed the matter as "questions about words and names and your own law" and sent them away (Acts 18:15). At this point the crowd—πάντες apparently refers to the Gentile onlookers—attacked Sosthenes, the ruler of the synagogue, and began to beat him in front of the βῆμα, all of which Gallio disdainfully ignored (Acts 18:17).

The Ministry of Apollos

After ministering in Corinth "many days longer" (Acts 18:18), Paul departed for Syria. With the Apostle's departure the focus shifts to Apollos. All further information about Paul's interactions with the Corinthians must be gleaned from his epistles, for after 18:18 Acts is silent on the subject. But the information about Apollos in Corinth is pointed.

Apollos first appears in Ephesus. Luke introduces him as "a certain Jew" followed by four defining phrases: (1) Apollos by name, (2) Alexandrian by nationality, (3) an eloquent man (ἀνὴρ λόγιος)[5] and (4) powerful in the Scriptures (δυνατὸς ἐν ταῖς γραφαῖς, Acts 18:24). While it is fallacious to assume without evidence that we are permitted to read Philonic doctrines into the picture merely because Apollos was an Alexandrian Jew,[6] it appears undeniable that by this description Luke is seeking to emphasize the erudition of Apollos, and in particular his eloquence and forcefulness as a speaker. Luke holds Apollos at a certain distance (e.g., τις, 24; οὗτος, 25; οὗτος, 26) in his account as if he was something of a phenomenon in the church, a phenomenon moreover that focused almost entirely on the man's public speaking. Though Apollos did not at first completely understand the gospel, the parts he did understand he spoke and taught (ἐλάλει καὶ ἐδίδασκεν) with accuracy (ἀκριβῶς) and great fervency (ζέων τῷ πνεύματι, Acts 18:25). He entered the synagogue and began to speak out boldly (παρρησιάζομαι). Upon hearing him and recognizing the deficiencies of his understanding of "the way of God,"[7] Priscilla and Aquila took him aside and tutored him (Acts 18:26). Thus equipped, Apollos received the enthusiastic support of "the brethren" in Ephesus, so much so that when he decided to travel to Achaia—and to Corinth in particular, Acts 19:1—they encouraged him and wrote to the Christians there to give him a warm welcome (Acts 18:27). The Corinthians apparently did welcome Apollos, and his public speaking ministry

---

[5]So Plutarch of Cicero (*Lives*, Cicero 49.3). On the meaning of this term in Hellenistic Greek, Bruce (1979, p. 68) summarizes: "'A man of culture' is Moulton and Milligan's suggested rendering of *aner logios*, otherwise translated 'a learned man' (RV, NIV) or 'an eloquent man' (AV, RSV, NEB). Of these two translations the former corresponds to the sense of the adjective in classical Greek, but the latter agrees with its meaning in Hellenistic and Modern Greek"; cf. Bruce (1975, pp. 356-57).

[6]See appendix one. The same may be said, perhaps even more emphatically, of any claims that Apollos used a Philonic approach to the interpretation of Scripture. Against this assumption Barrett (1982, p. 4) rightly says that the fact that Apollos "was Ἀλεξανδρεὺς τῷ γένει is probably insignificant, for there is no ground for supposing that every Alexandrian Jew was a potential Philo (though some writers seem to think so)"; cf. also Munck (1959, pp. 143-44); Lake (1930, p. 112).

[7]See Acts 18:25; cf. also Acts 9:2; 16:17; 19:9, 23; 22:4; 24:14, 22.

in Corinth went extraordinarily well. Luke says that Apollos contributed "greatly" to the believers (τοῖς πεπιστευκόσιν) there (Acts 18:27). In what way did he help them? By forcefully confuting (εὐτόνως ... διακατηλέγχετο) the Jewish opposition, publicly demonstrating through the Scriptures (δημοσίᾳ ἐπιδεικνὺς διὰ τῶν γραφῶν) that Jesus is the Christ (Acts 18:28).

The final mention of Corinth in Acts is in 19:1. Luke curiously juxtaposes Paul and Apollos with regard to Corinth: "And it happened that while Apollos was at Corinth, Paul . . ." Perhaps this is no more than a literary bridge to bring the focus of the account back to the Apostle, but the contrast of Paul's experience in Corinth with that of Apollos is nonetheless striking. As Barrett says, Paul encountered in Corinth "as difficult and dangerous a situation as he had ever faced."[8] His frustration in the synagogue and a developing fear regarding his speaking threatened to silence him. But with Apollos the picture was quite the opposite. He was an eloquent speaker, and this had its effect in Corinth. The opponents fell before his eloquence, and this in turn pleased and impressed the Corinthian believers.

Hence we may observe that Acts complements 1 Corinthians 1–4 in several important ways, and at no point contradicts it. Public speaking is presented as central to Paul's ministry throughout. Moreover, it is a ministry of proclamation. Paul consistently announces Jesus as the Christ, usually but not invariably basing his message on an interpretation of Scripture. Repeatedly a proportion of the audience rejects the message while another proportion—"as many as were appointed to eternal life," comments Luke in Acts 13:48—embrace it in faith. It is precisely the approach Paul contrasts with the dynamic of Greco-Roman rhetoric in 1 Corinthians 1–2. His role is simply to placard Christ. It is the Spirit of God who must draw those who are called (τοῖς κλητοῖς, 1 Cor 1:24; cf. Rom 1:6) to himself.

Regarding Corinth itself, the book of Acts speaks explicitly of Paul's fear and weakness in relation to his preaching, confirming Paul's own testimony in 1 Corinthians 2:3. Neither Acts nor 1 Corinthians specifies the cause of this fear, but it was apparently unique to Paul's Corinthian experience.[9] We have no record of any similar experiences elsewhere, despite the fact that Paul often faced similar rejections and threats of personal harm. What Acts does tell us,

---

[8]Barrett (1973, p. 10).
[9]Though we may also note Paul's concern that Timothy might have a similarly fearful experience in Corinth (1 Cor 16:10), which he related to Timothy's being despised (ἐξουθενήσῃ, 16:11) by the Corinthians. It is perhaps no accident that this is the same word used by the critics to ridicule Paul's speech (2 Cor 10:10).

however, is that Apollos followed Paul in Corinth and apparently emerged as something of a hero to the Corinthians, an eloquent champion with whom they were much pleased. This too is consistent with the picture that has emerged from Paul's epistles.

On the other hand, it should also be noted that Acts supplies inadequate grounds for concluding that Apollos depended on the persuasive dynamic of Greco-Roman rhetoric in his preaching. If we may assume that Apollos was not only born in Alexandria but received his education there as well, then it is all but certain that he would have been trained in rhetoric, as Philo, for example, certainly was.[10] Yet the preaching of Apollos is described by Luke (albeit more briefly) in much the same way as is Paul's. The twice-repeated stress on the role of the Scriptures in Apollos's preaching (Acts 18:24, 28) especially identifies his approach with Paul rather than the rhetoricians. Luke clearly enough affirms that Apollos was eloquent, and this could only have had meaning within the general standards of eloquence known to the readers of that day. But it would require moving beyond our evidence to conclude that Apollos depended in any full-fledged way in Corinth on the dynamic of Greco-Roman persuasion. We may only observe that, according to Acts, the Ephesian and especially the Corinthian Christians—not to mention Apollos's opponents and even Luke himself—were much impressed by the quality and effectiveness of the man's eloquence. Beyond this, without further evidence all else is speculation.[11]

---

[10]See Smith (1974, pp. 75, 110).

[11]Mihaila (2009, p. 188) rejects the possibility that Apollos may have played even an unintentional part in the Corinthian dissensions. Says he, "If the cross requires the style of one's presentations to be in weakness, devoid of rhetorical eloquence, as Paul's, it is impossible to see how the cross would allow for a style that is powerful, conforming to contemporary standards of an accomplished orator." But such an all-or-nothing approach is unnecessary. Well short of accusing Apollos of fully conforming to contemporary standards of oratory, it is not at all impossible that, unlike Paul's (2 Cor 10:10), Apollos's bodily presence and speech were more than presentable. Apollos may have shown strengths the Apostle did not, strengths that need not have contradicted Paul's core concerns as expressed in 1 Cor 1–4. For a more nuanced analysis of these core concerns, see above, chap. 17.

Appendix Three

Paul's Epistemology

Epistemology is that branch of philosophy focused on the nature of knowledge and belief. In his extended analysis of Paul's contribution to this important subject, Ian Scott observes that there are two passages in the Pauline epistles that for centuries have been recognized as having especially strong epistemological implications: Romans 1:18-32 and our passage, 1 Corinthians 1:17–2:16.[1] Scott's treatment of Paul's implicit epistemology in these two passages is insightful and deeply relevant to our own study. The following is a condensed summary, largely in his own words, of Scott's most salient points.

ROMANS 1:18-32

The thrust of this important passage is to emphasize how much humanity has lost. Paul is speaking here of the universal state of humankind. In doing so he presents a vision of humanity whose entire existence is characterized by the "vanity" that the Old Testament associates with idols.

In this passage Paul launches an accusation against humanity for its culpable lack of knowledge about God. Due to their rebellion, human beings have become chronically incapable of seeing religious things clearly. In their preference for worshiping the creature rather than the creator, humans can no longer even diagnose their own situation. The race continues to boast about itself despite its hopeless ignorance of God. Thus human reason remains, at least in the present state of things, constitutionally unable to reach truth about God.

The root problem is not an intellectual one, however. It's a moral problem. The human preference for idols is a vice for which human beings are morally responsible. The decisive moment in religious knowing is the moral struggle to

---

[1]The following is adapted from Scott ([2006] 2009, pp. 15-48); used by permission. Cf. Polhill (1983, p. 329).

respond rightly to the truth about God. It is this moral effort that fallen human beings are no longer able to exert. The result is their blindness to religious truth.

This moral failure in turn affects how humans are able to reason. The reasoning process is influenced by the reasoner's moral character. The strength and direction of our moral will distorts our reasoning. Reason is not in Paul's view an impartial arbiter capable of standing outside the influence of the self and returning a perfectly objective judgment. Instead, the strength and direction of one's moral will often determines the range of ideas one is willing to accept. Human religious thought is thus corrupted by a chronic and powerful aversion to giving the Creator proper honor and worship.

In Paul's view, the underlying human problem is our illegitimate desire for independence and autonomy from God; that is, a refusal to accept our status as created beings subject to the Creator. One aspect of this desire for autonomy is an intellectual arrogance that demands that God be entirely comprehensible and intellectually controllable. This arrogance reflects our profound discontent with our creaturely limitations. We prefer to compete with God in the business of being God.

This deep-seated aversion to acknowledging God for who he is constitutes a congenital flaw in our moral constitution, which, left to itself, corrupts all of our thinking about God. Human reason is a faculty that is, in principle, capable of attaining truth about God, but in its present state it is crippled by the idolatrous tendencies of the moral will. If one's moral faculties were repaired, one's reason might be free to operate as it was intended; to a renewed mind the truths of the gospel might well be compatible with the fruits of rational inquiry. This is possible, however, only if the endemic human rebellion against God were somehow overcome.

1 Corinthians 1:17-2:16

In this important passage Paul is both defending himself against Corinthian criticisms and addressing factionalism within the Corinthian church. The Apostle hoped to address these two issues in one stroke by correcting the problem that lay at the root of both: a misunderstanding of wisdom.

Paul's main tactic in this passage is to draw a sharp opposition between the wisdom of the world and the wisdom of God. His point is that the kind of wisdom that most people, including some of the Corinthians, value so highly is actually of no use in the quest for salvation. Ordinary thought and discourse cannot recognize the gospel for what it is—the power of God for salvation—because the word of the cross stands in absolute, uncompromising contradiction to human wisdom. What God has done in "Christ crucified" is a direct contradiction of human ideas of wisdom and power; yet it achieves what human wisdom and power always fail to achieve.

What is it about ordinary human thought and discourse that so incapacitates them? God's action in Christ assumes a different set of intellectual and moral standards from those human beings normally employ. The Apostle implies that both the Greek and Jew expect God's action to be characterized by power, not weakness, so that they find the message of a crucified savior incredible. There is something about this event that does not fit human expectations about divine action.

For Paul, the underlying human problem is the expectation that God should subject his action to human standards of authentication, standards that arise from within human frames of reference. But God's wisdom does not subject itself to human criteria; it confounds all such criteria. In answer to this demand that truth be authenticated on our human terms, Paul presents a message of weakness that is offensive. God chooses to act in ways that will appear foolish to the world, he says, ways that frustrate ordinary human expectation about the divine. He does this in order to force human beings to let go of their typical frames of reference and adopt a new vantage point.

The problem, then, is not the human attempt to understand. Nowhere does the Apostle condemn reason or understanding in and of themselves. It is the wisdom *of the world* God makes futile, not wisdom itself. God has designed the gospel precisely to frustrate the race's prideful unwillingness to accept the limits of human autonomy. Humans long for control over their own existence, but this inclination to secure one's position over against the Creator is inherently idolatrous. It is this moral failure, endemic in fallen humanity, that inevitably corrupts the values and standards of reasonableness with which human wisdom operates. The word of the cross is designed to frustrate any attempt at confirmation from the realm of human experience and values. In order to accept the crucified Christ, one is forced to adopt a whole new frame of reference.

Rather than being incomprehensible, then, the gospel is simply unjustifiable in terms of standard human systems of evaluation and plausibility. Paul nowhere rejects wisdom itself; what he rejects is any system of wisdom that is corrupted by human epistemic vices—in other words, reason that has been hijacked by human demands for autonomy. Human wisdom is incorrigibly egocentric. Thus the message of the cross, while not antirational, is calculated to subvert these essentially idolatrous tendencies, tendencies that pervert all fallen human thought. To accept the gospel, one must be willing to abandon humanity's typical standards of evaluation. The *kerygma* is foolishness to the perishing, not because it is unintelligible, but because it is all too intelligible: it calls for a reversal of the human standard by which humans typically determine what will count as wisdom.

Paul's position is therefore not fideistic, if by that term we mean an appeal to faith as an alternative to rational thought. To be sure, the Apostle does affirm that given the present state of humanity, rational inquiry cannot on its own achieve reliable knowledge of God. What's more, God has chosen to act in such a way that ordinary human inquiries will always mistake the truth about God's action for nonsense. The message of Christ crucified simply redefines what counts as plausible and valuable. It's not that the message is rationally incoherent or that Paul's presentation avoids rational explanation. His hearers cannot comprehend its rationality unless they first overcome certain moral vices that are endemic to humanity, since it is these vices that consistently distort human intellectual standards.

God has intentionally arranged things such that the saving power of the apparently foolish gospel forces a reconsideration of all ordinary standards of reasonableness, incapacitating, reversing and turning upside down the values of this world. This situation is precisely what God intended. It is God who makes the wisdom of the world look foolish. It was he who decided to save those who believe through an apparently foolish message of the cross, straightforwardly proclaimed.

Paul's simple presentation of the gospel, then, was an intentional strategy geared to ensure that his preaching did not undermine God's subversion of the world's corrupt wisdom. Paul deliberately chose not to use eloquent rhetoric or sophisticated reasoning. Instead he wished to rely on a straightforward heralding of "Christ and him crucified," to be accepted or rejected. Why? Because he refused to frame his preaching within the values and standards of reasonableness that characterize other systems of thought. His proclamation of the gospel was deliberately designed to be incompatible with idolatrous human vices and the systems of value and plausibility those vices spawn. Paul therefore rejected both ordinary standards for rational verification and the rhetorical flair that was expected if those arguments were to carry force. Such ordinary human standards for evaluating the truth or falsehood of a message break down and become counterproductive when they encounter the gospel. This is why Paul repudiated an oratory that made its case by appeal to human frameworks of value and reasonableness. The Apostle was determined to depend instead on the Spirit, whose work is necessary not as a substitute for rationality but as a cure for the moral vices that determine what kind of divine action human beings are willing to accept as plausible and persuasive.

Hence, Paul says, it was not his rhetorical force that originally convinced the Corinthians; it was the direct activity of the Holy Spirit working on the hearer to produce belief in the gospel. Recognition of the truth of the gospel is like direct vision. The need is not for arguments; the need is to open one's eyes. But this opening of the eyes requires the work of the Spirit. In this transaction it's not that the Spirit somehow overrides human rationality, producing a belief in an irrational message. The Spirit redirects the listener's moral orientation so that the message that would otherwise appear foolish can be seen and understood as wisdom. Human rationality has been so corrupted by endemic moral failures that, left to itself, the human mind consistently resists interpreting the world in terms the gospel requires. What the Spirit of God offers Paul's audience is a powerful demonstration, a "proof" of the gospel's truth that is produced by strengthening and reorienting the listeners' moral wills. This allows them to grasp and embrace as true an interpretation of the world they would otherwise reject.

The Spirit's role, then, is to perform a moral restoration of believers that allows them to move into a new system of values within which the gospel is rational and plausible. Paul understands the believer to gain a new ability to consider and appraise things in the world because the gospel has provided a new standard by which all things can be measured. The human epistemic challenge is therefore not the discovery of truth about God, but the recognition (and embrace) of that truth as God's wisdom when it is presented. The Spirit's indispensible role is not to uncover hidden content, but rather to enable believers to recognize the openly proclaimed message as true. The Spirit's revelation, his uncovering, is simply a matter of opening human eyes to the truth of the message when they encounter it.

Appendix Four

Implications for Preaching

The most obvious contemporary implications of the Pauline model must surely relate to the subject of preaching. This was after all the issue in Corinth that generated the Pauline argument we have explored in this book. Yet applying Paul's argument to our contemporary setting is not as simple as it might seem.

Contrary to first impressions, the historical and cultural differences between our situation and Paul's are not the primary challenge. Paul did not ground his argument to the Corinthians in premises that were culturally and historically bound—that is, on premises that were specific and perhaps even unique to a particular time and place. He argued his case on fundamental theological premises about God's chosen *modus operandi* in the world in general. The Corinthians were only another example of what God had already universally demonstrated in the crucified Christ: his determination to frustrate humanity's pride by accomplishing his purposes, not through those human efforts the world considered impressive, but through Spirit-empowered means the world considered of no account—so that when those divine purposes were accomplished no mortal could boast. Such theological grounds are the opposite of culturally or historically bound. They speak to deep-seated issues of human pride and God's refusal to accommodate it in every time and place (see appendix three). They are every bit as relevant—though perhaps even more counterintuitive—to inhabitants of our twenty-first century as they were to the first-century Corinthians.

Our challenge in discerning the contemporary relevance of Paul's argument in 1 Corinthians 1–4 for our preaching is therefore not the cultural and historical gap between then and now. Our challenge relates to the equivocal nature of our English term *preaching*.

The exercise Paul is addressing in 1 Corinthians 1–4 is primarily the proclamation of the gospel to unbelievers. By contrast, the exercise many have in mind today when they speak of preaching is a Sunday sermon to churchgoers. In English we tend to refer to both as preaching, but biblically and theologically the two settings require differentiation.¹ Without plunging into a detailed exploration of the issues, it is enough to observe that according to the Bible, the role of the Holy Spirit in bringing unbelievers (ψυχικὸς ἄνθρωπος, 1 Cor 2:14) to faith is distinguishable from the Spirit's role in maturing believers (ὁ πνευματικός, 2:15). Paul's argument in 1 Corinthians 1–4 is primarily addressing the first of these settings, the proclamation of the gospel to the unconverted. This is what we usually have in mind when we speak of *evangelism*, an English term transliterated from the Greek word for "gospelizing" (εὐαγγελίζω). When this is the setting we have in mind, Paul's insights are more directly relevant to our contemporary practice. When our focus, is the second setting (addressing those who are already believers and thus possess the Holy Spirit), though the insights of 1 Corinthians 1–4 remain relevant, a degree of extrapolation is required. Moreover, when this second setting is our focus, the many biblical references to "teaching" (διδαχή) come into play (for example, 1 Cor 4:17).

In any case, given our present purposes we are limited in how much we can say about either setting. The issues are complex and difficult to pin down. A book on contemporary preaching that focused on these issues might provide room enough to sort through the larger questions, weighing one strategy against another. But our space here is more restricted. I must settle in this appendix and the next for offering a few suggestive examples of how the Pauline model might work itself out in contemporary practice.

Practical Application

What follows is an adapted version of an article originally published in *Christianity Today*.² I wrote it when I was still a young homiletics professor with a newly minted PhD in rhetorical theory. The article was prompted by a week of troubling evangelistic services that seemed to demand a response.

I was no stranger to such revivalist meetings. As a teenager I had witnessed a series of so-called evangelists who were little more than charlatans. They

---

¹See Craig Evans (1981); Hunter (1943, pp. 24-26). Says Porter (2013, p. 330): Paul's "letters are contextually sensitive discourses addressing a particular set of circumstances within an early Christian community, while his significance speeches ... are almost always (with one exception) addressed not to fellow Christians but to those outside the Christian community, either as promoting his mission or as apologetic defences."
²See the preface above, p. 15. Adapted from Litfin (1977). Used by permission.

would whirl into town and draw a crowd to the local fair grounds. Night after night for a week or so they would whip the audience into a frenzy in order to fleece them of money. I and some of my friends would show up for the entertainment value, but the experience always left me troubled.

Yet these later evangelistic services were different. They were not the fly-by-night scam of a transient hustler; they were held in a good church and seemed to be much appreciated by the members who attended. Fresh from my studies in classical rhetoric, however, I witnessed them through different eyes. What I heard were a series of messages that were delivered, once the preacher got wound up, in what the ancients would have recognized as the "grand style." The preacher came on strong and fast. His messages were crammed with emotive language and moving, well-honed stories. Every night he would build to an emotional crescendo, which produced dramatic results: people wept and many came forward at the wide-ranging invitation. The meetings were considered by all to be wonderfully successful and the preacher himself no doubt claimed them as such in his next prayer letter. The only thing those meetings seemed to lack was the gospel itself.

To be fair, if one had gone back and studied a transcript of the preacher's messages, one might have been able to cobble together a loose version of the biblical gospel. There was, after all, much God-talk, and the evangelist repeatedly referred to the Bible. But as the week unfolded I finally realized that proclaiming a clear gospel was not the evangelist's goal. He was after a response from his audience, and it did not seem to trouble him that the response he received might be to his own rhetorical stratagems rather than to the "word of the cross."

What I experienced that week was a minor contemporary version of what Cicero had in mind when he spoke of that "kind of eloquence which rushes along with the roar of a mighty stream."[3] When this evangelist was finished, what his listeners appeared to take away was an emotional experience induced by a talented speaker; they were moved by what they had heard and were impressed by the delivery man. What none could have taken away, unfortunately, at least on the basis of those meetings, was a clear understanding that "Christ died for our sins in accordance with the Scriptures, that he was buried, that he was raised on the third day in accordance with the Scriptures" (1 Cor 15:3-4).

Two millennia earlier Quintilian had spoken of those persuaders who could

---

[3] Cicero, *Or. Brut.* 97.

"sweep the [listener] with them, lead him to adopt that attitude of mind which they desire, and compel him to weep with them or share their anger." This is the one, said Quintilian, who "will inspire anger or pity, and while he speaks the [listener] will call upon the gods and weep, following him wherever he sweeps him from one emotion to another."[4] For a week I had watched this ancient and modern phenomenon unfold before me, and it worked: the speaker got his results. But the question was, *What should we make of such results?* This was the concern that dogged me all week long.

These evangelistic meetings finally triggered the following article. I had been thinking about these issues for years and it was time to put something into print. Though it was originally composed decades ago and its references are drawn from that period, the article's point—my first attempt at presenting the argument of this book—has not weakened over time. The issues it raises are as pertinent today as they were when the article first appeared. I have adapted the article to improve its fit in the flow of this book, but for the most part its argument remains intact.

Preaching and Persuasion

As we have seen throughout this book, the study of human persuasion has a long and often noble heritage. For most of its history the subject was pursued under the banner of rhetoric, but in more recent times it has been studied by social scientists under such rubrics as persuasion theory, attitude change and social influence.

The relation between secular views of persuasion and preaching is also of long standing. Christianity was conceived in a Jewish womb, and its first preachers, audiences and modes of discourse were all Jewish. Yet the new faith was born into a world dominated by Greco-Roman influence and immediately began to take on some of the characteristics of its environment. One of the most obvious of the church's adaptations was its appropriation of what was then the crown of a liberal education—rhetoric—for its own use in preaching.

This appropriation is not necessarily bad. The apostles never intended to provide a comprehensive theory of homiletics. Our situation is not that of the New Testament preachers either culturally or chronologically, and we would be foolish to try to copy them to the letter. Moreover, the work of rhetoricians and persuasion theorists, many of whom have themselves been preachers, abounds with wonderfully valuable insights into human communication. To the extent

---

[4]Quintilian, *Inst. or.* 12.10.61-63.

we can use their work to make our proclamation more effective, we not only should but must do so. But can we do it unquestioningly?

From the beginning nonreligious theories of persuasion have been designed to enable communicators to influence their audience more effectively. They are avowedly instrumental, utilitarian or goal oriented. Responsible rhetoricians have seldom condoned outright manipulation, but their efforts have been frankly directed toward drawing forth particular decisions, attitudes or behavior from their audiences.

Interestingly, some contemporary homileticians tend to agree. They hold that the goal of the preacher is essentially similar to that of the secular persuader—that is, to elicit a desired response from the listener—and that it is quite proper to use a broad range of rhetorical techniques to achieve this goal. This assumption lies beneath much of the modern writing on homiletics. For example, one homiletician writes: "Before the preacher understands the approach to be made to disbelieving audiences, he must first understand the sources through which people accept belief, so that he can organize his material in such a way as to gain the desired response." In another place he says, "If a good talk made a good sermon the preacher's lot would be an easy one. It is the fact that a sermon has to achieve a certain change of will that puts on the preacher the double compulsion of knowing both the response he desires and the countless techniques which will help him achieve his goal. Persuasion becomes an art."[5]

While we may grant that the secular persuader can proceed in this way, using his techniques to gain a particular response, are there not additional considerations for the preacher? One may ask whether the preacher should use *any* technique in an effort to induce the desired response from his audience—whether, in fact, gaining "the response he desires" should be the preacher's goal at all. For is it not possible that setting this as our goal increases the likelihood that the results we see will be of human beings and not of God?

For the sake of illustration, let us consider an extreme example. In his book *Hypnosis: Fact and Fiction*, Frederick L. Marcuse reports a research study conducted at a large eastern university.[6] The researchers attempted through hypnotic suggestion to induce a convinced and vocal atheist to become "religious." But the attempt was so successful that it was halted and all suggestion removed from the subject's mind. When his entire attitude toward religious faith changed

---

[5]Sleeth (1956, pp. 17, 45).
[6]Marcuse (1970, p. 115).

after only three sessions and for the first time in his life he began to attend church, the investigators decided that the ethics of the situation prevented them from pursuing their research any further.

The example is overly dramatic, but it serves to raise a monstrous question: would it be possible through hypnotic suggestion to create a "believer," quite apart from any work of the Holy Spirit? Would such a person genuinely be a Christian? Such questions are not simply academic. Psychologist James McConnell has said, "The time has come when if you give me any normal human being and a couple of weeks . . . I can change his behavior from what it is now to whatever you want it to be, if it's physically possible. I can't make him fly by flapping his wings, but I can turn him from a Christian into a Communist and vice versa."[7]

It is clearly possible to employ means that go too far in seeking results, means that tend to bypass some essential element in the human convictional process and therefore render any results less than satisfactory. Modern researchers have shown that audiences are not nearly so malleable as was once thought. Yet skilled persuaders, including some who stand in the pulpit, are often able to exert powerful influence on other human beings. And they do not have to resort to such dramatic methods as hypnotism. Consider, for example, the words of the well-known social scientist Milton Rokeach:

> Suppose you could take a group of people, give them a 20-minute pencil-and-paper task, talk to them for 10 to 20 minutes afterward, and thereby produce long-range changes in core values and personal behavior in a significant portion of this group. Suppose, further, that you could ascertain quickly and that you could predict accurately the nature and direction of these changes. . . .
>
> My colleagues and I have in the last five years achieved the kinds of results suggested [above]. As a result we must now face up to the ethical implications that follow from the fact that it now seems to be within man's power to alter experimentally another person's basic values, and to control the direction of the change.[8]

Rokeach gives too much credit to modern researchers; persuaders have long been able to influence the values, attitudes and behavior of their fellow human beings. But he is correct in asserting that modern techniques have reached a new level

---

[7] Quoted by Karlins and Abelson (1970, p. 1).
[8] Rokeach (1971, p. 68).

of sophistication and scientific accuracy. Moreover, the techniques he used were as simple as he says and they are only a sample of those available to any preacher.

All this suggests that through the use of certain techniques it is possible to get results, even where the Holy Spirit may not be active at all. But according to the Scriptures, God has said that his work is to be accomplished "not by might, nor by power, but by my Spirit" (Zech 4:6). The psalmist wrote, "Unless the LORD builds the house, those who build it labor in vain" (Ps 127:1). Paul later applied this principle to preaching when he avowed to the Corinthians that "my speech and my message were not in plausible words of wisdom, but in demonstration of the Spirit and of power, so that your faith might not rest in the wisdom of men but in the power of God" (1 Cor 2:4-5). Paul obviously understood that those persuasive "words of wisdom" so highly prized in the rhetorically oriented Corinthian culture could never bring men and women to Christ. Only the straightforward presentation of the gospel could do that. The use of persuasive techniques might indeed win a response, but it would be a response based on the "wisdom of men" and not the "power of God." Paul had the insight to see that such results would inevitably void the very gospel he preached.

Many Christians are troubled today by the seeming impermanence of much of what is accomplished by modern evangelistic methods. Perhaps a certain amount of the attrition can be explained by Christ's parable of the sower, but is it not also possible that the results we achieve may be the product not of God's Spirit but of our own "might and power" as persuaders? And are not such false results, as the Apostle Paul suggests, worse than no results at all?

The story is told that D. L. Moody was accosted on the streets of Chicago one day by a drunk who exclaimed, "Aren't you Mr. Moody? Why, I'm one of your converts!" Said Moody in reply, "That must be true, for you don't appear to be one of the Lord's." Perhaps we need more of Moody's honesty in facing the fact that it is possible for people to respond to the messenger and his techniques instead of to the gospel and the Savior it sets forth.

How can this pitfall be avoided? It's a function of the fact that God has chosen to use fallible human beings as instruments to reach other human beings. I suggest, however, that the danger can be minimized by a careful rethinking of the goal of preaching.

Earlier I suggested that homileticians, borrowing from secular persuasion theorists, have often set up the eliciting of a desired response as the goal of preaching. The trouble with such thinking is that it places the responsibility for obtaining results too much on the preacher. J. I. Packer analyzed this error perceptively in his book *Evangelism and the Sovereignty of God*. Says Packer,

> To proclaim salvation, we must never forget that it is God who saves.... Our evangelistic work is the instrument that He uses for this purpose, but the power that saves is not in the instrument: it is in the hand of the One who uses the instrument. We must not at any stage forget that. For if we forget that it is God's prerogative to give results when the gospel is preached, we shall start to think that it is our responsibility to secure them. And if we forget that only God can give faith, we shall start to think that the making of converts depends, in the last analysis, not on God, but on us, and that the decisive factor is the way in which we evangelize. And this line of thought, consistently followed through, will lead us far astray.
>
> Let us work this out. If we regarded it as our job, not simply to present Christ, but actually to produce converts—to evangelize, not only faithfully, but also successfully—our approach to evangelism would become pragmatic and calculating. We should conclude that our basic equipment, both for personal dealing and for public preaching, must be twofold. We must have, not merely a clear grasp of the meaning and application of the gospel, but also an irresistible technique for inducing a response. We should, therefore, make it our business to try and develop such a technique.... We should regard evangelism as a battle of wits between ourselves and those to whom we go, a battle in which victory depends on our firing off a heavy enough barrage of calculated effects.[9]

Much of the contemporary writing and preaching theory demonstrates the very tendencies Packer describes. But this need not happen. Let us examine the problem more closely.

We earlier introduced William McGuire's analysis of the five-step process of persuasion: *attention, comprehension, yielding, retention* and *action* (see above, p. 278). The traditional approach to homiletics sometimes seems to suggest that the goal of preaching is the third step, *yielding*; that is, the preacher's goal is to induce the listener to yield to, and ultimately to act on, a particular value, attitude or belief. But the approach outlined by Packer would suggest that the preacher's goal should not be viewed as the *yielding* step at all but simply the previous step, *comprehension*.

One might protest that this renders preaching merely a sterile intellectual

---

[9]Packer (1961, p. 27).

exercise, one focused on a mere exchange of information. But this is to miss the point. The preacher must deal with the whole person, including emotions. My point is that the goal of preaching should be so to present the gospel that the listener comprehends, sees, is grasped by the issues involved. This may well include and even require the use of emotional appeals, but those appeals will be directed toward helping the listener to comprehend, not toward inducing him to yield. Technique may play a valid role in bringing about *attention* and *comprehension*, but techniques focused on the yielding step should start raising red flags.

Preaching should always be a fork-in-the-road experience for the listener. He or she must be so clearly and powerfully confronted with the truth that it cannot be evaded or ignored. Comprehension is pressed on listeners, and they are required to make a decision. But the decision is the listener's to make, a matter between the hearer and the Holy Spirit. The preacher has shown the choice; now the listener must decide to accept, evade or reject.

What the preacher must not do is use the available persuasive techniques to shuttle the listener down one path instead of the other, even though the preacher deeply wills the listener to choose that path. At worst, such an approach may violate the listener's freedom by manipulating him or her. But even at its best this approach may involve shouldering an intolerable burden, one that belongs only to the Holy Spirit. It is to take upon oneself the responsibility of obtaining results.

In the end the preacher is a herald or ambassador for Christ, a function inherent in the words used in the New Testament for preaching: the preacher comes to tell or disclose the good news (εὐαγγελίζω); to solemnly proclaim (καταγγέλλω) the gospel; to bear witness to (μαρτυρέω) the crucified Lord; to announce (κηρύσσω) the living Word of God. As the appointed messenger the herald is responsible for seeing that all hear and that, to the best of his or her ability, all understand. But eliciting the desired response is not the messenger's affair. That transaction must remain between the hearer and the One whose message the herald is proclaiming. The voice may be that of the herald, but ultimately the Spirit is the one addressing the listeners through the preacher: "We are ambassadors for Christ, God making his appeal through us" (2 Cor 5:20).

Training in ancient rhetoric was designed to help the speaker mold his efforts to the needs and values of the audience so as to produce the desired response. The Christian preacher, on the other hand, molds his efforts to his audience for a different reason: to ensure that they comprehend the King's message. The preacher should use all the techniques at his disposal to put the message in terms his audience can understand, to break through the hearer's defenses so as to confront him or her with the truth. But having done this he dare go no further. Only the Holy Spirit can properly tread beyond this point.[10]

But, some may object, why can't God use a speaker's persuasive techniques to bring people to Christ? The answer, of course, is that he can and sometimes does. He does not require such "help," but he may use it in spite of us.

But what about all those misguided persons who respond to the messenger instead of the message because of our calculated efforts to gain results? Are we not at least partially responsible for leading them astray, for encouraging them to rest their faith on the wisdom of human beings rather than the power of God, and will we not be judged for our well-intended efforts that went beyond legitimate boundaries? We need not refrain from urging, entreating, exhorting or beseeching our listeners to follow Christ. The essence of the gospel is invitation, and some of the terms used in Scripture—for example, παρακαλέω (Acts 2:40) and δέομαι (2 Cor 5:20)—clearly portray this aspect of the preacher's ministry. Nothing we have said is meant to deny the validity of straightforward encouragement or exhortation to receive the gospel. After all, invitation in and of itself can scarcely be viewed as a persuasive technique designed to induce, rather than simply be the agent of, *yielding*. But we would do well to maintain serious reservations about practices such as these:

- *Gatherings centered on a charismatic, pseudo-celebrity communicator who revels in the spotlight.* Says Packer, "Those who have begun to understand the sovereignty of God . . . seek to efface themselves in all their work for God. They thus bear a practical witness to their belief that God is great, and reigns, by trying to make themselves small, and to act in a way which is itself an acknowledgment that the fruitfulness of their Christian service depends wholly on God."[11]

- *Styles of preaching or music that tend to rev up the emotions but short-circuit the listener's engagement with the gospel.*

- *Sentimental, story-laden messages that captivate the audience but fail to direct them to Christ.*

---

[10]H. Robinson (1986) on the balance required by the preacher: "Certainly methodologies are not neutral, and the gospel sits in judgment on the means used to proclaim it. Yet, effective communication requires that the cultural background of the hearer must be the starting point for the communicator. . . . Unless we produce a theology of method as well as message, we flirt with two dangers: delivering the pure milk in contaminated bottles, or not delivering any milk at all."
[11]Packer (1961, p. 27).

- *Empty, anthropocentric pulpit therapy that draws the listener in by purporting to deal with life's issues while lacking the gospel's biblical and theological substance.*
- *Interminable invitations designed to wear down resistance until someone, anyone, responds.*
- *Such techniques as asking people to raise their hands to be prayed for and then urging all who raised their hands to come forward.* Unwittingly—or perhaps not so unwittingly—those who do this are using a sophisticated psychosocial technique based on a cognitive consistency model. Having publicly admitted her need by the raising of a hand, the listener is induced by social and psychological pressure to comply when the second invitation is given. Such practices are aimed at inducing yielding and should be avoided by those who want to avoid false results.

A famous IBM advertisement once portrayed a business executive in a pensive mood. The copy read, "No one can take the ultimate weight of decision-making off your shoulders. But the more you know about how things really are, the lighter the burden will be. IBM. Not just data, reality."

In a sense, the goal of the preacher should be to function for the listener the way IBM purported to function for executives. The preacher cannot, must not, encroach upon the role of the Holy Spirit by employing persuasive strategies designed to promote yielding. But the preacher can and should do everything possible to build comprehension of the reality of Christ's claims upon the listener. This is what it means to be a faithful herald of the gospel.

Appendix Five

Broader Implications

As we approached the turn of the century, I was invited by the American Society for Church Growth (ASCG) to address their annual convention. I inquired as to whether they had any idea of what I might be likely to say on such an occasion, whereupon they replied that they did; they had run across my book, *St. Paul's Theology of Proclamation*, and they thought its argument might be of some benefit to their members. They were intent on thinking through where the Church Growth movement needed to go in the twenty-first century and so were interested in hearing from some of their friendly critics. I admired their response and accepted the invitation.

I took this speaking occasion as an opportunity to offer the requested counsel. "I stand before you as an outsider," I said to them.

> I have never been a part of the Church Growth movement; in fact, on occasion I have been among your critics. But more often I have been simply an interested observer. From its inception I have watched your movement rather closely, and while I make no formal effort these days to keep up with developments within the movement or to stay abreast of your literature, it does matter to me what you folks say and do.

Why did the Church Growth movement matter to an outsider like me? For two reasons. First, because its focus was the church. As a Christian, this is an institution that is near to my heart. It's also an institution, I said to them, "upon which you continue to exert a significant influence. It can be said of you that what you do matters—you have made a difference in the contemporary American church. Thus your work is of genuine interest to me; you have my attention."

The second and more specific reason the Church Growth movement mattered to me was that some of the principles that seemed to undergird it, and over which it has continued to tangle with its critics, dealt with the very issues to which I had given a sizable segment of my professional focus, both as a scholar and as a practitioner. "My goal," I said to them, "is to strike to the heart of these issues and see if we can pinpoint what it is that most worries the critics of the Church Growth movement. The criticisms themselves may be 'old hat' to you, but perhaps we can shed some useful light on the theoretical concerns that undergird them." So this is what I did. To their credit, the audience gave my address a gracious hearing and the society later published it in their journal.[1]

What follows is a revised version of the second half of that message. Had the ASCG not published it, I would not have included it here; I have no desire to exceed what was intended as constructive criticism of a movement that has accomplished much good. But the ASCG as such no longer exists. In 2009 it was transformed into the Great Commission Research Network, and its journal was renamed *Great Commission Research Journal*. What's more, as the reader will see, the relevance of the issues raised in this message reaches well beyond its original recipients. These issues speak to practices that continue to be taken for granted across wide swaths of the church today. Thus, while the following is couched in terms of that earlier discussion, it speaks to perennial issues that are with us today.

Trends and fads tend to come and go quickly in the modern church. The Church Growth movement was itself a successor to an earlier "Church Renewal" trend. Then, in reaction to what some perceived as Church Growth's overemphasis on measuring churches numerically, in the latter decades of the twentieth century there developed a counter-emphasis on developing "healthy" or "effective" churches. As the new century was dawning there then arose the so-called emergent church, bent on engaging our twenty-first-century postmodern culture. And as I write, this already passing moment is being supplanted by a "missional" emphasis. The missional movement stresses the church's role in the *missio Dei* ("mission of God") in the world.[2]

Each such development represents, more or less, a re-visioning of what the church is (or ought to be) and a re-prioritizing of what it's supposed to be doing. On the surface of things it cannot be a mark of the contemporary church's strength to see such core issues in a constant state of flux. But more to our present point, each new emphasis generates a waxing or waning of interest in the ministry issues Paul addresses in 1 Corinthians 1–4. In my estimation, how any of these trends deals

---

[1] The following is adapted from Litfin (1995, pp. 85-99). Used by permission.
[2] For both the positive and negative aspects of this complex movement, see Van Gelder and Zscheile (2011).

with (or ignores) these ministry issues becomes a fruitful measure, at least in part, of what we should think of that trend. For space reasons we cannot attempt to take those measures here, but I offer the following as one example of how we might weigh our contemporary thinking and practice in the light of 1 Corinthians 1–4.

I spent the first half of the ASCG address laying out a condensed version of the argument of this book, demonstrating how the Apostle had radically revised the persuader's stance. Then I turned to the broader implications of that revision, implications not just for our preaching but for ministry in general. The following paragraphs pick up approximately halfway through the address and the subsequent article.

THE CORE CRITICISM

So far [I said to the ASCG], we have been talking about Paul's preaching. But we should note that the Apostle is working here with a principle that has much wider application, a principle that he is merely *applying* to his ministry of preaching. What Paul is working out here is a principle so fundamental that it deserves to shape our entire philosophy of ministry. The results-driven approach Paul rejects is one we all understand and take for granted. Indeed, it is the most natural thing in the world. But it is also an approach to ministry the Apostle was required by his own theology to reject, precisely because it is so "natural" (1 Cor 2:14). It is the product of a merely anthropocentric way of thinking and doing, and as such it is out of concert with God's way of working. Moreover, it is fraught with the potential for obtaining false, merely natural results.

There are many positive things that even your worst critics are willing to commend about the Church Growth movement. As a whole the movement is made up of people who are forward looking, open, teachable and willing to work hard. You tend to be creative, unintimidated by the past and unafraid to try new things. At its best the Church Growth movement is fueled by a genuine desire to further the cause of Christ, and it has undoubtedly helped many people and many churches. Yet still your critics persist. Why? Let me put my answer as directly as I can.

It is my view that, without necessarily having thought through Paul's argument to the Corinthians, and certainly without posing their criticism in these terms, *your critics intuitively perceive the Church Growth movement to have lost sight of the contrast that so alarmed the Apostle Paul. They perceive you often to be operating out of the very persuader's stance Paul disavowed.*

Having offered this pointed observation, let me immediately soften it with two qualifications. I say "often" because the Church Growth movement has not shown itself completely oblivious to the dangers of the persuader's stance. There are times when the concerns Paul raises seem to be acknowledged in Church Growth materials. And yet, I must also say that in my estimation the Church Growth movement remains vulnerable to complaints that it has largely embraced the persuader's stance. If one looks not to what can merely be found somewhere within Church Growth literature but to *the constant and distinctive emphases of the Church Growth movement*, what one finds is a characteristically pragmatic, methodologically neutral stress on results-oriented strategies that "work." Despite the inevitable disclaimers, it is an approach that does seem to show the telltale signs of the persuader's stance.

Some Examples

At this stage, I am obligated to cite some examples. I cannot document my observations in full; that would require an entire volume. If I had more time I would walk us through some of the polling and market analysis that seems so fascinating to Church Growth advocates; or the "nickels and noses" growth techniques espoused by some of the growth gurus in their popular seminars; or the "bigger is better" obsession manifested by the megachurch "wannabes" who flock to these seminars; or the outright distortions of New Testament teaching on the subject of preaching one sometimes finds in the writings of some Church Growth advocates. But since we do not have the space for that, let me illustrate directly the sort of material that prompts your critics to worry that you have embraced the persuader's stance. For brevity I have limited myself to a few passages from some well-known and representative figures.

Here is a passage from a section titled "Fierce Pragmatism" in professor Peter Wagner's book *Church Growth and the Whole Gospel: A Biblical Mandate*:

> Since God's goal is clear, church growth people approach the task of accomplishing it in a fairly pragmatic way. The word "pragmatic," however, has drawn some criticism. Perhaps it is not the best word, but since it is being used, it should be explained. My dictionary defines pragmatic as "concerned with practical consequences or values." This is the way church growth understands the term.[3]

---

[3] P. Wagner (1981, p. 71).

Professor Wagner then quotes Donald McGavran:

> Donald McGavran said, "We devise mission methods and policies in the light of what God has blessed—and what he has obviously not blessed." He expressed concern about methodologies that are supposed to bring people to Christ and multiply churches, but don't. Or those that are designed to improve society, but don't. The best thing to do with such methods, he argued, was "throw them away, and get a method that works and brings glory to God." He then summed it up by saying, "As to methods, we are fiercely pragmatic."[4]

Later, in a section titled "Planning Strategy for Results," Professor Wagner declares,

> Those who fear pragmatism are concerned lest the end be taken as justifying the means. However, a knee-jerk rejection of this concept may be too hasty. In Christian work it is axiomatic that immoral means are not to be used for any end. But while immoral means may not be used in God's work, on what basis does one choose between several equally moral or value-free methodological options for accomplishing a certain goal? The approach of consecrated pragmatism recommends the option which most effectively and efficiently accomplishes the goal. In that sense, but only in that sense, the end is the only thing that can possibly justify the means. A means that fails to accomplish the goal is not, by anyone's measurement, a justifiable means.[5]

Let us see if we have this right, then: Church Growth advocates are fiercely pragmatic, a term that you define as being deeply concerned with practical consequences or results. You want methods that "work," that is, that achieve the desired results. If your efforts do not achieve the desired results, the only explanation must be that there is something wrong with your methods. Therefore these are to be discarded in favor of strategies that do achieve the desired results. To be sure, you do not want to use immoral methods, but that is the only criteria you need worry about—everything else is methodological fair game. In the end, you have no commitment to any particular method or strategy and no concern beyond the possibility of something being immoral. In your fierce pragmatism you evaluate strategies only on the basis of their ability to generate the desired results.

Have I overstated Professor Wagner's views? Apparently not. In his book *Strategies for Church Growth*, Professor Wagner addresses my point directly. He distinguishes among the three Ps of evangelizing: Presence Evangelism, Procla-

---

[4]Ibid., pp. 71-72.
[5]Ibid., p. 75.

mation Evangelism and Persuasion Evangelism. The approach Wagner calls Proclamation Evangelism is essentially what the Apostle Paul identifies as the approach required by his theological presuppositions. But it is also this approach that Dr. Wagner finds insufficient. Proclamation Evangelism focuses on obedience to God's call as a herald and leaves the results in the hands of the Holy Spirit—but Wagner argues that we must do more. We must have Persuasion Evangelism. "The bottom line," he says, "is how many disciples are made as the result of a given evangelistic effort."[6] To be sure, Professor Wagner wants to avoid manipulation: "I want to distance myself as far from that as possible. I do not approve the use of unfair or fraudulent influence to make people Christians."[7] Yet Wagner still insists on a persuasion-oriented definition of evangelism, one that emphasizes strategizing to achieve desired results. "I am goal-oriented," he says, "and I like the 'so to . . . that' [clauses in the definition]," the goal-oriented clauses that build the focus on results into the very definition of evangelism itself.[8]

A Response

If this is the stuff of the Church Growth movement, is it any wonder that your critics perceive you to be operating out of the persuader's stance that so alarmed the Apostle? Think for a moment about how out of step the above is with Paul's analysis of his own ministry. For Paul, issues of method were not simply up for grabs; his understanding of his methods was derived from, and thus profoundly anchored in, his understanding of God and of God's own methods in the world. What's more, Paul did not disavow the persuader's stance because it was immoral or manipulative; he rejected it because it was based on *a purely human dynamic that produced human results*. Has the Church Growth movement adequately come to grips with these issues?

Many of your critics think not. They find your notion of "consecrated pragmatism" facile and inadequate, indebted more to American consumerism than to a biblical theology. Suppose, for example, we were to apply your consecrated pragmatism standard to Paul's method. Did Paul's method "work"? In the vast majority of cases, apparently not. No one who had suffered with Paul from Philippi, to Thessalonica, to Berea, to Athens, to Corinth, would have concluded that his method was "working." The only thing it seemed to be "effectively and

---

[6]Wagner (1987, p. 122).
[7]Ibid., p. 127.
[8]Ibid., p. 130.

efficiently" accomplishing was more suffering for the Apostle. In fact, before the Lord himself appeared to Paul in Corinth and instructed him not to stop speaking, Paul was apparently ready to call it quits. Despite the tiny struggling congregations he left behind in a few cities, the great majority of those who listened to Paul along the way rejected him outright, finding his message unimpressive, absurd or even scandalous.

Should we, then, construe this as an indictment of Paul's method? Should we conclude that Paul's method was somehow the wrong one, worthy only of the trash heap? Only if we were operating out of the persuader's stance would we conclude such a thing. The truth is, Paul had agonized over these issues and had arrived at his methods for profoundly theological reasons. His methods were nothing less than *entailments* of his theology. Are we so thoroughly Americanized and so impoverished theologically that we cannot even *conceive* of such criteria playing a role in our methodological decisions? If the Apostle was so exercised about avoiding methods that engendered merely human results, why aren't we? How is it that we do not share Paul's reticence about wading into the realm of the Holy Spirit?

Paul's concern about our human potential for achieving merely human results appears to be lost on many growth gurus today. In their pragmatic rush to use whatever "works," they apparently assume that as long as they avoid the "immoral," the "unfair" or the "fraudulent" they are free to use any method to achieve their goals. But a concern to avoid the immoral, unfair and fraudulent scarcely rises above the pagans; noble-minded rhetoricians of Paul's day such as Quintilian would have concurred. As a standard for our methodological decision making in Christ's church, such concerns are necessary but insufficient. For a Christian there exists a crucial added dimension that the results-driven approach largely ignores. It is the concern for preempting the work of God by unduly crowding our human methods into the process.

Do we suppose this cannot happen? Paul knew better. In 1 Corinthians 1:17 he says, "For Christ did not send me to baptize but to preach the gospel, and not with words of eloquent wisdom, *lest the cross of Christ be emptied of its power.*" Later (1 Cor 2:5) he reminds the Corinthians that he very carefully chose his methods lest he wind up with a situation where their faith rested on his own human ingenuity rather than the Spirit's work. Can we allow Paul's warnings to register with us here for a moment? The issue in these passages was not the *content* of the gospel, which Paul affirms the Corinthians held fast; the issue was one of *methods*, methods that held the potential of either *displaying* or *displacing* the power of the cross. Can there be higher stakes?

With the stakes so high, one would think that discussions of the crucial issues would be widespread in Church Growth circles, and that Church Growth advocates would have become sophisticated over the years in evaluating various methods, not merely on their moral quality, but on their theological fit and their potential for engendering merely human results. Yet even summative works like Thom Rainer's *The Book of Church Growth* show little awareness that such issues even need to be addressed, much less finessed. Instead, one finds an enthusiastic and headlong endorsement of seemingly any and all morally acceptable methods that appear to "work," regardless of their source and regardless of their presuppositions.

While Paul was unwilling to base his approach to ministry on the pragmatic insights of classical rhetorical theory, the Church Growth movement seems to harbor no such reservations. In fact, the movement often appears to be sold out to classical rhetoric's closest modern counterpart, the world of advertising and marketing, and leans on it constantly for advice and strategy. Listen, for example, to George Barna, one of Church Growth's most commonly quoted sources:

> Most churches' inability to grow is not due to a lack of desire, or even a lack of resources. The truth is, we simply have not grasped the basic principles of marketing and applied them to the Church. The opportunities for successful church marketing are plentiful. All we as a community of believers need to do is gain a proper perspective on the Church and how it can be marketed effectively.[9]

What are the "basic principles" of marketing theory from which Mr. Barna will draw the insights for building Christ's church?

> To successfully market your product, you have to identify its prospective market. The key to market identification . . . is to be as specific as possible in selecting the audience to whom you will market the product. By matching the appeal of your product to the interests and needs of specific population segments, you can concentrate on getting your product to your best prospects without wasting resources on people who have no need or interest in your product.[10]

Here the thoughtful reader is bound to ask, In the light of such counsel, what should we make of Christ's parable of the sower? But Mr. Barna continues:

---

[9]Barna (1988, p. 40).
[10]Ibid., p. 42.

Without effective promotion, your product does not stand a chance of succeeding, because your target audience will either remain unaware of your product or will not have compelling reason to evaluate or try your product. Promotion is the way in which you persuade people that the product is available, worthy, a good value, and the way you explain how to acquire it.[11]

"Marketing, then," says Mr. Barna, "is a systematic series of active responses to existing conditions that is geared toward reaching specific goals." Hence one's "marketing plan" must outline "not just the marketing team's goals and objectives, but also the strategies and specific tactics by which they will satisfy their goals."[12]

These emphases are as old as the ancient Greeks. They are little more than echoes in our modern world of the very principles the Apostle repudiated as a basis for his approach to ministry. Paul's concern was not that these principles were evil; they need be no such thing. At its best the art of persuasion can be a splendid thing. In the hands of an honorable lawyer, politician or advertiser, persuasive techniques can be entirely appropriate. Paul's difficulty was not that these principles were inherently immoral but that *they were dependent on an essentially human dynamic*. They inserted the human agent into the process in an inappropriate way, potentially usurping the work of the Holy Spirit and generating false, merely human results.

Conclusion

This, then, is the issue I believe lies at the heart of much of the criticism of the Church Growth movement. In one way or another, despite your obvious and heartfelt commitment to Christ and his church, your critics perceive you to have committed a fundamental error of judgment. Like the ancient Corinthians, you are seen to have unwittingly embraced the persuader's stance in ministry without realizing that such a *modus operandi* is out of step with your own theology.

What can you do to blunt this criticism? Perhaps you do not care to. Perhaps your embracing of the persuader's stance is not unwitting, but rather is a conscious one, and you remain unconvinced there is anything inappropriate about it.

But if you do not approve of the persuader's stance as a basis for your ministry, then you will have to be much more careful in how you talk about some of the methodological issues. Prove your critics wrong by repudiating with Paul the persuader's role. Show yourselves to be *obedience* driven, not *results* driven.

---

[11]Ibid., p. 43.
[12]Ibid., p. 44.

By all means make plans and focus on goals, but resist stating your goals in terms of the *results* you want to achieve. Instead, state your goals in terms of *what God has called you to be and to do*, and then state your plans in terms of *how you intend to be that and do that*, leaving the results to the Lord. If you were to make this simple but dramatic shift, it would keep your efforts properly focused, and much of the criticism of the Church Growth movement would simply fade away, leaving the good that you do to speak for itself.

Works Cited

Abbott-Smith, G. (1921). *A Manual Greek Lexicon of the New Testament.* Edinburgh: T & T Clark.

Adams, Edward, and David G. Horrell, eds. (2004). *Christianity at Corinth: The Quest for the Pauline Church.* Louisville: Westminster John Knox Press.

Adams, Sean A. (2008). "Crucifixion in the Ancient World: A Response to L. L. Welborn." In *Paul's World,* edited by Stanley E. Porter, pp. 111-29. Leiden: Brill.

Aernie, Jeffrey W. (2012). *Is Paul Also Among the Prophets? An Examination of the Relationship Between Paul and the Old Testament Prophetic Tradition in 2 Corinthians.* London: T & T Clark.

Alexander, Loveday. (1995). "Paul and the Hellenistic Schools: The Evidence of Galen." In *Paul in His Hellenistic Context,* edited by Troels Engberg-Pedersen, pp. 60-83. Minneapolis: Fortress.

Amador, J. D. H. (1999). "Interpretive Unicity: The Drive Toward Monological (Monotheistic) Rhetoric." In *The Rhetorical Interpretation of Scripture,* edited by Stanley E. Porter and Dennis L. Stamps, pp. 48-62. JSNT Supplement 180. Sheffield: Sheffield Academic Press.

Anderson, Graham. (1993). *The Second Sophistic: A Cultural Phenomenon in the Roman Empire.* London: Routledge.

Anderson, R. Dean, Jr. (1998). *Ancient Rhetorical Theory and Paul.* Rev. ed. Leuven: Peeters.

Anderson, Raymond. (1963). "Kierkegaard's Theory of Communication." *Speech Monographs* 30 (1): 1-14.

Andrews, M. E. (1934). "Paul, Philo, and the Intellectuals." *Journal of Biblical Literature* 53 (2): 150-69.

Archer, David. (2010). *The Global Carbon Cycle.* Princeton: Princeton University Press.

Augustine, Saint. (1886). *The City of God.* In *A Select Library of the Nicene and Post-Nicene Fathers of the Christian Church.* Edited by Philip Schaff. Buffalo: The Christian Literature Co.

Aune, David Charles. (2008). "Passions in the Pauline Epistles: The Current

State of Research." In *Passions and Moral Progress in Greco-Roman Thought*, edited by John T. Fitzgerald, pp. 221-37. London: Routledge.
Baird, William. (1957). "What Is the Kerygma? A Study of 1 Cor 15:3-8 and Gal 1:11-17." *Journal of Biblical Literature* 76 (3): 181-91.
———. (1959). "Among the Mature: The Idea of Wisdom in I Corinthians 2:6." *Interpretation* 13 (4): 425-32.
———. (1990). "'One Against the Other': Intra-Church Conflict in 1 Corinthians." In *The Conversation Continues: Studies in Paul and John in Honor of J. Louis Martyn*," edited by Robert T. Fortna and Beverly R. Gaventa, pp. 116-36. Nashville: Abingdon Press.
Ballard, C. Andrew. (2014). "Tongue-tied and Taunted: Paul, Poor Rhetoric and Paltry Leadership in 2 Corinthians." *Journal for the Study of the New Testament* 37 (1): 50-70.
Barclay, John M. G. (1992). "Thessalonica and Corinth: Social Contrasts in Pauline Christianity." *Journal for the Study of the New Testament* 47: 49-47.
Barna, George. (1988). *Marketing the Church*. Colorado Springs: NavPress.
Barrett, C. K. (1968). *A Commentary on the First Epistle to the Corinthians*. Harper's New Testament Commentaries. New York: Harper and Row. 2nd ed., 1971. London: Adam and Charles Black.
———. (1970). *The Signs of an Apostle*. London: Epworth.
———. (1973). *A Commentary on the Second Epistle to the Corinthians*. London: Adam and Charles Black.
———. (1980). Comments in "Discussione." In *Paolo a una Chiesa Divisa (1 Cor 1–4)*, passim. Serie Monografica di Benedictina, 5. Edited by L. DeLorenzi. Rome: S. Paolo.
———. (1982). *Essays on Paul*. London: SPCK.
———. (1987). "Proclamation and Response." In *Tradition and Interpretation in the New Testament: Essays in Honor of E. Earle Ellis*, edited by Gerald F. Hawthorne and Otto Betz, pp. 3-15. Grand Rapids: Eerdmans.
Bauer, W. (1979). *A Greek-English Lexicon of the New Testament and Other Early Christian Literature*. 2nd edition. Translated and adapted by W. F. Arndt and F. W. Gingrich. Revised by F. W. Gingrich and F. W. Danker. Chicago: University of Chicago Press.
Baumann, Rolf. (1968). *Mitte und Norm des Christlichen: Eine Auslegung von 1 Korinther 1,1-3,4*. Munich: Aschendorff.
Baur, F. C. (1863). *Kirchengeschichte der drei ersten Jahrhunderte*. Tübingen: L. F. Fues.

———. (2001). *Paul the Apostle of Jesus Christ: His Life and Works, His Epistles and Teachings*. 2 vols. Peabody, MA: Hendrickson; reprinted 2003.

Beardslee, William A. (1994). "What Is It About? Reference in New Testament Literary Criticism." In *The New Literary Criticism and the New Testament*, edited by Edgar V. McKnight and Elizabeth Struthers Malbon, pp. 367-86. Sheffield: Sheffield Academic Press.

Best, Ernest. (1980). "The Power and the Wisdom of God: 1 Corinthians 1.18-25." In *Paolo a una Chiesa Divisa (1 Cor 1-4)*, pp. 9-39. Serie Monografica di Benedictina 5. Edited by L. De Lorenzi. Rome: S. Paolo.

Betz, Hans Deiter. (1975). "The Literary Composition and Function of Paul's Letter to the Galatians." *New Testament Studies* 21 (3): 353-79.

———. (1986). "The Problem of Rhetoric and Theology According to the Apostle Paul." In *L'Apôtre Paul: personnalité, style et conception du ministère*. Edited by A. Vanhoye. Leuven: Leuven University Press.

Bird, Michael F. (2008). "Reassessing a Rhetorical Approach to Paul's Letters." *Expository Times* 119 (8): 379.

Bitzer, Lloyd F. (1974). "The Rhetorical Situation." In *Rhetoric: A Tradition in Transition*, edited by W. R. Fisher, pp. 247-60. Lansing: Michigan State University Press.

Black, David Alan. (1984). *Paul, Apostle of Weakness: Astheneia and Its Cognates in the Pauline Literature*. New York: Peter Lang.

Blass, F., and A. Debrunner. (1961). *A Greek Grammar of the New Testament and Other Early Christian Literature*. Translated and revised by R. W. Funk. Cambridge: Cambridge University Press.

Bloomer, W. Martin. (2011). *The School of Rome: Latin Studies and the Origins of Liberal Education*. Berkeley: University of California Press.

Booth, Wayne C. (1963). "The Rhetorical Stance." *College Composition and Communication* 14 (3): 139-45.

Bornkamm, Günther. (1958). "Faith and Reason in Paul's Epistles." *New Testament Studies* 4 (2): 73-100.

———. (1966) "The Missionary Stance of Paul in 1 Corinthians 9 and in Acts." In *Studies in Luke-Acts*, edited by L. E. Keck and J. L. Martin, pp. 194-207. Nashville: Abingdon Press.

———. (1969). "Faith and Reason in Paul." In *Early Christian Experience*, pp. 29-46. Translated by P. L. Hammer. London: SCM Press.

Bouyer, Louis. (1990). *The Christian Mystery: From Pagan Myth to Christian Mysticism*. Translated by Illtyd Trethowan. Petersham, MA: Saint Bede's Publications.

Bowersock, G. W. (1969). *Greek Sophists in the Roman Empire*. Oxford: Clarendon Press.

Breytenbach, Cilliers. (2009). "Explaining the Foolishness of the Cross (1 Cor 1:18): New Material on the Origin of Paul's Metaphors on the Death of Christ." In *Saint Paul and Corinth: 150 Years Since the Writing of the Epistles to the Corinthians*. International Scholarly Conference Proceedings, vol. 1, pp. 347-56. Edited by Constantine J. Belezos. Athens: Psichogios Publications.

Briggs, Richard S. (2001). "The Uses of Speech-Act Theory in Biblical Interpretation." *Current Research: Biblical Studies* 9: 229-76.

Brockriede, Wayne E. (1955). "Bentham's Criticisms of Rhetoric and Rhetoricians." *Quarterly Journal of Speech* 41 (4): 377-82.

Broneer, Oscar. (1937). "Studies in the Topography of Corinth at the Time of St. Paul." *ARKHAIOLOGIKE EPHEMERIS*, 125-33.

———. (1939). "An Official Rescript from Corinth." *Hesperia* 8 (2): 181-90.

———. (1951). "Corinth: Center of Paul's Missionary Work in Greece." *Biblical Archaeologist* 14 (4): 78-96.

Brookins, Tim. (2010). "Rhetoric and Philosophy in the First Century: Their Relation with Respect to 1 Corinthians 1-4." *Neotestamentica* 44 (2): 233-52.

———. (2011). "The Wise Corinthians: Their Stoic Education and Outlook." *The Journal of Theological Studies* 62 (1): 51-76.

Brown, Peter. (1992). *Power and Persuasion in Late Antiquity: Towards a Christian Empire*. Madison: University of Wisconsin Press.

Brown, Raymond E. (1958). "The Semitic Background of the New Testament Mysterion (1)." *Biblica* 39 (4): 426-48.

Bruce, F. F. (1971). *1 and 2 Corinthians*. New Century Bible. London: Oliphants.

———. (1975). "Apollos in the New Testament." *Ekklesiastikos Pharos* 57: 354-66.

———. (1979). *Men and Movements in the Primitive Church*. Exeter: Paternoster.

Bryant, Donald C. (1974). "Rhetoric: Its Functions and Its Scope." In *Rhetoric: A Tradition in Transition*, edited by W. R. Fisher, pp. 195-230. Lansing: Michigan State University Press.

Bullinger, E. W. (1898). *Figures of Speech Used in the Bible*. London: Eyre & Spottiswoode.

Bullmore, Michael. (1995). *St. Paul's Theology of Rhetorical Style: An Examination of 1 Corinthians 2.1-5 in the Light of First Century Graeco-Roman Rhetorical Culture*. San Francisco: International Scholars Publications.

Bultmann, Rudolf. (1965). "πείθω." In *Theological Dictionary of the New Tes-

tament, edited by G. Kittel, translated by G. W. Bromiley, vol. 6, pp. 1-11. Grand Rapids: Eerdmans.

Caird, G. B. (1980). *The Language and Imagery of the Bible*. Philadelphia: Westminster Press.

Calvin, John. (1960). *The First Epistle of Paul the Apostle to the Corinthians; Calvin's Commentaries*. Translated by J. W. Fraser. Edited by D. W. Torrance and T. F. Torrance. Edinburgh: Oliver and Boyd.

Carson, Donald A. (1984). *From Triumphalism to Maturity: An Exposition of 2 Corinthians 10-13*. Grand Rapids: Baker.

Cavadini, John C. (1995). "The Sweetness of the Word: Salvation and Rhetoric in Augustine's *De doctrina christiana*." In *De doctrina christiana: A Classic of Western Culture*. Edited by Duane W. H. Arnold and Pamela Bright. Notre Dame, IN: University of Notre Dame Press.

Chadwick, Henry, trans. (1953). *Origen: Contra Celsum*. Cambridge: Cambridge University Press.

———. (1965–1966). "St. Paul and Philo of Alexandria." *Bulletin of the John Rylands Library* 48: 186-307.

Chance, J. Bradley. (1982). "Paul's Apology to the Corinthians." *Perspectives in Religious Studies* 9 (2): 144-55.

Chapman, David W. (2008). *Ancient Jewish and Christian Perceptions of Crucifixion*. Grand Rapids: Baker Academic.

Chester, Stephen J. (2003). *Conversion at Corinth: Perspectives on Conversion in Paul's Theology and the Corinthian Church*. London: T & T Clark.

Chevallier, Max-Alain. (1966). *Esprit de Dieu, Paroles d'Hommes*. Neuchatel: Delachaux Niestlé.

Ciampa, Roy E., and Brian S. Rosner. (2010). *The First Letter to the Corinthians*. Grand Rapids: Eerdmans.

Clarke, Andrew D. (2006). *Secular and Christian Leadership in Corinth: A Socio-Historical and Exegetical Study of 1 Corinthians 1-6*. Milton Keyes: Paternoster.

Classen, Carl Joachim. (1991). "Paulus und Die Antike Rhetorik." *Zeitschrift für die Neutestamentliche Wissenschaft* 82 (1-2): 1-33.

———. (1992). "St. Paul's Epistles and Ancient Greek and Roman Rhetoric." *Rhetorica* 10 (4): 319-44. Reprinted in (1993) *Rhetoric and the New Testament: Essays from the 1992 Heidelberg Conference*, edited by Stanley E. Porter and Thomas H. Olbricht, pp. 265-91. Sheffield: JSOT Press.

———. (2002). *Rhetorical Criticism of the New Testament*. Leiden: Brill, 2002.

Coenen, Lothar. (1990). "Κηρύσσω." In *Theologisches Befriffslexikon zum Neun*

Testament, edited by Lothar Coenen, Erich Beyreuther and Hans Bietenhard, vol. 2, pp. 1276-83. Wuppertal: R. Brockhaus.

Collins, Raymond F. (1999). *First Corinthians*. Collegeville, MN: The Liturgical Press.

Connor, W. R. (1971). *The New Politicians of the Fifth-Century Athens*. Princeton: Princeton University Press.

Conzelmann, Hans. (1969). *An Outline of the Theology of the New Testament*. Translated by J. Bowden. London: SCM Press.

———. (1973). *History of Primitive Christianity*. Translated by J. E. Steely. London: Darton, Longman and Todd.

———. (1975). *1 Corinthians*. Hermeneia Series. Translated by J. W. Leitch. Philadelphia: Fortress.

Corcoran, Paul E. (1979). *Political Language and Rhetoric*. St. Lucia, Queensland: University of Queensland Press.

Costa, Tony. (2013). "'Is Saul of Tarsus Also Among the Prophets?' Paul's Calling as Prophetic Divine Commissioning." In *Christian Origins and Hellenistic Judaism: Social and Literary Contexts for the New Testament*, edited by Stanley E. Porter and Andrew W. Pitts, pp. 203-35. Leiden: Brill.

Crouch, Frank. (1996). "The Persuasive Moment: Rhetorical Resolutions in Paul's Defense Before Agrippa." *Society of Biblical Literature Seminar Papers* 35: 333-42. Atlanta: Scholars Press.

Cullmann, Oscar. (1950). "'Kyrios' as Designation for the Oral Tradition Concerning Jesus." *Scottish Journal of Theology* 3 (2): 180-97.

Dahl, Nils A. (1967). "Paul and the Church at Corinth According to 1 Corinthians 1:10–4:21." In *Christian History and Interpretation: Studies Presented to John Knox*, edited by W. R. Farmer, C. F. D. Moule and R. R. Niebuhr, pp. 313-35. Cambridge: Cambridge University Press.

———. (1977). *Studies in Paul: Theology for the Early Christian Mission*. Minneapolis: Augsburg.

Davis, James A. (1984). *Wisdom and Spirit: An Investigation of I Corinthians 1:17–3:20 Against the Background of Jewish Sapiential Tradition in the Hellenistic Period*. Lanham, MD: University Press of America.

De Boer, Martinus C. (1994). "The Composition of 1 Corinthians." *New Testament Studies* 40 (2): 229-45.

Deissmann, Adolf. (1901). *Bible Studies: Contributions Chiefly from Papyri and Inscriptions to the History of the Language, the Literature and the Religion of Hellenistic Judaism and Primitive Christianity*. Edinburgh: T & T Clark.

———. (1907). *New Light on the New Testament, from Records of the Graeco-*

Roman Period. Edinburgh: T & T Clark.

Delling, G. (1972). "τέλειος." In *Theological Dictionary of the New Testament*, edited by G. Kittel, translated by G. W. Bromily, vol. 8, pp. 67-78. Grand Rapids: Eerdmans.

DeWitt, N. W. (1954). *St. Paul and Epicurus*. Minneapolis: University of Minnesota Press.

Dibelius, Martin. (1953). *Paul*. Edited by W. G. Kümmel. Translated by F. Clarke. London: Longmans, Green and Co.

Dickson, John P. (2003). *Mission-Commitment in Ancient Judaism and in the Pauline Communities*. Tübingen: Mohr Siebeck.

Dodd, C. H. (1936). *The Apostolic Preaching and Its Developments*. New York: Harper.

Dominik, William J. (1997). "The Style Is the Man: Seneca, Tacitus and Quintilian's Canon." In *Roman Eloquence: Rhetoric in Society and Literature*, edited by William J. Dominik, pp. 150-68. London: Routledge.

Doty, William G. (1972). *Contemporary New Testament Interpretation*. Englewood Cliffs, NJ: Prentice-Hall.

Dover, K. J. (1974). *Greek Popular Morality in the Time of Plato and Aristotle*. Oxford: Basil Blackwell.

Du Toit, Andreas B. (1989). "Persuasion in Romans 1:1-17." *Biblische Zeitschrift* 33 (2): 192-209.

———. (2000). "A Tale of Two Cities: 'Tarsus or Jerusalem.'" *New Testament Studies* 46 (3): 375-402.

Duhamel, Albert P. (1965). "The Function of Rhetoric as Effective Expression." In *Philosophy, Rhetoric and Argumentation*, edited by Maurice Natanson and Henry W. Johnstone Jr., pp. 80-92. University Park: Pennsylvania State University Press.

Dunn, James D. G. (1995). *1 Corinthians*. Sheffield: Sheffield Academic Press.

———. (1996). Review of Saint Paul's Theology of Preaching. *Epworth Review* 23 (1): 116-17.

———. (2004). "Reconstructions of Corinthian Christianity and the Interpretation of 1 Corinthians." In *Christianity at Corinth: The Quest for the Pauline Church*, edited by Edward Adams and David G. Horrell, pp. 295-310. Louisville, KY: Westminster John Knox Press.

Dutch, Robert S. (2005). *The Educated Elite in 1 Corinthians: Education and Community Conflict in Graeco-Roman Context*. London: T & T Clark.

Ellingworth, Paul, and Howard Hatton. (1985). *A Translator's Handbook on*

Paul's First Letter to the Corinthians. London: United Bible Societies.

Ellis, Earle. (1978). *Prophecy and Hermeneutic in Early Christianity: New Testament Essays*. Tübingen: J. C. B. Mohr.

Engberg-Pedersen, Troels. (2000). *Paul and the Stoics*. Edinburgh: T & T Clark.

———. (2008). "The Logic of Action in Paul: How Does He Differ from the Moral Philosophers on Spiritual and Moral Progression and Regression?" In *Passions and Moral Progress in Greco-Roman Thought*, edited by John T. Fitzgerald, pp. 238-66. London: Routledge.

Enos, Theresa, ed. (1996). *Encyclopedia of Rhetoric and Composition*. New York: Routledge.

Eriksson, Anders. (1998). *Traditions as Rhetorical Proof: Pauline Argumentation in 1 Corinthians*. Stockholm: Almqvist & Wiksell International.

Evans, C. F. (1956). "The Kerygma." *Journal of Theological Studies*, New Series 7 (1): 25-41.

Evans, Craig A. (1981). "'Preacher' and 'Preaching': Some Lexical Observations." *Journal of the Evangelical Theological Society* 24 (4): 315-22.

Fantham, Elaine. (1997). "The Contexts and Occasions of Roman Public Rhetoric." In *Roman Eloquence: Rhetoric in Society and Literature*, edited by William J. Dominik, pp. 111-28. London: Routledge.

Fee, Gordon D. (1987). *The First Epistle to the Corinthians*. The New International Commentary on the New Testament. Edited by F. F. Bruce. Grand Rapids: Eerdmans.

———. (1994). "Another Gospel Which You Did Not Embrace." In *Gospel in Paul: Studies on Corinthians, Galatians, and Romans for Richard N. Longenecker*, edited by L. Ann Jervis and Peter Richardson, pp. 111-33. JSNT Supplement Series 108. Sheffield: Sheffield Academic Press.

———. (2007). *Pauline Christology: An Exegetical-Theological Study*. Peabody, MA: Hendrickson.

Findlay, George G. (1900). *St. Paul's First Epistle to the Corinthians*. In *The Expositor's Greek Testament*. London: n.p. Reprint, Grand Rapids: Eerdmans, 1961.

Finney, Mark T. (2010). "Honor, Rhetoric and Factionalism in the Ancient World: 1 Corinthians 1-4 in Its Social Context." *Biblical Theology Bulletin* 40 (1): 27-36.

Fiore, Benjamin. (1985). "'Covert Allusion' in 1 Corinthians 1-4." *Catholic Biblical Quarterly* 47 (1): 85-102.

Fiorenza, Elisabeth Schüssler. (2005). "Disciplinary Matters: A Critical Rhetoric and Ethic of Inquiry." In *Rhetoric, Ethic, and Moral Persuasion in Biblical*

Discourse: Essays from the 2002 Heidelberg Conference, edited by Thomas H. Olbricht and Anders Eriksson, pp. 9-32. New York: T & T Clark.

———. (2007). *Scripture and the Rhetoric of Empire*. Minneapolis: Fortress.

Fitzmyer, Joseph A. (1998). *To Advance the Gospel: New Testament Studies*. 2nd ed. Grand Rapids: Eerdmans.

Forbes, Christopher. (2003). "Paul and Rhetorical Comparison." In *Paul in the Greco-Roman World: A Handbook*. Edited by J. Paul Sampley. Harrisburg, PA: Trinity Press International.

———. (2010). "Ancient Rhetoric and Ancient Letters: Models for Reading Paul, and Their Limits." In *Paul and Rhetoric*, edited by J. Paul Sampley and Peter Lampe, pp. 143-60. London: T & T Clark.

Fortin, Ernest L. (2008). "Augustine and the Problem of Christian Rhetoric." In *The Rhetoric of Saint Augustine of Hippo: De Doctrina Christiana and the Search for a Distinctly Christian Rhetoric*, edited by Richard Leo Enos and Roger Thompson, pp. 219-33. Waco, TX: Baylor University Press.

Frank, Glenn. (1919). "The Parliament of the People." *The Century Magazine* 98: 401-16.

Freese, John Henry, trans. (1925). *The "Art" of Rhetoric*, by Aristotle. Loeb Classical Library. Cambridge, MA: Harvard University Press.

Frestadius, Simo. (2011). "The Spirit and Wisdom in 1 Corinthians 2:1-13." *Journal of Biblical and Pneumatological Research* 3: 52-70.

Friedrich, Gerhard. (1965). "κῆρυξ, κηρύσσω, κήρυγμα." In *Theological Dictionary of the New Testament*, edited by G. Kittel, translated by G. W. Bromiley, vol. 3, pp. 683-719. Grand Rapids: Eerdmans.

Furnish, Victor P. (1963). "Prophets, Apostles, and Preachers: A Study of the Biblical Concept of Preaching." *Interpretation* 17: 48-60.

———.(2009). *Theology and Ethics in Paul*. Louisville: Westminster John Knox.

Gärtner, Bertil E. (1968). "The Pauline and Johanine Idea of 'to Know God' Against the Hellenistic Background." *New Testament Studies* 14 (2): 209-31.

Gillespie, Thomas W. (1990). "Interpreting the Kerygma: Early Christian Prophecy According to 1 Corinthians 2:6-16." In *Gospel Origins and Christian Beginnings: In Honor of James M. Robinson*, edited by James E. Goehring, Charles W. Hedrick and Jack T. Sanders, pp. 151-66. Sonoma, CA: Polebridge Press.

Gitay, Yehoshua. (1991). "Rhetorical Criticism and the Prophetic Discourse." In *Persuasive Artistry: Studies in New Testament Rhetoric in Honor of George A. Kennedy*, edited by Duane F. Watson, pp. 13-24. Sheffield: Sheffield Academic Press.

Given, Mark D. (2001*). Paul's True Rhetoric: Ambiguity, Cunning, and Deception* *in Greece and Rome*. Emory Studies in Early Christianity 7. Harrisburg, PA: Trinity Press International.

Glover, T. R. (1925). *Paul of Tarsus*. London: Student Christian Movement.

———. (1945). *Springs of Hellas and Other Essays*. Cambridge: Cambridge University Press.

Godet, F. L. (1886). *Commentary on St. Paul's First Epistle to the Corinthians*. Translated by A. Cusin. 2 vols. Edinburgh: T. & T. Clark.

Goldammer, Kurt. (1957). "Der Kerygma-Begriff in der ältesten christlichen Literatur." *Zeitschrift für die neutestamentliche Wissenschaft* 48 (1): 77-101.

Gooch, Paul W. (1987). *Partial Knowledge: Philosophical Studies in Paul*. Notre Dame, IN: University of Notre Dame Press.

Goodenough, E. R. (1962). *Introduction to Philo Judaeus*. 2nd ed. Oxford: Basil Blackwell.

Gorman, Michael J. (2004). *Apostle of the Crucified Lord: A Theological Introduction to Paul and His Letters*. Grand Rapids: Eerdmans.

Goulder, Michael D. (1991). "Σοφία in 1 Corinthians." *New Testament Studies* 37 (4): 516-34.

———. (2001). *Paul and the Competing Mission in Corinth*. Peabody, MA: Hendrickson.

Graindor, P. (1930). *Un Milliardaire Antique: Hérode Atticus et sa Famille*. Cairo: n.p.

Grant, Robert M. (1951). "The Wisdom of the Corinthians." In *The Joy of Study: Papers on New Testament and Related Subjects Presented to Honor Frederick Clifton Grant*, edited by S. E. Johnson, pp. 51-55. New York: Macmillan.

Grass, Tim. (2012). *F. F. Bruce: A Life*. Grand Rapids: Eerdmans.

Grassi, Ernesto. (1980). *Rhetoric as Philosophy: The Humanist Tradition*. Translated by John Michael Krois and Azizeh Azodi. Carbondale: Southern Illinois University Press.

Graves, Michael. (2010). "The Literary Quality of Scripture as Seen by the Early Church." *Tyndale Bulletin* 61 (2): 161-82.

Green, R. P. H., trans. (1997). *On Christian Teaching*, by Augustine. Oxford: Oxford University Press.

Grindheim, Sigurd. (2002). "Wisdom for the Perfect: Paul's Challenge to the Corinthian Church (1 Corinthians 2:6-16)." *Journal of Biblical Literature* 121 (4): 689-709.

Grosheide, F. W. (1954). *Commentary on the First Epistle to the Corinthians*. 2nd ed. London: Marshall, Morgan and Scott.

Gupta, Nijay K. (2009). "The Theo-Logic of Paul's Ethics in Recent Research:

Crosscurrents and Future Directions in Scholarship in the Last Forty Years." *Currents in Biblical Research* 7 (3): 336-61.

Guthrie, W. K. C. (1971). *The Sophists*. Cambridge: Cambridge University Press.

Gwynn, Aubrey. (1926). *Roman Education from Cicero to Quintilian*. Oxford: Clarendon Press.

Habinek, Thomas. (2005). *Ancient Rhetoric and Oratory*. Oxford: Blackwell.

Hall, David R. (2003). *The Unity of the Corinthian Correspondence*. London: T & T Clark.

Hanson, A. T. (1980). *The New Testament Interpretation of Scripture*. London: SPCK.

Harris, William V. (1989). *Ancient Literacy*. Cambridge, MA: Harvard University Press.

Harvey, A. E. (1968). "The Opposition to St. Paul." *Studia Evangelica*, edited by F. L. Cross, vol. IV, pp. 319-32. Texte und Untersuchungen zur Geschichte der altchristlichen Literatur 102. Berlin: Akademie.

Hauser, Alan J., and Duane F. Watson, eds. (1994). *Rhetorical Criticism of the Bible: A Comprehensive Bibliography with Notes on History and Method*. Leiden: E. J. Brill.

Hays, Richard. (1997). *First Corinthians*. Louisville, KY: John Knox.

Heinrici, C. F. G. (1896). *Der erste Brief und die Korinther: Kritisch-exegetischer Kommentar über das Neue Testament*. 8th ed. Göttingen: Vandenhoeck und Ruprecht.

Henderson, Ian. (2011). "The Second Sophistic and Non-Elite Speakers." In *Perceptions of the Second Sophistic and Its Times*, edited by Thomas Schmidt and Pascale Fleury, pp. 23-35. Toronto: University of Toronto Press.

Hengel, Martin. (1977a). *Christ and Power*. Translated by E. R. Kalin. Philadelphia: Fortress.

———. (1977b). *Crucifixion in the Ancient World and the Folly of the Message of the Cross*. Translated by J. Bowden. Philadelphia: Fortress.

———. (1989). *The "Hellenization" of Judaea in the First Century After Christ*. London: SCM Press.

———. (1991). *The Pre-Christian Paul*. London: SCM Press.

Hock, Ronald F. (1978). "Paul's Tentmaking and the Problem of His Social Class." *Journal of Biblical Literature* 97 (4): 555-64.

———. (1979). "The Workshop as a Social Setting for Paul's Missionary Preaching." *Catholic Biblical Quarterly* 41 (3): 438-50.

———. (1980). *The Social Context of Paul's Ministry: Tentmaking and Apostleship*. Philadelphia: Fortress.

———. (2003). "Paul and Greco-Roman Education." In *Paul in the Greco-Roman World: A Handbook*, edited by J. Paul Sampley, pp. 198-227. Harrisburg, PA: Trinity Press International.

———. (2008). "The Problem of Paul's Social Class: Further Reflections." In *Paul's World*, edited by Stanley E. Porter, pp. 7-18. Leiden: Brill.

Horrell, David G. (1996). *The Social Ethos of the Corinthian Correspondence: Interest and Ideology from 1 Corinthians to 1 Clement*. Edinburgh: T & T Clark.

Horsley, Richard A. (1977). "Wisdom of Word and Words of Wisdom in Corinth." *Catholic Biblical Quarterly* 39 (2): 224-39.

———. (1978). "'How Can Some of You Say That There Is No Resurrection of the Dead?': Spiritual Elitism in Corinth." *Novum Testamentum* 20, Fasc. 3: 203-31.

Hudson, Hoyt H. (1965). "The Field of Rhetoric." In *Philosophy, Rhetoric and Argumentation*, edited by Maurice Natanson and Henry W. Johnstone Jr., pp. 20-31. University Park: Pennsylvania State University Press.

Hunter, A. M. (1943). *The Unity of the New Testament*. London: SCM Press.

Hurd, J. C. (1965). *The Origin of 1 Corinthians*. London: SPCK.

———. (1967). "Pauline Chronology and Pauline Theology." In *Christian History and Interpretation: Studies Presented to John Knox*, edited by W. R. Farmer, C. F. D. Moule and R. R. Niebuhr, pp. 225-48. Cambridge: Cambridge University Press.

Inkelaar, Harm-Jan. (2011). *Conflict over Wisdom: The Theme of 1 Corinthians 1–4 Rooted in Scripture*. Leuven: Peeters.

Jaeger, Werner. (1945). *Paideia: The Ideals of Greek Culture*. Translated by G. Highet. Oxford: Basil Blackwell.

Jasinski, James, ed. (2001). *Sourcebook on Rhetoric: Key Concepts in Contemporary Rhetorical Studies*. Thousand Oaks, CA: Sage Publications.

Jasper, David. (1990). "'In the Sermon Which I Have Just Completed, Wherever I Said Aristotle, I Meant Saint Paul.'" In *The Bible as Rhetoric: Studies in Biblical Persuasion and Credibility*, edited by Martin Warner, pp. 133-52. London: Routledge.

Johnstone, Henry W., Jr. (1959). *Philosophy and Argument*. University Park: Pennsylvania State University Press.

———. (1965). "Persuasion and Validity in Philosophy." In *Philosophy, Rhetoric and Argumentation*, edited by Maurice Natanson and Henry W. Johnstone Jr., pp. 138-48. University Park: Pennsylvania State University Press.

———. (1982). "Bilaterality in Argument and Communication." In *Advances in Argumentation Theory and Research*, edited by J. Robert Cox and Charles Arthur Willard, pp. 95-102. Carbondale: Southern Illinois University Press.

Jones, A. H. M. (1940). *The Greek City from Alexander to Justinian*. Oxford: Clarendon Press.

———. (1960). "The Roman Civil Service (Clerical and Sub-Clerical Grades)." In *Studies in Roman Government and Law*, pp. 153-75. New York: Barnes and Noble.

Judge, E. A. (1968). "Paul's Boasting in Relation to Contemporary Professional Practice." *Australian Biblical Review* 16 (1): 37-50.

———. (1960–1961). "The Early Christians as a Scholastic Community." *Journal of Religious History* 1 (3): 4-15, 125-37.

———. (1983). "The Reaction Against Classical Education in the New Testament." *Journal of Christian Education*, Papers 77: 7-14.

Kaibel, G. (1878). *Epigrammata Graeca*. Berlin: G. Reimer.

Kammler, Hans-Christian. (2003). *Kreuz und Weisheit: Eine exegetische Untersuchung zu 1 Kor 1,10-3,4*. Tübingen: Mohr Siebeck.

Kant, Immanuel. (1952). *The Critique of Judgement: Part I, Critique of Aesthetic Judgement*. Translated by James Creed Meredith. Oxford: Clarendon Press.

Karlins, Marvin, and Herbert Abelson. (1970). *Persuasion*. New York: Springer.

Kaster, Robert A. (1988). *Guardians of Language: The Grammarian and Society in Late Antiquity*. Berkeley: University of California Press.

Keil, Henrich, ed. (1857). *Grammatici Latini*. Leipzig: B. G. Teubner.

Kennedy, George A. (1963). *The Art of Persuasion in Greece*. London: Routledge and Kegan Paul.

———. (1972). *The Art of Rhetoric in the Roman World*. Princeton: Princeton University Press.

———. (1980). *Classical Rhetoric and Its Christian and Secular Tradition from Ancient to Modern Times*. Chapel Hill: North Carolina University Press.

———. (1984). *New Testament Interpretation Through Rhetorical Criticism*. Chapel Hill: University of North Carolina Press.

———. (1990). "'Truth' and 'Rhetoric' in the Pauline Epistles." In *The Bible as Rhetoric: Studies in Biblical Persuasion and Credibility*, edited by Martin Warner, pp. 195-202. London: Routledge.

———. (1994). *A New History of Classical Rhetoric*. Princeton: Princeton University Press.

———. (2001). "Historical Survey of Rhetoric." In *Handbook of Classical Rhetoric in the Hellenistic Period, 33 B.C.–A.D. 400*, edited by Stanley E. Porter, pp. 3-41. Leiden: Brill.

Ker, Donald P. (2000). "Paul and Apollos—Colleagues or Rivals?" *Journal for the Study of the New Testament* 22 (77): 75-97.

Kerényi, Karl. (1962). *The Religion of the Greeks and Romans*. Translated by C. Holme. London: Thames and Hudson.

Kerferd, G. B. (1981). *The Sophistic Movement*. Cambridge: Cambridge University Press.

Kern, Philip. (1998). *Rhetoric and Galatians: Assessing an Approach to Paul's Epistles*. SNTSMS 101. Cambridge: Cambridge University Press.

Kimball, Bruce A. (1995). *Orators and Philosophers: A History of the Idea of Liberal Education*. New York: The College Board.

Kinneavy, James L. (1987). *Greek Rhetorical Origins of Christian Faith: An Inquiry*. New York: Oxford University Press.

Knox, R. A. (1950). *Enthusiasm: A Chapter in the History of Religion, with Special Reference to the Seventeenth and Eighteenth Centuries*. New York: Oxford University Press.

Knox, W. L. (1925). *St Paul and the Church of Jerusalem*. Cambridge: Cambridge University Press.

———. (1937). "Pharisaism and Hellenism." In *Judaism and Christianity*, vol. 2 of *The Contact of Pharisaism and Other Culture*, edited by H. Loewe, pp. 61-111. London: Sheldon Press.

———. (1939). *St Paul and the Church of the Gentiles*. Cambridge: Cambridge University Press.

Kolbert, Paul. R. (2006). "Formal Continuities Between Augustine's Early Philosophical Teaching and Late Homiletical Practice." In *Studia Patristica*, XLIII, edited by F. Young, M. Edwards and P. Parvis, pp. 149-54. Leuven: Peeters.

Krentz, Edgar. (2003). "Logos or Sophia: The Pauline Use of the Ancient Dispute Between Rhetoric and Philosophy." In *Early Christianity and Classical Culture: Comparative Studies in Honor of Abraham J. Malherbe*, edited by John T. Fitzgerald, Thomas H. Olbricht and L. Michael White, pp. 277-90. Leiden: Brill.

Kümmel, Werner G. (1965). *Introduction to the New Testament*. 14th ed. Translated by A. J. Mattill Jr. Nashville: Abingdon.

Kwon, Oh-Young. (2010). "A Critical Review of Recent Scholarship on the Pauline Opposition and the Nature of Its Wisdom (σοφία) in 1 Corinthians 1–4." *Currents in Biblical Research* 8 (3): 386-427.

Labberton, Mark. (2014). *Called: The Crisis and Promise of Following Jesus Today*. Downers Grove, IL: InterVarsity Press.

Lake, Kirsopp. (1930). *The Earlier Epistles of St. Paul*. 2nd ed. London: Rivingtons.

Lamp, Jeffery. (2000). *First Corinthians 1–4 in Light of Jewish Wisdom Tradition:*

Christ, Wisdom and Spirituality. Studies in Bible and Early Christianity 42. Lewiston, NY: Edwin Mellen Press.

Lampe, Peter. (1990). "Theological Wisdom and the 'Word About the Cross': The Rhetorical Scheme in 1 Corinthians 1-4." *Interpretation* 44 (2): 117-31.

———. (2010). "Rhetorical Analysis of Pauline Texts—Quo Vadit?" In *Paul and Rhetoric*, edited by J. Paul Sampley and Peter Lampe, pp. 3-21. London: T & T Clark.

Lanham, Richard A. (1991). *A Handlist of Rhetorical Terms*. 2nd ed. Berkeley: University of California Press.

Lattimore, Richmond. (1942). *Themes in Greek and Latin Epitaphs*. Urbana: University of Illinois Press.

Lausberg, Heinrich. (1998). *Handbook of Literary Rhetoric: A Foundation for Literary Study*. Translated by Matthew T. Bliss, Annemiek Jansen and David E. Orton. Edited by David E. Orton and R. Dean Anderson. Leiden: Brill.

Levison, John R. (1991) "Did the Spirit Inspire Rhetoric?" In *Persuasive Artistry: Studies in New Testament Rhetoric in Honor of George A. Kennedy*, edited by Duane F. Watson. JSNT Supplement 50, pp. 25-40. Sheffield: Sheffield Academic Press.

Lewis, C. S. (1970). "Bulverism." In *God in the Dock: Essays on Theology and Ethics*, edited by Walter Hooper, pp. 271-77. Grand Rapids: Eerdmans.

Lewis, George, trans. (1911). *The Philocalia of Origen*. Edinburgh: T & T Clark.

Lightfoot, J. B. (1868). *St. Paul's Epistle to the Philippians*. London: Macmillan.

———. (1904). *Notes on Epistles of St. Paul*. London: Macmillan.

Litfin, Duane. (1977). "The Perils of Persuasive Preaching." *Christianity Today* 21 (9): 14-17.

———. (1994). *St. Paul's Theology of Proclamation: 1 Corinthians 1-4 and Greco-Roman Rhetoric*. Cambridge: Cambridge University Press.

———. (1995). "Understanding Your Critics: An Outsider's Analysis of a Core Criticism of the Church Growth Movement." *Journal of the American Society for Church Growth* 6: 85-99.

———. (2011). "Swallowing Our Pride: An Essay on the Foolishness of Preaching." In *Expository Preaching: In Honor of R. Kent Hughes*, edited by Leland Ryken and Todd Wilson, pp. 116-26. Wheaton, IL: Crossway.

———. (2012). *Word Versus Deed: Resetting the Scales to a Biblical Balance*. Wheaton, IL: Crossway.

Ljungman, Henrik. (1964). *Pistis: A Study of Its Presuppositions and Its Meaning in Pauline Use*. Lund: C. W. K. Gleerup.

Locke, John. (1894). *An Essay Concerning Human Understanding*. 2 vols. Edited by Alexander Campbell Fraser. Oxford: Clarendon Press.
Marcuse, Frederick L. (1970). *Hypnosis: Fact and Fiction*. Baltimore: Penguin.
Marrou, H. I. (1956). *A History of Education in Antiquity*. Translated by G. Lamb. London: Sheed and Ward.
———. (1981). "Education and Rhetoric." In *The Legacy of Greece: A New Appraisal*, edited by M. I. Finley, pp. 185-201. Oxford: Clarendon Press.
Marshall, Peter. (1987a). *Enmity in Corinth: Social Conventions in Paul's Relations with the Corinthians*. Tübingen: J. C. B. Mohr.
———. (1987b). "Invective: Paul and His Enemies in Corinth." In *Perspectives on Language and Text*, edited by E. W. Conrad and E. G. Newing, pp. 359-73. Winona Lake, IN: Eisenbrauns.
Martin, Dale B. (2001). "Review Essay: *Justin J. Meggitt, Paul, Poverty and Survival*." *Journal for the Study of the New Testament* 84 (2): 51-64.
Martin, Thomas F. (2000). "Vox Pauli: Augustine and the Claims to Speak for Paul: An Exploration of Rhetoric at the Service of Exegesis." *Journal of Early Christian Studies* 8 (2): 237-72.
Martin, Troy W. (2010). "Invention and Arrangement in Recent Pauline Rhetorical Studies: A Survey of the Practices and the Problems." In *Paul and Rhetoric*, edited by J. Paul Sampley and Peter Lampe, pp. 48-118. London: T & T Clark.
Martyn, J. Louis. (1997). *Galatians: A New Translation with Introduction and Commentary*. The Anchor Yale Bible. New Haven, CT: Yale University Press.
Mason, Jeff. (1989). *Philosophical Rhetoric: The Function of Indirection in Philosophical Writing*. London: Routledge.
Masson, Charles E. (1957). "L' évangile et la sagesse selon l'apôtre Paul d'aprés 1 Cor 1,17 á 3,23." *Revue de Theologie et de Philosophie* 7 (2): 95-110.
McComiskey, Bruce. (2002). *Gorgias and the New Sophistic Rhetoric*. Carbondale: Southern Illinois University Press.
McCracken, George E., trans. (1949). *The Case Against the Pagans*, by Arnobius of Sicca. Westminster, MD: The Newman Press.
McDonald, James I. H. (1980). Kerygma *and* Didache: *The Articulation and Structure of the Earliest Christian Message*. SNTS 37. Cambridge: Cambridge University Press.
McDonald, Mary Francis, trans. (1964). *The Divine Institutes*, by Lactantius. Washington, DC: The Catholic University of America Press.
McGuire, William J. (1969). "The Nature of Attitudes and Attitude Change." In *Handbook of Social Psychology*, edited by G. Lindzey and E. Aronson, vol. 3,

pp. 136-314. 2nd ed. Reading, MA: Addison-Wesley.

McKane, W. (1965). *Prophets and Wise Men*. London: SCM Press.

Meeks, Wayne A. (1982). "The Social Context of Pauline Theology." *Interpretation* 36 (3): 266-77.

———. (1983). *The First Urban Christians: The Social World of the Apostle Paul*. New Haven, CT: Yale University Press.

———. (2009). "Taking Stock and Moving On." In *After the First Urban Christians: The Social-Scientific Study of Pauline Christianity Twenty-Five Years Later*, edited by Todd D. Still and David G. Holler, pp. 134-46. London: T & T Clark.

Meggitt, Justin J. (1998). *Paul, Poverty and Survival*. Edinburgh: T & T Clark.

———. (2001). "Response to Martin and Theissen." *Journal for the Study of the New Testament* 84 (2): 85-94.

Meinardus, O. F. A. (1973). *St. Paul in Greece*. Athens: Lycabettus Press.

Merritt, Benjamin Dean, ed. (1931). *Greek Inscriptions, 1896–1927*. Vol. 8, part 1 of *Corinth: Results of Excavations Conducted by the American School of Classical Studies at Athens*. Cambridge, MA: Harvard University Press.

Meyer, H. A. W. (1870). *Kritisch exegetisches Handbuch über den ersten Brief an die Korinther*. 5th ed. Göttingen: Vandenhoeck & Ruprecht.

Mihaila, Corin. (2009). *The Paul-Apollos Relationship and Paul's Stance Toward Greco-Roman Rhetoric: An Exegetical and Socio-historical Study of 1 Corinthians 1–4*. London: T & T Clark.

Milgrom, Jacob, and Daniel Isaac Block. (2012). *Ezekiel's Hope: A Commentary on Ezekiel*. Eugene, OR: Cascade Books.

Millar, Fergus. (1998). *The Crowd in Rome in the Late Republic*. Ann Arbor: The University of Michigan Press.

Miller, Anna C. (2013). "Not with Eloquent Wisdom: Democratic Ekklesia Discourse in 1 Corinthians 1–4." *Journal for the Study of the New Testament* 35 (4): 323-54.

Mitchell, Margaret M. (1991). *Paul and the Rhetoric of Reconciliation: An Exegetical Investigation of the Language and Composition of 1 Corinthians*. Tübingen: J. C. B. Mohr.

———. (1994). "Rhetorical Shorthand in Pauline Argumentation: The Functions of 'The Gospel' in the Corinthian Correspondence." In *Gospel in Paul: Studies on Corinthians, Galatians, and Romans for Richard N. Longenecker*, edited by L. Ann Jervis and Peter Richardson, pp. 63-88. JSNT Supplement 108. Sheffield: Sheffield Academic Press.

———. (2002). *The Heavenly Trumpet: John Chrysostom and the Art of Pauline*

Interpretation. Louisville: Westminster John Knox Press.

———. (2003). "The Corinthian Correspondence and the Birth of Pauline Hermeneutics." In *Paul and the Corinthians: Studies on a Community in Conflict*, edited by Trevor J. Burke and J. Keith Elliot, pp. 17-54. Leiden: Brill.

Moffatt, J. (1938). *The First Epistle of Paul to the Corinthians.* London: Hodder and Stoughton.

Morgan, Teresa. (1998). *Literate Education in the Hellenistic and Roman Worlds.* Cambridge: Cambridge University Press.

Moule, C. F. D. (1959). *An Idiom Book of the New Testament.* 2nd ed. Cambridge: Cambridge University Press.

Munck, Johannes. (1959). *Paul and the Salvation of Mankind.* Translated by F. Clarke. London: SCM Press.

Murphy, C. T. (1938). "Aristophanes and the Art of Rhetoric." *Harvard Studies in Classical Philology* 49: 69-113.

Murphy, James J. (2008). "St. Augustine and the Debate About a Christian Rhetoric." In *The Rhetoric of St Augustine of Hippo: De Doctrina Christiana and the Search for a Distinctly Christian Rhetoric*, edited by Richard Leo Enos and Roger Thompson, pp. 205-18. Waco, TX: Baylor University Press.

Murphy-O'Connor, Jerome. (1964). *Paul on Preaching.* London: Sheed and Ward.

Mussies, G. (1972). *Dio Chrysostom and the New Testament.* Leiden: Brill.

Natanson, Maurice. (1965). "The Limits of Rhetoric." In *The Province of Rhetoric*, edited by J. Schwartz and J. A. Rycenga, pp. 55-66. New York: The Ronald Press.

Nauck, Augustus. (1867). *Lexicon Vindobonense.* Petropolis: Academiae Scientiarum Petropolitanae.

Neville, Graham, trans. (1964). *On the Priesthood*, by St. John Chrysostom. Crestwood, NY: St. Vladimir's Seminary Press.

Neyrey, Jerome H. (2003). "The Social Location of Paul: Education as the Key." In *Fabrics of Discourse: Essays in Honor of Vernon K. Robbins*, edited by David B. Gowler, Gregory Bloomquist and Duane F. Watson, pp. 126-64. Harrisburg, PA: Trinity Press International.

Nock, A. D. (1933). *Conversion.* Oxford: Clarendon Press.

Norden, Eduard. (1909). *Die Antike Kunstprosa.* 2 vols. Leipzig: B. G. Teubner.

North, H. F. (1979). *From Myth to Icon: Reflections of Greek Ethical Doctrine in Literature and Art.* Ithaca: Cornell University Press.

Ober, Josiah. (1989). *Mass and Elite in Democratic Athens: Rhetoric, Ideology, and the Power of the People.* Princeton, NJ: Princeton University Press.

Oke, C. C. (1956). "Paul's Method Not a Demonstration but an Exhibition of the

Spirit." *Expository Times* 67 (2): 35-36.

Olbricht, Thomas H. (2005). "The Foundations of the Ethos in Paul and in the Classical Rhetoricians." In *Rhetoric, Ethic, and Moral Persuasion in Biblical Discourse*, edited by Thomas H. Olbricht and Anders Eriksson, pp. 138-59. New York: T & T Clark.

Olson, Gary A. (2002). *Justifying Belief: Stanley Fish and the Work of Rhetoric*. Albany: State University of New York Press.

Ong, Walter J. (1983). Foreword to *The Present State of Scholarship in Historical and Contemporary Rhetoric*, edited by Winifred Bryan Horner. Columbia: University of Missouri Press.

Orr, W. F., and J. A. Walther. (1976). *1 Corinthians*. The Anchor Bible. Garden City, NJ: Doubleday.

Outler, Albert C., trans. (1955). *Confessions and Enchiridion*, by Augustine. Library of Christian Classics, Vol 7. Philadelphia: Westminster Press.

Packer, James I. (1961). *Evangelism and the Sovereignty of God*. London: Inter-Varsity Press.

Paige, Terrence. (1992). "Stoicism, ἐλευθερία and Community at Corinth." In *Worship, Theology and Ministry in the Early Church: Essays in Honor of Ralph P. Martin*, edited by Michael. J. Wilkins and Terence Paige, pp. 180-93. JSNT 87. Sheffield: Sheffield Academic Press.

Painter, J. (1982). "Paul and the Pneumatikoi at Corinth." In *Paul and Paulinism: Essays in Honor of C. K. Barrett*, edited by M. D. Hooker and S. G. Wilson, pp. 237-50. London: SPCK.

Papadopolos, Styulianos G. (2009). Prologue to *Saint Paul and Corinth: 150 Years Since the Writing of the Epistles to the Corinthians*, edited by Constantine J. Belezos, pp. 19-23. International Scholarly Conference Proceedings, vol. 1. Athens: Psichogios Publications.

Pascuzzi, Maria. (2009). "Baptism-based Allegiance and the Divisions in Corinth: A Reexamination of 1 Corinthians 1:13-17." *Catholic Biblical Quarterly* 71, no. 4: 813-29.

Patrick, Dale, with Allen Scult. (1999). "Rhetoric and Ideology: A Debate Within Biblical Scholarship over the Import of Persuasion." In *The Rhetorical Interpretation of Scripture*, edited by Stanley E. Porter and Dennis L. Stamps, pp. 63-83. JSNT Supplement 180. Sheffield: Sheffield Academic Press.

Pearson, Birger A. (1973). *The Pneumatikos-Psychikos Terminology in I Corinthians: A Study of the Theology of the Corinthian Opponents of Paul and Its Relation to Gnosticism*. SBL Dissertation Series 12. Missoula, MT: Scholars Press.

———. (1975). "Hellenistic-Jewish Wisdom Speculation and Paul." In *Aspects of Wisdom in Judaism and Early Christianity*, edited by R. L. Wilken, pp. 43-66. Notre Dame, IN: University of Notre Dame Press.

Perelman, Chaim. (1982a). "Philosophy and Rhetoric." In *Advances in Argumentation Theory and Research*, edited by J. Robert Cox and Charles Arthur Willard, pp. 287-97. Carbondale: Southern Illinois University Press.

———. (1982b). *The Realm of Rhetoric*. Translated by William Kluback. Notre Dame, IN: University of Notre Dame Press.

Perelman, Chaim, and Luci Olbrechts-Tyteca. (1969). *The New Rhetoric: A Treatise on Argumentation*. Translated by John Wilkinson and Purcell Weaver. Notre Dame, IN: University of Notre Dame Press.

Peterson, Brian K. (1998). *Eloquence and the Proclamation of the Gospel in Corinth*. SBL Dissertation Series 163. Atlanta: Scholars Press.

Pickett, Raymond. (1997). *The Cross in Corinth: The Social Significance of the Death of Jesus*. JSNT Supplement 143. Sheffield: Sheffield Academic Press.

Pippin, Tina. (1997). "Ideological Criticisms, Liberation Criticisms, and Womanist and Feminist Criticisms." In *Handbook to Exegesis of the New Testament*, edited by Stanley E. Porter, pp. 267-75. Leiden: Brill.

Pitts, Andrew W. (2008). "Hellenistic Schools in Jerusalem and Paul's Rhetorical Education." In *Paul's World*, edited by Stanley E. Porter, pp. 19-50. Leiden: Brill.

Plank, K. A. (1987). *Paul and the Irony of Affliction*. Atlanta: Scholars Press.

Plantinga, Alvin. (2011). *Where the Conflict Really Lies: Science, Religion, and Naturalism*. New York: Oxford University Press.

Pogoloff, Stephen M. (1991). "Isocrates and Contemporary Hermeneutics." In *Persuasive Artistry: Studies in New Testament Rhetoric in Honor of George A. Kennedy*, edited by Duane F. Watson, pp. 338-62. JSNT Supplement 50. Sheffield: Sheffield Academic Press.

———. (1992). *Logos and Sophia: The Rhetorical Situation of 1 Corinthians*. SBL Dissertation Series 134. Atlanta: Scholars Press.

Polhill, John B. (1983). "The Wisdom of God and Factionalism: 1 Corinthians 1–4." *Review and Expositor* 80 (3): 325-39.

Porter, Stanley E. (1999a). "Paul as Epistolographer *and* Rhetorician?" In *The Rhetorical Interpretation of Scripture*, edited by Stanley E. Porter and Dennis L. Stamps, pp. 222-48. JSNT Supplement 180. Sheffield: Sheffield Academic Press.

———. (1999b). *The Paul of Acts: Essays in Literary Criticism, Rhetoric, and Theology*. Tübingen: Mohr Siebeck.

———. (2013). "Hellenistic Oratory and Paul of Tarsus." In *Hellenistic Oratory:*

Continuity and Change, edited by Christos Kremmydas and Kathryn Tempest, pp. 319-68. Oxford: Oxford University Press.

Porter, Stanley E., and Bryan R. Dyer. (2012). "Oral Texts? A Reassessment of the Oral and Rhetorical Nature of Paul's Letters in Light of Recent Studies." *Journal of the Evangelical Theological Society* 55 (2): 323-41.

Provence, T. E. (1982). "'Who Is Sufficient for These Things?': An Exegesis of 2 Corinthians ii 15–iii 18." *Novum Testamentum* 24 (1): 54-81.

Prümm, Karl. (1963). "Das neutestamentliche Sprach- und Begriffsproblem der Vollkommenheit." *Biblica* 44 (1): 76-92.

Purcell, Nicolas. (1983). "The *Apparitores*: A Study in Social Mobility." *Papers of the British School at Rome* 51: 125-73.

Rainer, Thom S. (1993). *The Book of Church Growth: History, Theology, and Principles*. Nashville: Broadman.

Rauh, Nicholas K. (1989). "Auctioneers and the Roman Economy." *Historia: Zeitschrift für Alte Geschicht* 38 (4): 451-71.

Reed, Jeffrey T. (1993). "Using Ancient Rhetorical Categories to Interpret Paul's Letters: A Question of Genre." In *Rhetoric and the New Testament: Essays from the 1992 Heidelberg Conference*, edited by Stanley E. Porter and Thomas H. Olbricht, pp. 292-324. Sheffield: Sheffield Academic Press.

Rengstorf, Karl Heinrich. (1952). *Apostleship*. Translated by J. R. Coates. London: Adam and Charles Black.

———. (1969). *Apostolate and Ministry: The New Testament Doctrine of the Office of the Ministry*. Translated by P. D. Pahl. St. Louis, MO: Concordia.

Rescher, Nicholas. (2001). *Philosophical Reasoning: A Study in the Methodology of Philosophizing*. Oxford: Blackwell Publishers.

Resner, André, Jr. (1999). *Preacher and Cross: Person and Message in Theology and Rhetoric*. Grand Rapids: Eerdmans.

Robertson, Archibald, and Alfred Plummer. (1911). *A Critical Commentary and Exegetical Commentary on the First Epistle of St. Paul to the Corinthians*. New York: Charles Scribner's Sons.

Robertson, A. T. (1934). *A Grammar of the Greek New Testament in the Light of Historical Research*. Nashville: Broadman.

Robertson, C. K. (2001). *Conflict in Corinth: Redefining the System*. Studies in Biblical Literature 42. New York: Peter Lang.

Robinson, Haddon. (1986). "More 'Religion,' Less Impact." *Christianity Today* 30 (1): 4-6.

Robinson, James M. (1959). *A New Quest of the Historical Jesus*. London: SCM Press.

Rokeach, Milton. (1971). "Persuasion That Persists." *Psychology Today* 5 (4): 68-73.
Romilly, Jacqueline de. (1975). *Magic and Rhetoric in Ancient Greece*. Cambridge, MA: Harvard University Press.
Roukema, Riemer. (2013). "The Foolishness of the Message About the Cross (1 Cor. 1:18-25): Embarrassment and Consent." *Studia Patristica* 63: 55-67.
Russell, D. A. (1981). *Criticism in Antiquity*. London: Duckworth.
———. (1983). *Greek Declamation*. Cambridge: Cambridge University Press.
Saussure, Ferdinand de. (1959). *Course in General Linguistics*. Translated by Wade Baskin. New York: Philosophical Library.
Schouls, Peter A. (1969). "Communication, Argumentation, and Presupposition in Philosophy." *Philosophy and Rhetoric* 2 (4): 183-99.
Schweizer, E. (1960). *Spirit of God*. Translated by A. E. Harvey. London: Adam and Charles Black.
Scott, Ian W. (2006). *Implicit Epistemology in the Letters of Paul: Story, Experience and the Spirit*. Tübingen: Mohr Siebeck. Reprinted as *Paul's Way of Knowing: Story, Experience, and the Spirit*. Grand Rapids: Baker Academic, 2009.
Scranton, R. L. (1951). *Corinth: Monuments in the Lower Agora and North of the Archaic Temple*. Princeton: The American School of Classical Studies at Athens.
Scroggs, Robin. (1967). "Paul: ΣΟΦΟΣ AND ΠΝΕΥΜΑΤΙΚΟΣ." *New Testament Studies* 14 (1): 33-55.
———. (1988). *Christology in Paul and John*. Philadelphia: Fortress.
Sellin, Gerhard. (1982). "Das 'Geheimnis' der Weisheit und das Rätsel der 'Christuspartei' (zu 1 Kor 1-4)." *Zeitschrift für die neutestamentliche Wissenschaft* 73 (1-2): 69-96.
Shaw, Graham. (1982). *The Cost of Authority: Manipulation and Freedom in the New Testament*. Philadelphia: Fortress.
Sider, Robert Dick. (1971). *Ancient Rhetoric and the Art of Tertullian*. Oxford: Oxford University Press.
Siegert, Folker. (1985). *Argumentation bei Paulus: Gezeigt an Röm 9-11*. Wissenschaftliche Untersuchungen zum Neuen Testament 2.34. Tübingen: J. C. B. Mohr (Paul Siebeck).
Simcox, W. H. (1890). *The Writers of the New Testament: Their Style and Characteristics*. London: Hodder and Stoughton.
Sleeth, Ronald E. (1956). *Persuasive Preaching*. New York: Harper.
Sloane, Thomas O., ed. (2001). *Encyclopedia of Rhetoric*. Oxford: Oxford University Press.
Smiley, Charles Newton. (1906). "*Latinitas* and Ἑλληνισμός." *Bulletin of the Uni-*

versity of Wisconsin, Philology and Literature Series 3: 205-72.

Smit, Joop F. M. (2002). "'What Is Apollos? What Is Paul?' In Search for the Coherence of First Corinthians 1:10–4:21." *Novum Testamentum* 44 (3): 231-51.

———. (2003). "Epideictic Rhetoric in Paul's First Letter to the Corinthians 1–4." *Biblica* 84 (2): pp. 184-201.

Smith, Robert W. (1974). *The Art of Rhetoric in Alexandria: Its Theory and Practice in the Ancient World*. The Hague: Martinus Nijhoff.

Spencer, W. D. (1989). "The Power in Paul's Teaching (1 Cor 4:9-20)." *Journal of the Evangelical Society* 32 (1): 51-61.

Stamps, Dennis L. (1999). "The Theological Rhetoric of the Pauline Epistles: Prolegomenon." In *The Rhetorical Interpretation of Scripture*, edited by Stanley E. Porter and Dennis L. Stamps, pp. 249-59. JSNT Supplement 180. Sheffield: Sheffield Academic Press.

———. (2002). "The Christological Premise in Pauline Theological Rhetoric: 1 Corinthians 1.4–2.5 as an Example." In *Rhetorical Criticism and the Bible*, edited by Stanley E. Porter and Dennis L. Stamps, pp. 441-57. London: Sheffield Academic Press.

Stanley, Christopher D. (2013). "The Ethnic Context of Paul's Letters." In *Christian Origins and Hellenistic Judaism: Social and Literary Contexts for the New Testament*, edited by Stanley E. Porter and Andrew W. Pits, pp. 177-201. Leiden: Brill.

Stanley, David M. (1956). "The Conception of Salvation in Primitive Christian Preaching." *Catholic Biblical Quarterly* 18 (3): 231-54.

Stanton, G. R. (1973). "Sophists and Philosophers: Problems of Classification." *The American Journal of Philology* 94 (4): 350-64.

Still, Todd D. (2012). "Why Did Paul Preach 'Christ Crucified' in Corinth? A New Answer to an Old Question from an Unexpected Place." *Perspectives in Religious Studies* 39, no. 1: 5-13.

Stirewalt, M. Luther, Jr. (1969). "Paul's Evaluation of Letter-Writing." In *Search the Scriptures: New Testament Studies in Honor of Ramond T. Stamm*, edited by J. M. Myers, O. Reimherr and H. N. Bream, pp. 179-96. Leiden: E. J. Brill.

———. (2003). *Paul, the Letter Writer*. Grand Rapids: Eerdmans.

Sullivan, Sister Thérèse. (1930). *S. Avreli Avgvstini, hipponiensis episcopi, De doctrina christiana, liber qvartvs; A Commentary, with a Revised Text, Introduction, and Translation*. Washington, DC: The Catholic University of America.

Syme, Ronald. (1958). *Tacitus*. 2 vols. Oxford: Clarendon Press.

Theissen, Gerd. (1974). "Soziale Schichtung in der korinthischen Gemeinde: Ein

Beitrag zur Socialogie des hellenistischen Urchristentums." *Zeitschrift für die neutestamentliche Wissenschaft* 65 (3-4): 232-72.

———. (2001). "The Social Structure of Pauline Communities: Some Critical Remarks on J. J. Meggitt, *Paul, Poverty and Survival*." *Journal for the Study of the New Testament* 24 (84): 65-84.

———. (2003). "Social Conflicts in the Corinthian Community: Further Remarks on J. J. Meggitt, *Paul, Poverty and Survival*." *Journal for the Study of the New Testament* 25 (3): 371-91.

Thiselton, Anthony C. (2000). *The First Epistle to the Corinthians: A Commentary on the Greek Text*. Grand Rapids: Eerdmans.

———. (2006). *First Corinthians: A Shorter Exegetical and Pastoral Commentary*. Grand Rapids: Eerdmans.

Thorgerson, Erika Jean. (1993). "Sortis Ultimae Homo: Roman Praecones and the Dissemination of Information in the Republic and Empire." MA thesis, University of Georgia.

Thrall, Margaret E. (2002). "The Initial Attraction of Paul's Mission in Corinth and of the Church He Founded There." In *Paul, Luke and the Graeco-Roman World: Essays in Honour of Alexander J. M. Wedderburn*, edited by Alf Christophersen, Carsten Claussen, Jörg Frey and Bruce Longenecker, pp. 59-73. JSNT Supplement 217. Sheffield: Sheffield Academic Press.

Thurén, Lauri. (2002). "Romans 7 Derhetorized." In *Rhetorical Criticism and the Bible*, edited by Stanley E. Porter and Dennis L. Stamps, pp. 420-40. London: Sheffield Academic Press.

Tomlin, Graham. (1997). "Christians and Epicureans in 1 Corinthians." *Journal for the Study of the New Testament* 20 (68): 51-72.

Torrance, T. F. (1950). "A Study in New Testament Communication." *Scottish Journal of Theology* 3 (3): 298-313.

Turner, Nigel. (1976). *Style*. Vol. 4 of *A Grammar of New Testament Greek*, edited by J. H. Moulton. Edinburgh: T & T Clark.

Usher, Stephen. (1969). "Oratory." In *Greek and Latin Literature: A Comparative Study*, edited by J. Higginbotham, pp. 342-89. London: Methuen.

Van Gelder, Craig, and Dwight J. Zscheile. (2011). *The Missional Church in Perspective: Mapping the Trends and Shaping the Conversation*. Grand Rapids: Baker Academic.

Vanhoozer, Kevin J. (1998). *The Bible, The Reader, and the Morality of Literary Knowledge: Is There a Meaning in This Text?* Grand Rapids: Zondervan.

Van Unnik, W. C. (1971). "First Century A.D. Literary Culture." *Nederlands Theologisch Tijdschrift* 25: 39-40.

Vos, Johan S. (1996). "Die Argumentation des Paulus in 1 Kor 1,10–3,4." In *The Corinthian Correspondence*, edited by R. Bieringer, pp. 87-119. Leuven: Leuven University Press.

———. (2010). "Rhetoric and Theology in the Letters of Paul." In *Paul and Rhetoric*, edited by J. Paul Sampley and Peter Lampe, pp. 161-79. London: T & T Clark.

Wagner, J. Ross. (2002). *Heralds of the Good News: Isaiah and Paul "In Concert" in the Letter to the Romans*. Leiden: Brill.

Wagner, Peter. (1981). *Church Growth and the Whole Gospel: A Biblical Mandate*. San Francisco: Harper & Row.

———. (1987). *Strategies for Church Growth: Tools for Effective Mission and Evangelism*. Ventura, CA: Regal.

Wallace, Karl. R. (1963). "The Substance of Rhetoric: Good Reasons." *Quarterly Journal of Speech* 49 (3): 239-49.

Wanamaker, Charles A. (2003). "A Rhetoric of Power: Ideology and 1 Corinthians 1–4." In *Paul and the Corinthians: Studies on a Community in Conflict*, edited by Trevor J. Burke and J. Keith Elliot, pp. 115-37. Leiden: Brill.

Watson, Duane F. (1999). "The Contributions and Limitations of Greco-Roman Rhetorical Theory for Constructing the Rhetorical and Historical Situation of a Pauline Epistle." In *The Rhetorical Interpretation of Scripture*, edited by Stanley E. Porter and Dennis L. Stamps, pp. 125-51. JSNT Supplement 180. Sheffield: Sheffield Academic Press.

———. (2010a). "The Role of Style in the Pauline Epistles: From Ornamentation to Argumentative Strategies." In *Paul and Rhetoric*, edited by J. Paul Sampley and Peter Lampe, pp. 119-39. London: T & T Clark.

———. (2010b). "The Three Species of Rhetoric and the Study of the Pauline Epistles." In *Paul and Rhetoric*, edited by J. Paul Sampley and Peter Lampe, pp. 25-47. London: T & T Clark.

Weima, Jeffrey A. D. (1997). "What Does Aristotle Have to Do with Paul? An Evaluation of Rhetorical Criticism." *Calvin Theological Journal* 32 (2): 458-68.

———. (2000). "The Function of 1 Thessalonians 2:1-12 and the Use of Rhetorical Criticism: A Response to Otto Merk." In *The Thessalonians Debate: Methodological Discord or Methodological Synthesis?*, edited by Karl P. Donfried and Johannes Beutler, pp. 114-31. Grand Rapids: Eerdmans.

Weiss, Johannes. (1909). *Paul and Jesus*. Translated by H. J. Chaytor. London: Harper and Brothers.

———. (1959). *Earliest Christianity: A History of the Period A.D. 30-150*. 2 vols. Translated and edited by F. C. Grant. New York: Harper and Brothers.

Welborn, L. L. (1987). "On the Discord in Corinth." *Journal of Biblical Literature* 106 (1): 85-111.

———. (1997). *Politics and Rhetoric in the Corinthian Epistles*. Macon, GA: Mercer University Press.

———. (2005). *Paul, the Fool of Christ: A Study of 1 Corinthians 1–4 in the Comic-Philosophical Tradition*. London: T & T Clark.

Whitmarsh, Tim. (2005). *The Second Sophistic*. Oxford: Oxford University Press.

Wilckens, Ulrich. (1959). *Weisheit und Torheit*. Tübingen: J. C. B. Mohr.

———. (1965). "σοφία." In *Theological Dictionary of the New Testament*, edited by G. Kittel, translated by G. W. Bromiley, vol. 7, pp. 464-539. Grand Rapids: Eerdmans.

———. (1979). "Zu 1 Kor 2,1-16." In *Theologia Crusis—Signum Crusis*, edited by C. Anderesen and G. Klein, pp. 501-39. Tubingen: J. C. B. Mohr. Revised from a paper delivered at the VI. Colloquium Paulinum in Rome, later published in *Paolo a una Chiesa Divisa (1 Co. 104)*. Serie Monografica di "Benedictina" 5, edited by L. De Lorenzi. Rome: S. Paolo, 1980.

Wilken, Robert L. (2003). *The Christians as Romans Saw Them*. 2nd edition. New Haven, CT: Yale University Press.

Williams, H. H. Drake, III (2001). *The Wisdom of the Wise: The Presence and Function of Scripture Within 1 Cor 1:18–3:23*. Leiden: Brill.

Williams, Michael Allen. (1996). *Rethinking "Gnosticism": An Argument for Dismantling a Dubious Category*. Princeton, NJ: Princeton University Press.

Winter, Bruce W. (2001). *After Paul Left Corinth: The Influence of Secular Ethics and Social Change*. Grand Rapids: Eerdmans.

———. (2002). *Philo and Paul Among the Sophists*. 2nd ed. Grand Rapids: Eerdmans.

———. (2003a). "The Toppling of Favorinus and Paul by the Corinthians." In *Early Christianity and Classical Culture: Comparative Studies in Honor of Abraham J. Malherbe*, edited by John T. Fitzgerald, Thomas H. Olbricht and L. Michael White, pp. 291-306. Leiden: Brill.

———. (2003b). "The 'Underlays' of Conflict and Compromise in 1 Corinthians." In *Paul and the Corinthians: Studies on a Community in Conflict*, edited by Trevor J. Burke and J. Keith Elliot, pp. 139-55. Leiden: Brill.

Wire, Antoinette. (1991). *The Corinthian Women Prophets: A Reconstruction Through Paul's Rhetoric*. Minneapolis: Augsburg Fortress.

Witherington, Ben, III. (1995). *Conflict and Community in Corinth: A Socio-Rhetorical Commentary on 1 and 2 Corinthians*. Grand Rapids: Eerdmans.

———. (2009a). *New Testament Rhetoric: An Introductory Guide to the Art of Persuasion in and of the New Testament.* Eugene, OR: Cascade Books.

———. (2009b). *What's in the Word: Rethinking the Socio-Rhetorical Character of the New Testament.* Waco, TX: Baylor University Press.

Wuellner, W. (1970). "Haggadic Homily Genre in 1 Corinthians 1–3." *Journal of Biblical Literature* 89 (2): 199-204.

———. (1973). "The Sociological Implications of 1 Corinthians 1:26-28 Reconsidered." In *Studia Evangelica* VI, edited by E. A. Livingstone, pp. 666-72. Texte und Untersuchungen zur Geschichte der altchristlichen Literatur 112. Berlin: Akademie.

———. (1979). "Greek Rhetoric and Pauline Argumentation." In *Early Christian Literature and the Classical Intellectual Tradition, in Honorem Robert M. Grant,* edited by William R. Schoedel and Robert L. Wilken, pp. 177-88. Paris: Editions Beauchesne.

Young, Frances M. (1985). "John Chrysostom on First and Second Corinthians." In *Studia Patristica, XVIII,* edited by Elizabeth A. Livingstone, vol. 1, pp. 349-58. Kalamazoo, MI: Cistercian Publications.

———. (1997). *Biblical Exegesis and the Formation of Christian Culture.* Cambridge: Cambridge University Press.

Author Index

ANCIENT SOURCES
Acts of Paul and Thecla, 144
Aelius Donatus, 145
Ambrose, 50, 147
Aristides, 70, 71, 76, 77, 87, 177, 214, 269
Aristophanes, 63
Aristotle, 50, 58, 67, 72, 73, 95, 135, 177, 184, 187, 217, 229, 261, 280, 290, 292, 296, 303, 304, 311, 315
Arnobius, 146
Basil, 50
Cassius Dio, 122, 123, 199
Cicero, 58, 61, 66, 67, 71, 72, 77, 88-90, 95-98, 99-100, 101, 102, 105-6, 108-9, 115, 135, 136, 145, 184, 202, 215, 227, 228, 252, 260, 261, 277, 291, 301, 310, 311, 312, 341
Clement of Alexandria, 50
Clement of Rome, 34, 156, 219, 247
Cyprian, 50
Demetrius, 135
Dio Chrysostom, 23, 77, 79, 83-84, 86, 92, 99, 101, 103-5, 110, 122, 123, 125, 185, 191, 214, 215, 230, 233, 286, 311, 313, 329
Diogenes Laertius, 50
Diomedes, 145
Dionysius of Halicarnassus, 101, 116, 229, 277
Epictetus, 145, 218
Eusebius, 146
Favorinus, 125-28, 154
Galen, 211, 233
Gorgias, 76
Herodotus, 185
Homer, 59
Isocrates, 50, 64-67, 87, 128, 151, 202, 215, 217, 223, 228, 302, 329
Jerome, 50, 146
John Chrysostom, 28-29, 51, 142-43, 192-93, 230, 268, 298-301
Josephus, 207

Justin Martyr, 50, 191
Juvenal, 57, 207
Lactantius, 50, 146
Longinus, 77-78, 101, 150, 184
Lucian, 110, 149, 233
Martial, 196
Origen, 146, 233, 235
Pausanius, 122, 123
Petronius, 86-87
Philo, 124, 325-26
Philostratus, 69, 76, 83, 99, 101, 105, 110, 120, 123, 125-26, 142, 144, 150, 215, 228, 232
Plato, 43, 61, 63, 64, 71, 73, 76, 81, 82-83, 88, 136, 185, 207, 215, 232, 237, 269, 286, 287, 292, 295, 296, 310
Pliny, 84-85, 99, 101, 110, 135, 136, 217, 277
Plutarch, 87, 101, 105, 215, 229, 251, 274, 286, 331
Polybius, 145
Quintilian, 23, 43, 50, 68, 71, 72, 74, 76, 78-79, 83, 90, 101, 106-7, 110, 115, 131, 136, 191, 202, 204, 227, 260, 261, 277, 280, 287, 291, 301-2, 310, 311, 312, 342
Seneca, 86, 101
Strabo, 119-20, 122, 123
Suetonius, 101, 207
Synesius of Cyrene, 50
Tacitus, 71, 80, 83, 84, 85, 91-93, 98-99, 101, 103, 109-10, 121, 184, 291, 213
Tertullian, 50
Thucydides, 82, 156
Titian, 50
Xenophon, 63, 286

MODERN SOURCES
Abbott-Smith, G., 200
Abelson, H., 344
Adams, E., 122
Adams, S. A., 191, 211
Aernie, J. W., 286
Alexander. L., 211
Amador, J. D. H., 27
Anderson, G., 151

Anderson, R., 31
Anderson. R. D., 24, 42, 141, 144, 295
Andrews. M. E., 325
Archer, D., 30
Aune, D. C., 278
Baird, W., 201, 219, 237
Ballard, C. A., 234
Barclay, J. M. G., 250
Barna, G., 357-58
Barrett, C. K., 29, 124, 156, 159, 178, 186, 189, 198, 222, 225, 230, 237, 255, 264, 303, 332
Bauer, W., 237
Baumann, R., 19, 172
Baur, F. C., 33, 168, 218
Bearedslee, W. A., 24
Best, E., 192
Betz, H. D., 16, 34, 43, 175, 297
Bird, M. F., 131
Bitzer, L. F., 141
Black, D. A., 227
Blass, F., 143, 183, 199
Block, D., 30
Bloomer, W. M., 68
Booth, W. C., 44, 272-76
Bornkamm, G., 265, 267, 303, 305
Bouyer, L., 227
Bowersock, G. W., 151
Breytenbach, C., 191
Briggs, R. W., 22
Brockriede, W. E., 232
Broneer, O., 125
Brookins, T., 34
Brown, P., 155
Brown, R. E., 244
Bruce, F. F., 17-18, 234, 331
Bryant, D. C., 262
Bullinger, E. W., 42, 202, 203
Bullmore, M., 19, 203-4
Bultmann, R., 200, 221
Caird, G. B., 16, 28
Calvin, J., 229
Carson, D. A., 244
Cavadini, J. C., 275
Chadwick, H., 235, 325
Chance, J. B., 131
Chapman, D. W., 211

Chester, S. J., 171
Chevallier, M., 225
Ciampa, R. E., 208, 213
Clarke, A. D., 125, 148
Classen, C. J., 98, 121, 136, 287, 298
Coenen, L., 206
Collins, R. R., 24, 200, 230
Connor, W. R., 57
Conzelmann, H., 124, 162-63, 192, 198, 216, 329
Corcoran, P. E., 211-12
Costa, T., 285
Crouch, F., 262
Cullmann, O., 196
Dahl, N. A., 31, 130, 131, 169, 327
Davis, J. A., 19, 237
De Boer, M. C., 34, 130-31
Debruner, A., 143, 183, 199
Deissmann, A., 21
Delling, G., 237, 238
DeWitt, N. W., 231-32
Dibelius, M., 122
Dickson, J. P., 133, 186, 248, 252
Dodd, C. H., 195-97
Dominik, W. J., 83
Doty, W. G., 196
Dover, K. J., 23, 153
Du Toit, A. B., 22, 120, 288
Duhamel, A. P., 31
Dunn, J. D. G., 156, 290
Dutch, R. S., 148
Dyer, B. R., 120-21, 132, 136
Ellingworth, P., 198, 259
Ellis, E., 191
Engberg-Pedersen, T., 248
Enos, T., 262
Eriksson, A., 26
Evans, C. A., 340
Evans, C. F., 201
Fantham, E., 45, 136-37
Fee, G. D., 33, 186, 198, 208
Findlay, G. G., 200
Finney, M. T., 173
Fiore, B., 248
Fiorenza, E. S., 27
Fitzmyer, J. A., 178, 189
Forbes, C., 136, 147, 303, 304
Fortin, E. L., 52
Frank, G., 103
Freese, J. H., 95
Frestadius, S., 38, 173
Friedrich, G., 200, 201, 205, 316
Furnish, V. P., 185, 252
Gärtner, B. E., 238, 241

Gillespie, T. W., 190, 238, 267
Gitay, Y., 21
Given, M. D., 231
Glover, T. R., 142, 145, 233
Godet, F. L., 267
Goldammer, K., 211
Gooch, P. W., 302
Goodenough, E. R., 326
Gorman, M. J., 198
Goulder, M. D., 33
Graindor, P., 125
Grant, R. M., 325
Grass, T., 18
Grassi, E., 209, 210
Graves, M., 145, 147, 158
Green, R. P. H., 50
Grindheim, S., 168, 240, 243
Grosheide, F. W., 197
Gupta, N. K., 252
Guthrie, W. K. C., 62, 295
Gwynn, A., 291
Habinek, T., 58, 128, 205
Hall, D. R., 131
Hanson, A. T., 241
Harris, W. V., 207
Harvey, A. E., 16, 167-68
Hatton, H., 198, 259
Hauser, A. J., 18-19, 36
Hays, R., 156, 161, 208, 236-37, 238, 239, 290
Heinrici, C. F. G., 190
Henderson, I., 24
Hengel, M., 120, 178, 191
Hock, R. F., 120, 144
Horrell, D. G., 122, 184
Horsley, R. A., 325
Hudson, H. H., 136
Hunter, A. M., 37, 197, 205, 340
Hurd, J. C., 248
Inkelaar, H., 198, 224
Jaeger, W., 63
Jasinski, J., 262
Jasper, D., 43
Johnstone, H. W., 209, 215
Jones, A. H. M., 123, 207
Judge, E. A., 15, 119, 142, 149-50, 204, 232, 252, 303
Kaibel, G., 154
Kammler, H., 19
Kant, I., 296
Karlins, M., 344
Kaster, R. A., 119
Keil, H., 145
Kennedy, G. A., 15, 21, 70, 83, 112, 114, 141, 151, 172, 204, 210, 285, 286, 287, 293, 297, 298

Ker, D. P., 144, 156
Kerényi, C., 215
Kerferd, G. B., 63, 64
Kern, P., 132
Kimball, B. A., 295
Kinneavy, J. L., 121, 178, 262
Knox, R. A., 11-12
Knox, W. L., 325
Kolbert, P. R., 51
Krentz, E., 295
Kümmel, W. G., 130, 131
Kwon, O., 34
Labberton, M., 318
Lake, K., 331
Lamp, J., 19, 33
Lampe, P., 21, 136, 173, 294-97
Lanham, R., 42
Lattimore, R., 154
Lausberg, H., 42, 262
Levison, J. R., 290
Lewis, C. S., 24
Lewis, G., 233
Lightfoot, J. B., 197, 241
Ljungman, H., 178
Locke, J., 296
Marcuse, F. L., 343
Marrou, H. I., 65-66, 120
Marshall, P., 136, 229, 232
Martin, D. B., 148
Martin, T. F., 51
Martin, T. W., 28, 172
Martyn, J. L., 132, 179-81, 232, 288-89
Mason, J., 31, 297
Masson, C. E., 237
McComiskey, B., 295
McCracken, G. E., 145, 146
McDonald, J. I. H., 196, 201
McDonald, M. F., 146
McGuire, W. J., 278-80, 284, 292, 301, 304
McKane, W., 192
Meeks, W. A., 148
Meggitt, J. J., 120, 148
Meinardus, O. F. A., 125
Merritt, B. D., 124
Meyer, H. A. W., 197
Mihaila, C., 19, 144, 156
Milgrom, J., 30
Millar, F., 202
Miller, A. C., 204
Mitchell, M. M., 28, 41, 131, 143, 196, 218, 227, 268, 300
Moffatt, J., 197, 237
Morgan, T., 65
Moule, C. F. D., 241
Munck, J., 215, 217, 228, 331
Murphy, C. T., 291

Murphy, J. J., 50, 283, 291
Murphy-O'Connor, J., 185
Mussies, G., 232
Natanson, M., 37-38, 41, 271
Nauck, A., 145
Neville, G., 298
Neyrey, J. H., 120
Nock, A. D., 154, 155, 184, 264
Norden, E., 119, 122, 260, 303
North, H. F., 23
Ober, J., 23, 103
Oke, C. C., 229
Olbrechts-Tyteca, L., 44, 184, 212, 261, 264, 265, 269, 280, 287
Olbricht, T. H., 24, 40, 136
Olson, G. A., 295
Ong, W. J., 44, 114, 178
Orr, W. F., 198
Outler, A. C., 50
Packer, J. I., 346, 348
Paige, T., 34
Painter, J., 244
Papadopolos, S. G., 157
Pascuzzi, M., 171
Patrick, D., 25, 23
Pearson, B. A., 237, 325
Perelman, C., 44, 184, 212, 215, 261, 264, 265, 269, 280, 287, 292
Peterson, B. K., 34
Pickett, R., 22-23, 248
Pippin, T., 27
Pitts, A. W., 120
Plank, K. A., 253
Plantinga, A., 30
Plummer, A., 197
Pogoloff, S. M., 19, 143-44, 156, 157-59, 182, 255, 293
Polhill, J. B., 210, 334
Porter, S. E., 36, 39-40, 42, 120-21, 131, 132, 136, 288, 327, 340

Provence, T. E., 238
Prümm, K., 236
Purcell, N., 207
Rainer, T. S., 357
Rauh, N. K., 207
Reed, J. T., 132, 136
Rengstorf, K. H., 188, 285
Rescher, N., 209
Resner, A., 37
Robertson, A., 197
Robertson, A. T., 200, 241
Robertson, C. K., 148, 173
Robinson, H., 348
Robinson, J. M., 201
Rokeach, M., 344
Romilly. J. de, 75
Rosner, B. S., 208, 213
Roukema, R., 147
Russell, D. A., 17, 44-45, 68
Saussure, F. de, 293
Schouls, P. A., 209
Schweizer, E., 242
Scott, I. W., 41, 266-67, 334-38
Scranton, R. L., 125
Scroggs, R., 191, 194, 238
Scult, A., 25, 231
Sellin, G., 325
Shaw, G., 232
Sider, R. D., 291
Siegert, F., 294
Simcox, W. H., 143
Sleeth, R. E., 343
Sloane, T. O., 262
Smiley, C. N., 277
Smit, J. F. M., 173-74, 291
Smith, R. W., 120, 333
Spencer, W. D., 254
Stamps, D. L., 34, 36
Stanley, C. D., 214
Stanley, D. M., 188
Stanton, G. R., 151
Still, T. D., 223-25, 329
Stirewalt, M. L., 34, 136

Sullivan, Sr. T., 49, 50, 51, 282, 283
Syme, R., 128
Theissen, G., 120, 148
Thiselton, A. C., 198, 204, 241, 260-61
Thorgerson, E. J., 206
Thrall, M. E., 267-68
Thurén, L., 223
Tomlin, G., 34
Torrance, T. F., 201
Turner, N., 144
Usher, S., 291
Van Gelder, C., 351
Van Unnik, W. C., 156
Vanhoozer, K. J., 22
Vos, J. S., 23, 175, 295
Wagner, J. R., 286
Wagner, P., 353-55
Wallace, K. R., 265
Walther, J. A., 198
Wanamaker, C. A., 173
Watson, D. F., 18-19, 36, 131, 132, 136, 143
Weima, J. A. D., 132
Weiss, J., 216, 303, 325
Welborn, L. L., 19, 148, 250
Whitmarsh, T., 69
Wilckens, U., 19, 35, 221, 225, 229, 237
Wilken, R. L., 232
Williams, H. H. D., 19, 229
Williams, M. A., 34
Winter, B. W., 19, 69, 126, 143, 144, 147, 150-53, 169, 178, 325
Wire, A., 287
Witherington, B., 21, 34, 120, 131, 136, 156, 160, 178, 179, 229, 230, 242, 286, 288
Wuellner, W., 131, 148, 221
Young, F. M., 28
Zscheile, D. J., 351

Scripture Index

OLD TESTAMENT
Numbers
21:8-9, *224*

Nehemiah
3, *319*
6:15, *319*

Job
5:13, *248*
11:2-3, *156*

Psalms
127:1, *345*

Isaiah
29:14, *192*

Jonah
1:2, *188*

Micah
3:5, *188*

Zechariah
4:6, *229*, *345*

NEW TESTAMENT
Matthew
3:1, *188*
4:7, *188*
4:17, *285*
5:37, *23*
10:7, *188*
10:19-20, *241*
10:27, *188*
12:41, *197*, *208*
24:14, *188*
25:21, *319*
25:23, *319*

Mark
1:14, *285*
1:38, *285*
3:14, *188*
14:9, *246*
15:32, *214*
16:15, *188*
16:20, *188*

Luke
4:18-19, *188*
11:32, *197*, *208*
12:11-12, *241*
19:17, *319*
23:13, *239*
23:34, *239*
24:45, *267*

John
1:7, *188*
1:12, *186*
1:34, *188*
1:47, *23*
2, *301*
3:14-15, *224*
5:41-44, *25*
6:40, *224*
7:18, *25*
8:28, *224*
10:26-27, *268*
12:23, *224*
12:32, *224*
12:33, *224*
14:15, *318*
15:26, *188*
15:27, *188*
17:5, *224*
18:37, *188*
20:25, *214*
20:29, *214*

Acts
1:8, *188*
2:40, *348*
3:17, *239*
4:13, *142*
4:20, *264*
4:33, *188*
8:25, *188*
9:1-19, *328*
9:2, *331*
9:20, *328*
9:27, *328*
9:28, *328*
10:36-43, *188*
10:42, *188*
10:43, *188*
12:21, *125*

13:4, *328*
13:5, *328*
13:27, *239*
13:43, *189*
13:44-48, *330*
13:48, *267*, *332*
15:35, *328*
15:36, *328*
16:6, *328*
16:10, *328*
16:13-14, *328*
16:14, *267*, *281*
16:17, *328*, *331*
16:19, *239*
16:21, *328*
16:32, *328*
17, *159*, *308*, *309*, *327*
17:1-3, *224*
17:2, *308*, *328*
17:2-3, *328*
17:2-4, *190*
17:3, *308*, *309*, *328*
17:3-4, *281*, *328*
17:4, *189*, *308*
17:5-9, *308*
17:11, *308*, *328*
17:12, *328*
17:13, *308*, *328*
17:16, *329*
17:16-34, *239*
17:17, *308*, *329*
17:17-34, *328*
17:18, *309*, *329*
17:18-20, *308*
17:19-21, *329*
17:21, *82*
17:22-31, *329*
17:23, *309*, *329*
17:30, *329*
17:31, *309*
17:32, *329*
17:34, *329*
18, *156*, *246*, *323*
18:1, *330*
18:1-17, *157*, *227*
18:1-18, *328*
18:4, *124*, *189*, *281*, *330*
18:5, *330*
18:6-7, *330*

18:8, *330*
18:9, *227*
18:9-10, *330*
18:11, *130*, *330*
18:12-16, *125*
18:12-17, *130*, *239*
18:13, *330*
18:15, *330*
18:17, *330*
18:18, *130*, *331*
18:24, *156*, *331*, *333*
18:24-28, *143*, *324*
18:25, *331*
18:26, *331*
18:27, *331*, *332*
18:28, *332*, *333*
19:1, *324*, *331*
19:8, *189*
19:9, *331*
19:23, *331*
22:4, *331*
22:15, *188*
23:11, *188*
24:14, *331*
24:22, *331*
26:15-16, *187*
26:16, *188*
28:23-24, *189*, *281*
28:25-28, *330*
28:31, *328*

Romans
1, *41*
1:1, *186*
1:6, *187*, *332*
1:16, *176*, *178*, *190*, *201*
1:16-17, *180*
1:18, *210*
1:18-32, *41*, *267*, *334*
1:21-22, *248*
3:27, *218*
6:17, *254*
8:17, *253*
10, *184*, *186*
10:8, *186*
10:9-13, *224*
10:12-17, *186*
10:14, *178*
10:17, *178*, *181*, *186*, *187*

Scripture Index

11:33-36, *164, 239*
13:3, *239*
16:18, *142*
16:25-26, *240*

1 Corinthians
1, *188, 266, 325*
1–2, *141, 219, 230, 237, 255, 291, 296, 332*
1–4, *15, 16, 19, 20, 21, 25, 29, 32, 33, 34, 35, 38, 39, 40, 41, 42, 43, 45, 46, 47, 49, 50, 51, 52, 53, 58, 67, 72, 117, 120, 122, 124, 129, 130, 131, 132, 133, 134, 135, 137, 139, 140, 141, 143, 145, 146, 147, 149, 151, 152, 153, 155, 156, 157, 159, 160, 161, 164, 166, 169, 170, 171, 172, 173, 174, 175, 178, 179, 184, 204, 207, 210, 219, 220, 221, 224, 231, 233, 234, 244, 248, 254, 255, 259, 260, 261, 265, 274, 278, 282, 283, 289, 291, 294, 296, 297, 301, 302, 304, 305, 306, 316, 317, 321, 323, 324, 325, 327, 332, 333, 339, 340, 351, 352*
1:1, *186*
1:1-17, *161*
1:2, *216*
1:4, *172*
1:5, *172*
1:6, *141, 170, 183, 190*
1:10-16, *172*
1:10–2:5, *236*
1:10–4:13, *254*
1:10–4:21, *131, 173*
1:11, *34, 130, 184, 244, 324*
1:12, *324*
1:13, *167, 170, 290*
1:14-16, *170, 171*
1:17, *32, 33, 51, 133, 137, 159, 171, 172, 174, 175, 176, 178, 179, 182, 183, 193, 220, 221, 222, 238, 240, 241, 242, 259, 276, 318, 356*
1:17-20, *182*
1:17–2:5, *15, 33, 34, 46, 144, 172, 231, 234, 237, 259, 260, 265, 270, 271*
1:17–2:6, *237*
1:17–2:16, *41, 198, 267, 334, 335*
1:18, *176, 178, 183, 187, 190, 193, 210, 213, 216, 222, 225, 238, 239, 265, 276, 283, 305*
1:18-21, *210*
1:18-24, *268*
1:18-25, *216*
1:18-31, *222*
1:18–2:5, *175, 184, 198, 233, 236, 290, 323*
1:19, *248*
1:19-20, *191*
1:19-21, *163*
1:19-31, *222*
1:20, *162, 208, 305*
1:21, *164, 179, 188, 193, 195, 197, 198, 201, 207, 208, 211, 239, 259, 305*
1:21-25, *164*
1:22–2:5, *214*
1:23, *133, 180*
1:23-24, *164, 226, 238, 318*
1:24, *176, 178, 187, 237, 238, 245, 265, 332*
1:26, *216, 217, 219, 221, 318*
1:26-28, *217*
1:27, *217*
1:27-29, *163, 164, 184, 219, 268*
1:27-38, *248*
1:28, *217, 239*
1:29, *218*
1:30, *141, 164, 216, 218, 226, 237, 238, 245*
1:31, *218, 234, 246*
2, *237*
2:1, *133, 137, 216, 221, 222, 223, 227, 241, 259, 294, 301*
2:1-4, *158, 159*
2:1-5, *26, 140, 175, 193, 203, 204, 221, 225, 290*
2:2, *179, 223, 238, 245, 269, 276, 300*
2:3, *138, 142, 227, 229, 323, 329, 332*
2:3-4, *287*
2:3-5, *227*
2:4, *51, 133, 180, 189, 201, 221, 222, 225, 229, 230, 259, 267, 268, 294, 300, 301*
2:4-5, *138, 172, 190, 225, 242, 345*
2:5, *152, 159, 176, 178, 186, 229, 234, 261, 276, 295, 296, 356*
2:6, *133, 178, 236, 237, 238, 239, 242, 244, 245*
2:6-7, *237, 240*
2:6-8, *164*
2:6-9, *164*
2:6-16, *236, 238, 241, 243*
2:6–4:21, *236*
2:7, *133, 239, 240*
2:7-10, *240*
2:8, *240*
2:8-9, *239*
2:9, *239*
2:10, *238, 239, 245*
2:10-11, *239*
2:10-12, *164*
2:12, *240, 242, 245*
2:13, *133, 138, 172, 222, 240, 241, 259, 296, 326*
2:14, *47, 164, 220, 240, 242, 244, 289, 305, 306, 340, 352*
2:14-15, *221, 238*
2:14-16, *245*
2:15, *242, 243, 245, 289, 306*
2:16, *242*
3:1, *133, 220, 221, 239, 244, 306*
3:1-2, *284, 303*
3:1-4, *243, 245, 250*
3:2, *244, 245*
3:3, *220, 231, 244*
3:3-4, *220*
3:4, *244, 250*
3:4–4:5, *323, 324*
3:4–4:6, *323*
3:5, *246*
3:5-9, *246, 248*
3:6, *267*
3:6-7, *246*
3:6-9, *247*
3:7, *52, 281*
3:8, *249*
3:8-9, *247*
3:9, *247*
3:10, *247*
3:10-15, *248*
3:10-17, *247*
3:13, *164, 247*
3:13-15, *249*
3:15, *247*
3:17, *247, 324*
3:18, *155, 164, 248, 250, 251*
3:18-21, *323*
3:18-23, *248*
3:19-21, *163*
3:20, *248*
3:21, *155, 167, 246, 249*
3:22, *324*
3:23, *249, 324*
4, *252*
4–7, *143*
4:1, *249*
4:1-2, *133*
4:1-5, *249, 316*
4:2, *249, 272, 319*
4:3, *134, 250*
4:3-5, *155, 249*
4:4, *231, 249*
4:5, *134, 164, 233, 249, 250*
4:6, *134, 155, 167, 247, 250, 255, 323*
4:6-13, *250, 254*
4:7, *155, 250, 251*
4:8, *251, 252, 253, 290*
4:8-10, *252*
4:9, *253*
4:9-13, *253, 254*
4:10, *155*
4:11-13, *253*
4:14, *253*
4:14-16, *244*
4:14-21, *253*
4:15, *254*
4:16, *253, 254*
4:17, *254, 340*
4:18, *155, 254*
4:19, *155*
4:19-20, *254, 255*
4:21, *141*
5–16, *139*
5:2, *155*
5:9, *130*
6, *143, 168*
6:1-8, *169*
7:1, *34, 130*
7:31, *163*
8:1-3, *155*
9, *140*
9:3, *134*

9:14, *133*
9:16, *133*
9:16-18, *133*
9:18, *133*
9:19-23, *284, 303*
9:23, *133*
9:27, *133*
10:11, *252*
11, *168*
11:18, *219*
11:23, *254*
12:1, *244*
12:8, *172*
12:12, *167, 318*
13:11, *245*
13:12, *164*
14:11, *238*
14:20, *237, 244*
14:26, *172*
15, *166, 251*
15:1, *133, 254*
15:1-2, *245*
15:1-11, *141*
15:2, *133*
15:3, *133, 185, 254*
15:3-4, *341*
15:3-8, *245*
15:8, *163*
15:11, *133*
15:14, *133*
15:15, *133*
15:19, *163*
15:29, *171*
15:32, *163*
15:34, *163*
16:10, *332*
16:12, *247, 248, 324*
16:17, *34, 130*

2 Corinthians
1:1, *186*
1:12, *24, 138, 231, 241, 296*
1:13-14, *134*
1:14, *134, 231*
1:19, *133, 189*
2:14-17, *226, 227, 238*
2:15-16, *305*
2:17, *133, 138, 231, 232, 233, 296*
3:6, *163*
3:12, *233*
3:14-18, *164*
3:16, *164*
4:1, *163*
4:2, *25, 139, 152, 229, 233, 248, 274, 296*
4:3-4, *164, 190, 234, 240*
4:4, *133*
4:5, *133, 233, 234*
4:6, *163*
4:7, *133, 139, 162, 220, 227, 233, 241, 301*
4:7-12, *253*
4:13, *133, 233*
4:18, *163*
5:7, *163, 215*
5:9-10, *249*
5:9-12, *249*
5:11, *189*
5:12, *134*
5:13, *234*
5:16, *163*
5:18-20, *133*
5:20, *163, 189, 347, 348*
6:4, *249*
6:4-10, *253*
7:14, *133*
10–13, *135, 160*
10:1, *323*
10:3-4, *139, 234*
10:3-5, *163*
10:5, *163*
10:7, *169*
10:10, *23, 24, 40, 51, 135, 137, 144, 158, 176, 227, 288, 307, 332, 333*
10:12, *234*
10:16, *133*
10:18, *164, 249*
11:3, *231*
11:4, *133*
11:6, *23, 51, 142, 143, 144, 147, 158, 227, 245, 299, 300, 301, 323*
11:7, *133*
11:23-29, *253*
11:30, *253*
12:1-10, *163*
12:5, *253*
12:9, *253*
12:9-10, *229, 253*
12:11, *134*
12:12, *230*
12:19, *134*
12:20, *134*
13:3, *160*
13:6, *134*
13:7, *135*

Galatians
1:1, *186*
1:1-12, *163*
1:2, *165*
1:6, *166, 189*
1:6-7, *165*
1:10, *189, 288*
3:1, *165, 189, 216, 225*
3:2, *180, 181*
5:8, *189, 190*
5:16–6:1, *243*
5:19-21, *244*
5:20-21, *220*
5:22-23, *220*
6:1, *243*

Ephesians
4:13-15, *245*

Colossians
1:9, *245*
1:26-28, *240*
1:28, *238, 245*
2:3, *245*

1 Thessalonians
1:4-5, *189, 216, 269*
1:5, *141, 225, 232*
1:8, *232*
1:10, *224*
2:2, *232*
2:3, *233, 234*
2:3-6, *227, 249*
2:4, *232, 233*
2:5, *296*
2:6, *234*
2:8, *232*
2:9, *232*
2:13, *141, 189, 216, 225, 232, 269*

2 Thessalonians
2:13-14, *189*
2:15, *254*
3:6, *254*

2 Timothy
2:10, *268*
2:14, *51*
2:18, *251*

Titus
3:13, *324*

Hebrews
5:11-14, *237, 246*

James
5:12, *23*

1 Peter
2:2, *245*

1 John
1:2, *188*
4:14, *188*
5:9-11, *188*
5:20, *267*

www.ingramcontent.com/pod-product-compliance
Lightning Source LLC
Chambersburg PA
CBHW020605300426
44113CB00007B/519